THE

DOCTRINE AND LITERATURE

OF

THE KABALAH

BY

ARTHUR EDWARD WAITE

AUTHOR OF

"THE LIFE OF LOUIS CLAUDE DE SAINT-MARTIN, THE UNKNOWN
PHILOSOPHER," AND TRANSLATOR OF THE WORKS OF
ÉLIPHAS LÉVI.

1902.

The Doctrine and Literature of the Kabalah
Arthur Edward Waite

A Cornerstone Book
Published by Cornerstone Book Publishers
An imprint of Michael Poll Publishing

Cornerstone Book Publishers
New Orleans, LA
www.cornerstonepublishers.com

Photographic Reproduction of the 1902 edition

First Cornerstone Edition - 2015

IISBN:1613422393
ISBN-13:978-1-61342-239-7

MADE IN THE USA

CONTENTS

BOOK III

SOURCE AND AUTHORITY OF THE KABALAH.

BOOK IV

THE WRITTEN WORD OF KABALISM : FIRST PERIOD.

BOOK V

THE WRITTEN WORD OF KABALISM : SECOND PERIOD.

BOOK VI

THE WRITTEN WORD OF KABALISM : THIRD PERIOD.

BOOK VII

SOME CHRISTIAN STUDENTS OF THE KABALAH.

BOOK VIII

THE KABALAH AND OTHER CHANNELS OF ESOTERIC TRADITION.

PREFACE

FEW educated persons, and certainly none belonging to the class of students for which this work is more especially designed, will require to be told that the Kabalah is a form of esoteric philosophy, that it makes for itself a high claim, or that this claim has, from time to time, been admitted by persons who are entitled to our consideration. Nor will it be needful to state that the literature called Kabalistic rose up among the Jews during the Christian centuries which succeeded their dispersal and the destruction of their Holy City. It offers a strong contrast to the sacred scriptures of Israel, which are direct, beautiful and simple, while Kabalism is involved, obscure and in many ways repellent as regards its outward form. The Bible is in focus with humanity ; the Kabalah is distorted out of all correspondence with the simple senses, and we must grind our intellectual lenses with exceeding care if we would bring it into perspective.

From whatever point of view it may be approached, the Kabalah is, however, of importance : it connects with literatures which are greater than itself and with pregnant issues of history. It is part of the history of philosophy, and as such it once entered into the thought of Europe. It is responsible, broadly speaking, for all that strange tissue of symbolism and ceremonial which made up the magic of the Middle Ages ; at a later period it sought to transform alchemy ; it tinctured many of those conventional practices and beliefs which we term superstition generically, and the guise in which we know them is therefore chiefly a Kabalistic guise. If we might dare to suppose for a moment that behind magic, behind alchemy, behind astrology there is any mystery of secret and real knowledge, then it is entitled to peculiar respect, because, by the hypothesis of some of its defenders, it is through this seemingly impassable literature that the road to the secret lies.

A comprehensive account of the Kabalah, in the main bibliographical and historical, but seeking to establish its connections with other forms of occult philosophy and to determine its influence and importance from more than one standpoint, is the design of the present work, in which special regard has been also paid to the limitations and requirements of English readers —in other words, of those unacquainted with the languages, dead and living, in which Kabalistic literature has been, with few exceptions, available heretofore. The subject is exceedingly abstruse, and has been presented by some of its expositors after a highly technical fashion ; in this case there is no knowledge assumed in the reader, and hence all technicalities have been avoided, while the scope of the enterprise much exceeds the one or two attempts—mostly in foreign tongues—which have been made to simplify the study of the Kabalah. It is the result of an inquiry undertaken, in the first instance, for my own personal requirements ; and I must add, in fairness to my readers and in gratitude to early labourers in this obscure field of research, that the abounding difficulties of the Hebrew and Aramaic originals have been simplified by recourse to the vast storehouses of Rabbinical lore entombed for some centuries in such Latin collections as those of Buxtorf, Bartolocci,

Pistorius and Rosenroth; a very large proportion of the materials necessary for an intelligent familiarity with Jewish esoteric tradition are, indeed, to be found in these. These and other resources have been strengthened subsequently by a considerable range of reading among modern writers in England, France and Germany who, directly and indirectly, have concerned themselves with the subject. The work has therefore the learner's advantage of being without pretence and without ambition, but it is believed at the same time to contain all that the ordinary student is likely to require in order to appreciate at their proper worth the various claims preferred on behalf of the Kabalah by those who take it seriously at this day. It is necessary to add that it has been written by a transcendentalist and chiefly for the use of transcendentalists; in offering materials for their judgment, it also indicates the lines of the conclusions to which the writer leans himself, and seeks to enforce some of them. It has been preceded in England by only two books dealing directly with the subject; one is the slight but not inconsiderable essay of Dr. Ginsburg,* which is critical rather than descriptive, and is, on the whole, hostile in its tendency. It has been, moreover, long out of print. The other is the " Kabbalah Unveiled " † of Mr. S. L. MacGregor Mathers, which is largely translation and commentary, and, in addition to other limitations, embraces therefore only

---

* " The Kabbalah." By C. D. Ginsburg. London, 1865. 8vo.

† " The Kabbalah Unveiled, containing the following books of the Zohar : 1. The Book of Concealed Mystery ; 2. The Greater Holy Assembly ; 3. The Lesser Holy Assembly, Translated into English from the Latin version of Knorr v . Rosenroth, and collated with the original Chaldee and Hebrew Text." By S. L. MacGregor Mathers, London, 1887. 8vo. The Commentary is partly that of Rosenroth, and partly the work of the translator.

a small portion of an extensive literature. The present comprehensive account fulfils a distinct purpose, and may, it is hoped, be held to occupy, not altogether unworthily, a vacant place from which there is a wide prospect, by no means deficient in importance for those who are not transcendentalists, for the student of philosophy and history, and for the curious in paths of literature which the elder D'Israeli, despite the bias of his birthright, forebore to enter.

The works containing the esoteric tradition of Israel, as distinguished from the exoteric tradition embodied in the Talmud and its dependencies, fall, under two heads :

a. The Sepher Yetzirah, or " Book of Formation."

b. The Zohar, or " Splendour."

Connected with the " Book of Formation " are its commentaries, foremost among which are those of Saadya Gaon, Rabbi Azariel Ben Menahem and Rabbi Abraham Ben Dior. The treatise itself is comprised within a few pages.

The Zohar proper is a commentary on the five books of Moses,* but a number of distinct treatises are connected with or embedded therein. There are also supplements and additions which must be considered to some extent separate from the original collection.

With the Zohar, furthermore, are connected certain important developments and commentaries, some of which are included in the *Kabbala Denudata* of Rosenroth. They fall under two heads :

1. Those which deal with the subject-matter of

---

* This at least is its conventional description ; Graetz, the German historian, seems uncertain as to its correctness, but does not offer an alternative. It is really a theosophic medley connected with the Pentateuch, and arising therefrom.

the work, and are designed to elucidate certain of its most obscure treatises.

2. Those which expound and extend the doctrines of Pneumatology which are established in the Zohar.

These commentaries are, of course, the work of later Kabalists whose dates can be fixed with more or less certainty. Such Zoharistic writings have been sometimes confused with the Zohar.†

Some classifications of the Kabalah also include and give prominence to :

c. The *Sepher Sephiroth*—i.e., the "Book of Numerations," or "Emanations."

d. A treatise entitled *Æsh Metzareph*, or "Purifying Fire."

Whatever their authority and importance, there is no warrant for placing these works among the great classics of the Kabalah. The "Book of Emanations" is more properly set down among the dependencies of the Sepher Yetzirah, while that of "Purifying Fire" occupies a peculiar position, as it is almost without a history, and as it is perhaps the only Kabalistic treatise which deals directly with alchemy. Its date is doubtful and its authorship entirely unknown.

A short but comprehensive account of all the works which have been mentioned above will be found in Books IV., V., and VI. ; an attempt at such a formal tabulation has not been made previously in the English language. The first three books contain a historical and critical survey of the entire subject,

† Thus in the "Kabbalah Unveiled," Mr. Mathers mentions the "House of God," or of "The Elohim," and the "Book of the Revolutions of Souls," among the most important sections of the Zohar. (Introduction, p. 15.)

showing the philosophical system embodied in the Kabalah, the method by which it was developed, its connections with previous theosophies, designed, like itself, to explain the fundamental mysteries of the universe, and the evidences for its antiquity.

The seventh book is devoted to the Christian students of the Kabalah, and collects for the first time the opinions of the chief Christian scholars whose names have been connected with Kabalism. The design of this book is to exhibit a consensus of opinion among all those authorities who are most in vogue with occultists as to what is of value in the Jewish esoteric traditions and as to what is waste substance. On this point there has never been any real difference of sentiment, except in the modern school of transcendentalism, which, devoid of a proper criterion of judgment, and regarding the entire subject from a new standpoint, has been disposed to accept everything indiscriminately as part of the genuine tradition, and has thus esteemed the apparatus of *Gematria* and *Notaricon* as no less important and mysterious than the Zoharistic philosophy of the unconditioned summed up in *Ain Soph*.

The eighth book deals briefly with other channels through which the esoteric tradition is believed to have been perpetuated in the West and their connection with the channel of Kabalism.

To those who may approach the work from the historical and bibliographical standpoint the presence of its leading motive and its appeal to a single class of students may require some explanation. It has, I believe, been suggested that since the appearance of Dr. Ginsburg's destructive criticism there has been no

interest among English scholars in the subject of the
Kabalah. Among mere scholars — that is to say,
within the region of research which has only a
scholastic horizon—there was no interest which calls
for special mention at the period which preceded that
work immediately, and it is quite true that there has
been as little subsequently to its publication, but not
mainly on account of Dr. Ginsburg's criticism. There
has been always, or, speaking exactly, since the days
of Thomas Vaughan, Cudworth and the Cambridge
Platonists, a certain class of thinkers for whom the
claims made by and on behalf of the Kabalah have
possessed great interest and importance, and this
class is now much larger than at any date prior to
1865. It also forms intellectually a more respectable
and considerable body than the academical reader
might be disposed to imagine in the absence of much
acquaintance with the literature by which it is
represented. One is obliged to speak of these
thinkers under the generic designation of occult
students, though the phrase is somewhat inexact and
has been used to describe persons who have little
title to earnest consideration. A proscribed mode of
thought is here, as in other cases, identified
ungenerously with the meaner capacities that follow
it, and an unpopular subject is classed according to
the waste and drift which has collected about it. But
the class to which I have adverted does not in itself
deserve either ridicule or contempt; it is that which
believes in the perpetuation of a secret religious, or,
more correctly, theosophical, tradition from an early
period of human history, and this is not manifestly
an unwarrantable consequence to draw from the
study of religions undertaken philosophically. Now,

the Kabalah is not only, as I have said, the occult philosophy of Jewry, it is not only one of the chief sources from which occult science and philosophy have drawn in the western world, but it has been further represented to be the channel of such a tradition as I have just mentioned. It is therefore not merely reasonable to suppose, but it is true as a fact, that to occultists, and to them almost exclusively, an inquiry like the present must appeal. Other interests are accidental; their interest is vital. To determine the claims of the Kabalah as a department and inspiring centre of occult philosophy is to determine that which is of most real moment regarding it.

It is for this reason that I have been led to consider the Kabalah, not, indeed, as an occultist in the accepted sense, but from the occult standpoint, and to recur with so much frequency to the belief in a secret doctrine of religion, as well as to some other connected questions which need reconsideration at the hands of those who hold them. If I have had in the course of the inquiry to reduce certain illusions to their proper place in the realm of the fantastic, more especially if I have contracted the sphere of what is called Mysticism within its proper dimensions, I trust that I shall be justified, so far as regards my intention, by those whom I have sought to disabuse. From its nature the foundation of Mysticism cannot be in occult science or in occult philosophy, while it is on the historical side alone that it connects with any traditions of the past, popular or achromatic.*

---

* The reason is indicated by Schopenhauer, when he remarks on the astonishing unanimity of mystics in all ages, unlike in everything except those principles which constitute mysticism, and yet not holding those principles as a sect clings to its tenets, for they are not and can never be a sect.

In the course of the general inquiry I have endeavoured to elucidate the most curious Kabalistic teachings on the subject of the soul, its origin and destiny, the primal state of man, the life of the world to come and the Messianic dream of Jewry.

I should add that this study is mainly concerned with the documents, and as such it cannot deal exhaustively with all the issues. It is also bibliographical rather than philosophical. The exhaustive study of the Kabalah would have to be made in connection with that of comparative religion, demanding qualifications to which I can make no claim and a space for its development which would have been, under any circumstances, impossible. I could wish my inquiry to be regarded rather as the note-book of a student methodised. Finally, the work has been performed in a spirit of impartiality, and this is perhaps the only side on which it leans towards perfection. There has been no interest at stake which I have felt myself compelled to defend, and it is therefore free from the animus of extreme hostile criticism, as well as from the unreasoned assumptions of those—in the main non-critical believers—who still have the cause of the Kabalah at heart. I claim, furthermore, that I have considered honestly and sympathetically all the interests at stake, including those which the bias of modern scholarship is inclined to overlook, or to dismiss in an intolerant spirit.

I should add that the history of this book has been chequered and somewhat unfortunate. The manuscript was completed for press at the end of 1898, and in the year following the greater part had been set up and a number of the sheets machined, which were wholly destroyed in a fire at the printer's.

The delay which thus occurred was considerable in itself, and was increased still further through the suspension of the publishing house by which it was to be issued. In the interval which has elapsed during the course of those fresh negotiations which have resulted in its production under the auspices of the Theosophical Publishing Society, and during the resetting of the entire work, Dr. S. Karppe has published in Paris his elaborate *Etude sur les Origines et la Nature du Zohar*, which approaches the subject from a standpoint entirely different to my own, but is at the same time a valuable contribution to our knowledge of Jewish theosophy, and I note with satisfaction that there are many debated points on which, working thus independently, we have reached the same conclusion. Dr. Karppe's study is designed for the scholar and the philosopher, while my own, as already explained, is intended, primarily at least, for the occult student. The Jewish mysticism which led up to and preceded the Zohar is very fully presented by him, but of the influence exercised by that work and of its after history he has nothing to tell us. On the other hand, the scheme of my own treatise has led me of necessity to pass lightly over pre-Zoharic theosophy, over Saadyah, Ibn Gebirol, Judah Ha Levi, Aben Ezra, Maimonides, &c., because they did not affect materially the occult thought of Europe, and to give prominence to Kabalistic literature in its later phases, to the Christian students of the subject, and to its influence upon other channels of esoteric tradition in Europe. Among the points of agreement between Dr. Karppe and myself may be mentioned the common recognition of the heterogeneous nature of the Zohar, which has

justified me in terming it a medley ; of the specifically
Jewish character of Zoharic mysticism, which has
justified me in denying that it is referable exclusively
to any one school of thought outside Jewry ; of the
rapid deterioration of the Kabalah, subsequent to the
appearance of the Zohar, into a thaumaturgic system;
of the undue prominence which has been given to the
commentaries on the Zohar and the false impressions
which have been the result ; of the preconception
which governed the mind of most Christian students
of the literature, by which they were led to regard it
as an unacknowledged depository of Christian
doctrine ; of the absence in the Sepher Yetzirah of
any distinctive pantheism or emanationism. There is
also considerable similarity, both of thought and
treatment, in the development of the Kabalistic and
typically Zoharic doctrines concerning God and the
universe, more especially concerning *Ain Soph* and
creation *ex nihilo*. It would be easy to multiply these
instances, nor less easy to furnish numerous points
of divergence, for, on the other hand, Dr. Karppe
has, I think, laid too much stress on his distinction
between the early Jewish mysticism and that of the
Zoharic period, not because such a distinction is either
non-existent or unimportant in itself, but because
I cannot find that it has been challenged by any
qualified writer. And I must, of course, as a mystic,
take exception to the conception of mysticism
expressed or implied throughout the whole work.
Mysticism is not a double doctrine, whether of
monotheism for the initiate and of many deities for
the vulgar, or of any other such antithesis as the
priestcrafts may have derived in the past, but it is
outside possibility to do more in the present place than

refer to this point and register the bare fact that the students to whom personally I appeal will join issue with Dr. Karpe as to all that follows from his conception, whether it be a matter of simple definition, such as that mysticism is a reprisal of faith against science, or of historical criticism, as for example, when he observes that the doctrine of ecstacy is almost unknown to Jewish theosophy, a statement, however, which the author himself abundantly, though not explicitly, modifies at a later stage of his study. To this exception may be added certain points of critical importance, to which, personally, I have only had occasion to refer in passing. The student will also notice a tendency in certain instances to pass over questions of criticism as if there had never been a dispute regarding them : on the one hand the commentary of Hay Gaon is made use of as if no scholar had challenged its authenticity ; and, on the other, the late date of the *Bahir* is taken for granted. Criticism may not have said its last word on either subject, but Dr. Karppe ignores the criticism.

The limits of the present work which, as regards the original intention, have been already exceeded, have necessitated the omission of a number of subsidiary yet not unimportant matters. I will mention two only : certain developments of pneumatology and eschatology which are representative of the doctrinal or systematic part—let us say, the hells of Kabalism : certain historical consequences, such as the mission of Sabbatai Zevi, the Neo-Pietists and the Zoharists. But in each case these omissions are without real consequence for the occult student.

BOOK I

POST-CHRISTIAN LITERATURE
OF THE JEWS

ARGUMENT

The literature of Kabalism has a philosophical, historical and, within certain limits, an exegetical interest for ordinary students, but it has a living interest only for those who believe ; (*a*) That a secret religious tradition has been perpetuated from the early ages of history, and (*b*) That Kabalistic literature has been one of its vehicles. Such persons are here termed occult students. The purpose of the present book is to show that whatever be the value of the first view (*a*), imperfect investigation has placed the second (*b*) in a false position. The occult estimate of the Talmud is cited as a case in point, and the divisions of the Kabalah are distinguished to make clear the issues and to correct some other misconceptions.

I. INTRODUCTORY

THE construction of the exile placed by the " princes of the exile " upon the sacred oracles of ancient Israel cannot be dismissed as unimportant. From the period of the dispersal of the Jews after the destruction of Jerusalem by Vespasian down even to our own times, Hebrew literature has developed in many of the chief centres of Europe, but outside the scattered remnant of the children of the covenant it has remained largely unknown. Many persons, not otherwise ill-formed, would be astonished to discover that so far back as the end of the seventeenth century there were nearly four thousand works* written in the Hebrew tongue which were individually known and quoted by one authority on rabbinical bibliography, namely, Julius Bartolocci, of the Reformed Order of St. Bernard.† Almost every conceivable department of human learning and intellectual activity is represented in this literature,‡ which, in things secular as in things sacred, has the seal of the sanctity of Israel upon all its leaves. It is otherwise an extremely curious and in some respects a profound literature, which translation has done little to make known, which is represented incompletely enough even in the great and authoritative text-books of Hebrew history. There is no need to add that its extent and its difficulties make it a formidable subject of approach. It is, indeed, an undiscovered country, still awaiting its Columbus ; § a land full of wealth and mystery, of strange shrines and sanctuaries shining weirdly far away through the darkness of our ignorance with a light which might well be a reflection of the Shekinah, so foreign does it seem to that which enlightens most men who are born into the modern world.

---

* It is perhaps unnecessary to say that they were for the most part in MS.

† *Bibliotheca Magna Rabbinica.   De scriptoribus et scriptis rabbinicis, ordine alphabetico Hebraice et Latine digestis, auctore* D. Julio Bartoloccio de Cellerio, 4 vols.   Roma, 1678-1692.   The work is printed from right to left, after the Hebrew manner.

‡ For one of the accessible collections which give some idea of its variety, see the " Catalogue of Hebraica and Judaica in the Library of the Corporation of the City of London."   With a Subject-Index by the Rev. A. Lowy.   London, 1891.

§ The work of Dr. Moritz Steinschneider, the German bibliographer of rabbinical literature, is the most important contribution to our knowledge which has been made during this century.

Within this literature there is, so to speak, another and stranger literature included, the report of which has been amongst us for several centuries, and in a certain way and measure it must be admitted that it is known to some of us, chiefly because it has been made available by the fathers of bibliographical erudition, the Latin-writing scholars of the past. This storehouse of Hebrew theosophy, for such it is, has exercised a peculiar fascination on many great minds of Christendom, and its Gentile students, even at the present day, may, for all that we can tell, be as numerous as its Jewish disciples. It is called the Kabalah, of which term there is more than one explanation suggested by the makers of romance in etymology. For example, the word has been derived from the name of the Hindoo teacher Kapila,* to whom a philosophy of numbers is ascribed, seemingly on the slender ground that one branch of Kabalistic literature also deals largely with this subject. Another equally fanciful suggestion makes the term an analogue of Cybele,† the mythological Queen of Heaven, who is thus connected with the Jewish personification of Wisdom under a female aspect. As to the true derivation there is no room for uncertainty, and it possesses that simplicity which is so often the seal of truth in things of language as it has been said to be in

---

* Mr. C. W. Heckethorn has made himself responsible recently for this view in the new and enlarged edition of his very unequal work, "Secret Societies of all Ages." See vol. i. p. 83.

† The responsibility in this case rests with the late Edward Vaughan Kenealy, whose anonymous "Book of God" and its sequels are quoted frequently as an authority by occult writers. Its philology is of the period of Godfrey Higgins, of the author of "Nimrod" and of Bryant's "Ancient Mythology." See Kenealy's "Introduction to the Apocalypse of Adam-Oannes," p. 613.

those of Nature and Art. The word comes from a Hebrew root which signifies to receive. Kabalah equals reception.* The knowledge embodied in the literature which passes under this title purports to have been transmitted orally from generation to generation. The literature as it exists is the tradition put into writing, and in this form it is supposed to be veiled—that is to say, the meaning which appears on the surface is not the true sense.†

The Kabalah then claims to be the light of a secret traditional knowledge‡ preserved among the "chosen people,"§ and the subjects with which it is concerned, as might be expected, are sacred and divine subjects; they include, indeed, the most profound mysteries of God and the emanations of the Deity; the celestial economy; the process of creation; the scheme of Providence in regard to man; the communications of God in revelation and to the just in his church; the offices and ministries of good and evil angels; the nature and pre-existence of the soul, its union with matter and its metempsychosis; the mystery of sin and its penalties; the Messiah, his

---

* The "Encyclopædia Perthensis" observes that the word is written also as Gabella, which is, of course, a nonsensical corruption, and would not be worth noting if it were not true in fact that it occurs in this form among a few old writers on magic. See "Encyc. Perth." iv. 543, 544.

† We shall see afterwards that this view must be received with a certain amount of caution.

‡ One of the titles ascribed to it was ChKMH NSThRH, that is, secret wisdom; the initials of these words gave another title, signifying Grace. See Kitto's "Cyclopædia of Biblical Literature," s.v. Kabbalah. (Third edition, London, 1864.)

§ The recipients of this knowledge were termed Mekkubalim, a name which will be familiar to the readers of the Astrologer Gaffarel. On this point see the worthless article, s.v. Kabbalah, in T. H. Blunt's "Dictionary of Doctrinal and Historical Theology." London, 1872.

kingdom and his glory to be revealed; the state of
the soul after death and the resurrection of the dead.
It is needless to say that by a literature so considerable in its capacity there are many other subjects
embraced, but these are the heads of the instruction
as I find them set forth in an excerpt from a Latin
epistle in the collection of Baron von Rosenroth.*
The Kabalah, in a word, is the hidden thought of
Israel upon the doctrines of the Jewish religion, which
are in most cases Christian doctrines, and upon the
proper understanding of that Written Word which is
referred to a divine origin both in Christendom and
Jewry. It is therefore obvious that in a general sense
it may be expected to cast light of some kind upon
the problems of Christian faith; but its Christian expounders have held that it does this also in a more
special way, that the New Testament and the writings
of the early fathers of the church did not only derive
from the inspired memorials of the first covenant, but
from the construction placed on those memorials by
this esoteric tradition.†

According to the literature which embodies it, the
tradition in question originated with God himself, by

---

* *Kabbala Denudata, seu Doctrina Hebræorum Transcendentalis
et Metaphysica,* vol. i. *Apparatus in Librum Sohar, pars secunda,*
pp. 3-5.

† "It is apparent from the many similarities in this Qabbalistic
philosophy to the doctrines in the New Testament and early Patristic
literature that both of the latter most probably have had a common
germ and origin in the esoteric teachings of the Israelites, as well
as in the more open and exoteric teachings of the Hebrew Holy
Writings." Isaac Myer, LL.B., "The Philosophical Writings of
Solomon Ben Yehudah Ibn Gebirol," Philadelphia, 1888, 8vo., p. 7.
The letter of St. Jerome to Paulinus, which dwells consecutively
upon the mysteries contained in all the books of the Old and New
Testaments, has been sometimes regarded as a case in point.

whom it was communicated to chosen ministers in the angelical world; and it was imparted by divine revelation to Adam in his unfallen state. When he lapsed from that pure condition he lost this precious deposit, but it was subsequently restored to him in order that he might return towards perfection. It was handed down through Noah to Abraham and thence derived to Moses. It is the concealed sense of the Mosaic Pentateuch, the secret of which was entrusted by the law-giver to the seventy elders, and from these in due course it passed onward to David, and was possessed in an especial manner by Solomon. It was not committed to writing until after the destruction of the second temple.* A genealogy of this kind will, of course, recall the fabulous origins ascribed to institutions like Freemasonry, the appeal made by the alchemists to the sages of antiquity, and many other fictions which deserve to be classed as monstrous. We should beware, however, of fixing imposture on an esoteric literature because its attribution is mythological; it should be remembered that we are dealing,

---

* The legend has many variations and has been loosely reproduced by many inexact writers. Naturally enough, it takes occasionally the guise of a book delivered to Adam. An old Jewish tradition tells us that this volume was brought by the Angel Razael. Mr. John Yarker, in his "Notes on the Scientific and Religious Mysteries of Antiquity" (London, 1872, p. 21), connects this myth with the pre-Zoharic "Book of Razael," not the imposture of Ceremonial Magic sometimes referred to under this name, but presumably the ancient legendary Midrash, afterwards developed by Eleazar of Worms and reproduced under various forms by debased Kabalism. Compare E. V. Kenealy's mythical notice of a Book of the Wisdom of Adam, received in an ecstasy and "full of mysteries and signs expressive of the most profound knowledge." See "Book of God," p. 243. See also *ibid.*, p. 273 *et seq.*, for a rabbinical account of a staff given to Adam, which is supposed to signify the support of a secret knowledge.

by the hypothesis, with a body of symbolism, and the genealogy may be itself an evasion.   Moreover, an oral tradition is peculiarly liable to the exaggeration of its antiquity, and we must distinguish therefore between the possible fact of its existence at a remote period and the growth of legend about it.   We have the testimony of Christ Himself as to the existence of a tradition in Israel, and we have also His judgment upon its value.   It is in one sense ·he purpose of this inquiry to determine whether the later literature of the reception is entitled to be included in the condemnation of the Divine Rabbi.

II. THE OCCULT STANDPOINT

As the Kabalah claims to be a tradition long received in secret by one generation from another and reduced at length into writing, so one of its classics informs us,* because of the bad state of the affairs of Israel, but yet written after a concealed manner,† it is to be expected that its literary methods will offer difficulties to the ordinary student.   It has, indeed, proved so unintelligible upon its surface that, on the one hand, it has been considered merely meaningless jargon, while a few who pretend to have penetrated to its real sense have, on the other, found pleasure in believing that it is sealed to uninitiated persons, for whom it must ever remain a matter of curious and unrewarded research, though not perhaps wanting

---

* The *Sepher Yet.irah* or " Book of Formation," but the state ment is probably the explanation of a commentator.

† Obscurities, complexities and confusions do not necessarily point to the existence of a double sense.

some gleams of unexpected suggestion.   The first view suggests that more patience and greater pains were needed ; the second, that the faculty for pains-taking is a kind of peculiar election which is possible only to the few, and this appears unwarranted.

Specialists in cryptography assure us, and we have even higher warrant in the testimony of reason itself, that no cipher writing devised by human in-genuity is incapable of solution also by human ingenuity, but the assumption, of course, supposes good faith in the cipher ; it must follow a certain method and conceal a definite sense.   There is also no system of symbolism and no form of philosophical speculation, however complex, which will not sur-render its secrets to the searchlight of analysis, pro-vided always that the symbolism is systematic and that the speculation is methodised, however curious in its involutions.   There are cryptic philosophies and con-cealed metaphysics, even as there is cryptic writing ; but if they possess a meaning, it cannot escape ulti-mately the penetration of the patient and skilled critic, subject, however, to the distinction which must subsist of necessity between the sense of a cipher—which is unmistakable from the moment that it is disengaged —and the construction of a speculative hypothesis which in its minor issues may always be open to debate.*   In regard to occult philosophies it is usual

---

* The best example of a really cryptic literature is that concerned with Alchemy, and yet it is not cryptic in the sense of cipher-writing. It has a perfectly simple surface meaning ; the concealment is the significance of certain conventional words and recipes.   This also is its great difficulty ; while cryptography must disclose its secret to skill and patience, it is nearly impossible to say what the word Vitriol, for example, may represent to any writer, if it be not the ordinary substance passing under that name.

to say that they are unintelligible till the key is supplied, which in its legitimate meaning is true ; but just as cipher writing will surrender its secret to analysis, which is the master-key to all cryptography, so will occult philosophy also disclose its mystery,* without conventional initiation, though supposing the existence of a royal road of this kind, it might be regarded as a labour-saving apparatus which, if accessible, it would not be prudent to set aside.

There are, however, two considerations on the surface of a question like the present which will at once arrest attention. The first is whether the occult philosophies are not inherently unmeaning, and unable therefore to disclose what, in fact, they do not possess. Or alternately, in the case that they are methodised, whether the mystery which they cover is not out of all proportion to the enormous intellectual cost of unravelling it.† Of these two points one at least must be determined according to individual predilection. For my own part, after spending some years among strange pathways of human ingenuity, I know certainly that the occult sciences do constitute a methodised system which is singularly inwrought,‡ and since *la science est une noblesse qui oblige*, I must bear testimony to this fact, even though an imaginative reader may transfigure the statement and interpret too liberally the narrow concession which I have here made to sincerity. About the second point it is

---

* In most cases this mystery is merely the difficulty of the single sense.

† I refer here to the unravelling of the first sense ; the existence of any other is a matter of conjecture.

‡ In the sense that, for example, numerical mysticism runs through all departments of occultism.

extremely difficult to indicate even a personal opinion. So far as knowledge is its own reward, I suppose that it may be worth its cost ; but if any department of research should be ruled out of the sphere of operation possessed by this truism, it is occult science and philosophy, so far, at least, as the majority are concerned. The labour involved by their exhaustive study repays those who undertake it only in a few cases. In the pursuit of occult knowledge Campaspe is never finished. But it is precisely for this reason that an inquiry like the present may be held to deserve a welcome, because it offers to all those who may be disposed to concern themselves with one important department of occult philosophy an intelligible statement of the issues which will save most of them the need of personal research.

The importance of the written tradition of Kabalism can be regarded only from two standpoints. There is that which it may possess for the sacred scriptures of the Jewish and Christian religions and for the exoteric doctrines which more or less derive from these.* Under this first head may be also included its significance, if any, for the science of comparative theology and for the history of human thought. Besides such obvious and unquestioned grounds upon which it is entitled to consideration,

---

* From the occult standpoint this is of more consequence than from that of ordinary exegesis. Adolphe Bertet, in his *Apocalypse du bienheureux Jean . . . devoilée* (Paris, 1861, p. 51), gives the position very clearly. "We find on every page of the five books of Moses Kabalistic expressions which proclaim that everything must be taken in a figurative sense, yet in none of these books do we possess a complete treatise of initiation, whence it follows that prior to Moses oral tradition was alone charged with transmitting the secret of initiation." Bertet owed his inspiration and frequently his language to Eliphas Levi.

there is another warrant in the interest which it possesses for the seeker after occult knowledge. And here it is necessary to determine what is meant and involved by occultism. The study of the large literature of the secret sciences is pursued by many persons from many motives, but few of these can, in the proper sense of the term, be regarded as occult students. Nor, indeed, does the attempted practice of any of the secret sciences in itself constitute a claim to that title. In a very large number of cases such practices suggest titular distinctions which are not of a flattering kind. As I understand him, the true student of occultism believes in the existence of a knowledge—which in effect is occult science—handed down from remote ages,* and that it concerns, broadly speaking, the way of union between man and God. It has, according to its legend, assumed, for various reasons, the disguise of many veils; it is not confined to one country or people, nor is it the interior sense of any single religion or of any single cycle in literature to the

---

* The best aspects of this belief are, as might be expected, quite modern ; it can scarcely be said to have existed prior to the end of the eighteenth century, but even then it had taken no definite shape. One of its aspects was developed in a remarkable manner by M. de Briere, who in his *Essai sur le symbolisme antique de l' Orient, principalement sur le symbolisme Egyptien* (Paris, 1847), maintained : (*a*) A common origin for all religions ; (*b*) The existence of sacerdotal sciences as the exclusive patrimony of the priesthood ; (*c*) The existence among all eastern priests of a common idiom of high antiquity, which passed as a theurgic, magical and efficacious language ; (*d*) The reproduction of this language by hieroglyphics which were also theurgic and magical ; (*e*) A dual sacerdotal method of expressing the principles of priestly sciences, and chiefly of theology : (1) Imitation of words = hieroglyphs of the texts ; (2) Imitation of thoughts = images, idols, emblematic figures of gods ; (*f*) The existence of the sacred language and hiero- glyphic writing among all peoples possessing sacerdotal sciences, the Phœnicians and Chaldeans for example.

exclusion of all others; there are traces of its existence in all times, among all nations, through all religions;[*] it is behind the conventional occultism of Magic and the transcendental physics of Alchemy; among occult philosophies, Kabalistic literature is one of its most important vehicles.

From this standpoint the true message of the Kabalah is not exegetical or historical; it is not of systems, schools, or interpretations; it is of a living and spiritual kind. This is, indeed, the only vital point of view from which the subject can be regarded, and it redeems the whole circle of occult science from the charge of vanity.

Given this standpoint, Kabalistic literature is indescribably momentous, and yet to concede the position is impossible for ordinary criticism, and should not, indeed, be expected by those who hold it intelligently. It is, in truth, very difficult to defend, because heretofore it has been occupied either on the warrant of a knowledge which cannot be made public, and is therefore idle to proclaim, or on that of evidence which is without much title to serious consideration. If we take, for example, the expository literature of Kabalism which has been written from the occult standpoint in any modern language, there is not a single work which does not break down at once in the hands of the most temperate criticism. Mr. Mathers, in England, has translated a small portion of the Zohar, and has prefixed an introduction which

---

* As regards the Christian religion, see Eckartshausen concerning "a more advanced school," or "invisible celestial Church," to which the "deposition of all science has been confided." *The Cloud upon the Sanctuary*, Letter I. Translated by Isabel de Steiger, London, 1896.

takes the whole claim for granted, while he leaves on the mind of his readers an indistinct impression that Dr. Ginsburg, who errs on the side of hostility, is not only one of its supporters, but gives credit to the most fabulous side of Kabalistic legend. In America, Isaac Myer, whose erudition entitles him to our respect, is forced on crucial points to assume many things that are required for his hypothesis.* In France the real questions at issue are scarcely skirted in the otherwise careful tabulation attempted by Papus.† In Germany, which exhausts everything, I do not know that in any true sense of the term the position has a single defender. It is not my purpose either to question or maintain the general fact alleged, namely, that a secret doctrine has been transmitted from antiquity; it would be scandalous as a reasonable person to challenge the possibility. I propose only to determine whether there is ground for believing that the Kabalah has been a channel of such tradition, and if this view must be abandoned, to place those who are willing to follow me in possession of a method of regarding it which will make its existence at least intelligible without taking anything for granted and without appealing to any source of knowledge which is not fully in evidence.

---

* He assumes in fact the existence, antiquity and general but con cealed diffusion of a Wisdom Religion, a term borrowed from modern theosophy, and one which, in the last analysis, is not entirely sati factory to the mystic.

† *La Kabbale. Tradition Secrete de l'Occident. Résumé Méthodique.* Paris, 1892, 8vo.

III. THE KABALAH AND THE TALMUD

The post-Christian literature which is of authority in Israel must, of course, be distinguished from the multifarious productions of its scholars and *literati* which it was the object of rabbinical bibliographies, like those of Bartolocci and Wolf,* to resume in brief. In order to understand the place occupied by the Kabalah it is necessary to say something of that great and authoritative collection which is known to everyone as the Talmud. The latter is a larger as it is also an older growth. Its starting-point has been placed by a moderate criticism shortly before the birth of Christ,† and, to use a somewhat conventional phrase, its two canons were fixed in the fourth and sixth centuries, A.D., at which periods, although there are evidences in abundance of a more esoteric doctrine, it cannot be shown conclusively that Kabalistic literature, according to the restricted sense in which the term is here applied, had as yet come into existence. Put shortly, the sources of the Talmud are said to be " the customs and regulations practised by the authori-

---

* *Bibliotheca Hebræa, sive notitia tum auctorum Hebraicorum cujuscumque ætatis, tum scriptorum, quæ vel Hebraice primum exarata, vel ab aliis conversa sunt, ad nostram ætatem deducta.* 4 vols., Leipsic and Hamburg, 1715, 4to.

† There are critics outside occult circles who ascribe a similar antiquity to the Kabalah, as, for example, the author of the article *s.v. Cabale* in the *Grand Dictionnaire Universel du* XIXe *Siècle* (Pierre Larousse), t. iii. Paris, 1867. " In reality the Kabalah originated among the Jews five centuries before our era. Formed of the mixture of oriental ideas and Mosaism at the epoch of the captivity, it was elaborated silently, and in the main among the sect of the Karaites, but did not attain its definite development till the period of Philo and the schools of Alexandria." The inspiration here is Franck.

ties in their administration of religious and civil
affairs."* It is claimed that this source goes back to
the period of Esdras, and there can, at least, be no
doubt that the materials embodied in the literature
are far older than their earliest collected forms.
These materials were certain *Mishnayoth*, a term
signifying repetitions—namely, notes of academical
teachings, which received subsequently many additions.† About the year 220, A.D., a considerable proportion of these was engarnered by Rabbi Judah the
Prince,‡ by whom they were methodised carefully,
short comments of his own being also occasionally
added.§   In this way the collection received the
impression of his peculiar views, from which other
authorities differed. He endeavoured to destroy all
rival *Mishnayoth*, but some of them were preserved in
secret and came to light after his death. In this way
we have—

(*a*) The *Mishna*, or repetition, being the methodised selection of Rabbi Judah.

(*b*) The *Tosephtoth*, or additions, also called
Baraithoth,‖ outsiders, or secondary matter, terms

* "The Babylonian Talmud." English Translation. By Michael
L. Rodkinson. Vol. i. New York, 1896, 8vo., pp. xv., xvi.

† In the *Halichot Olam* it is said that Jewish teachers had little
schedules or scrolls of parchment, in which they set down all the tradi
tions, sentences, statutes, decisions and so forth which they learned
from their masters and that these scrolls were called the volume   i
thing. cret.

‡ He was the third patriarch of the Western Jews, and a legend
says that, having converted the Emperor Marcus Aurelius, he compiled
the Mishna at the command of that Prince. See I. II. I. Imer:
"History of the Jewish Nation," London, 1883, pp. 204, 205.

§ For an old account of this labour, see David Ganz: *Germen
Davidis, sive Chronologia Sacra et Prophana.* Leyden, 1644.

‖ And extravagances, in the sense of things extraneous.

applied by the followers of Rabbi Judah to the rival *Mishnayoth*, by which the original collection is said in the course of time to have been almost extinguished. Their rival claims were ultimately harmonised by later rabbis, and thus arose

(*c*) The *Gemara*—*i.e.*, conclusions or completion.*

The union of the *Gemara* and the *Mishna* forms the Talmud,† or instruction, from a word signifying "to teach," of which there are two versions, the *Mishna* being the same in each. The *Gemara* collected by Jerusalem rabbis, representing the school of Tiberias and R. Johanon Ben Eliezer, with the *Mishna*, forms the Jerusalem Talmud, and belongs to the end of the fourth century. The *Gemara* collected by Babylonian rabbis, and especially by Rabhina, R. Ashi and R. Jose, with the *Mishna*, forms the Talmud of Babylon, four times larger than that of Jerusalem.‡ It was begun in the fifth and completed in the sixth century, but even subsequently to this period much additional material was gathered into it.

It is exceedingly important that we should understand the position which is occupied by the great collections of the Talmud in respect of the literature which is termed technically the Kabalah. In the first place, this name, technical or conventional, as I have said, has suggested many errors of comparison. By

---

* Simeon ben Jochai is represented as asserting that the study of the *Gemara* was more meritorious than that of the *Mishna* or the sacred Scriptures. But here a later predilection has perhaps sheltered itself under an earlier name.

† Strictly speaking, the term Talmud applies only to the *Gemara*, but it has obtained the wider application because the *Gemara* always accompanies the *Mishna*, the text being essential to the note.

‡ The proportion of the Babylonian *Gemara* to the original *Mishna* is about eleven to one.

the hypothesis of both literatures the Talmud is Kabalah even as the Zohar is Kabalah, because both are a reception by tradition.* But to say that the Talmud is Kabalistic in the sense of the Zohar is extremely misleading. The cycles are distinct and almost divergent. There is no question as to the age and the great authority of the one,† while some cen- turies of inquiry have not as yet determined the claims of the other. Moreover, if we assume the equal antiquity of both, the nature of the tradition is still generically different. The Talmud is not, at least, primarily a philosophical system; ‡ it is law and com- mentary; it is the construction placed by authority on the jurisprudence, ecclesiastical and political, of old Israel.§ It is sociology, not metaphysics, even though it has admitted metaphysics and has accretions which can be termed mystical. To place it by the arbitrary

---

"In older Jewish literature, the name (Kabalah) is applied to the whole body of received religious doctrine with the exception of the Pentateuch, thus including the prophets and Hagiographa, as well as the oral traditions ultimately embodied in the Mishna." —*American Encyclopædia*, iii., pp. 521, 522.

† I do not mean that there has never been a question, for the French ecclesiastic Morin, proceeding on the principle that the Jews cannot be believed in anything relating to the age of their literature, endeavoured to refer the Mishna to the beginning of the sixth century and the Gemaras to some two hundred years later.—*Exercitationes Biblicæ*, Paris, 1660.

‡ Hence all the conspicuous philosophical doctrines of the Kabalah have no place therein. For example, the Sephirotic system, with which we shall be concerned later on, and the theory of emanation which it involves, cannot be traced in the Talmud. Consult Edersheim : "History of the Jewish Nation," third edition, p. 406.

§ It has been described as "a *corpus juris* in which the law has not yet been differentiated from morality and religion." See Farrar's "Life of Christ," illustrated edition, *n.d.*, p. 758.

It is possible to institute a comparison between the Talmud and the Kabalah as between Freemasonry and late Western Occultism. The Talmud is not mysticism, but it became the asylum of some

use of a conventional term in the same category as the literature which discusses the mysteries of the "Supreme Crown," the evolution of "negative divine subsistence," so-called, into positive being, the emanation of the *Sephiroth* and the origin, metempsychosis and destiny of souls, is to make a foolish and deceiving classification. M. Isidore Loëb* offers us the equivalent of an admirable distinction between the two literatures in his observations upon the comparative position of the French and Spanish Jews at the period of the promulgation of the Zohar. Talmudic Israel was, he tells us, circumscribed by the circle of the Law; it had no horizon and no future; it had no place in the life of philosophy.† The Zohar gave to Israel the splendid impulsion of the ideal; it gave philosophy; it created a wide horizon; it brought the

---

mystic traditions. Freemasonry is not Occult Science, but under the standard of the Craft all occult science of the eighteenth century found not only a refuge, but a field of work and of development. The way of entrance in the one case was the Haggadic morality, in the other it was the high grades.

    * *La Grande Encyclopédie*, Paris, 4to, *s.v. Cabbale*, vol. viii.

    † "In the immense collections which have come down to us from the fifth or sixth centuries of the Christian era, in the Talmud as in the allegorical interpretations of the Bible, there is no trace of philosophical speculations. If we find reminiscences of the Kabalah, they concern, so to speak, the exoteric portion, or angelology; the existence of the speculative part is shown in these books solely by the reference to the mysteries contained in *Bereshith*, or the first chapter of Genesis, and in the *Mercavah*, or Vision of Ezekiel."—S. Munk: *La Philosophie chez les Juifs*, Paris, 1848, p. 8. The author was an informed and accomplished defender of the existence of Kabalistic tradition in Talmudic times. It should be added that the Talmudic references to the Work of the Creation and the Work of the Chariot would, if collated, go far to verify the opinion that such a tradition was known as regards the fact of its existence, but it was referred to only enigmatically, and its nature does not really transpire. While the Talmud records occasionally that there were conversations between the doctors of Israel thereon, it does not report the utterances.

exiled Jew into correspondence with the thought of the world; it communicated the Eternal.

The first result of the confusion in question is to place a wrong construction upon Talmudic literature, to affirm that, as believed of the Kabalah proper, it possesses a double meaning, and that we are to look below its literal sense.* It has been well pointed out that it would be as reasonable to admit a metaphysical construction in the Common Law of England, the deliberations of a Holy Synod in the collections of State Trials, and a theory of transmutation in Conveyancing. Yet this is what has been done actually in the case of the Talmud by the one Kabalistic expositor whose influence with occult students in France and England is so paramount as to have been considered almost beyond appeal. To Eliphas Levi, who, as a fact, misstated so much, we owe a grandiose presentation of the Talmudic system which does grave outrage to good sense.† He lays down that the first Talmud, the only truly Kabalistic one, was collected during the second century of the Christian era by " Rabbi Jehudah Hakadosh Hanassi—that is, Judah

---

* Edersheim divides Talmudic traditionalism into two portions : Halakha = the legislative enactments of the Fathers ; and Haggada = free interpretation.—" History of the Jewish Nation, p. 136. Some of the Haggadic legends may possess an inner meaning, that is, they are allegorical stories ; the history of the salting of Leviathan is so absurd in its literal sense that one is driven out of mere generosity to suppose that it meant something which does not appear on its surface. Compare " Israel among the Nations," by Anatole Leroy-Beaulieu, p. 24. As Halakha is rule, *norma*, so Haggada is legend, s.iga, " a collection of miscellaneous utterances touching on every possible subject." The Halakha alone is law.

† *La Clef des Grands Mysteres.* Paris, 1861, 8vo, p. 351, *et seq.* See also Waite : " Mysteries of Magic." Second edition, London, 1897, 8vo, pp. 112-120.

the most holy and the prince "—who " composed his book according to all the rules of supreme initiation." He "wrote it within and without, as Ezekiel and St. John have it, and he indicated its transcendental sense by the sacred letters and numbers corresponding to the Bereshith of the first six *Sephiroth*."* This asserted Sephirotic correspondence has no place in fact. The Mishna comprises six sections, of which the first concerns tithes, the beasts which it is unlawful to pair, the seeds which must not be sown together in the earth, the threads which must not be interwoven, the fruits which must not be gathered till the trees have passed their third year, and so forth. It is by no means chiefly, much less exclusively, agricultural, as Levi, who had obviously not read it, represents. Nor has it any special correspondence with *Kether*, except on the thin ground that " in the notion of the Supreme Crown is contained that of the fructifying principle and of universal production." Any attribution could be accredited after this fashion.

The second book concerns the festivals of Israel, the meats which are prohibited on these, the days of fasting and so forth. There is no attempt to justify the attribution which connects it with *Chokmah*. The third book concerns marriage and divorce, or, in the

* I should note that, long prior to Éliphas Lévi, Adrianus Relandus (*Analecta Rabbinica*, 1702) and Galatinus (*De Arcanis Catholicæ Veritatis*, 1656) supposed a second sense in the Talmud. It was not, however, metaphysical or mystical, but was a concealment prompted by the necessities of a persecuting time. This supposition is not less idle than the other, for the first thing which prudence would have suggested would be to hide the real feelings of Talmudic Jews towards Christians, and these are not dissembled in the Talmud. There are, of course, many histories in the Talmud which must not be construed literally, but, as in the case previously cited, they belong merely to the domain of allegory.

words of Lévi, "it is more particularly consecrated to women and the fundamental basis of the family." The fourth book deals with civil contracts, general jurisdiction, civil and criminal actions, penalties, &c. Eliphas Lévi says that it is superior to any code of the Middle Ages and accounts for the preservation of Israel through all its persecutions. According to the natural order of the *Sephiroth*, it corresponds with *Chesed* or Mercy, but as it looks better under the attribution of Justice, the Sephirotic system is reversed accordingly. The fifth book, which is allotted to Mercy by this transposition, treats, according to the French transcendentalist, of consoling beliefs and things holy, which creates a completely false impression concerning it. As a matter of fact, it is dedicated to votive offerings. The sixth book treats of purifications, which Levi terms "the most hidden secrets of life and the morality which directs it." *

It is procedures of this kind which have made occult criticism deservedly a byword among scholars.†

---

* The exegesis thus inaugurated loses nothing in the hands of later occult writers. For example, an occult *opusculum* observes that the key which will alone open the revelations of the Christian Scriptures and manifest their interior sense, "exists in a book proscribed by the Christian Church—the Jewish Talmud." See "The Astral Light," by Nizida. Second edition, London, 1892, pp. 50, 51. It is just to add that this work is not regarded as of consequence by the circle to which it makes appeal.

† Some criticism which is not the work of occultists deserves the same condemnation. Mr. C. W. Heckethorn, author of the "Secret Societies of all Ages and Countries" (new edition, 2 vols., 1897), has presumed to treat the subject of the Kabalah in the absence of elementary knowledge. Thus, he tells us that the literal Kabalah is called the Mishna (vol. I. p. 85), which, as we have seen, is the traditional commentary on the legislative part of the Mosaic *Thorah*. So also Walton, in his eighth prolegomena to the "Polyglot Bible," observes that the terms Kabalah and Massorah are applied to one science by the Jews. Richard Simon draws attention to this error, saying that

The Talmud has its correspondences with the Kabalah, but they are of method rather than material. It is highly desirable to study it in connection with the Zohar, but it is a consummate act of ignorance to confound and to regard them as written upon the same principle and with the same objects.

Another writer, also an occultist, but governed by very different sentiments of scholarship, Mr. Isaac Myer, makes an exceedingly proper distinction when he affirms that the Kabalah and the Zohar " allow a great margin to speculative thought." He means to say that they are purely speculative philosophy, while the Talmud " deals with everyday life and humanity under the Law ; " that the one " starts from a spiritual point of view, contemplating a spiritual finality as regards the Law and its explanation," but that the other is " eminently practical in both its starting-point and end, and having, in the face of ignorance, want of perception and natural waywardness of the masses, nothing but the strict observance of the Law in all its details in view." *

IV. DIVISIONS OF THE KABALAH

Before we can proceed with our subject it will be necessary to remove some further false impressions which, unlike the transcendental aspect attributed to

---

the Massorah is the criticism of the Hebrew text.—*Histoire Critique du Vieux Testament*, p. 498.   Amsterdam, 1685.

* " Philosophy of Ibn Gebirol," p. 35.   Compare W. B. Greene, " The Blazing Star," 1872, 12mo.   " The Massorah is in every respect the converse of the Kabalah.   The Massorah is that which was openly delivered by the Rabbi ; the Kabalah is that which was secretly and mysteriously received by the disciple," p. 29.

the Talmud, are not errors peculiar to occult writers, and have consequently a wider sphere of operation. They concern the nature and applications of the tradition which is supposed to have been perpetuated in Israel. For most popular writers, for almost all encyclopædias which have not had recourse to a specialist, the Kabalistic art is simply the use of sacred names in the evocation of spirits,* or it is that at least above all and more than all.† We find it in standard sources of reference like the great dictionary of Calmet,‡ while it obtains still in many slipshod accounts which pass from book to book, without any attempt at verification on the part of those who reproduce them. It illustrates the importance which is everywhere attributed to magic, for in the last analysis all occult science and all its oral traditions are resolved by the popular mind into a commerce with the denizens of the unseen world. I have done full justice elsewhere§ to the enormous influence exercised by the belief in this commerce, so that the vulgar instinct is not entirely at fault. In a higher sense than that of ceremonial magic the ends of all occult science are assuredly in the unseen, and as to the

---

* Compare Frinellan : *Le Triple Vocabulaire Infernal* (Paris, *n.d.*), p. 30 : "What is termed the Kabalah is the art of commercing with elementary spirits."

† Sometimes, however, it is closely united with astrology, and to speak of this occult science is considered equivalent to speaking of Kabalistic matters. Such, apparently, was the notion of Démeunier, *L' Esprit des Usages et des coutumes des différens Peuples, tom.* ii. lib. xi. London, 1776.

‡ "Dictionary of the Bible." For convenience of reference, consult C. Taylor's translation, London, 1823, vol. i. *s. v.* Cabbala.

§ "The Book of Black Magic and of Pacts," part i. c. i. p. 5 *et seq.* London, 1898, 4to. It must be admitted that the term Kabalah was applied early in its history to some form of theurgic practice.

processes of evocation I have said already that they are largely Kabalistic processes.* They are, however, either late and corrupt derivatives which are not the esoteric tradition, but applications, and hence accidents thereof ; or, if we must admit that there were magical practices involving a conventional procedure and a formal ritual prevalent among the Hebrews at a remote period,† which were also handed down, and are therefore entitled to be classed, in a sense, as Kabalah, then that reception must be distinguished very carefully from the Kabalah with which we are here concerned.‡ The tradition of the " Book of Formation " and the " Book of Splendour " is not of magic but of philosophy. It has not been incorrectly described, though by an unknown writer, in the following terms : " The Kabalah claims to be that spontaneous philosophy which man, quoad man, naturally affirms now, always has affirmed, and always will affirm so long as man is man. The worlds confessed by the Kabalah are worlds known to man, worlds upon which man has set the seal of his own nature, worlds related to man and of which man is the

---

* Refer to preface.

† It is to these practices that I suppose Richard Simon alludes, when he says that "the ancient Jewish doctors brought many superstitious sciences from Chaldea," p. 93. This author can be hardly regarded as an authority on Kabalistic questions ; indeed, he seems to confess (op. cit., pp. 116, 117) that he had not thought it worth while to expend time over "the ancient allegorical books of the Jews," such as the Zohar and the Bahir.

‡ The opposite is held by an American writer, T. K. Hosmer, who says : " From this source all Jewry was overrun with demonology, thaumaturgy, and other strange fancies."—The Jews in Ancient, Mediæval and Modern Times, London, 1890, pp. 222, 223. Speaking generally, it is most in consonance with the facts to regard the magic which Europe received at Jewish hands as a debased application of Kabalism.

authentic form.   There is nothing in the Kabalah
which is not found also in the nature of man." *

As we have found it expedient to set aside the
Kabalah of the Talmud in order to clear the issues, so
also, or at least till a later stage of our inquiry, we
must ignore the Kabalah of magic. We are dealing
with an attempted explanation of the universe, which
is something entirely distinct from all formulæ of
evocation. The theurgic and talismanic use of divine
names and the doctrine of efficacious words belongs
to a distinct category, and is liable to be encountered
everywhere in Jewish Theosophy. As will be seen
later on, there is no question as to the antiquity of
these notions.

By another error the subject-matter of the secret
tradition is confused with certain exegetical methods
by which a scriptural authority is found for it. These
methods obtained very widely, and there is no doubt
that many of their most curious results contributed to
swell the volume of the tradition, but the method
which deals with material, and may even occasionally
supply it, must be held distinct therefrom. They
were, however, a matter of tradition, and as such
are Kabalah, but they are not the doctrinal Kabalah,
and in the attempt to methodise our subject these
also must be held as embodying things distinct.†

---

* W. B. Greene : "The Blazing Star," p. 57. It follows from the
specific teaching of the chief storehouse of Kabalism, the Zohar, that
apart from the human form, permanence and organisation are impossible
to finite existences, whence, also, it is the form in which God communicates Himself.

† P. J. Hershon divides the Kabalah into two parts, symbolical and
real. The first teaches the secret sense of Scripture and the thirteen
rules by which the observance of the Law is expounded Kabalistically,
i.e, Gematria, Notaricon, Themurah, &c. The real Kabalah he sub-

It follows from the above discriminations that there are, broadly speaking, four separate groups or species of tradition in Israel which, by virtue of the meaning of words, are entitled to rank as Kabalah : *

1. The administrative tradition of the Talmud, the authoritative regulations as to the laws, customs, ceremonies and civil life of the Jewish nation. The literature of this tradition is of great historical value, but it has little place in philosophy.

2. The magical tradition of the Hebrews, very important to the history of occult science, very obscure in its history, very much exaggerated by those who write about it, possessing little literature prior to the fourteenth century of the Christian era, by which time it had lost most of its antique elements."†

3. Certain exegetical and other traditional

---

divides into theoretical and practical ; the one is concerned with the emanations and worlds of Kabalism, the nature and names of God, the celestial hierarchy and its influence on the lower world, the mysteries of creation and so forth ; the other deals with the mystical properties of divine and angelic names and the wonders performed with these.— "Talmudic Miscellany," London, 1880.

* Dr. Wynn Westcott, in his work on "Numbers, their Occult Power and Mystic Virtue," observes (p. 11) that the word Kabalah "includes the Hebrew Doctrines of Cosmogony and Theology as well as the Science of Numbers." The first he terms the Dogmatic and the second the Literal Kabalah. The Kabalistic Science of numbers is included in *Gematria*.

† The indefectible title of magic to a place in Jewish Kabalah is enforced by all modern occultists, who have helped very much to confuse the issues in question. So far back as the end of the seventeenth century the distinction between the magical tradition and the philosophical or doctrinal was recognised by R. Simon (*Histoire Critique du Vieux Testament*. Amsterdam, 1685, 4to), who said : "There is another sort of Kabalah which is more dangerous and forms part of that which is commonly called Magic. It is a mere illusion, the prepossession of certain persons who believe they can perform miracles by means of it." (p. 374).

methods by which a secret sense was extracted from the letter of Holy Scripture.   Very curious results were sometimes obtained by these solemn follies which appear so childish and ridiculous at the present day.*   They comprise :

a. Gematria, by which the letters of a word were converted into numbers, and the arithmetical value was used to explain its internal sense.

b. Notaricon, by which each letter of a word was taken as the initial of another word, or, conversely, the initial letters of an entire sentence were combined to form a word, which word was held to throw light on the sentence.

c. Themurah, that is, the transposition of letters in a given word or sentence.

It is obvious that the field of these methods is not confined to one language or one literature ; their application to the plays of Shakespeare might produce results which would exceed even the pretensions of the " Great Cryptogram." It is a little humiliating to find an important subject and a fascinating literature connected with such diversions, but we shall see later on that the peculiar views of the Hebrews upon the divine character of their language invested them with a certain speciousness, while, for the rest, our inquiry is fortunately not concerned with them.   These methods are sometimes termed the artificial or prac-

---

* The Kabalistic method of interpreting scripture, "which reduces the sense of the sacred books to vain and ridiculous subtletie-, the mysteries contained in letters, in numbers, and in the dismemberment of certain words," was supposed by Simon to have passed from the school of Platonism to that of the Jews, chiefly in Europe.   There is no ground for this view.   IIe adds (*op. cit.*, p. 374) that this " specu-lative Kabalah " was, in his own day, still highly esteemed by the Jews of the Levant."

tical Kabalah.* Their antiquity, like that of the Hebrew vowel-points, is a debated question. By some critics their traces have been discerned even in Holy Scripture.† One point, however, which should be especially noted is that recourse to these methods is met with comparatively seldom in the Zohar.

4. The philosophical tradition, embodied in the "Sepher Yetzirah" and the "Zohar" cycles. To this only, in the interests of clearness, should the conventional term Kabalah be applied, and it is this which is really signified by every well-informed writer who uses it. It is divided by the Kabalists themselves into

a. The Doctrine of Creation,

b. The Doctrine of the Chariot—i.e., the chariot of Ezekiel's vision.‡

These divisions are concerned respectively with the natural and the transcendental world, and are sometimes termed collectively the theoretical Kabalah.

---

* They assumed sometimes the most extravagant forms. For example, the middle letter of any sacred book was written in an unusual position or of an unusual size, and was regarded as possessing a deep spiritual meaning. See "The Bible Handbook," by Joseph Angus, D.D., 1860, p. 499. "The modes by which the Kabalah educes the secret meaning veiled under the words of the Hebrew scriptures are manifold, extending to every peculiarity of the text. Even in what we should regard as critical marks or as errors or fancies of some transcriber, as when a letter is written too large or too small, is inverted or in any way distinguished, an occult intent was presumed." *American Encyclopædia*, iii. 521, 522.

† The Chaldaic paraphrase of Jonathan ben Ouziel has recourse occasionally to a species of transliteration when dealing with certain obscure scriptural names.

‡ Both these divisions are mentioned in the Mishna by name (*Chagiga*, xi. 2), and are said to be secret doctrine, but the *Maasse Bereshith* and the *Maasse Mercabah* there referred to are not a written tradition, nor does that of the written Kabalah necessarily represent it. The Zohar identifies the *Mercabah* with the *Sephiroth* or Ten Emanations, which see.

It is this which gave to Israel the intellectual horizon which was impossible to the Talmudic Jew, and it is this also which gave the Children of the Exile a place in Western philosophy.   When we hear that the Kabalah once fascinated some of the great minds of Christendom, it is to this only that the statement can be applied.*   It is this, finally, which it is the purpose of the present inquiry to elucidate.†   It should be added that outside the cycle of the Zohar there is a large Jewish theosophical and mystical literature, of which the Sepher Yetzirah is an instance.   It was this which led up to the Zohar, and was embraced thereby.   But whether it was Kabalistic in the sense of the latter is one of the disputes of scholarship.

---

* Drach distinguishes three uses of the term Kabalah for which authority can be cited : (1) It is frequently applied by the Talmud to the books of the Old Testament outside the Pentateuch ; (2) The rabbins apply it to the legal or talmudic tradition ; (3) It signifies especially the "mystic, esoteric, acroamatic portion of the oral tradition."—*De l'Harmonie entre l'Eglise et la Synagogue. Par le* Chevalier P. L. B. Drach, 2 vols., Paris, 1844.

† I must not pass over the division of the Kabalah proposed by Dr. Papus in one of his latest publications, though I regard it, critically speaking, as fantastic. The Kabalah is, in his opinion, attributable to Moses, and the written word of Scripture is therefore naturally a part of the tradition. We have thus : (a) The written word ; (b) The oral word ; (c) An intermediate portion, being rules insuring the preservation of the text, *i.e.* Massorah. The last is the body of the oral tradition ; the Mishna and Gemara are its life ; the Sepher Yetzirah and the Zohar are its spirit. Unfortunately Dr. Papus has not made his thesis so clear as he does usually, and he seems to assume some of the most important points at issue. See *Traité Elémentaire de Science Occulte,* 5e édition, Paris, 1898.

BOOK II

THE DOCTRINAL CONTENT OF
THE KABALAH

ARGUMENT

The fundamental doctrines of the Kabalah are shown to be :
(*a*) The Philosophy of the Absolute ; (*b*) The evolution of the
universe by way of emanation ; (*c*) The distinction of the emanation
into Four Worlds issuing one from another. The subsidiary
doctrines connected with these are : (1) The contrast between
God in Himself and God as revealed to His people ; (2) The
Sacramental nature of the conventional symbols of the human
Logos ; (3) Certain ways and methods by which knowledge and
wisdom are attainable ; (4) A complex system of pneumatology.
These subjects are regarded from the occult standpoint, but a
sufficient warrant is not found for the view that they represent an
occult doctrine of Absolute Religion.

I. THE UNMANIFEST GOD

THE conventional division of Kabalistic doctrines into
transcendental and physical, though valuable for purposes of tabulation, must not be held to signify that
there is a clear line of demarcation in virtue of which
the literature branches off into divergent paths, much
less that the Kabalah offers a natural history of the
universe. Its physics, so far as it can be said to have
any, are transcendental physics. Admitting of no
separation between God, Man and Nature,* the

---

* That is to say, the mystic communication is permanent, but
the pantheistic doctrine of identity is quite foreign to the position of
Kabalism.

science which explains them is likewise one, and the best manner of studying it is to follow its view as to the eternal order. It begins in that Absolute which it is the purpose of all fundamental wisdom to make known or communicate to man; it attempts to exhibit the transition from the Absolute to the related, from the noumenal to the phenomenal, and to establish a chain of correspondence between the infinite and the finite. It is, however, more than a philosophical attempt to bridge over the gulf which separates the timeless from the temporal; that is the side on which it connects with philosophy, as commonly understood. The intermediaries of the transition are the ladder of ascent by which man returns to the Divine; hence also it is more than an explanation of the universe; it is, speaking correctly, a sum of religion, and as it is founded, no matter how, on those Scriptures which Jew and Christian have recognised equally as the peculiar revelation of God, the text-book of true religion, we shall see readily what depth and mystery are sought to be infused by the Kabalah into the Bible. We shall also agree with those discerning critics who describe it as, strictly speaking, a system of theosophy; it is the application of the wisdom of Israel to the unsearchable mystery of God, and it begins, as we might have expected, by confessing that it is unsearchable, that beyond our best conceptions of all that is most divine, as beyond so many veridic illusions, there is the unknown and unknowable God.*

---

* According to the Zohar, it is impossible to know that which there is in this principle, for it never stoops to our ignorance and is above even wisdom. See "The Lesser Holy Synod," when treating, for example, of the *Caput quod non est caput* . . . *quod non comprehenditur Sapientia nec intellectu. Kabbalæ Denudatæ Tomus Secundus*, p. 528.

Even in the mystic communication possible between the divine and man, which is an old doctrine of Jewish mysticism, long anterior to the Zohar, at least in its present form, the essence escapes our apprehension. We can, indeed, know God, but not as He is in Himself, our knowledge being made possible through the manifestation of the Deity, and this takes place after two manners—by the mediation of the Law of Nature, that is to say, in the physical universe; and by the Law of Grace, which is the manifestation of God in his relation with the souls of his elect. It will be seen that both these methods are sacramental, and the sacramental system is the form of all mysticism. For the Kabalistic Jew the Law and the Covenant were signs or mysteries capable of a plurality of interpretations, while the whole outward world was omen and metaphrasis. It is therefore to be expected that in the written word we must look for another meaning than is conveyed by the outward sense. It was also a part of Jewish mental bias to look for an inward significance which was opposed to the external, and strikes unfailingly the modern observer as strained and unnatural.

In the eternity which preceded either of the manifestations which I have mentioned, the Deity was withdrawn into Himself and subsisted after a manner which entirely transcends the conception of human faculties.* The names which are ascribed to the

---

* The tract entitled the " Faithful Shepherd," which forms part of the Zohar, says, on the authority of R. Simeon ben Jochai, that before God created the archetypal idea which underlies the form of the world, He was alone, without form or similitude, and hence there could be no cognition of him. (*Rayah Mehemnah*, in the Cremona edition of the Zohar, pt. ii. col. 73). There was, of course, no intelligence to

Deity in this abyssal condition are not names which present either the condition or the Divine Nature; they are the conventions of the philosophical hypothesis; they are terms which serve to indicate that God, prior to manifestation, is nameless, even as He is beyond reach.* He is the Ancient One, and the most Ancient of all the Ancients, but this describes only the eternity of His subsistence; He is the Hidden of all the Hidden Ones, but this concerns only His concealment; He is *Ain Soph*, a phrase which Rosenroth renders *fine carens*,† the unlimited or infinite, but it also includes, by the separate significance of the word *Ain*, the abstract competition of nothingness, and this registers only the inconceivable nature of His infinite mode.‡ According to the "Book of Concealment," His dwelling is the place which is not a place, or more literally, *locus qui non est.*§ There is at first sight a touch of atheistical impiety in this attempt to describe God as the

---

comprehend Him, but the idea which underlies the confusion is that the supposed period of God's eternal rest is now beyond the comprehension of the human mind. We are unable to conceive a state or period in which the world was not, but God alone.

* The interrogative pronoun *Who?* is ascribed by the Zohar to this state of the Supreme. Earlier mysticism speaks of God being alone with his Name, *i.e.*, the Divine Tetragram, which, according to Maimonides, preceded the whole creation.

† *Apparatus in Librum Sohar pars prima, Kabbala Denudata*, vol. I. p. 81.

‡ Zoharic teaching specifically affirms this point. It is said, for example, that prior to the creation of the world, prior to the production of any image, God was alone, formless and resembling nothing. In this state it is forbidden to represent Him by any image or under any form whatsoever, even by His Holy Name, or by any letter or any point.—*Zohar*, ii., 42 *b.*, Mantua.

§ *Liber Occultationis, seu Mysterii*, c. i. § 5. *Kabbala Denudata*, vol. ii. p. 348.

Non-Ens dwelling in the *Non Est*, but it is really a philosophical subtlety which seeks, by successively stripping off every attribute pertaining to manifest existence, to attain some idea of unmanifest, unconditioned, abstract being. The key is given in the treatise entitled *Pardes Rimmonim*, by R. Moses of Cordova,* which says that the Cause of Causes is called *Ain Soph* because His excellence is without bound, and there is nothing which can comprehend Him.

It will be seen that the Kabalistic conception is one which is familiar to later forms of transcendental philosophy under the name of the Absolute, a term which, in the last analysis, is not wanting in similar intellectual difficulties, or, rather, it symbolises our intellectual recognition of that which exceeds our intelligence.† In this Absolute resides the essence or potentiality of all ; ‡ it is not accurate to say that it is the subsistent principle which underlies the objective state termed existence, because existence is a condition of the finite and the created, though there is a true and real sense in which God may be said to

---

* *Pardes Rimmonim, i.e.*, Paradise of Pomegranates, Tract iii. c. i. Moses of Cordova belonged to the more modern school of Kabalists, and his treatise is exegetical and not authoritative in Kabalism.

† See, however, Dr. Noah Porter : "The Human Intellect," London, 1868, who argues that in its proper definition the Absolute becomes knowable. Our idea of the Absolute belongs, nevertheless, to that region of our consciousness which Herbert Spencer terms indefinite and escaping formulation.

‡ Hœne Wronski, whose mathematical transcendentalism is of high authority with French occultists, affirms that the reality of the Absolute is the first principle of reason, and in the absence thereof every assertion made by reason would be valueless. On this principle, as on an indispensable condition, he establishes absolute philosophy in his work entitled *Apodictique.*

encompass, overstand and subtend the visible world.*
Ain Soph is the subsistent state of Deity itself,†
whence it follows that there is from the Kabalistic
standpoint a manifested state of the Divine Nature,
and this is certainly not the visible world. Where
this manifestation occurs will be indicated in the next
section.

It will be obvious that all ordinary notions of a
personal God are destroyed or transcended by this
Non-Ens or *Non-Ego* of the Kabalists; it is absolutely
simple, unity without any multiplication, above all
number, above Wisdom, which, as we shall see, is,
however, one of its first emanations. It is also without sex, and it is therefore, strictly speaking,
inaccurate to make use of the masculine pronouns in
reference thereto. According to Moses of Cordova,
the angels are neither simple nor without multiplication in comparison with it. The book entitled
"Faithful Shepherd"‡ says: "Woe unto him who
makes God to be like unto any mode or attribute
whatever, even if it be one of His own; but woe still
more if he make Him like unto the sons of men, whose
elements are earthly, and so are consumed and perish!
There can be no conception attained of Him, except
in so far as He manifests Himself when exercising

---

* According to the Zohar, God is immanent in all that he
created or emanated, and yet is transcendent to all.

† Occultists should beware of giving further currency to the
absurd description of this state as " negative existence." So far back
as 1867 Herbert Spencer established clearly in l   Principles "
that "the Unconditioned must be represented   e and not
negative."

‡ Quoted in *Beth Elohim*, or the " House of the Gods,"
Dissertatio i. c. i. See *Kabbala Denudata*, vol. ii. ; *Partis l i
Tractatus* i., *i.e.*, *Pneumatica Kabbalistica*, p. 187.

dominion by and through some attribute. Abstracted from this there can be no attribute, conception, or ideal of Him. He is comparable only to the sea, filling some great reservoir, as, for example, its bed in the earth, wherein it fashions for itself a certain concavity, so that thereby we may begin to compute the dimensions of the sea itself."

It remains for me to state that the doctrine of *Ain Soph* is not found in the earliest Kabalistic literature, and appears to have been first developed by the commentators on the Sepher Yetzirah and in the school of Isaac the Blind.

II. THE DOCTRINE OF THE TEN EMANATIONS

Having thus postulated the existence of the Absolute and the Unconditioned, the next concern of the Kabalah is the mode of the manifestation of that withdrawn and inconceivable nature. Having attained its ultimate and fundamental conception of the Deity by the process of elimination to which reference has been made already, it was inevitable that the attribution of absolute reality to that which had been stripped of all realism should have produced as a result something which was outside intellectual comprehension. It is perhaps open to question whether this fact justified the transcendency with which *Ain Soph* was invested, as it is also doubtful whether the methical and elaborated antithesis of anthropomorphism thus created was not as much a convention of the human mind as that which it sought to replace.

The intellectual difficulty was, however, the ground
for the exaltation of the conception at the expense of
the human mind by which it had been devised so
laboriously.* Now, the Jew was confronted by at
least two problems which called for the exercise of his
further ingenuity as regards the *latens Deit.is* of *Ain
Soph.* He had to account for the bond of connection
between this abyss of the Godhead and the visible
universe, having man for its mouthpiece, but so far
this is only the common problem of all philosophy
which begins and ends in the unconditioned. He had
further a problem peculiar to his own inheritance and
election, and this was to establish another bond of
connection between the absolute transcendency of
Ain Soph, apart from all limitation, outside all human
measurement, isolated from all relationship, and the
anthropomorphic Lord of Israel, whose stature and
measurements were not beyond the ingenuity of rabbinical calculations, and most of whose members are
mentioned with sufficient fulness and frequency in the
sacred writings for any devout student to possess a
clear notion of the " body of God," and to describe it,
did he please, and we shall see later on that he did,
with considerable precision, in a book dedicated to
the question. For the moment, however, we are concerned only with the first problem, namely, the difficulty of conceiving why the abyssal state in which
God unmanifest had been sufficient from eternity to
Himself should at any period have had another mode
superadded to it. I say superadded by convention

* The Zohar says that it is called *Ayin*, not on the ground of
nonentity, but, it may be inferred, because that which is wholly
outside our knowledge is for us as nothing.

based on the notion of sufficiency; it is not a reasonable term to make use of in such a relation, to which
no terminology is suitable. The *non ens* dwelling in
the *non est* is like the cipher of the decimal system ;*
of itself it is nothing, and its extension produces
nothing; so also it is not possible to add to it, but it
gives power to all numbers. The solution offered by
Kabalism does not differ materially from that which
has been always given. It is, in a word, the movement of the Divine Will. "In this," says Myers,
"the Unknown Absolute, above all number, manifested itself through an emanation in which it was
immanent, yet as to which it was transcendental."†
We are dealing here with a system of speculative
philosophy, and, traditional or otherwise, it must not
be supposed to be free from the disabilities of other
philosophies or from the crudities of its particular
period. The Kabalistic hypothesis supposes an
eternity antecedent to this initial operation of the
Divine Will, and in the latent subsistence of *Ain Soph*
it would appear an inconsequence to assume that
there was either will‡ or consciousness possible.§
Both, however, by a common and almost inevitable
anachronism, are attributed to *Ain Soph*, despite the
warning of the Zohar already quoted: "Woe unto
him who shall compare Him with any mode or

---

* The circle is, in fact, a Kabalistic symbol of *Ain Soph*.

† "Philosophy of Ibn Gebirol," p. 266.

‡ The Zohar, however, says expressly that "in the beginning was
the will of the King." Cremona edition, i., fol. 56.

§ "Exceeding comprehension it must be regarded as the *non-
Ego* rather than the *Ego*. All that is in man depends from it,
but it transcends consciousness; it transcends what we conceive by
the terms personal and individual." Myer: "Philosophy of Ibn
Gebirol."

attribute, even with one of his own."* The later
commentators on the Zohar either do not recognise or
are content to ignore the difficulty. Thus a treatise
entitled "The Royal Valley," by Rabbi Naphthali
Hirtz, says: "Blessed be His Holy Name! Before
anything was, He, by His simple will, proposed to
Himself to fashion the worlds. For the King is not
given without the people, as it is written in Proverbs
xiv. 28: 'In the multitude of the people is the King's
honour.' And it is the nature of the Supreme Goodness to dispense good. Now, if the world were not,
on whom could He bestow it?"† The exegetical
literature, treatises like the "Gates of Light," indicate
that the exertion of the Divine Will in the production
of the emanations is a path so secret that no creature,
not even Moses himself, can understand it.‡ At the
same time, that will is *beneplacitum*, or good pleasure,
and *beneplacitum termine carens*, without end or
limit. Hence the motive by which the universe is
accounted for is the same motive which communic
the mercy of God to them that fear Him, after which
it will be unnecessary to say that optimism is the
fundamental characteristic of Kabalism, or that,
according to to the Zohar, this is, in some respects,
the best of all possible worlds.

Seeing then that the transition of the Divine
Being from the state of the *non ens* was accomplished,
like the conversion of man from the condition of a
merely material creature, by an operation of the

---

* Zohar, pt. ii. (*Rayah Mehemna*), col. 73, Cremona edition.
† *Kabbala Denudata*, tom. ii., *partis* pr   undus,
§1, *De Mundo Infinito primo*, p. 152.
‡ *Kabbala Denudata*, tom. i.. *Apparatus in Librum Sohar pars
prima*, pp. 691, 692.

mystery of the will, we have next to ascertain something of the nature of this process, and this leads us
to the word which I have already mentioned in-
advertently, namely, emanation.* In specifying what
followed from the motion of the Divine will, we must,
I think, in an elementary treatise, set aside too subtle
inquiries into the sense in which terms were used. It
must be allowed in any case that the Kabalah re-
pudiates implicitly the axiom *ex nihilo nihil fit*, for the
non ens dwelling in the unconditioned state wherein
is neither time nor place† is the fulness which contains
the all. *Ex plenitudine ista omnia fiunt.* In this
divine plenitude pre-existing eternally was the substance of all the worlds, which therefore came forth
from God. Hence the Kabalistic system is one of
emanation.‡ When it is said that emanation is not

---

* In which the idea of pantheism is almost always, but not, I
think, of necessity involved. There is, of course, a certain sense in
which that notion is not escaped even on the hypothesis of creation,
and further there is a higher sense of pantheism from which no spiritual
philosophers could wish to escape. But as regards Jewish mysticism,
while there is always some doubt in what way it made use of the term
emanation, there seems to me no doubt that its system does not answer
to what is commonly understood by pantheism, though it has often a
pantheistic aspect. God was all for the Kabalist, as he is for the
Christian, and yet the theosophic Jew no more than the orthodox
theologian would admit that God was one with the material world.
When, therefore, Solomon Munk (*Dictionnaire de la Conversation*)
says that the Kabalah issued from the amalgamation of oriental
pantheism with the religion of the Hebrews, we can accept this only
by supposing that the pantheism in question had suffered a peculiar
alteration.

† " The No-Thing is not, however, an absolute negative or void, but
some-Thing unknown to man." Myer : " Philosophy of Ibn Gebirol,"
p. 378. It should be added that Nachmanides was one of the few
Kabalists who maintained creation *ex nihilo*.

‡ In Book IV. § 2, we shall see that this statement is subject to a
reservation regarding the most ancient document of the Kabalah, and
it should be noted in this connection that at least one scholar of

its only foundation, for it rests also on the identity of thought and existence,* or otherwise the doctrine of Divine Immanence, there is much in the literature which would tempt us to endorse this view, after due allowance has been made for the confusion and ob scurity of the originals.† But it is not necessary to follow it at any length ; it is enough for the present purpose to say that the term emanation is more in harmony with the doctrine of the Kabalah than is that of creation, and the rejection of the axiom already mentioned is perhaps little more than a play upon words.

We are not, however, concerned as yet with the evolution of the physical universe. The first consequence which followed the operation of the Divine will was the manifestation or unfolding of the Divine attributes—in a word, the transition of Deity from the latent to the active state. As in the one He was above all number, so in the other He may be said to have produced numbers, and the decade is the emanation of *Ain Soph*. We must not be so crude as to suppose that the mere arithmetical numerals are here intended ; it was powers, forces, vitalities, virtues, attributes, principles, which were thus produced,+ and in the first instance the *Sephiroth*, as they are termed,

---

authority has rejected the general view, and does not regard the Kabalah as a system of emanation. See Joel, *Philosophie Religieuse du Zohar.*

   * Isaac Myer : " Philosophy of Ibn Gebirol," p. 266.

   † That is to say, the terms emanation, creation, formation and such like. signifying distinct ideas, are used somewhat indiscriminately by the Kabalists.

   ‡ Azariel, in his work on the Canticle of Canticles, terms them "measures and organs," and in the Zohar itself they appear as divine emanated essences.

belong solely to the world of Deity.   The names
which are assigned to them are:

    I. KETHER, the Supreme Crown.
    II. CHOKMAH, Wisdom.
    III. BINAH, Intelligence or Understanding.
    IV. CHESED.   Mercy, otherwise Gedulah, Magni-
        ficence or Benignity.
    V. GEBURAH, Severity.
    VI. TIPHERETH, Beauty.
    VII. NETZACH, Splendour.
    VIII. HOD, Victory.
    IX. JESOD, the Foundation.
    X. MALKUTH, the Kingdom.

The conjunction of *Chokmah* and *Binah* produced a quasi-emanation called *Daath*, knowledge,
but it is not one of the *Sephiroth*.*

To these ten emanations or numerations various
profound meanings are attached; indeed, the study
of the Kabalistic system of the *Sephiroth* constitutes
a science by itself, and one which is full of complexity.
We are not concerned here with its exhaustive presentation, which would fill volumes, or with more than
its elementary symbolism.   We are concerned, in a

---

* A term derived from a word signifying "to number," though
late Kabalists offer other etymologies, as, for example, the Greek
σφαῖραι The singular is *Sephira*.   The emanations are regarded as
vessels, receptacles of the Divine Power and attributes as they
developed, and there is no doubt that these vessels were usually
considered spherical.   See especially the treatise *Beth Elohim* concerning *Kether*, in which the idea of circularity is involved.   The
author of the "Gates of Light" refers the term to the Hebrew word
signifying sapphire, which stone, on account of its brightness and
purity, is a symbol of the *Sephiroth*.   Other rabbinical authorities
have supported this view.   See Jellinek : *Beiträge zur Geschichte der
Kabbala*.   Leipsic, 1851.

word, not with what it may have been designed to conceal for the benefit of a circle of initiates, which is the claim of occult science, but with what it was intended to explain, and this explanation may offer some warrant for concluding that outside it there is only the province of fantasy.

Beyond a certain point it is not reasonable to suppose a double meaning in any literature; the theory of many-sided allegories does credit only to the ingenuity of the critic, and of its general value we have had a typical instance in Talmudic exegesis.[*]

The initial purpose of the Sephirotic system was undoubtedly to provide intermediaries between the Deity and the material world. It is that of all doctrines of emanation. But while we reject conjectures for which no warrant is produced we must be careful not to fall into the opposite error. To bridge the gulf between the finite and the infinite, and to effect a correspondence by stages between the inconceivable purity of the Divine Nature and the uncleanness attributed to matter by all the old theosophies, was not the sole purpose of the Sephirotic system, a point which is sometimes missed by the merely academical critic.

It is affirmed by hostile writers, for example, by

* After an exhaustive study of modern occult literature, I doubt much whether the occultist really concerns himself with the discovery of a concealed sense in the Kabalah. It is a sufficient exercise of his patience to codify and harmonise the outward sense, which is perhaps a little irradiated and transcendentalised by his methods, but is assuredly not removed. Take, for example, the conception of *Ain Soph* : he certainly does not look for any notion more withdrawn than that of divine latency therein. The inner meaning of the Kabalah is its proper and single sense, which has been confused by the obscurity of its style and its subject.

Dr. Ginsburg,* that as the earliest Kabalistic literature does not contain the doctrine of *Ain Soph*, so also
it wants that of the *Sephiroth*, but it is above challenge that the germ of the Sephirotic scheme must be
sought in the Sepher Yetzirah. The ten numerations
of that treatise are, in fact, the *Sephiroth*, and it seems
quite impossible to maintain the contrary opinion.†

III. THE DOCTRINE OF THE FOUR WORLDS

The Sephirotic system was concerned first of all,
as I have indicated, with the mystery of Divine Evolution.   From that unsearchable condition which is
above consciousness, by a mysterious operation, the
Uncreated Will moved outward, and subsequently
three manifestations or relations of Deity were established.   By the first manifestation the *Ain Soph*
passed from latency into activity ; the *non-Ego*
became *Ego*, subsisting still, however, in a condition
which is humanly inconceivable, in the state of pure
abstract thought.   The concentration of this thought
is depicted in *Kether*, which is also the Divine Will
in its primordial manifestation.   The Supreme
Crown‡ is, symbolically speaking, the base or sphere

---

* More especially in his article, *s.v.* Kabbalah, contributed to the
third edition of Kitto's " Cyclopædia of Biblical Literature."

† William Postel, the first translator of the Sepher Yetzirah,
indubitably regarded the Ten Numerations as identical with the
Sephiroth of more evolved Kabalism.

‡ In the treatise entitled the " Gates of Light," it is said that the
name of *Kether* is applied to the first *Sephira*, because even as the
crown encircles the head so does *Kether* encircle every *Sephira*. It is

of the Divine Consciousness. By the second manifestation the abstract thought entered into or de
veloped the relationship of time, so that it could be
now regarded as that which was, which is and is to
come.   Lastly, it established a relation with Nature—
that is to say, its development produced the universe.

By a slight extension of the symbolism *Kether*
is also regarded as the Throne of the Ancient of
Days,* and as the Divine Consciousness is the veil of
the subsistent state, *Ain Soph* is further represented
as the central point of *Kether*, regarded as a sphere,
and the circumference is infinity, which is, as it were,
the Divine Vestment. The later Kabalists explain
that this is because *Kether* has no vessel or receptacle
wherein it may be contained.†   Hence also it is
beyond all cognition.   The " Book of Formation,"
however, affirms that the properties of all the
Sephiroth are infinite, " the infinite of beginning, the
infinite of ending, the infinite of good, the infinite of

the world of " Direction," which encompasses all things.   This
statement involves the view that the *Sephiroth* were emanated as a
series of concentric circles, a point which will be dealt with later on.

* The term Throne is applied to several of the *Sephiroth*.   Thus
Malkuth is the throne of judgment, *Tiphereth* that of mercy.   Sometimes, however, *Binah* is termed the throne of mercy, because it is as
a seat under the supernal dilections.   *Tiphereth* is also called the
throne of glory when it receives the influence of the thirty-two paths of
wisdom.   See Bk. i. § 10.   The same name is applied to *Malkuth*,
because it is the seat of *Tiphereth*.   The term throne taken simply
signifies *Malkuth*, and *Binah* which is the seat of Malkuth.   *Kabbala
Denudata, Apparatus in Librum Sohar*, s.v. *Thronus*, vol. i. p. 483.
These points are cited only to show the chameleon character of the
symbolism.

† I owe this statement to the " Morals and Dogma of the
Ancient and Accepted Scottish Rite," compiled by Albert Pike. Grand
Commander of the Southern Jurisdiction of the U.S.A.   The authority
is not stated, but it is, I believe, from " The Royal Valley," by R.
Napthali Hirtz.

evil, the infinite in elevation, the infinite in depth, the infinite at the East, the infinite at the West, the infinite at the North, the infinite at the South, and the Lord alone is above all; as a faithful King He governs all from the height of His throne in the ages of ages."* As the vessel of the Divine Consciousness, which itself is contained by nothing,† *Kether* contains all things;‡ it is the egg in which reposes the germ of the universe, to borrow the symbolism of another system. In particular it contains the remaining *Sephiroth*, which are the sum of all things. The Word of God circulates in all, and *Kether* is, in a special sense, the Spirit of the Living God.

The second *Sephira* is Wisdom, but seemingly of a middle quality, for the highest of all, the truly celestial Wisdom, can be referred only to *Kether*. That of *Chokmah* is, notwithstanding, so transcendent that no creature can attain it. It was concealed from Moses, and the Wisdom for which Solomon was magnified belongs to an inferior order, which connects with the lowest of the *Sephiroth*. The *Sephira*

---

* Sepher Yetzirah, c. i. par. 4.

† This appears paradoxical, but just as Fichte and Carl du Prel have maintained that the human ego is not wholly embraced in self-consciousness, so *Kether* is presumably the vessel of the Divine Consciousness in the sense that it receives an influx therefrom. Readers will remember the Universal Solvent which yet could be contained in a phial, a diverting incident in one of the "Tales of the Genii." According to the "Royal Valley," *Ain Soph* had full consciousness and appreciation, prior to their actual existence, of all the grades and impersonations contained unmanifested within Itself.

‡ There is hence, as Isaac de Acco observes in his treatise on "The Enlightenment of the Eyes," a unity of the ten *Sephiroth* in themselves, which unity is concentrated always in *Ain Soph*. It must, perhaps, be admitted that this idea is contained implicitly in the Zoharic statement that *Ain Soph* is the beginning and end of all degrees in the creation.

Chokmah is described by the " Book of Formation "
as the Breath of the Spirit of God.

Binah, Intelligence or Understanding, is symbolically represented by the same fundamental authority
as the moisture of the Breath of the Spirit. It is the
highest *Sephira* with which man can establish correspondence, but it contains at the same time one
mystery which was also concealed from Moses. The
root of all roots and the foundation of all foundations
is by it communicated to man, who could otherwise
have no knowledge of the antecedent states of the
Divine Nature.*

Magnificence or Mercy, *Gedulah* or *Chesed*, the
fourth emanation, is the warmth or fire contained
within the moisture breathed forth by the Spirit of
God. It expresses the eternal love and compassion,
connecting with life and vitality. It is the base of the
beneplacitum termine carens mentioned in the last
section and supposes implicitly the free will of the
Divine Agent. It follows from this as a consequence
that the universe was made or emanated, not because
anything was wanting to the Divine completeness, but
out of the fulness of goodwill, which is, however, in
distinct opposition to some of the later Kabalists,
especially Isaac de Loria.+ Symbolically speaking,
Chesed is therefore the *Sephira* by which God constituted the world.

* All things, according to the commentary of Isaac de Loria, in a
certain and most abstruse manner, consist and reside and are contained
in *Binah*, which projects them and sends them downwards, species by
species, into the several worlds of Emanation, Creation, Formation and
Fabrication. *Binah* is hence represented as a great reservoir or o
it is the source of prophetic inspiration, as *Chokmah* is that of revelation.

† See *Liber Drushim*, a metaphysical introduction to the Kabalah,
Kabbala Denudata, vol. i. pt. 2 Also Book vi. § 1 of this work.

The fifth *Sephira* is *Geburah*, signifying Judgment, Justice, Judicial Power, known also as *Pachad*, or Fear. It is the supernal tribunal before which nothing can subsist.

Tiphereth, or Beauty, the sixth *Sephira*, is, in a sense, the conjunction of Mercy and Judgment and summarises the Divine goodness; it is the heart of the pillar of benignity.

But the Divine Benignity is manifested by the victory signified in *Netzach*, the seventh *Sephira*. There are three rays diffused from the splendour of Providence—Benignity, Beauty and Victory. When they shine and are diffused over the *Sephiroth* the whole world is filled with joy and perfection, for the Divine goodness itself looks forth upon all creatures, and all the worlds are in fulness and completeness.* This *Sephira* is also termed Eternity.

The eighth *Sephira*, *Hod*, signifies Glory, Adornment, Splendour. In combination with *Netzach* it is termed the armies of Jehovah. All the salutations and praises contained in the Psalter of David belong to this emanation. It is the place of praise, the place of wars and victories, and of the treasury of benefits.†

Jesod, the Basis or Foundation, the ninth *Sephira*, is the storehouse of all forces, the seat of life and vitality, and the nourishment of all the worlds.‡

---

* *Apparatus in Librum Sohar. Kabbala Denudata*, s.v. *Superatio*, i.e. *Netzach*, p. 589 *et seq.*

† *Ibid.* s.v. *Decus, Gloria*, i.e. Hod, p. 268 *et seq.* According to the Zohar *Netzach* and *Hod* correspond to extension, multiplication and force, and thence issue all the forces of the universe, for which reason these *Sephiroth* are also termed the Armies of the Eternal. *Zohar*, iii., 296 a, Mantua.

‡ *Kabbala Denudata, Apparatus*, s.v. *Fundamentum*, i.e., *Jesod*, p. 439 *et seq.*

Malkuth is the tenth *Sephira*, signifying Dominion, Royalty, Kingdom. In the " Lesser Holy Synod " it is termed " the Mother of all the Living." It is the final manifestation, emanation, or development of the Divine Nature taking place in the Divine World, and is, therefore, that point at which the more external orders make contact with the supernal.*

To this brief general description, which rests on the authority and reproduces the words of the Kabalists, I will now add the heads of an occult interpretation, which is, of course, conjectural, but has a very reasonable aspect.

Ain Soph, the Unknowable and Absolute, manifests through the efflux of the spiritual and material universe, using the *Sephiroth* as its media. The first emanation symbolises Abstract Thought, the Absolute assuming consciousness to manifest outwardly. The second emanation represents the association of abstract ideas in the intellect, which association is Wisdom. The third emanation is Mind receiving the impression of the abstract ideas. These three constitute the Spirit of the World. The second triad of *Sephiroth*, Mercy, Judgment and Beauty, includes the principles of construction and symbolises the abstract dimensions of matter, length, breadth, depth and their double polarity. *Chesed* and *Geburah* are the centripetal and centrifugal energies between the poles of the dimensions. In their junction with *Tiphereth* they represent all ethical life and perfection. They correspond to the Soul of the

* Hence it is said that the tenth *Sephira* is the *Shekinah*, that is, the place of the manifestation of Deity.

World.   The third triad is dynamic ; its *Sephiroth*
signify the Deity as universal potentiality, energy and
productive principle.   They answer to the idea of
Nature, the *natura naturans*, however, and not the
natura naturata.   The tenth *Sephira*, or *Malkuth*,
represents the Concrete, and is the energy and execu-
tive power of the Abstract Intellect.*

The important point to remember as regards
both tabulations is that, although their wording is
open occasionally to another significance, they are
neither concerned as yet with any material evolution,
but solely with that development of the Divine Principles which found its ultimation at last on the
material plane, between which and the Divine there
was the intervention, as we shall see, of two mediate
worlds.†

Now, it must be confessed that the distinction
seems absolute between the Sephirotic system and
any anthropomorphic conception of Deity ; it is
arbitrary to the point of fantastic, but it seems outside
all human correspondences.   Its point of view is that
the visible world is the last consequence in the
development of the attributes of God, or that God in
order to create had to pass outward from his eternal
subsistence.   The *Sephiroth* are the symbolism of the
attributes, and the course of their efflux is the history

---

* Summarised from Isaac Myer's " Philosophy of Ibn Gebirol,"
§ xiii.

† So also it is said by the later Kabalists that God called Himself
Wisdom in *Chokmah*, Intelligent in *Binah*, in *Chesed* He took the
character of Great and Benignant, in *Geburah* of Rigourous, in
Tiphereth of Beautiful, in *Netzach* of Overcoming, in *Hod* of our
Glorious Author, in *Jesod* of our Support, by Jesod all vessels and
worlds being upheld, while in *Malkuth* He applied to Himself the
title of King.

of the Divine evolution.* This course or sequence is the subject of much discussion among Kabalistic writers. It is generally held that the *Sephiroth* were contained originally one within the other, that is, *Kether* enclosed all those below it, *Chokmah* enclosed *Binah*, while *Binah* contained the seven last, produced by a successive efflux. " Originated by points, they expanded in circular shape—ten circles under the mystery of the ten *Sephiroth* and between them ten spaces."†

The entire emanation, unlikely as it may seem, was collected together under the notion of a heavenly man, Adam Kadmon, archetypal and primordial. It was similarly collected under the notion of a supreme world, termed *Atziluth*, the World of Deity,‡ of which Adam Kadmon§ was the sole occupant.‖ This in a special manner is termed the World of Emanations. From this proceeded a second world, having also its Sephirotic decade, that of Creation, called *Briah*, but not, as I infer, to be understood in the usual acceptation of that term, for *Briah* also came forth or was emanated. It was, in fact, a consequence of the superior world, namely, of the effectuating energies of the Supreme Will, resident in the Archetypal World. The Sephirotic forces were carried forward in *Briah* and by this prolonged emanation was the world of highest finite intelligence, technically that of the arch-

* It is in this sense that the ten *Sephiroth* are said to form a strict unity among themselves and also with *Ain Soph*.

† *Introductio in Librum Sohar, i.e., Vallis Regia.* See *Kabbala Denudata*, vol. ii. p. 152 *et seq.*

‡ The " intelligible world," of the Zohar.

§ That is, the Man from the I ..

‖ Myer : " Philosophy of Ibn Gebirol," p. 418.

angels, produced. But the Sephirotic prolongation was continued into a third world, that of *Yetzirah*, or formation, the abode of the angelic choirs. Though further removed from Supreme Perfection, there is not a taint of the material in this abode of incorporeal beings. It is otherwise with the World of Action, the fourth product of the tenfold emanation, *Assiah*, the region of matter and also the dwelling of the demons, called shells or *Cortices* by the Kabalists. In common with many other systems of emanation this material world is regarded as the gross purgations of the upper regions. It should be observed, however, that the *Sephiroth* permeate the four systems, but they deteriorate as they proceed further from *Ain Soph* and the corruption of the infernal world, the formless region and the seven hells of Kabalism are the extreme limits of the emanation which begins in *Kether*. Thus, in order to explain the imperfections found in the world-craft of a perfect author the deterioration of his infinite energy is not disdained as a resource. It is easy to criticise such a system, or to set it down as beneath criticism, but, again, the disability is common to the dreams of all emanationists. It remains to say that we have the distinct authority of the Zohar for regarding the demons as products of the will of God and designed for a specific purpose; but this point may be reserved for further consideration at a later stage.*

Broadly speaking, the Four Worlds of the Kabalah may be regarded as corresponding in the physical order:

---

* We have already seen that, according to the "Book of Formation," the ten *Sephiroth* are the infinite of evil as well as of good.

(*a*) ATZILUTH, to the Primum Mobile.
(*b*) BRIAH, to the sphere of the Zodiac.
(*c*) YETZIRAH, to the planetary chain.
(*d*) ASSIAH, to the world of the four elements.

Thus, astronomy is at the basis of the conception.

The doctrine of the Four Worlds was developed between the period of the Sepher Yetzirah and that of the promulgation of the Zohar, and it received many increments from the commentators on the latter work. It is first met with in the " Book of Emanation," which is a product of the school of Isaac the Blind.   This treatise is ascribed to R. Jacob Nazir. Its distribution of the Four Worlds differs from the above tabulation in one or two respects, as, for example, by referring the souls of the just to *Briah*, the archangelic world.   It should be added that the Zohar also recognises a distribution of the *Sephiroth* into Three Worlds—(1) Intelligible, (2) Moral, (3) Natural.

IV. THE DOCTRINE OF THE
COUNTENANCES

The Four Worlds are also depicted in a single Sephirotic scheme, and this leads us to another order of symbolism established for a distinct purpose, namely, the vindication of the relationship between man and God. This vindication is founded, it will be superfluous to say, on God's providence regarding the Jewish nation, as it is recorded in the sacred literature of the First Covenant.   There are many respects, however, in which it is not at all peculiar to that nation, and there are indeed traces of a very liberal and almost Catholic doctrine in the books which form the Kabalah. The Chosen People is the channel by which all grace and favour are communicated from above, but the gifts of the Divine Mercy derive through Israel to the world at large; the union of the divine potency with Zion incorporates all things together, so that they are as one body, and by this union the whole universe is found to be in joy.* Again, it is said that a certain light falls from the supernal which blesses the whole world, so that wrath is no longer found in the universe; "all the worlds rejoice and are fulfilled with all perfection."

The relations of God with man are, however, those which are delineated in the dealings between Jehovah and Jewry, and the conception of the God of Abraham, Isaac and Jacob had to be harmonised with the exalted or at least recondite Godhead of *Ain Soph* and the Sephirotic system. Now, *Ain Soph*, as such, the *latens Deitas*, being essentially unknowable and outside the region of correspondence and relationship, enters by manifestation into a quasi-knowable but still unsearchable and transcendent state in the supernal triad of the *Sephiroth*. Therefore, this triad is taken to represent the entire Sephirotic system of the Atzilutic world. We have seen that this world is regarded as the abode of *Adam Kadmon*, who is also its sole denizen. In the alternative symbolism with which we are now dealing, this notion of the Body of

---

* See "The Lesser Holy Synod," § xxii., *Kabbala Denudata*, II., p. 592 *et seq.*

God is replaced by that of a Vast Countenance,* resident in *Kether* and termed the *Macroprosopus*. By this head, devoid of all lower conformation, the antithesis of anthropomorphic Deity is shadowed forth, and the qualities ascribed to it are also the antithesis of the embodied Jehovah. As *Ain Soph* is the Closed Eye of the Unknown Darkness, so in the Vast Countenance the eye is open aud never closes.† for the subsistence of the universe and all its worlds depends upon the light which shines therefrom.‡ In this Vast Countenance there is neither wrath nor judgment, while all wrath and judgment which operate in the world and in humanity are held in check by the mercy and longanimity of *Macroprosopus* to such an extent that they may be regarded as counterbalanced and annulled in the last disposition. There is no need to expatiate here on the symbolism, to which reference must be made again. It is sufficient to note that the first Sephirotic emanation, corresponding to the self-consciousness and abstract thought of the Supreme Being, is a God described by the Kabalists in terms which are intentionally the reverse of the salient characteristics ascribed to the Old Testament Deity. From *Macroprosopus*, through the *Sephira* Wisdom, under the aspect of a masculine potency, and through the third *Sephira*, the feminine *Binah*, Understanding,§ there is

* Called *Arik Anpin* in the Zohar and its dependencies.
† "Book of Concealment," c. i. v. 14.
‡ The same notion is found in Indian mythology, and readers of Southey's "Curse of Kehama" will remember what followed the sudden veiling of the eyes of Seeva.
§ These are the Supernal Father and the Supernal Mother, who must be regarded, however, as modes of the manifestation of *Macroprosopus*.

emanated the Lesser Countenance,* or *Micro-prosopus*, possessing bodily configuration and extended through the six emanations from *Chesed* to *Jesod* inclusive. It embraces, therefore, the two inferior triads of the *Sephiroth*, the worlds of Creation and Formation. But as *Kether* in the world of *Atziluth* is attributed specially to the Vast Countenance, so is *Tiphereth* in *Briah* to the Lesser Countenance. As longanimity is the characteristic of *Macroprosopus*, so is "swiftness to wrath" that of the inferior being, *parvam faciem habens, cito irascens.*† These comparative qualities are typified by length and shortness of face. *Microprosopus* is regarded by modern occultism as the shadow or reflection of the superior manifestation, but this view is not entirely borne out by Kabalistic literature. Making due allowance for all inexactitude, it repre-sents in a general manner what is designed to be enforced by the symbolism, and the sole point which we are concerned in establishing here is that *Micro-prosopus* is the mediator between God and Man. It is not, however, in the Christian sense of mediation, that of intercession, for wrath, vengeance and judg-ment are not in the Vast Countenance, even as they are not in *Ain Soph*. The mediation is communica-tive or sacramental. In the natural order it is the human conception of Deity, to which God con-descends and may be said in a sense to verify and even to inform.‡ Conversely, as regarded from above, it is the construction of the Divine Nature, so that its

---

* Called *Zair Anpin* in the Zohar.

† *Apparatus in Librum Sohar, Kabbala Denudata*, vol. i. p. 312, s.v. *Macroprosopus*.

‡ Éliphas Lévi, *Le Livre des Splendeurs*, Paris, 1894, p. 69.

knowledge and its power may be derived to mankind. It is the adjustment of the infinite being to finite possibilities, so that the limited may receive a certain measure of the boundless. It is so much of God as man by his constitution and estate is capable of comprehending; it is Divine Providence leading humanity by an administration suited to humanity, by the way of contest and prize, by the way of kindness and severity, of reward and punishment. God in Himself is above all these things, but they are necessary to His froward children. In a word, it is so much of the *Principia* of Newton as would be understood in a village school, namely, the illustration of the falling apple.

That this is the significance of the symbolism is evinced further by the Sephirotic allotment of certain Divine Names which occur continually in the Bible. The affirmation of self-existence and self-consciousness is made in the Name which signifies, I am that I am, AHIH,* and this is referred to *Kether*, while the world of *Atziluth* generally embraces the mysterious name, never uttered and therefore re garded as incomprehensible and unpronounceable, JOD, HE, VAU, HE.† When the Israelite comes to this name in the Bible, he omits it altogether, or substitutes ADNI, Adonai, the Lord.   The word

---

* "It is possible," says Maimonides, "that in the Hebrew language, of which we have but a slight knowledge now, *Tetragrammaton*, in the way it was pronounced, conveyed the meaning of absolute existence." — M. Friedlander: "The Guide of the Perplexed of Maimonides," vol. i. (*Moreh*, part i. c. 61) p. 228.

† It is unpronounceable, because its real vowels are unknown. See Renan: "History of Israel," note to c. vi.   More accurately, the first three letters belong to the supernal Sephiroth and the fourth to the inferior seven.   The attributions, however, vary.

which we render Jehovah belongs, therefore, to the symbolism of the Vast Countenance, to the God who is not as man is. But AL and its derivatives, Jehovah, or the Lord of Hosts, those lesser names of which the contents can be grasped by the human mind and can therefore be uttered, are the Names of the Lesser Countenance. The relation between *Macroprosopus* and *Microprosopus* is the philosophical hypothesis of the correspondence between the absolute as it is and the absolute as conceived by man. The disparity between them registers the inadequacy of all human conceptions of the Divinity, fully recognised by every Kabalist as abounding in that book which he regarded as more Divine than any.

Like the Sephirotic system, the doctrine of the Four Worlds and the two Countenances is curiously involved, and though in its elements it is exceedingly simple, in its elaborations it is highly technical. As in the single Sephirotic scheme with which we have been dealing here the first triad of emanations is held to represent the world of *Atziluth*, so the second triad comprehends *Briah* and the third the world of Formation, or *Yetzirah*. *Assiah*, the fourth world, is contained in *Malkuth*. Now, with *Microprosopus* there is associated the symbol of a Bride, who is in fact *Malkuth*, or the Kingdom, in which sense it would follow that the visible creation is the Spouse of God, or rather of that lesser Divine Manifestation which alone communicates with man. The *locus sanctorum*, the organ of nuptial intercourse, is, however, " the place called Zion and Jerusalem,"* and it is,

---

* Laurence Oliphant quoted these and similar passages to prove the sanctity and mysticism with which the notion of sexual conjunction,

therefore, in Israel only that the communication is received. The office of Israel is hence the dispensation of the divine to the world and men.*

The doctrine of the Countenances is the subject of special development in the "Book of Concealment" and its supplements, being tracts introduced into the Zohar; it was unknown to the Sepher Yetzirah or its early commentators.

V. THE INSTRUMENTS OF CREATION

It must be confessed that, so far, Kabalistic literature deserves to be called philosophical. The doctrine of *Ain Soph* may be classed with Platonic conceptions; the Sephirotic system will not suffer by comparison with any other dream of emanation and may even challenge all; the motive which underlies the metaphysics of the two Countenances is singularly profound and may be regarded as the chief glory of the Kabalah. We must now, however, approach its fantastic portions. We have seen that the World of *Briah* is that of Creation, but whatever reservations may be inferred from Kabalistic writers on the axiom *ex nihilo nihil fit*,† we have seen also that their use

and the act itself, was invested, as he said, from the earliest times. But his opinion of the Kabalah was derived only from Mr. Mathers' translation of the "occultation" series, and he had probably never heard of the controversial history of the Zohar. See "Scientific Religion," London, 1888, Appendix I.

* This is a further development of the Talmudic doctrine that Zion is not only the centre of the earth but the starting point of the universe. Consult also the *Kuzari*, of R. Judas Ha Levi.

† According to Myer, the speculative or metaphysical Kabalah is an attempt to harmonise Hebrew monotheism with the "fundamental

of the term Creation does not at all correspond to the sense of Christian cosmology, because that which they called Nothing evasively was the plenitude in which the All lay latent. Further, the world of *Briah* was not that in which anything material was formed, emanated, or otherwise brought into actual being; it was rather the Elohistic world, that of Panurgic force and intelligence, which became formative in *Yetzirah*, but did not produce matter except in the fourth world. Now the materials used and shaped, or, perhaps, more properly speaking, the instruments, the matrices of the material world, are said by the Kabalists to have been the letters of the Hebrew alphabet. According to the Sepher Yetzirah, God imparted to them form and weight by combining and transforming them in divers manners, *Aleph* with all the rest and all the rest with *Aleph*; *Beth* with all and all with *Beth*; and so of the rest.* Some hundreds of permutations were obtained in this manner, which are the origin not only of all languages but of all creatures. As these permutations can, by the hypothesis, be reduced to a single name, that of *Tetragrammation*, the JOD, HE, VAU, HE, which I have had occasion to mention previously, it is said that the entire universe proceeds from this name.† The

---

principle of ancient philosophy," namely, the axiom quoted above. "Philosophy of Ibn Gebirol," p. 230. This was also the design of Maimonides in his "Guide of the Perplexed."

    * Sepher Yetzirah, c. ii. par. 4. Cf. the Talmudic teaching that the present world was created by God with the letter *He* and the world to come with the letter *Jod*.

    † And thus the comprehension of this name gives all knowledge according to the Kabalists. Compare Éliphas Lévi. who reduces the doctrine to an axiom: "All knowledge is in a word, all power in a name; the intelligence of this name is the Science of Abraham and Solomon." *Clefs Ma·eures*, Paris, 1895.

reader will discern at once the nature of the device, which may be methodised by a simple process:

The world came forth from God:
But the name of God is יהוה ;
Therefore the world came forth from יהוה.*

The fundamental letters of the Book of Formation are not, however, those which compose the Divine Name; they are *Aleph* (א), *Mem* (מ) and *Shin* (ש), distinguished as the Three Mothers and corresponding to Air, Water and Fire. The heavens are formed of Fire, the Earth is of Water, and the Air of the mediate Spirit.

Their correspondences are: in the year, the torrid, frigid and temperate seasons; in man, the head, belly and breast.

Besides the Three Mothers there are seven double letters—*Beth* (ב = B), *Ghimel* (ג = G). *Daleth* (ד = D), *Kaph* (כ = K), *Pe* (פ = P), *Resh* (ר = R) and *Tau* (ת = T, Th). These seven signs stand in the Book of Formation for:—

Life			Death
Peace			Strife
Knowledge			Ignorance
Wealth	and their opposites		Poverty
Grace			Sin
Fruitfulness			Sterility
Dominion			Slavery

---

* It will be unnecessary to point out that this is a logical *non sequitur*, but it must be added that for the Kabalistic Jew the true name of God, as indeed of any existence, was a manifestation of its essence and, as such, inseparable therefrom.

Their correspondences in the universe are : —

East	Depth
West	North
Height	South

and the Holy Palace, fixed in the centre and sustaining all things. When the seven double letters had been shaped by the Deity, He combined and created therewith the planets in the heaven; the days in the year—*i.e.*, the seven days of creation; and the gates in man—*i.e.*, eyes, ears, nostrils and mouth.

There are, finally, twelve simple letters, having the following correspondences in man and the world : —

HE	=	ה, E =	Sight	=	N.E.
VAU	=	ו, V =	Hearing	=	S.E.
DZAIN	=	ז, Z =	Smell	=	E. Height
CHETH	=	ח, Ch =	Speech	=	E. Depth
TETH	=	ט, T =	Digestion	=	N.W.
JOD	=	י, I =	Coition	=	S.W.
LAMED	=	ל, L =	Action	=	W. Height
NUN	=	נ, N =	Motion	=	W. Depth
SAMEK	=	ס, S =	Wrath	=	S. Height
AIN	=	ע, =	Mirth	=	S. Depth
TSADE	=	צ, Ts =	Meditation =	N. Height
QUOPH	=	ק, Q =	Sleep	=	N. Depth

By means of the twelve simples there were created the signs of the zodiac, the twelve months and the twelve directors of man—*i.e.*, the two hands, the feet, the two kidneys, the liver, the gall, the spleen, the colon, the bladder and the arteries.

I must leave my readers to decide how this

bizarre system is to be interpreted.   It has been regarded by one or two critics who have no occult leanings as a serious attempt to devise a philosophical cosmology;* but for myself I must confess that I do not see in what manner it is superior to the familiar fable of the elephant and the tortoise.   There are those, of course, who discern in it a secret meaning, who remember, for example, that the letters of the Hebrew alphabet stand also for numerals, and do not fail to cite the scriptural statement that God made everything by weight, number and measure.

Indeed, the Sepher Yetzirah may be regarded as a commentary on this declaration. As a rule, however, I think that the Kabalists, like other makers of philosophy, meant that which they said, and if they did not say all that they meant the unexpressed residuum was along the lines of the sense expressed. When they affirmed, therefore, that the world was made by means of the letters of the alphabet, they really meant what they stated ; but if it be asked whether they understood by those letters the symbols of arcane powers, it must be answered that they did. The letters are, however, more than mere symbols ; they are vessels or manifestations of the concealed powers. The sense is therefore true *ex hypothesi* in a literal and arcane manner.

The warrant of the hypothesis must be sought in the Talmudic system, which believed that the body of the sacred text was divine like the sense which was

---

* Dr. Alfred Edersheim seems to speak in this sense in his " History of the Jewish Nation after the Destruction of Jerusalem." I have used the third, posthumous edition, revised by the Rev. H. A. White, M.A.   London.   1896.   See p. 408.

its soul, which soul had, like man himself, an inner spirit, the highest of all, namely, the concealed meaning. Now, the letters of the alphabet were the materials of the textual body, to the care and preservation of which the traditional science of the Massorah was devoted.* For the mystical Jew, who discerned strange abysses of mystery in the smallest peculiarities of the *Thorah*, there was a weird fascination in the fact that all the wonders and sanctities of the Law and the Prophets resulted from the diverse combinations of twenty-two letters, and he came to regard this handful of conventional hieroglyphs as so many sacraments or instruments by which the divine wisdom was communicated to man. In a word, for him they ceased to be conventions ; a divine revelation required a divine language to express it, and the alphabet of that language was a derivation from the noumenal world, vessels of singular election, instruments of Deity, from which it was an easy transition to suppose that such channels of spiritual grace and life must have fulfilled some exalted office in the shaping of the universe itself.

---

* The Massorah was concerned with the body of the text, the rules as to reading and writing the *Thorah*, and special considerations on the mystic sense of the sacred characters. It was hence the criticism of the Hebrew text. It was also, as already seen, that which was openly delivered by the rabbins in contradiction to that which was supposed to have been communicated secretly. Thus it taught the true reading of doubtful passages, the true pronunciation of uncertain words, the correct subdivisions of the books, and so forth. Buxtorf's work entitled "Tiberias" (Basiliæ, 1620, 4to) deals with the Massorah. Compare Molitor's "Philosophy of Tradition." Occultists pretend that its exoteric formulæ were designed to conceal every trace of a secret sense in the *Thorah*. See "Mission des Juifs," p. 646, by Saint-Yves d'Alveydre, who follows Fabre d'Olivet in *La Langue Hébraïque Restituée*. The Massorah compiled from MSS., alphabetically and lexically arranged, has been published by C. D. Ginsburg. 3 vols London. 1880-85.

This doctrine of the instruments of creation is the oldest part of Kabalistic literature, which, it follows, improved very much as it developed. It was intimately connected with the idea of the pre-existence of the *Thorah*, and to say that the world was created by the inscription of letters in the air was, in one sense, only another manner of saying that it was created by the *Thorah*, while the latter affirmation is not incapable of being regarded in a philosophical manner by the help of the Kabalistic doctrine of correspondences, for which the *Thorah* of Moses would be only the mundane type of the Eternal and Divine Law.

VI. THE PATHS OF WISDOM

In the Latin collection of Pistorius the marrow of philosophical Kabalism is presented in the form of certain terse propositions or dogmas,* according to one of which the ways of eternity are thirty-two—*Viæ æternitatis sunt triginta duo.*† These are the paths of the Sepher Yetzirah, namely, the ten *Sephiroth* and the letters of the Hebrew alphabet, The doctrine concerning them is a dependency of this fundamental treatise, but of much more recent date,

---

* They are the extremely interesting theses of Picus de Mirandola, which will be found in Book vii.

† They are referred to the *Sephirah Chokmah* and are termed occult channels, at once hidden and revealed. In the "Faithful Shepherd" *Chokmah* is called the highest of all paths, embracing and including all that are beneath it, and the influx of all is derived therefrom. The same treatise connects with *Chokmah* the words in Job, xxviii. 7 : "The bird hath not known the path, neither hath the eye of the vulture beheld it."—*Kabbala Denudata, Apparatus*, i. 601, 602

and without even an imputed authorship. It tabulates the special graces and illuminations which may be communicated to man from above by means of these channels, and is very interesting because it shows that the most philosophical part of Kabalism had a practical application to the human mind, and was not merely a speculative system. It is outside the province of this work to offer translations to the student, but as in the present instance it would be difficult to summarise the tabulation more briefly, I shall give it *in extenso*, premising only that it has been translated more than once into English, and is indeed available in a number of European languages.

The first path is called the Admirable Intelligence, the Supreme Crown. It is the light which imparts understanding of the beginning which is without beginning, and this also is the First Splendour. No created being can attain to its essence.

The second path is called the Illuminating Intelligence. It is the Crown of Creation and the splendour of the Supreme Unity, to which it is most near in proximity. It is exalted above every head and is distinguished by Kabalists as the Second Splendour.

The third path is called the Sanctifying Intelligence and is the foundation of Primordial Wisdom, termed the Creation of Faith. Its roots are אמן. It is the mother of Faith, which indeed emanates therefrom.

The fourth path is called the Arresting or Receiving Intelligence, because it arises like a boundary to receive the emanations of the higher intelligences which are sent down to it. Herefrom all spiritual virtues emanate by the way of subtlety, which itself emanates from the Supreme Crown.*

The fifth path is called the Radical Intelligence, because it is more akin than any other to the Supreme Unity and emanates from the depths of the Primordial Wisdom.†

The sixth path is called the Intelligence of Mediating Influence, because the flux of the emanations is multiplied therein.   It communicates this affluence to those blessed men who are united with it.‡

The seventh path is called the Hidden Intelligence, because it pours out a brilliant splendour on all intellectual virtues which are beheld with the eyes of the spirit and by the ecstasy of faith.

The eighth path is called the Perfect and Absolute Intelligence.   The preparation of principles emanates therefrom.§   The roots to which it adheres are in the depths of the Sphere Magnificence, from the very substance of which it emanates.

The ninth path is called the Purified Intelligence. It purifies the numerations, prevents and stays the fracture of their images,|| for it establishes their unity

---

* Dr. Westcott, following the Hebrew text of Rittangelius, makes this rendering : " The fourth path is named Measuring, Cohesive, or Receptacular ; and is so-called because it contains all the holy powers, and from it emanate all the spiritual virtues with the most exalted essences ; they emanate one from the other by the power of the primordial emanation," *i.e.*, *Kether*.

† Or, "the primordial depths of *Chokmah* "—Westcott, Sepher Yetzirah, p. 28.

‡ " It causes that influence to flow into all the reservoirs of the Blessings with which these themselves are united."—*Ibid.* p. 29.

§ According to Westcott "it is the means of the primordial."—*Ibid.*

|| Or, " proves and corrects the designing of their representations.'
—*Ibid.*

to preserve them from destruction and division by their union with itself.*

The tenth path is called the Resplendent Intelligence, because it is exalted above every head and has its seat in *Binah*; it enlightens the fire of all lights and emanates the power of the principle of forms.†

The eleventh path is called the Fiery Intelligence. It is the veil placed before the dispositions and order of the superior and inferior causes. Whosoever possesses this path is in the enjoyment of great dignity; to possess it is to be face to face with the Cause of Causes.‡

The twelfth path is called the Intelligence of the Light,§ because it is the image of magnificence. It is said to be the source of vision in those who behold apparitions.

The thirteenth path is called the Inductive Intelligence of Unity. It is the substance of glory, and it manifests truth to every spirit.‖

The fourteenth path is called the Illuminating Intelligence. It is the institutor of arcana, the foundation of holiness.

The fifteenth path is called the Constituting Intelligence, because it constitutes creation in the

---

* Or, "disposes their unity with which they are combined without diminution or division."—*Ibid.*

† "Causes a supply of influence to emanate from the Prince of Countenances."—*Ibid.*

‡ Westcott gives an entirely different version : " It is the essence of that curtain which is placed close to the order of the disposition, and this is a special dignity given to it that it may be able to stand before the face of the Cause of Causes."—*Ibid.*

§ Or of Transparency.—*Ibid.*

‖ "It is the consummation of the truth of individual spiritual things."—*Ibid.*

darkness of the world. *   According to the philosophers, it is itself that darkness mentioned by
Scripture (Job xxxviii. 9), cloud and the envelope
thereof.

The sixteenth path is called the Triumphant and
Eternal Intelligence, the delight of glory, the paradise
of pleasure prepared for the just.

The seventeenth path is called the Disposing
Intelligence,   It disposes the devout to perseverance
and thus prepares them to receive the Holy Spirit.†

The eighteenth path is called the Intelligence or
House of Influence,‡ and thence are drawn the arcana
 1 the concealed meanings which repose in the
shadow thereof.

The nineteenth path is called the Intelligence of
the Secret or of all spiritual activities.   The fulness
which it receives derives from the highest benediction
and the supreme glory.

The twentieth path is called the Intelligence of
Will.   It prepares all created beings, each individually,
for the demonstration of the existence of the
primordial glory.

The twenty-first path is called the Rewarding
Intelligence of those who seek.§   It receives the
divine influence, and it influences by its benediction
all existing things.

The twenty-second path is called the Faithful

---

* "It constitutes the substance of creations in pure darkness."—
Ibid., p. 30.

† Westcott adds: "It is called the foundation of excellence in
the state of higher things."—*Ibid.*

‡ Westcott adds: "By the greatness of whose abundance the
influx of good things upon created beings is increased."—*Ibid.*

§ Westcott gives "the Conciliating Intelligence."—*Ibid.*

Intelligence, because spiritual virtues are deposited and augment therein, until they pass to those who dwell under the shadow thereof.*

The twenty-third path is called the Stable Intelligence. It is the source of consistency in all the numerations.

The twenty-fourth path is called the Imaginative Intelligence. It is the ground of similarity in the likeness of beings who are created to its agreement after its aspects.

The twenty-fifth path is called the Intelligence of Temptation or Trial, because it is the first temptation by which God tests the devout.

The twenty-sixth path is called the Renewing Intelligence, for thereby God—blessed be He!—reneweth all which is capable of renovation in the creation of the world.†

The twenty-seventh path is called the Active Intelligence, for thence is created the spirit of every creature of the supreme orb, and the activity, that is to say, the motion, to which they are subject.‡

The twenty-eighth path is called the Natural Intelligence, whereby the nature of everything found in the orb of the sun is completed and perfected.§

The twenty-ninth path is called the Corporeal

---

* Westcott's literal rendering reads, "by it spiritual virtues are increased, and all dwellers on earth are merely under its shadow."—*Ibid.*

† "All the changing things which are renewed by the creation of the world."—*Ibid.*, p. 31.

‡ "The twenty-seventh path is the Exciting Intelligence, and it is so called because through it is consummated and perfected the nature of every existent being under the orb of the sun, in perfection."—*Ibid.*

§ This path is omitted both in the text of Rittangelius and in Westcott's version.

Intelligence; it informs every body which is incorporated under all orbs, and it is the growth thereof.

The thirtieth path is called the Collective Intelligence, for thence astrologers, by the judgment of the stars and the heavenly signs, derive their speculations and the perfection of their science according to the motions of the stars.

The thirty-first path is called the Perpetual Intelligence. Why is it so called ? Because it rules the movement of the sun and the moon according to their constitution and causes each to gravitate in its respective orb.*

The thirty-second path is called the Assisting Intelligence, because it directs all the operations of the seven planets, with their divisions, and concurs therein.

The modern accent of this tabulation will occur at once to the reader, but its quotation was necessary to exhibit the intellectual profit believed to follow from the study of Kabalism, and still more that it was in the last resource the understanding of man methodised,† and embracing, as such, the entire circle attributed to human knowledge.‡

* According to Eliphas Levi, this verse contains the secret of the great work of alchemy. The reason assigned is that path thirty-one corresponds to the Hebrew letter *Shin* (Sh), which represents the magic lamp, or the light between the horns of Baphomet. " It is the Kabalistic sign of God or the Astral Light, with its two poles and equili brated centre." The sun mentioned in the paragraph represents gold, the moon silver, and the planets correspond to the other metals.—*La Clef des Grand Mysteres*, p. 234. It is needless to say that the Sepher Yetzirah and its developments have nothing to do with alchemy.

† " Man is the Kabalistic balance," according to Mr. W. b. Greene.—" The Blazing Star," p. 51.

‡ However, it fell, as may be expected, into superstitious uses and became a kind of theosophic divination, based on the first chapter of Genesis, wherein the name Elohim is mentioned thirty-two times.

For the sake of completeness, and because an occult importance has been attributed to it, though in the absence of any real warrant, a word may be added concerning a somewhat conventional piece of Kabalistic classification, entitled the Fifty Gates of Understanding. It is referable to *Binah*, the third Sephira, and is an attempt to sketch the outlines of universal science, to embrace, as Eliphas Levi observes, all possible departments of knowledge and to represent the whole encyclopædia. At the present day such classifications have something of a ghostly aspect. There is, however, no intention to methodise human science after the impossible manner of Raymond Lully and his *Ars Magna Sciendi*. I infer also that, in spite of the exalted themes which are included in the scheme, it concerns only intellectual knowledge, acquired by the external way, and thus constitutes a kind of scholastic introduction to the paths of *Chokmah* or of Wisdom,* by which the holy men of God may, as Kircher observes, after long toil, long experience of divine things and long meditation thereon, penetrate to the concealed centres.† The principle of the enumeration must perhaps be sought in the symbolism of the Hebrew word *Koll*, which signifies All, and the consonants of which are equivalent to the number fifty.

The consultation of this chapter was accompanied by prayers extracted from the divine name in question, and, according to Kircher, by suitable ceremonies.

    * According to Papus, the thirty-two paths are deductive like the Sepher Yetzirah itself, which starts from the notion of God and proceeds thence to natural phenomena, while the fifty gates are established on the inductive principle, ascending from Nature to Deity. —*La Kabbale*, p. 132.

    † Kircher, *Œdipus Ægyptiacus*, Rome, 1623, fol.

The Gates of Understanding, considered as an introduction to the Paths of Wisdom, which diverge, as we have seen, from Chokmah, are essential to the higher knowledge approached by these.* It would serve no purpose to enumerate them all categorically; they begin with the first matter, the Hyle or Chaos, proceed through the various elements of ancient science to the theory of composite substances, thence to organic life and the physical, intellectual and psychic nature of man, afterwards to the heaven of the planets, that of the fixed stars and the *primum mobile*, then to the nine orders of the angelical world, and, finally, to the supermundane and archetypal world, that of *Ain Soph*, unseen by motal eye, transcending human intelligence. It is said that Moses did not attain to this, the fiftieth, gate, and some stress seems to be laid on this point, one would think a little superfluously, as it is obvious that what is beyond all finite capacity must have been beyond the law-giver of Israel.

The scheme of the Gates of Understanding is late in Kabalism; it is found in the treatise entitled " The Gates of Light,"† which is full of references to the mystery of the word *Koll* (KL). All created things, it explains, have come out of these gates, so that in a sense their knowledge connects with the mystery of universal generation, in reference to which it may be observed that the addition of the feminine letter H = 5 to the word KL = 50 gives KLH = the Bride of *Microprosopus*, the Lesser Countenance,

---

* They are called gates, because no one can attain to the paths unless he enters by these.—*Ibid.*

† By R. Joseph Gikatilla ben Abraham.

whence follows the whole mystery of spiritual generation in man, for KLH connects with KNSTL, *i.e.*, the
Church, *Ecclesia Israel*, and brings us back to that
place called mystically Zion and Jerusalem, in which
the divine is communicated to man, as stated in the
fourth section of this book. It is by little gleams of
suggestion of this kind that the barren science of
Gematria is illuminated occasionally.

VII. THE DOCTRINE OF PNEUMATOLOGY

We have now ascertained the heads of Kabalistic
instruction as to the essential nature of God, the
transition from the divine unmanifest into the manifestation of divinity, the extension of the powers and
attributes thus developed through the archetypal,
creative, formative and material worlds, the Kabalistic
hypothesis of creation and the doctrine of transcendental and natural science. It remains for us to
present in brief outline the doctrine of spiritual
essences according to Jewish theosophy. This is,
perhaps, the favourite and certainly the most recurring
subject of the Zohar, and it is this also which was
destined to receive fuller development than any other
in the later literature of Kabalism. The history of its
growth is also worth noting. Pre-existence and the
subdivision of the spiritual nature are found in the
Talmud, but the Sepher Yetzirah has nothing to tell
us on the subject, and there is very little in the first
commentators on that treatise. It may be said, with
considerable truth, that the book and its connections

were concerned rather with the physical forces which produced the universe, but the commentaries at least are sufficiently discursive to have included it in their scheme if they had anything to say upon the subject. It remains, therefore, that the fascinating hypothesis with which we are here dealing is in the main a late growth. The distinction between a holy intelligence and an animal soul in man is found, however, in the "Book of Concealment," * which, so far as can be judged from its form, is the most ancient portion of the Zohar. The latter cycle may be regarded, broadly speaking, as the chief source of pneumatology in Kabalism proper. The indications contained therein became a vast and ponderous system in the schools of Isaac de Loria and Moses of Cordova. This system has at all times exercised the greatest influence on occultists, and, chiefly, perhaps, because it has been made available in Latin by Rosenroth, has superseded that of the Zohar itself. Franck states that it is not true Kabalism and hints that it is full of distorted rabbinical reveries, but it may be doubted whether there is any real canon of criticism. The later speculations are in any case founded on the Zohar, and the following slight sketch contains the general elements of the subject.

We have seen that the world of *Briah* is that of Creation so-called, that is, of the emanation of creative forces. These forces are the *Elohim*, and *Briah* is

---

* "When the inferior man descends (namely, into this world) there are found (in him) two spirits, according to the supernal form. Man (therefore) is constituted from the two sides, the right and the left. As from the right side he has a holy mind, as from the left an animal soul." The extension of the left side was the consequence of the Fall. —"Book of Concealment," c. iv. par. 7-9.

therefore the Elohistic world; in other words, it is that of the lesser or secondary gods. It is also called the world of archangels. It would not be exact to say that the archangels are *Elohim*, much less that Michael, Raphael, Gabriel, Metatron and so forth, are deities according to the Kabalah.* The system is much too involved to admit of such clear identifications. In a general way it may perhaps be affirmed that the intelligent forces of the Briatic world, when assumed, so to speak, by the divine world, may be regarded as the *Elohim*. Thus, according to Kabalism, the three men who appeared to Abraham in the vale of Mamre to announce the destruction impending over the cities of the plain were three archangels, but they were also *Adni*, the Lord, for they were the forms assumed by the Divinity.

Of the hierarchy of spiritual beings outside humanity we meet with various classifications by different Kabalistic writers, the sources of which must be referred to Talmudic times; but, as regards the descending scale more especially, later authorities do not even hesitate to contradict Zoharic statements. The archangels of *Briah*, corresponding to the extension of the *Sephiroth* in that world, are usually enumerated as follows:

I. METATRON, Angel of the Presence, World-Prince, corresponding to *Kether*.†

---

* Isidore Loëb, however, describes *Metatron* as a species of *Demiourgos*, following presumably the heterodox opinions of the Talmudic R. Acher. Franck also regards him as a divine hypostasis.

† When written with a *Jod* (MITTRVN), the name *Metatron* signifies the *Shekinah*; without that letter it signifies the angel who is the "legate of *Shekinah*" also called NGHR = Boy, and hence *Metatron* is said to be a boy-angel.—*Kabbala Denudata, Apparatus*, i. 528.

II. RATZIEL, the Herald of Deity, corresponding to *Chokmah.*

III. TSAPHKIEL, Contemplation of God, corresponding to *Briah.*

IV. TSADKIEL, Justice of God, corresponding to *Chesed.*

V. SAMAEL, Severity of God, corresponding to *Geburah.*

VI. MICHAEL, Like unto God, corresponding to *Tiphereth.*

VII. HANIEL, Grace of God, corresponding to *Netzach.*

VIII. RAPHAEL, Divine Physician, corresponding to *Hod.*

IX. GABRIEL, Man-God, corresponding to *Jesod.*

X. SANDALPHON, Messias, the second phase of Metatron, corresponding to *Malkuth.*

As the Sephirotic forces of the Atziluthic world are represented as resumed under the likeness of a man, Adam Kadmon, so those of *Briah* are resumed under the form of a second Adam, who is regarded as the sole inhabitant of that world, as Adam Kadmon is of *Atziluth.*

The world of *Yetzirah* or Formation is said to be that of the angels, who are divided into nine choirs, which are very nearly identical with the hierarchy of pseudo-Dionysius, whose scheme has become part of Christianity.* Those who attribute a high antiquity to the Kabalistic tradition say that Dionysius drew

---

* It should be noted, however, that unlike Christian angelology, that of the Zohar represents the divine ꞏ ꞏ ꞏ ꞏ ꞏ together inferior to man and most certainly to the souls of the just, which ascend higher and attain a superior rank. See the Mantua edition, iii. 68 *b*.

from the oral doctrine of Israel; others pretend that Dionysius and the Kabalah both derive from Neoplatonism, but Greek and Hebrew thought had joined hands before the date of the Areopagite. Dionysius, perhaps, may be taken to represent the point of contact between Hellenism and Jewry after modification by Christianity. The Kabalah may represent, but at a much longer distance, in the form of its extant literature, the point of contact between Hellenism and Israel unmodified by Christianity.

According to the most usual attribution the choirs of *Yetzirah* are as follows :—

    I. CHAIOTH HA KADOSH, the holy living creatures, or animals of Ezekiel and the Apocalypse, corresponding to *Kether* and to the Christian Seraphim.

    II. OPHANIM, or Wheels, also mentioned in Ezekiel, corresponding to *Chokmah* and the Cherubim.

    III. ARALIM, or Mighty Ones, corresponding to *Briah* and the Thrones.

    IV. HASHMALIM, or Brilliant Ones, corresponding to *Chesed* and the Dominations.

    V. SERAPHIM, or Flaming Serpents, corresponding to *Geburah* and the Powers.

    VI. MELACHIM, or Kings, corresponding to *Tiphereth* and the Virtues.

    VII. ELOHIM, or Gods, corresponding to *Netzach* and the Principalities.

    VIII. BENI-ELOHIM, or Sons of God, corresponding to *Hod* and the Archangels.

    IX. CHERUBIM, the Seat of the Sons, corresponding to *Jesod*, the Foundation, and the Angels.

The tenth order required to complete the Sephirotic attribution is found in the ISHIM, or beatified souls of just men, corresponding to *Malkuth* and the great multitude of the redeemed seen by St. John in the Apocalypse.

These orders are also summarised in the notion of a third Adam, *Yetzirah* represented by the Malkuth of the Yetziratic world, man in the likeness of the angels—in a word, the unfallen Adam of Genesis.

The world of *Assiah*, or of matter, is that into which Adam descended at the Fall, the abode of the evil spirits, the Shells, Envelopes and *Cortices* of the Kabalah.* It contains the orders of retrograde spirits corresponding by inversion to the angels of *Yetzirah* and the arch-fiends corresponding after the same manner to the archangels of the Briatic world.† They are usually enumerated as follows :

I. THAUMIEL, the doubles of God, said to be two-headed and so named, because they pretend to be equal to the Supreme Crown. This is properly the title of the averse *Sephira* corresponding to *Kether*. The cortex is CATHARIEL, according to the supplements of the Zohar. Satan and Moloch are said to be the arch-demons, but the attributions are hopelessly confused throughout, partly owing to the obscure classifications of the Zohar and the contradictions of later Kabalists.

II. CHAIGIDIEL, a term connecting with the significance of *placenta*, or, according to other authori-

---

* For some information on Kabalistic demonology, see *Die Kabbala. Ihre Hauptlehren und ihr verhaltniss zu Christenthum.* Innsbruch, 1885.

† But there are also many material correspondences which are not of shells and demons.

ties, with that of obstruction, in the sense of an impediment to the heavenly influx. This averse *Sephira* corresponds to *Chokmah*. Its cortices are the OGHIEL or GHOGIEL, which cleave to illusory or material appearances in opposition to those of reality and wisdom. This explanation is, of course, very late. The arch-demon is said to be ADAM BELIAL, and so again is Beelzebuth. The Dukes of Esau are also connected with this number.

III. SATHARIEL, the concealment of God, meaning that this averse *Sephirah*, unlike *Binah*, or Intelligence, hides the face of mercy. In the Supplements of the Zohar it is termed SHEIRIEL, from the hirsute body of Esau. The Dukes of Esau are referred to this number, instead of to the averse correspondence of *Chokmah*, by the same work. LUCIFUGE is said to be the arch-demon, but this is obviously not a Kabalistic term ; it is known, however, to the grimoires and to some late demonologists of the Latin church.

IV. GAMCHICOTH, or GOG SHEKLAH, disturber of all things, the averse correspondence of *Chesed.* According to the Zoharic Supplements the cortex seems to be AZARIEL. The arch-demon is ASTAROTH in late Kabalism.

V. GOLAB, or burning, in the sense of incendiarism. This is the averse correspondence of *Geburah* and the antithesis of the Seraphim or Fiery Serpents. The cortex is USIEL. The arch-demon of late Kabalism is ASMODEUS.

VI. TOGARINI, wranglers, because, according to Isaac de Loria, this averse correspondence of *Tiphereth* strives with the supernal *Geburah*. The cortices are called ZOMIEL and the arch-demon is BELPHEGOR.

VII. HARAB SERAP, dispersing raven, referring to the idea that this bird drives out its young, the averse correspondence of *Netzach*. The cortices are the THEUMIEL and the arch-demon is BAAL CHANAN.

VIII. SAMAEL, or embroilment, corresponding to *Hod*, the supernal Victory. The cortices are THEUNIEL according to the Supplements of the ZOHAR, and ADRAMELEK is the name assigned to the arch-demon by late writers.

IX. GAMALIEL, the obscene, in averse correspondence with *Jesod*, which signifies the generation of the higher order. OGIEL, which other classifications attribute to the averse correspondence of *Chesed*, seems to be the cortex mentioned in the Zoharic Supplements, and the arch-fiend is LILITH, according to late Kabalism.

X. LILITH * is, however, according to another tabulation, the averse correspondence of MALKUTH, with whom later Kabalism connects NAHEMA,† the demon of impurity.

In Zoharistic doctrine, however, the chief personalities of *Assiah* are SAMAEL, who is to some extent the averse Adam Kadmon, though in a better sense we may presume that this title is applicable to natural humanity as a whole, and his bride LILITH. The Sephirotic attributions are obscure and incomplete,

---

* According to the Zohar she is a stryge who slays infants.

† A succubus who brings forth spirits and demons after con nection with men, says the Zohar, which in various places further develops this idea.

but in a general way it is said that as in the Holy Kingdom so is it in that of iniquity,* as in the circumcision so also in the uncircumcision. SAMAEL is said to be the uncircumcised and his bride is the prepuce, which, it adds significantly, is the serpent.†

I have given space to this portion of the pneumatic hypothesis of Kabalism, part of which is post-Zoharic, not because it is of any inherent importance, or can be regarded otherwise than as a disfigurement of the philosophical doctrine, but because we shall have later on to give account of the connection between the Kabalah and ceremonial magic, and the doctrine of angels and demons is necessary to the understanding of this connection.‡ It should be added that the doctrine of the celestial and infernal hierarchy is not found in the most ancient portions of the Zohar.

The psychological doctrine concerning the nature of man is of greater interest. It is now a matter of general knowledge that the belief in the soul's immortality, which is not found in the Pentateuch or the prophets, was held by the Jews in later times in connection with that of the resurrection of the body

---

* Hence the true name of Satan is said to be that of YHVH reversed.—Pike, "Morals and Dogma," p. 102.

† R. Simeon ben Jochai in *Tikkunim*, or "Supplements," No. 18. See *Beth Elohim*, by R. Abraham Cohen Irira, c. ii., *Kabbala Denudata*, ii., Part 3, Tract 1, *i.e.*, *Pneumatica Kabbalistica*, p. 188 *et seq.*

‡ The Talmuds abound with legendary history and teaching on this subject, for they are as much a storehouse of folk-lore as of jurisprudence. It has been even proposed that the mediæval notion of vampirism is to be traced to Talmudic fables concerning stryges. See A. Brierre de Boismont, "Des Hallucinations," &c. Second ed. p. 395. Paris. 1852.

and appears freely in the Talmuds.* Occultists, who remember that Moses was learned in all the wisdom of the Egyptians, conceive it to be impossible that he should have known nothing of doctrines which were known to all Egypt, and they hold accordingly that he communicated them secretly to a circle of initiation, by which they were perpetuated in the oral way. Others incline to the notion that they were acquired by the Jews in Babylon. In the Græco-Egyptian period it was, of course, impossible that the learned rabbins of Alexandria should not have been acquainted with the great speculation of a future life. In one way or another it was inevitable that the Jews should have acquired it, which they did accordingly, and the particular date or circumstances are a minor question, about which there can be no certainty. The doctrine, as taught by the Talmud, though recognising five divisions of the soul having names familiar to Kabalism, is comparatively of a simple kind; it does not possess, for example, that philosophical aspect which we find in Philo, and even those who discern Greek influence in early Kabalism must admit that its pneumatology, after allowing for pre-existence, shows very little trace of Platonism.†

Broadly speaking, the Kabalistic hypothesis

---

* "The immortality of the soul and the resurrection of the body figure in the Talmud as tenets of the Synagogue. They form the thirteenth and last article in the profession of faith of Maimonides." Leroy-Beaulieu, "Israel among the nations," p. 17. This is not quite accurate, as that article concerns the resurrection only. "I firmly believe that there will be a resurrection of the dead, at the time when it shall please the Creator, blessed be His name!"—M. Freidlander, "Text Book of the Jewish Religion." 4th ed. London. 1896.

† For a good summary of Kabalistic pneumatology the German student may consult, *inter alia*, Leiningen's *Leelenlehre der Qabalah*. Leipsic. 1887.

divides man into body, soul and spirit,* and thus the triad reigns in things below as in those which are above. These divisions are the animal nature, *Nephesh* ;† the rational nature, *Ruach* ; and the seat of individuality, *Neshamah*. The system is, however, in reality far more complicated. In the first place, *Nephesh* is the animal soul rather than the physical body, or, more exactly, it contains also the triad. There is thus a *Neshamah* of *Nephesh*, which is the principle of the whole, there is a *Ruach* of *Nephesh*, and a *Nephesh* of *Nephesh*, which is the physical part.‡ The whole together is, according to the Zohar, the living man in this world.§ It may be gathered also from the same work that the natural man is complete in this one division, and that it depends upon himself to attain or receive the others. ‖   The true

---

* The most universal and natural of all extant classifications. The Kabalah also holds that the higher rules the lower.   Compare Mrs. Crowe's translation of Kerner's "Seeress of Prevost," pp. 125, 126, where the "revelation" given in the magnetic condition reads like a simplified Kabalism.

† Papus states that *Nephesh*, "the inferior principle," is not the material body, because matter has no existance essentially. I find this doctrine nowhere in Kabalism, for which matter was a vile reality. The text will explain further in what sense *Nephesh* is and is not the physical body.   But Papus also admits that *Nephesh*, *Ruach* and *Neshamah* are practically identical with the body, life, and will of "modern science."—*La Kabbale*, pp. 91, 92.

‡ The German Kabalist, Carl de Leiningen, in a communication addressed to the Munich Psychological Society, includes the material body under the *Nephesh* division. There can be no question that this view has the countenance of the Sepher Yetzirah by which the term is applied to the human body as long as it is alive.

§ Rosenroth, however, identifies *Nephesh* with *Psyche*, the vegetative soul and the plastic part of the soul.   He regards it also as the *Anima vivens* of the Zoharic Supplements.—*Apparatus, Kabbala Denudata*, i. 589.

‖ R. Isachar ben Napthali ; *Synopsis Libri Sohar, Titulus* xiii. *è dictis in Geneseos*, No. 22.   *Cum homo nascitur, non nisi Psychem*

Ruach, or rational principle, and the true *Neshamah*, or spiritual individuality, are for those " who deserve to do the work of the Master." *Neshamah* correponds to *Briah*, *Ruach* to *Yetzirah* and *Nephesh* to *Assiah*. The junction of *Ruach* with the natural man constitutes a state to which the term *Chiah* is given by the Kabalists. The junction of *Neshamah* with both adds another principle termed *Jechidah*. *Jechidah*, *Chiah* and *Neshamah* are also said to be the highest triad. The doctrine of the four worlds suggests, however, that there is a still more exalted part of man, coresponding to *Atziluth*, and of which the *Neshamah* is only a shadow reflected. This is called *Tsure*, which signifies Prototype, and it never quits its exalted abode in the archetypal world. It is connected with the *Neshamah* by an invisible thread, and the aspiration of the lower to the higher opens the path of ecstasy.* The doctrine of the Mystic Marriage in Christian transcendentalism has analogies with some developments of this speculation. But its immediate connections in Israel are with the Ten Degrees of contemplation described in the Babylonian Talmud, and with the later ritual of the *Pardes*.

In the hands of the later Kabalists Zoharic pneumatology became still more involved. The Sephirotic attribution of the triple triad and the supernal part is,

---

solam accipit, et prœterea nec spiritum nec mentem : cum autem deinde incedit in via virtutum, eidem super additur Spiritus et Mens.

   * Compare Tauler's " divine knot which binds happily the soul with the Saviour in the eternity of His kingdom."—*Institutiones Divinæ*, c. xxxix. in the collection of Surius, Cologne, 1548. It is a part of Kabalistic teaching that the path of ecstasy is not entirely closed to man even in this life, which may to some extent be held to follow from another doctrine, namely, that life draws at once from above and from below.—*Zohar* i, 60 *et seq.*, Mantua.

of course, obvious, though it is not methodised in the Zohar. It was, however, taken up by the school of Isaac de Loria, and the operation of the ten *Sephiroth* is elaborated in each of the ten divisions. It is not necessary to enter into these refinements.

It should be added that the Zohar teaches the pre-existence and foreknowledge of the soul* but the revolutions of Kabalism are not precisely what modern occultism understands by reincarnation.† The works of Isaac de Loria treat very largely of this subject, but have been regarded as full of innovations. ‡

It will be seen that the doctrines of the Kabalah, taken *per se*, are nearly all of consequence to occultists, but it is necessary to add that the aspects under which they are presented do not increase that consequence, while the presumption that they are part on their surface. There is nothing in the doctrine of of a tradition delivered from generation to generation, deriving from a remote past, by no means appears *Ain Soph* which will warrant us in placing it on a higher level than any other theory of the Absolute ;

---

* All souls, moreover, were created together. Later writers introduced the idea of transmigration. Thus the treatise entitled "The Royal Valley," says that the soul of a slanderer is transmigrated into a silent stone, and that of the murderer into water.

† They are still less what Christian mysticism understands by regeneration, a misapprehension peculiar, I believe, to the late Lady Caithness.—See "Old Truths in a New Light," p. 370. "We now know that the doctrine of regeneration was secretly taught among the Jews in the 'Mysteries,' or Sacred Kabalah," the regeneration in question being the transformations and mysterious trials, the goings and returnings of souls and spirits, described in the Zoharic "Discourse of the Ancient Man."

‡ In a general sense Mr. W. T. Flagg is correct when he states that "the Gnostics and Kabalists held that perfection was arrived at by means of successive reincarnations."—See "Yoga or Transformation." New York and London. 1898.

there is much in its modern presentation by some occultists, who most strenuously defend its antiquity, and even its divine derivation, which helps to place it outside philosophical consideration; in its fundamental nature it is the common inheritance of all human speculation; it needs neither revelation nor oral tradition to perpetuate it. The doctrine of the *Sephiroth*, on the other hand, is at most a degree better than any other system of emanation, and no such theory can be accepted as a satisfactory attempt to explain the universe. At the epochs when these theories were possible they were serious and excellent in their intention, and up to that point their interest is permanent for the history of human thought. To revive them at the present day is beside all reason. Just as the necessity of final causation, with all the difficulties which it involves, is not dispensed with by recourse to evolution, so the transition from infinite to finite, from eternal to temporal, from absolute perfection to the imperfect order of the physical and moral world, from God, in a word, to the material, is not assisted by supposing stages between them. This kind of compromise belongs to a period of human thought which has utterly passed away. It is the same with the doctrine of the two Countenances; it was admirable for its time as an *eirenicon* between the God of the philosophers and the God of old Israel, but at the present day there is not much need to bridge that gulf, and occultists in particular who have abandoned the orthodox in faith, who are also very proud of this fact, and very resolute as to its importance, are less in need than others of such an accommodation. Speaking generally, the Kabalah is an attempt to give depth and significance to a form of religious faith which occultism has, at least in its literal aspects, agreed to set aside.   Its pneumatology is important to those who take ceremonial magic seriously, and the doctrine of the virtue in words, contained by implication in that of the Instruments of Creation, is much in favour with a certain school of occultism; but, taken altogether, the content of the Kabalah does not possess the momentous character which has been ascribed to it by those whose beliefs have invested it with something of living interest. The next stage of our inquiry is to determine as far as possible its claims to antiquity.*

---

* It may be mentioned in conclusion that the reader who has a little knowledge of Hebrew will do well to consult the curious diagrams as well as the Latin text of the rare fourth part of Rosenroth's *Apparatus in Librum Sohar.*

BOOK III

SOURCE AND AUTHORITY OF THE KABALAH

ARGUMENT

The two chief cycles of Kabalistic literature, in spite of destructive criticism, are referable, by their materials, to Talmudic times. There is no reason why the "Book of Formation" should not be the work of R. Akiba, as tradition affirms. There is no solid evidence to support the theory that R. Moses de Leon wrote the Zohar at the end of the thirteenth century. At the same time, the belief of occult students that these works represent a tradition dating from an early period of history has also little to support it. The attempts to refer the Kabalah in a direct manner to some prior philosophical system must be largely set aside ; it has its antecedents everywhere, but its analogies with other systems are referable to a natural similarity between independent conclusions on fundamental problems of being. Antecedent Jewish influence through the school of Aristobulus and Philo must not be overlooked, but also it must not be exaggerated. The Kabalah is *sui generis*. It has its scholastic connections, and it has its Mohammedan corre spondences. If there be any preponderance in a given direction, its sphere of influence has been Christian rather than Jewish.

I. DATE AND DOCTRINE OF THE "BOOK OF FORMATION"

WE are now in possession of the most important elements of Kabalistic doctrine and the chief heads of its philosophical instruction. There is much, very much, more in its literature, some of which must be set aside altogether from consideration in a work which would exceed its purpose if it entered into abstruse and technical matters, while some has been postponed till a later stage of our study, because, although it is highly important to the right understanding of the subject, it does not involve the points with which we are concerned at the inception. First among these points is whether and how far we are warranted, by evidence that can be produced in the open day, in regarding the literature which contains the doctrines summarised by the preceding sections as possessing an authentic character, or the doctrines themselves as part of a tradition perpetuated in Israel from very early times.

For this purpose it will be convenient to accept the literature as divisible into four classes—(1) The " Book of Formation "; (2) The commentaries on that work which preceded the public appearance of the Zohar; (3) The Zohar itself; (4) The writings subsequent thereto.*

The report of an esoteric tradition in Israel did not begin to circulate through Christendom till the fourteenth century, and this, as we shall see later on, is explained by the fact that the chief collection of its archives was unknown, at least generally, in Jewry itself till about 1290, A.D. This collection is that

---

* Solomon Munk, one of the highest French authorities on Kabalism, tabulates the following classification in the *Dictionnaire de la Conversation*, s.v. *Kabbale*. (1) A symbolical portion, namely, mystical calculations, *i.e.*, *Themurah*, *Gematria*, *Notaricon*, on which refer to Book I. § 4; (2) A dogmatic or positive part, which is, in fact, concerned with the hypothesis of spiritual essences, *i.e.*, angels, demons, human souls and their transmigration; (3) A speculative and metaphysical part, namely, Sephirotic doctrine and so forth. It is not a satisfactory classification, but there is no need to criticise it here.

which is termed by Kabalists the work of the Chariot, in other words, the Zohar. The work of Creation—that is, the Sepher Yetzirah—was known, as we have ground for believing, to at least one Christian student so far back as the middle of the ninth century, but there was no consequence attached to it for Christendom. The Sepher Yetzirah is supposed to embody a tradition handed down from the time of Abraham, and there is no doubt that the uncritical spirit of several centuries represented the patriarch as its author. This does not seem, however, as some modern criticism has loosely supposed,* to have been the view universally adopted by the Jewish learning which accepted the document. That he received and he transmitted it was undoubtedly held, but the work itself does not pretend to have been reduced to writing till after the destruction of Jerusalem, and tradition has ascribed its formal authorship to Rabbi Akiba ben Joseph, the pupil of R. Joshua ben Chananja, who was himself the successor, as he was also once the opponent, of Rabban Gamaliel. There is nothing flagrantly improbable in this attribution, though it reaches us late in history. Akiba was a mystic with whose notions the scheme of the Sepher Yetzirah was in complete accordance, and he is the reputed author of another work dealing with the mysteries of the Hebrew alpha-

---

* Dr. Edersheim, "History of the Jewish Nation," observes that it is properly "a monologue on the part of Abraham, in which, by the contemplation of all that is around him, he ultimately arrives at the conviction of the unity of God." 3rd. ed. p. 407. So also Ginsburg says that it professes to be a monologue of the patriarch. It does nothing of the sort ; but the fifth chapter mentions "Abraham our father." Of course, the legend of patriarchal derivation became stereotyped quickly. In the twelfth century, R. Judah Ha Levi זהה הוא¹ of "the Book of the Creation which belongs to our father Abraham.

bet.* In his interpretation of Scripture he followed and exaggerated the principles of Hillel the Great and Nahum of Giso. He promulgated, or, at least, gave the weight of his authority to, the doctrine that " every sentence, word and particle in the Bible had its use and meaning."† His literary labours were also very great, for to him is attributed the arrangement and redaction of the Halakha. Subsequent generations were so impressed by his marvellous knowledge of divine things that he was asserted to have discovered much of which even Moses was ignorant, which, in the sense not intended, is indubitably true. If we admit the existence of a secret tradition in Israel, we shall not need to question that Akiba was initiated therein; if we admit the existence of the Sepher Yetzirah in the second century, we can imagine no more probable author for that work.‡ Nor is the date essentially disagreeable to a moderate criticism;§ it is merely unestablished for want of exact evidence, ‖

---

* It is called the alphabet of R. Akiba, being the letters allegorically explained. Buxtorf says that it was printed at Cracovia in 1597, with a *Commentarius Prolixus*. See *Bibliotheca Hebræa Rabbinica*. Basilia, 1618-19, 4 vols. fol. An earlier edition of the Alphabet appeared at Venice in 1546. See Bartolocci, iv. 274.

† Edersheim, "History of the Jewish Nation."

‡ Curiously enough, M. Nicolas admits the date necessary but not the authorship it suggests, on the ground that Akiba was a rigid and head-strong doctor of the Law and not likely to indulge in speculative lucubrations. This estimate, with which it is difficult to agree, has also the authority of Franck, on the ground that the Talmud reproaches Akiba for his incommensurate notions of God, but Franck is possibly more influenced by his belief in the earlier origin of the work.—*La Kabbale*, p. 87 *et seq.*

§ Quite independently of occult prepossessions it has been argued that the language of the Sepher Yetzirah is a Hebrew wholly analogous to that of the Mishnah.

‖ Dr. Schiller-Szinessy expressly says that the book no doubt belongs to Akiba, " both in substance and form."—*Encyclopædia Bri-*

which begins only with the ninth century, when there is tolerable reason to infer that it was known by St. Agobard.* It is not possible from any internal testimony to fix the work as belonging to the later period, for obviously any book may be far older than the date of its first quotation, while the fact, if established, that it was known in France in or about the year 850 † would create a presumption that it was in existence much earlier, for literature travelled slowly in those days. We must remember also that a Sepher Yetzirah is mentioned in both Talmuds in connection with the doctrine that heaven and earth were created by a mysterious combination of letters, and that Franck characterises the attempt of modern scholarship to

tannica, 9th ed., s.v. Midrashim, a term derived from a root signifying to seek out or to question. Munk also takes this view in the article s.v. Kabbale, contributed to the ninth volume of the Dictionnaire de la Conversation et de la Lecture, Paris, 1833.

* The English reader may consult Taylor's translation of Basnage's " History of the Jews," p. 590 et seq. London. 1708. Agobard was Archbishop of Lyons, and wrote against trials by ordeal and other superstitions of his period. See the Abbé Migne's Dictionnaire des Sciences Occultes, vol. i. col. 32. Despite this apparent enlightenment he figures among the persecutors of Jewry. See Basnage, Histoire des Juifs, t. v. pp. 1493, 1494.

† The evidence falls short of demonstration, and is confined to two short passages in the Epistola S. Agobardi . . . de Judaicis Superstitionibus. In the first, the Jews are branded for their gross notions of the Deity, on the ground that they believe Him to be possessed of a bodily form, having distinct members and lineaments, including organs of seeing, hearing, speaking and so forth ; also that they note only one difference between the body of God and that of man who is in His image, namely, that the fingers are inflexible, because God effects nothing with his hands. It seems certain that St. Agobard draws here from the " Description of the Body of God." In the second passage it is said : " Further, they believe the letters of their alphabet to have existed from everlasting, and before the beginning of the world to have received diverse offices, in virtue of which they should preside over created things."—S. Agobardi, Lugdunensis Episcopi, Opera Omnia. Patrologiæ Cursus Completus . . . accurante J. P. Migne. Paris, 1851, p. 78 et seq.

distinguish two works under an identical title as founded in gross ignorance.* If, however, we do not place the work in Talmudic times, we may concede that it came into existence within a measurable distance of the stormy period in which the great Talmudic canons were forcibly closed.

We have next to distinguish between the date which may be surmised for the treatise and that which must perhaps be attributed to the teaching embodied therein. Have we any ground for believing that the doctrine of the Sepher Yetzirah is older than the Egyptian captivity, as its legend affirms ? This question must be answered by an emphatic negative. The doctrine under notice gives prominence to the sacred and divine character of the Hebrew alphabet, and we have no warrant for supposing that the art of writing was possessed by Abraham ; every probability is against it and every authority is agreed on this point. But the Sepher Yetzirah contains, by implication at least, the doctrine of an occult power and sanctity inherent in certain divine names, and we know that this belief is very old in humanity, that it is found at an early period in Chaldea, Akkadia and so forth. It is afflicting to modern intelligence, but it is of great antiquity, and as it belongs to those countries with which Israel was in contact, we have reason to think that it became part of the religious baggage of the Hebrew people long before the Sepher Yetzirah, the Alphabet of Akiba, or the Mishna itself were dreamed of. Occultism has

---

* On this fact Franck insists very strongly, maintaining that these references demonstrate the existence of a work reserved to a few and that this work is identical with the Sepher Yetzirah as we now have it.—*La Kabbale,* Paris, 1843, p. 75 *et seq.*

attached itself to this doctrine,* and we must allow, therefore, to occultists that the most ancient document of Kabalism† does embody something of tradition from the past, perhaps even from the period of the Babylonian captivity, as the Talmud itself indicates. On the other hand, we have no evidence to show that the doctrine of the Instruments of Creation is much prior to the date of the treatise which develops it; it has no history previously, and can therefore be placed only in Talmudic—*i.e.*, in post-Christian—times. It should be added that the Sepher Yetzirah is part of a considerable literature of an occult or mystical complexion covering the period between the closing of the Talmudic Canon and the first report of the Zohar.

II. MODERN CRITICISM OF THE BOOK OF SPLENDOUR

The commentaries on the Sepher Yetzirah which preceded the publication of the Zohar make no claim

---

* And so also, it would seem, has the less pronounced form of modern Christian mysticism. See, for example, the interesting collection entitled "Letters from a Mystic of the Present Day," by an anonymous writer. Second edition, London, 1889, pp. 205-207. "We seem to have to learn the *various* names of God before we can grasp *the* Name. *The* Name grasps us, while the others are various outer courts through which we come into the Sanctuary or Name of God; in that name we find pasture wherever our outer life may take us." Compare Saint-Martin, *L'Esprit des choses*, tom. ii. 65 *et seq.*

† I ought not, perhaps, to omit that Mayer Lambert, one of the latest editors of the Sepher Yetzirah, affirms that it has nothing in common with the Kabalah, by which he understands a mysterious explanation of the Bible drawn from the letters of the text and a metaphysical theory which connects God with the world through a series of emanations of divinity. As regards its date, he agrees that it is one of the numerous *Midrashim* produced by the Talmudic period.

on antiquity, and may therefore be reserved for consideration in their proper place later on. The alleged traces of Kabalism in writers of known dates also prior to that event may in like manner be left till we deal with the documents consecutively. We may, therefore, proceed at once to the absorbing problems connected with the Book of Splendour. Chief among these are the vital questions : (1) Whether modern criticism is right in ascribing the Zohar to the thirteenth century as its period, and to R. Moses Shem Tob de Leon as its author. (2) Whether we have evidence that some at least of its doctrine was in existence at a much earlier period, or, as its legend states, at the time of the Roman Emperor Antoninus. To determine these points we shall do well to glance first of all at the history of the criticism which has befallen this vast document.

We shall get very little help from the insight of contemporary Israel as to either point. The Sepher Yetzirah was known and accepted before documentary criticism can be well said to have been born, and so also when the Zohar was promulgated it was among a mixed audience who either took or rejected it on *a priori* grounds. Those who loathed the yoke of Aristotle, which Abraham ben David Ha Levi, Aben Ezra and Moses Maimonides would have placed on the neck of Jewry, accorded it a glad welcome ;* all that great section of Jewry which was

* The contrariety of the two systems is best shown by this fact. Myer says : " Its opponents were almost universally Jewish Aristotelians who opposed the ancient secret learning of the Israelites because it was more in accord with the philosophy of Plato and Pythagoras, and indeed most likely emanated from the same sources, the Aryan and Chaldean esoteric doctrine."—*Philosophy of Ibn Gebirol*, p. 12. It is the fact

addicted to astrology and magic took it into their
heart of hearts : it was neither astrology nor magic,
but it harmonized with their transcendental aspirations.
On the other hand, it was hated by the Aristotelians
because it did not consort with their methods.* It is
not till recent times that we have any intelligent
defence on the part of Jewish thinkers—Konitz in
1815, Franck in 1843, David Luria in 1857, Munk in
1859; or, on the other hand, a strong and informed
hostility, as that of Graetz† in Germany, to quote only
one instance.

In the influence exercised by the Kabalah upon
certain minds of Christendom, the Sepher Yetzirah
must be distinguished from the Zohar. The former
has had no influence ; it was indeed introduced to our
knowledge by a monk of exalted erudition and of
eccentricity equally great, but it was not till the
sixteenth century and it found no sphere of operation.
Some of its Sephirotic developments, the com-

only which is of value ; Mr. Myer's explanation may be read in the
light of Book iii., § 5.

* " When the Saracens became the patrons of philosophy   . .
the attention paid both by Arabians and Christians to the writings of
Aristotle excited the emulation of the Jews, who, notwithstanding the
ancient curse pronounced on all Jews who should instruct their sons in
the Grecian learning . . . continued in their philosophical course
reading Aristotle in Hebrew translations made from the inaccurate
Arabic, for Greek was at this period little understood."—Gould,
" History of Freemasonry," London, 1885, ii. 66, 67 ; see also 69, 70.

† . . . ps it is more strong than it is well informed. I see no
tia . . . etz of any real acquaintance with the Kabalah, about which
he writes savagely and with the indiscrimination which we connect with
a savage. Thus, he terms the Zohar "a notorious forgery," whereas the
chief notoriety concerning it is that after eight centuries of criticism
scarcely two authorities can be found to agree in their estimate.
Throughout this part of his history we find continually things uncertain
lescribed in the language of certitude, and things for which there is
little evidence as if there were overwhelming testimony.

H

mentaries of Rabbi Abraham and Rabbi Azariel, met with a certain audience among a few men of learning, but they can bear no comparison with the appeal made by the larger cycle. For all Christian students the Kabalah was substantially the Zohar, and, as we shall see subsequently, the office attributed to it was almost exclusively evangelical; that is to say, the discovery that there had existed in Israel, from time immemorial, as it was alleged, a secret doctrine which appeared to contain analogies and even identities with fundamental dogmas of Christianity, put the Jews so clearly in the wrong, by their own showing, that their conversion was deemed inevitable.* Thus, the antiquity of the tradition was not at that time challenged in Christendom, and again it was not a period when documentary criticism was pursued with any keenness. The fourteenth century made the grave, but yet excusable, mistake of supposing that most people wrote the books attributed to them. They accepted the claim of the Zohar for much the same reason that they were persuaded of the antiquity of Homer. In the existing state of scholarship to have challenged one might have opened an abyss beneath the other, and could well have included all ancient literature in a common uncertainty. Of course, as time went on, and

---

* "Some Christians have also esteemed them (*i.e.*, the Kabalistic books and their connections) because they found them more favourable to the Christian religion than the recent commentaries of the Rabbins. But they failed to consider that these same allegorical books are filled with an infinitude of ridiculous fables, and that Jewish superstition is much more clearly proved from them than are the mysteries of our religion. William Postel has imposed on several theologians in this matter, having pretended to find Christianity in the books of the Zohar."—Richard Simon, *Histoire Critique du Vieux Testament*, p. 371.

the evangelical instrument proved to be of no effect, its validity began to be challenged, but even then it was scarcely on critical grounds. So also, even at the inception of the enthusiasm, some sceptical voices were raised, but again from uncritical and predetermined motives.* The Christians who rejected the Zohar were like the Jews who rejected it—the latter because they were Aristotelians, the former because they were Christians, who saw no good in the Ghetto, and only the final impenitence of the lost thief in the erudition of Toledo.†

The credulity, or at least the disability, of early students has been amply atoned for in the spirit which has governed the later critics of the Kabalah. I must confess that in some cases they seem, after their own manner, to have prejudged the question much as that laborious bibliographer Julius Bartolocci prejudged it in the seventeenth century. It was offensive to the dignity of the Latin Church to suppose that there was a rival tradition, full of illumination and wisdom, preserved unknown to the church in the rejected house of Israel. By a similar sentiment it has seemed intolerable to modern taste that any occult literature should possess a real claim on attention. It is there-

---

* Among writers who did not permit themselves to be deceived by the alleged instrument of conversion, a high place must be accorded to Petrus Galatinus and his *De Arcanis Catholicæ Veritatis contra Judæorum perfidiam*, first published in 1518.

† The connection between Christianity and the Zohar still finds an occasional expositor in occult circles. Consult Stanislas de Guaita, *Essias des Sciences Maudites. I. Au Seuil du Mystere. Nouvelle édition, corrigé. Paris.* 1890. "The Zohar has wedded the Gospel ; the spirit has fructified the soul ; and immortal works have been the fruits of this union. The Kabalah became Catholic in the school of St. John," &c. A romantic criticism inspired by Eliphas Lévi.

fore said out of hand that the Kabalah, represented by the Zohar, is a forgery of the thirteenth century. We must endeavour to comprehend precisely what is involved in this standpoint.

There are some literary fabrications which do not need a high degree of scholarship to expose them, for they may be said to betray themselves, often at every point. In the department of *belles lettres* it is sufficient to mention the so-called Rowley poems. These, as everybody is well aware, were forgeries pure and simple, and their disguise is so entirely spurious that it can be peeled off without any difficulty. It is not necessary to add that they possessed their believers, and not further back than the days of the Bell edition of Chatterton, the race of Rowleyites had still a few survivals, for we find the editor describing their characteristics in terms which have a wider application than he was concerned with at the moment. A true Rowleyite, he says, is not open to conviction, and the statement obtains in the case of all pertinacious defenders of spurious literary productions. The position of the Rowley MSS. is fairly paralleled by that of many occult documents, among which, as typical instances, we may select the handbooks of Ceremonial Magic. There are no works which betray themselves more transparently and abundantly than the "Key of Solomon" and the "Sacred Magic of Abramelin the Mage," and yet they possess at this day their believers, enthusiasts for the good faith of their claims to a high antiquity or a Hebrew origin, as the case may be.

There are again some fabrications which possess a certain basis in fact, over which a mass of forgery has been arranged. One ready instance in point is found in the poems of Ossian, for which there was indubitably a nucleus of floating Gaelic tradition which was wrought into his imposition by McPherson. The result may deceive for a moment even sound scholarship, but its full exposure is only a matter of time. In this case the epic of " Wallace " was fatal to the possibility of Fingal. Perhaps the Latin alchemical writings attributed to Geber may be regarded as typical instances in occult literature of this form of fraud. They have scarcely any resemblance to the Arabic originals, but such originals exist.

Finally, there are certain works which may or may not be fabrications, but they either incorporate so much genuine material belonging to the depart ment of literature which they pretend to represent, or else are so skilfully constructed that the balance of probability is poised pretty equally concerning them, and it is almost impossible to arrive, by impartial methods, at the determination of their claims. I do not know whether there is any good instance in *belles lettres* of this kind of alleged fabrication. Hogg's " Jacobite Relics of Scotland " is perhaps the nearest approach to a parallel. That collection undoubtedly contains a large proportion of genuine material, but it is suspected that the Ettrick Shepherd supplied a proportion of the collection by his own skill in verse-craft, and criticism, though it has not concerned itself very seriously, is perhaps fairly divided on the question. In occult literature we have several signal examples of this suspected writing which has not been found out to the satisfaction of the impartial mind.

For example, a few of the Hermetic books, which are usually classed by scholars as productions of the Alexandrian period, and therefore post-Christian, are held by others to represent occult traditions of considerable antiquity, and I do not think that the case has been decided for all time as regards some of these works. But the most renowned of all the instances is that with which we are here concerned—the Kabalah itself. Destructive criticism has maintained that its foremost work was forged by a single writer, of indifferent claims to our intellectual consideration, at the end of the thirteenth century. There is, as we shall see, no positive evidence on this point which is worth naming, and the presumptive evidence is not at all strong. There is very good proof of late writing, but the theory of the fabrication of the Zohar by Moses de Leon puts an almost impossible burden on the shoulders of that questionable personage, and is generally the work of writers who have not paid sufficient regard to the possible existence of much of the traditional doctrine which is summarised in the Zohar at a period preceding its appearance by some centuries.

We admit, therefore, that Kabalistic literature belongs to a suspected class, but how we are to regard its impeachment is a different question. The fact that this inquiry has been undertaken will indicate that, in my own opinion, the hostile critic must change the nature of his indictment. As regards its material, and usually as regards its motive, spurious literature belongs to the most accountable class. It falls into line readily. Where there are complex workings of the human mind, as in the Zohar, there sincerity is usually present. The Kabalah is much too singular in its mechanism to be referable to a solitary author. So far as there is evidence on the subject, that evidence tends to show that it grew, and that in its final state it was neither wholly old nor entirely new, but doctrine more or less familiar or following from familiar doctrine.* These facts are now in course of recognition outside occult circles, in the academic places which rule general opinion. Of this Dr. Schiller-Szinessy offers the best evidence when he observes that "almost all that the latest critics have said concerning the age of the various Targumim and Midrashim," including the Zohar, "will have to be unsaid."

III. THE DATE AND AUTHORSHIP OF THE BOOK OF SPLENDOUR

The theory which accounts for the Zohar on the ground that it was written by Moses de Leon in the latter half of the thirteenth century does not depend merely on internal evidence; it is not exclusively an inference made by modern criticism from allusions to late events found here and there in the work; it is

---

* This is very nearly the position of Solomon Munk, who maintains that the Zohar and its connections, that is, the various tracts and fragments which enter into the compilation, are not the inventions of an impostor, but that ancient documents were used by the editor, including Midrashim which are not now extant.—*Melanges de Philosophie, Juive et Arabe.* Paris. 1859, p. 275 *et seq.* In spite of this, Munk did not consider the Zohar, at least in its present form, as anterior to the seventh century, but rather that the Kabalistic development which it represents took place in the thirteenth century, and were either influenced by Gebirol or by sources common to both.—*Ibid.* pp. 276, 277.

not a presumption arising only from the fact that the Spanish Jew who is suspected of the splendid imposture lived by transcribing copies of it,* that it had never been heard of previously, or that the original MS. from which R. Moses claimed to have drawn has never come to light. It is based upon evidence which claims to be contemporary, or there abouts, with the appearance of the Zohar itself. It may be highly probable that in the absence of any such testimony the same point would have been reached independently, but the fact remains that it is not the discovery of modern criticism at all; it transpired without being sought for, and hence the case against the work is based both on external and internal grounds. It is not therefore at first sight a weak case, and I have sketched it fully and frankly that I may not be accused of any bias in the matter. At the same time it is my purpose to show that the indictment breaks down altogether.

Let us dispose first of all of the alleged external evidence. In the year 1566 there appeared in Hebrew at Constantinople a work entitled *Sepher Yuhasin*, or "Book of Genealogies," by R. Moses Abraham ben Samuel Zakut, who belongs to the

---

* Although I have called this a fact, because it is accepted by all critics who accept the account of the Zohar given in the *Sephir Yuhasin*, it seems to me that the statement has an air of fable. The Zohar is a very large work, and Moses de Leon must have employed a very large staff of copyists in order to transcribe it frequently. There is no evidence, however, that he employed any one; but if he worked single-handed, he could not have " made large sums," as alleged, by so slow a process. It has been suggested alternatively that he profited much by the patronage of the wealthy Jews, to whom he dedicated his works, but as to this there is no conclusive evidence. It is merely an inference from the fact that he dedicated several other works to co-religionists who were his patrons.

second half of the fifteenth century.* Its point of
view with regard to the Zohar is that the splendour
of that work is truly an illumination of the world;
that it contains the deep secrets of the Law and of
the concealed tradition in Israel; that it is conformed
to the truth as regards the written and oral law; that
it embodies the sayings of R. Simeon ben Jochai, of
the period of the Emperor Antoninus, under whose
name it appears, but is really the work of his
disciples; and that, finally, it did not become public
till after the death of Nachmanides, namely, the
second half of the thirteenth century. It is therefore
obvious that Zakut must not be classed among those
who opposed the Zohar, as some modern critics have
attempted.

It will seem almost incredible that in this work,
which so elaborately defends the Zohar, a narrative
should appear which represents it as an imposture
devised from mercenary motives by Moses de Leon,
yet such at first sight is the case, and as such it has
been accepted by those who impeach the Kabalah.
The explanation is in reality simple; the narrative in
question is a fragment, and the proof that its missing
conclusion is really to the credit of the Zohar, and
exculpatory as to the transcriber of that work, is found
in the fact that the person whose adventures it relates
became subsequently assured that the Zohar was not
a sordid forgery, as he embodied some of its principles
in one of his own treatises. The most biassed of

* That is to say, to the reign of Ferdinand and Isabella. He was
a Jew of Salamanca, but he taught at Saragossa. When the edict of
expulsion was published he retired into Portugal and was appointed
Royal Historiographer by King Emanuel. His work embraces the
entire period between the creation of the world and the year 1500 A.D.

modern critics, Dr. Graetz, admits the force of this fact.

The narrative is concerned with the adventures of Isaac de Acco,* a disciple of Nachmanides, who laid claim to the performance of miracles by a transposition of the Hebrew letters according to a system which he pretended that he had learned from the angels. Independently, therefore, of the Zohar, he was a Kabalist after his own fashion, and, we may suspect, a visionary. In either case, he was at Novara, in Italy, about 1293, when he heard that a Spanish Rabbin was in possession of the original Zohar MSS., and, being very anxious to see them, he made a journey into Spain. He there learned by report that the erudite Moses Nachmanides was said to have transmitted the book to his son in Catalonia from Palestine,† but that the ship which bore it was driven by the wind to Aragonia‡ or to Catalonia, and the precious volume came into the hands of Moses de Leon. At Valladolid Isaac de Acco made the acquaintance of the latter, who declared upon oath that he was in possession of the MS. and that it was at his home in Avila, where he would exhibit it to Isaac. They undertook a journey together with this object, but Moses de Leon died at Arevolo on the way.§ His companion proceeded to Avila, and there

---

* *I.e.*, Acre, besieged by the Sultan of Egypt in 1291. Isaac was one of the Jewish refugees from that city, and seems to have suffered imprisonment for a time.

† It is curious that the disciple should first learn that his master was in possession of such a treasure by a floating rumour from a great distance.

‡ The reference is probably to Tarragona, as Aragon has no seaboard.

§ So far the account represents Moses de Leon as acting with perfect sincerity in the matter.

prosecuted his inquiries among the relatives of the deceased. By one of these, namely, by David Rafon, of Corfu, he was informed that Moses de Leon had been a spendthrift who derived great profit from his writings, but neglected his wife and daughter, while as for the Zohar he had made it up out of his own head. How far Isaac was impressed by this statement does not appear explicitly, but he next had recourse to a wealthy Rabbin of Avila, named Joseph, who communicated with the widow and daughter of Moses, offering for the maiden the hand of his son and a substantial dowry if they would produce the original MS. of the Zohar. The women had been left in poor circumstances, and there was every reason to suppose that they would comply gladly. They, however, concurred in affirming that there was no such MS., that the dead man had composed the work out of his own head and written it with his own hand.* His quest having thus failed, Isaac de Acco left Avila and proceeded to Talavera, where he met with R. Joseph Hallevy, the son of a Kabalist named Todros, who, in reply to his inquiries, affirmed that the genuine Zohar was in the hands of Moses de Leon, as he had himself proved conclusively. The nature of the proof does not appear, and the account of Isaac breaks off abruptly in the middle of a sentence describing some testimony which he received at Toledo as to an ancient Rabbin, named Jacob, who had "testified by heaven and earth that the book

---

Hence he did not employ transcribers, and whatever price he may have obtained for copies of the work he could not have multiplied many. If assiduous, he could have had no time for squandering ; if idle, no money to spend.

Zohar, of which R. Simeon ben Jochai is the author * * *."

I have passed over purposely in this brief account several minor details which have awakened suspicion as to the honesty of the narrative, for it is unnecessary to confuse the issues. The point is that it closes with two solemn testimonies to the authenticity of the Zohar, and by the course which he subsequently took Isaac de Acco must have concluded to abide by these. Assuming that the narrative is truthful, the evidence which was set aside as insufficient by the one person who has recorded it cannot be accepted by impartial criticism unenforced by other considerations. So far therefore as the account in the *Sepher Yuhasin* is concerned, it is not proved that Moses de Leon wrote the Zohar "out of his own head."* Zakut himself mentions an opinion that he did write it under the guidance of the Writing Name, *i.e.*, by angelic revelation, but I do not conceive that it is necessary to discuss this possibility.

The state of the case as it stands is confused, and most persons who have taken part in the controversy have been led into more or less contradiction. Those who have regarded Moses de Leon as nothing more than a transcriber have had to reckon as they could with certain damaging references to late events which

---

† Outside this document there is, moreover, no proof, so far as I am aware, that he was even connected with it as transcriber. Further, speaking still under correction, the *Yuhasin* is the one authority by which we can fix so important a date as the death of Moses de Leon. Who was the Rabbi of this name and place, for whom Samuel, son of Isaac, transcribed a copy of the *Moreh*, *anno* 1452, which copy is still preserved in the Günglung Library, Paris? It is numbered 771, according to Friedlander's preface to the third volume of his version of Maimonides, p. xiv.

are found in the Zohar, and their explanations are often quite worthless; those who regard the transcriber as the concealed author have had to meet as they might the extreme difficulty of supposing that such a collection was the production of one individual, and that individual Moses de Leon. Their explanations also are of little value and are for the most part merely ingenious assumptions.

The internal evidence against the Zohar may be reduced under the following heads :

(1) It refers to the vowel points which are alleged to have been invented in post-Talmudic times.* (2) It quotes or borrows from a book entitled the "Duties of the Heart," written by a Jew of Saragossa,† about the middle of the eleventh century. (3) It mentions two kinds of phylacteries, or Tephilim, which fact is supposed to prove the late origin of the entire work.‡ (4) It quotes authorities posterior to its alleged period. (5) It is written in Aramaic, whereas at the period to which it is ascribed Aramaic was the vernacular, while Hebrew was made use of in religious writings.

---

* Elias Levita, a German Jew of the sixteenth century, was one of the first to affirm the late institution of the points, which he ascribed to the Jews of Tiberias about the beginning of the sixth century. In reply to this it has been advanced that at the period the schools of Judæa had been closed, and that Jewish learning was then centred at Babylon (see David Levi : *Lingua Sacra*, part i. c. iii. § 1, London, 1785). Ginsburg, however, adopts the theory of Levita, subject to the modification that they were introduced by the Karaite, R. Mocha, at the end of the sixth century. David Levi, on the other hand, makes their reception by the Karaite Jews a proof of their antiquity, because they were " professed enemies to tradition and innovation." Unfortunately, there are no pointed Hebrew MSS. prior to the tenth century.

† R. Behai ben Joseph Ibn Bakoda.

‡ For a general description of the *Tephilim*, see Basnage, *Histoire des Juifs*, tom. iii. p. 752 *et seq.*

These difficulties are met by defenders of the Zohar in the following way :

(1) The vowel points are not the invention of times posterior to the Talmud; the proof is that they are mentioned in the Talmud, and there is no question that this work is long anterior to the thirteenth century. In the Talmud they are said to have been a rule given to Moses on Mount Sinai.* The pre-Christian existence of the point system with the exception of a very few cases occurring in the Pentateuch, which, moreover, are not vowel-points, this is one thing, and must be left to those who affirm it; its existence in Talmudic times,† that is, prior to the close of the sixth century is another, and all that is required in the present case to destroy the validity of this objection to the genuine character of the Zohar.‡

(2) The treatise on the " Duties of the Heart " is certainly a work of the eleventh century, but it is advanced that its author himself borrowed from the Zohar in an early form, the existence of which is traceable, from Talmudic references, under the name

---

* Treatise *Nedareem*, also *Bab. Megillah*, *Bab. Berocoth*, and *Bab. Eruvin*. This is also the testimony of the Zohar, obviously reproducing current legend, or borrowing from the traditional storehouse of the Talmud.

† See David Levi, *op. cit.*, who says that in several places of the Babylonian Talmud mention is made of " the distinction of the accents, and, in particular, of the accents of the law, which might be shown and pointed at by the hand, consequently they must be visible marks or figures, and are to be understood both of the vowel points and accents." Though belonging to an early period of the controversy, Levi's defence is still worth reading. Basnage, tom. ii. p. 763, refers the invention to the eleventh century.

‡ The commentary of St. Jerome on Jeremiah is positive proof that the vowel signs were not in existence in his day.

of the *Midrash* of Rabbi Simeon Ben Jochai.*   It is also said that the author was a contemporary of Rabbi Abraham, who wrote a commentary of repute upon the Book of Formation, but this mysterious personage, the pretended instructor of Nicholas Flamel in the secrets of alchemy, died at the close of the twelfth century.   As it is obvious that the objection with which we are here concerned is equivalent to begging the question at issue, so it is fairly met by the opposite assumption.   It is unserious and may be dismissed.

(3) The existence of two kinds of phylacteries arose through a difference of rabbinical opinion as to the Scriptural passages to be used on them.   The question is whether this difference of opinion occurred in the eleventh century and later, or whether it originated in earlier Talmudic times.   Certain statements and inferences therefrom are set forth by defenders of the Zohar in support of the second view, but the use of two kinds of phylacteries before the tenth century has not been clearly demonstrated.

(4) The citation by the Zohar of late authorities belonging to the Amoraim school is met by representing it in its present form as the growth of several centuries, which is provably true of most early Hebrew literature, canonical or not.   The indirect strength of this view is considerable, but it is much weakened by its supporters when they attempt to argue that had the Zohar been forged by Moses de Leon he would

---

* According to Jellinek the great classic of the Kabalah has passed under three names : (*a*) *Midrash* of the Rabbi Simeon Ben Jochai ; (*b*) Midrash : Let there be Light ! (*c*) Zohar, *i.e.*, Splendour or Light, after Daniel xii. 3.—*Die Kabbala, oder die Religions philosophie der Hebraei von Franck*.   Leipsic, 1844.   The *Midrash* is a symbolical narrative or account.

have carefully avoided the citation of later authorities. The history of literary impostures points wholly in the opposite direction, and the objection demonstrates quite clearly that the work as we have it is later than its latest authority. For it to be otherwise is impossible. How the late authorities came to be included is a distinct matter.

(5) When Isaac de Acco set out on his quest for the original MS. of the Zohar, he is recorded to have said: "If it be written in the Jerusalem idiom it is genuine, but if in Hebrew it is not." The value of an objection to the Zohar founded on its use of Aramaic is here exhibited by the express statement of a Jewish *littérateur* in the thirteenth century.* It is argued furthermore, by its defenders: (*a*) That Aramaic is the language of the Targums, which are mystical. (*b*) That the common language is used to increase the symbolism, but this may be regarded as a subtlety. (*c*) That supposing the antiquity of the Zohar, the scribe of Simeon Ben Jochai was undoubtedly the Rabbi Abbah that it mentions, and he as a Babylonian must have been thoroughly conversant with Aramaic.† (*d*) That supposing the Zohar to be a forgery produced by Moses de Leon, he was more likely to have

---

* Compare the article *s.v. Midrashim* in the ninth edition of the "Encyclopædia Britannica," by Dr. Schiller-Szinessy, Reader in Talmudic at Cambridge. "The Zohar was begun in Palestine late in the second or early in the third century, A.D., and finished at the latest in the sixth or the seventh century. It is impossible that it should have been composed after that time and before the Renaissance, as both language and contents clearly show."

† There is no evidence for the editorship of R. Abbah, but if anything Zoharic was committed to writing in the second century there would be good ground for accepting the express statement of the "Lesser Holy Synod" that the recorder was the son of R. Simeon.

written it in Hebrew, which is the language of his other books.*

From these objections and these answers the general conclusion must be that the internal evidence for the late origin of the bulk of the Zohar as it stands is not of any real force. The two tabulations have by no means exhausted the difficulties or the counter-evidence, as to which, even at the present day, Franck is in many cases the best and certainly the most lucid expositor. The absence of Christian influence, if not absolutely of all reference to Christianity, the absence also of Aristotelian influence, and some points of the argument from the dialect in which the work is written, seem to possess as much force as they did originally in 1843. But the strength of the case in favour of the Zohar is also the strength of the chief objection against it. It does quote later authorities, but this may exhibit that it grew like the Talmudic writings and several of the canonical Hebrew books. It has been well urged that if contemporary with the Talmud, the latter ought to have mentioned it, and it is replied that it does, not, however, under the catch-

---

* On the entire question compare Munk, *Mélanges de Philosophie, Juive et Arabe*, pp. 280, 281. "The Aramean dialect of the Zohar is not that of Daniel and Ezra, of the Chaldaic paraphrase of Onkelos and Jonathan, of the Targums, the Talmuds, the *Midrashim* or the *Gueonim*, but an incorrect and most corrupt mixture of all." M. Munk also sees traces in the Zohar of unfamiliarity with the language used. By this a double and altogether intolerable burden seems placed on the shoulders of its reputed forger. On this subject the question raised by Franck in 1843 remains still pertinent and still unanswered :— How could Moses de Leon at the beginning of the fourteenth century treat matters of the most elevated order in an idiom which the most distinguished scholars had been for so long content merely to under stand and which, on this hypothesis, had not produced a single work capable of serving him as a model ?—*La Kabbale*, p. 104.

I

word of its late name, but by the title of the Secret Learning, and by other titles which have been mentioned in this section. It would exceed the province of an elementary work to pursue the subject further. The minute considerations are of course highly technical, and there are some on both sides which it is wise to abstain from pressing. One of these is the argument that Moses de Leon was an unlikely person to have written such a work as the Zohar, because he was intellectually and morally unfit.* I have noted that he was unlikely, but possibilities of this kind can only be determined by the event. Many great books have been accomplished by persons who were antecedently improbable, and after all, at the best, we know Moses de Leon only through the testimony of a hostile relative. There is no doubt that the Zohar was to some extent sprung upon the Jewish people at the period of its publication. The manner of its reception was not unmixed; it was the kind of reception which would be given to a work which was old as regards its materials, but unfamiliar—less or more—in its form, and this is sufficient to account for any silence of previous authorities, while in the shaping of those materials and the impressing of that form the individual who multiplied the copies may have had a hand.†

---

* Dr. Schiller-Szinessy shows that he was proud of the authorship of his books, and hence unlikely to conceal his hand in the composition of any, but this argument also must not be pressed too far. The same writer terms him an inferior Kabalist, and it seems admitted on all sides that his original books are poor in quality. From these works Jellinek has extracted passages which are parallel to others in the Zohar and some critics have thence concluded an identity of the authors. In any other branch of research such parallels would be held to prove nothing.

† And by those who accept this view it is considered that he interfered only to disfigure it.

IV. THE AGE OF ZOHARIC TRADITION

It must not be supposed that the field of criticism is entirely occupied by a hypothesis of unmixed fraud, or that this hypothesis has always fastened upon the same person.* The most favoured delinquent is, of course, Moses de Leon, because he is reported to have circulated the Zohar, but occasionally he appears as the tool of other conspirators. Thus, Samuel Cohen maintains that the Zoharic writings were composed by a convocation of converted Rabbins, convened for the purpose in a Spanish monastery, employing Moses as their publisher, and thus the Church itself seems to figure as an accomplice.† Others, like M. H. Landauer, argue that the true author was Abraham ben Samuel Abulafia, while the voice of Dr. Graetz is raised in favour of the school of Abraham ben David of Beaucaire. Abraham ben David of Posquiere and Isaac the Blind are also favoured names, to whom it is indubitable, in any case, that Kabalism owed some thing of development and of impulse. Meanwhile this extreme opinion in all its varieties is balanced by

* Basnage is inclined to refer the original Zohar to the tenth century, and, following Bartolocci (*Bibliotheca Rabbinica*, t. iv. p. 82), represents Moses de Leon as in possession of several exemplars which he amplified.—*Histoire des Juifs*, t. ii. 781 ; t. v. 1775, 1776.

† At the opposite extreme was Christianus Schœttgenius in his considerable work, *Horæ Hebraicæ et Talmudicæ in Theologiam Judæorum Dogmaticam antiquam et orthodoxam de Messia impensæ*, 2 vols., Dresden and Leipsic, 1733, 1742. See vol. ii. *Rabbinicorum Lectionum Liber Secundus*, c. ii., *docens R. Simeonem filium Jochai, auctorem Libri Sohar, Religionem fuisse Christianam*. There are eight heads to the argument, the most important being that the Zohar contains the precise, orthodox doctrine concerning the Messiah and His divine and human nature, and this not in one place or mys teriously, but in many and openly.

counterviews which also denaturalise the literature. It may be suspected, therefore, with reason that on both sides there is an error of enthusiasm: there are the children of intelligence who look to find the secret doctrine of Judea a mere transcript from that of Egypt, or whatever land is for them the well-spring of all truth and all truly sacred knowledge. These remember, for example, that Abraham was in Egypt, and, accepting at once the fairy-tale attribution of the " Book of Formation " to the patriarch, conclude that this document is older than the Ritual of the Dead. It is useless to reason with those whose confidence is not shaken in the face of impossibilities, whose imagination can bridge all gulfs in evidence by fantastic suppositions. On the other hand, there is the crass criticism which rules off a literature by a single stroke of the pen into the region of forgery and imposture, as it rules off all occult psychology into that of imposture or hallucination. It does not matter that this criticism is always in disgrace. It proved Troy town to be solar mythos till Troy town was excavated; it undermined, as it believed, the book of Daniel till fresh archæo-logical discoveries cast it into the pit which it had dug. It is truly not less stupid, and it is far less engaging, than the opposed excess.*

The importance of the Zohar does not depend so much upon the date of its documents as on the possible claims of its tradition. The collapse of its claim to antiquity, in that respect, and this only, will

---

* Its typical representative is Graetz, and one can scarcely conjecture by what principle he was guided in his estimate of Moses de Leon. It is the height of exaggeration, the account in the *Yuhasin* transcendentalised till it almost exceeds recognition.

reduce it to the full rank of imposture. It is clear that the speculations, for example, of mediæval or later Rabbins, if we waive the dishonesty of a false pretension, will have at most some literary, historical, or exegetical interest, but it will differ in kind rather than degree from that which must attach to a tradition which interlinks with the far past. We are therefore more concerned in ascertaining the state in which modern criticism has left the content of the Zohar than the form in which it is presented to us. The early students of the work, who accepted and defended its antiquity, did not make this saving distinction, and in many instances modern hostility does not make it either. Upon the surface of the history of Kabalistic criticism the first presumption is, of course, unfavourable to any hypothesis of antiquity, because this would seem to have been admitted in days when scholarship was insufficiently equipped for the determination of such a question. In the light of fuller knowledge it will be thought that the claim has lapsed, or remains only as a pious belief prevailing among an uncritical minority, a few persons being always found whose mental bias predisposes them to the defence of exploded views. In such a case, however, an indiscriminate rejection is not much less superficial than an unenquiring acquiescence in a non-proven claim. The history of debated questions of this kind teaches another lesson, and the closest approximation to truth is found usually in the mean of extreme views. Now, in the history of Zoharic criticism we find that the old students not only accepted the claim of the tradition to antiquity, and were disposed to understand the genealogy more or less literally, but that further they regarded the books which contain both as belonging to certain dates and produced by certain writers without much suspicion, on the simple authority of the literature.* Later scholars, on the other hand, having found something to countenance the modern origin of the documents, have frequently overlooked the possible antiquity of their tradition. The reference to this antiquity as something which deserves to be regarded apart from the date of publication will explain what I mean by the moderate and middle view in which the truth must be sought. If we fail entirely here we may regard the case as closed.

Now, I believe that a careful and unbiassed comparison of all the evidence will lead us to conclude that there are elements of old doctrine in the Zohar; their exact antiquity is, in part, highly speculative, but it is quite sufficient to invest them with considerable interest. Like the Sepher Yetzirah, some of it may even be referable to the period of Esdras. I refer here to the Yetziratic notions concerning the virtue of Divine Names, for this is also found in the Zohar, as it is abundantly found in the Talmud; a residuum of its teaching concerning angels and demons may be also an inheritance from Babylon. All this, however, is the worthless part of the Zohar, as it is the worthless, if curious, part of Talmudic literature. With

---

* Some modern ecclesiastical historians, for no solid reason, incline to this view. Thus, we have in Dean Hook's compilation, " A Church Dictionary " (fourteenth edition, London, 1887), the statement that the chief Kabalistic author was Simeon ben Jochai, and also that most of the heretics in the primitive Christian Church fell into the vain conceits of the Kabalah, particularly the Gnostics, Valentinians and Basilidians. There is more warrant for the second than the first view, as readers of Matter's *Histoire du Gnosticisme* and of King's " Gnostics " will not need to be told.

regard to the Scriptural exegesis which constitutes so large a portion of it, we shall not offend possibility by supposing that some of it may be a transmission from Talmudic times.* If we take the obscure but ample hints and references found in the Talmuds to the existence of a mystic tradition, and follow them through the large mystical literature which intervened between those works and the Zohar as we now have it, we shall be led not to the conclusion of the occultist, that there was a great body of secret doctrine which became revealed gradually, but that there was a kernel of tradition which was planted in the secret heart of Israel, which many watered and fostered, till the growth at length put forth, not without something of transformation and of suddenness, the strange flower of the Zohar. As regards form its most ancient part is probably the Book of Concealment, but it is entirely improbable that any conspicuous portion could have existed in writing till after the sixth century, while the growth of most of it is perhaps much later and subsequent to the latest date which can be ascribed to the Sepher Yetzirah.†   It is

---

* In other words, we may follow the learned author of the article on the *Midrashim* in the " Encyclopædia Britannica," who says that the nucleus of the work is of Mishnic times and that R. Simeon was its author in the same sense that R. Johanan was of the Palestine Talmud, namely, that he gave the first impulse to its composition."

† I mention this possibility because Dr. Schiller-Szinessy has not stated his reasons why it is impossible that it should have been later than the seventh century, and subject to the conclusiveness of those reasons. We may speculate what Dr. Szinessy would think of Mr. Zangwill did he read the epilogue to the " Children of the Ghetto," in which it is casually remarked that the Zohar was "forged by a Spanish Jew in the thirteenth century." By the way, are copies of the Zohar likely to be found in a small room, used as a synagogue, outside Jerusalem and so poor that it is bare even of seats ?

advanced, as we have seen, by its defenders that it is the subject of reference in several texts both of the Babylonian and Jerusalem Talmud under the name of the *Midrash* of Simeon ben Jochai, and the parallels between Talmudic sayings attributed to this Rabbi have been exhaustively compared with the Zohar, with a view to exhibit their identity. The existence of a work entitled the "Mysteries of Simeon ben Jochai" before the middle of the eleventh century and possibly much earlier, is acknowledged by Dr. Graetz. It is therefore reasonable to conclude that early written and oral materials entered into the composition of the work as we now possess it.* This is the most that can be urged, and this is sufficient to prove that no one person wrote it out of his own head.†

It must be confessed, on the other hand, that the legend which attributes its origin to R. Simeon ben Jochai seems to have made an unfortunate choice, for this great authority of the Talmud represents a reaction against the mystical tendencies of R. Akiba, and there is some evidence for believing that he did not investigate the hidden meaning of Scripture, but rather its rational principles. He is described by a

---

* An interesting article by M. Nicholas in Lichtenberger's *Encyclopédie des Sciences Religieuses*, t. xi. *s.v.* *Cabale* (Paris, 1877), regards it as certain that the philosophical speculations which compose the Kabalah generally began to form during the century which preceded the Christian era, but they were oral, imparted to a few only, and under the seal of secresy. Unfortunately, the article is not trustworthy, representing, as it does, the *Ain Soph* doctrine to be part of the Sepher Yetzirah.

† Compare Blunt's "Dictionary of Doctrinal and Historical Theology," which argues that the variety of style and the disjointed character of its contents show that the Zohar is the growth of ages. Unfortunately, Blunt's work indicates no real acquaintance with the Kabalah and its criticism.

modern writer as cold, exclusive and stoical. At the same time, if we accept the existence of a genuine tradition which became incorporated in the Zohar, it is difficult to reject its leading and central figure.*

If we turn now for a moment to the standpoint of modern occultism we shall see that so far we have no warrant for connecting the chief cycle of Kabalistic literature with the high antiquity to which occultists incline.† While we leave them once more in full possession of the alleged virtue inherent in divine names, and perhaps with some elements of legend concerning angels and demons, we are forced to take all that remains a considerable distance into the Christian era. But the Zohar, although it embodies the entire content of Kabalistic doctrine, is not the sole nor the earliest storehouse of that doctrine, and we have next to consider whether the antiquity of the philosophical tradition given in the second book is to be inferred from its points of contact and corre-spondence with other theosophical systems which have prevailed in the past.

* The author of the article "Cabala" in Herzog's *Real Encycklopädie* takes a middle view, namely, that the Zohar is not the work of Moses de Leon, nor is it of R. Simeon's period, though its doctrines are referable to him. It was completed in the eighth century. The evidence adduced for this view seems inconclusive, so far as this article is concerned.

† Take, for example, the following typical instance of the exaggerations which have found currency on this subject. "The origin of the Kabalah is lost in the night of time. Is it of India or of Egypt? We do not know; but it is certain that to Egyptians and Indians it was alike known. Pythagoras returned with it into Greece after his travels in the East, then the region of the light. One asks vainly whether its first revelation was divine or the product of inspiration."— Desbarrolles, *Les Mystères de la Main*, 14me *édition*, Paris, *n.d.* M. Desbarrolles knew nothing of the Kabalah, but he reflected his friend Levi, who claimed knowledge but wrote frequently in the same distracted strain.

V. ALLEGED SOURCES OF KABALISTIC DOCTRINE

We are now able to reach a specific conclusion with regard to our subject and to affirm that many of the materials collected in the Zohar are earlier than the period of their promulgation. We cannot say whether the Sepher Yetzirah is much anterior to the ninth century.* But both works are in connection with Talmudic times and, within the limits of the Christian centuries, there seems therefore to have been an esoteric tradition in Israel.† Whether it existed prior to Christianity itself is the next concern of our inquiry. At this point the difficulties begin to multiply, because the range of research is exceedingly large, and it has been covered in every direction by successive generations of hardy speculators. We must proceed step by step and shall do well to begin first of all by a general survey of the subject.

The doctrine of the Kabalah has been referred for its origin to almost every philosophic and religious system of antiquity, and its points of correspondence with each have been carefully tabulated. It has been shown to be derived from Akkadia, from India, from China, from ancient Egypt,‡ from Platonism and Neo-

---

* But we can say that one of the most pronounced opponents of Jewish theosophy assigns it to early Gnostic times.—See Graetz, *Geschichte der Juden*.

† One of the exponents of the English school of Kabalism states that, according to Hebrew tradition, the doctrines of the oldest portions of the Zohar are antecedent to the second Temple.—W. Wynn Westcott, *Sepher Yetzirah*. Translated from the Hebrew. Second edition. London, 1893.

‡ This is the view which obtains most widely among occultists. "It is in Egyptian science," says Stanislas de Guaita, "carried from

Platonism, from the categories of Aristotle, from early Christian Gnosticism.* The most philosophical conclusion which can, I think, be drawn from all this rival evidence is that it is not derived from any one of them specifically and exclusively, but rather that the human mind, when engaged on certain fundamental and perhaps insoluble problems of the universe, tends independently to reach conclusions that are similar and may even wear sometimes an aspect of literal identity; that the Kabalah is largely an outcome of such unaided research; that its results are in the main *sui generis*, but that they offer points of contact with other attempts of the kind in all ages and nations. We must, of course, distinguish the fundamental part of the Kabalah from its developments. Included in the first class are the doctrine of the Ten Emanations, that of *Ain Soph*, of the *Macroprosopus* and the *Microprosopus*, some of which may go far back in the history of post-Christian Jewish literature, indeed almost to Talmudic times. The subsequent developments possess a complexion derived from many sources, not excluding the scholastic philosophy of Christian Europe during the Middle Ages.† *Ain Soph* is that final concept of the Deity which is

---

Mitzraïm by Moses at the exodus of the Sons of Israel, that we must discern the source of that sacred tradition transmitted among the Jews from generation to generation, by the oral way, down to the disciples of Simeon ben Jochai, who wrote, at the dictation of this master, about the second century of the Christian era, the Great Book of the Light (Zohar)."—*Au Seuil du Mystère*, pp. 183, 184. The last statement is, of course, merely an assumption of the vital point at issue.

* Even the so-called "Symbols of Pythagoras" have been approximated to Kabalistic teaching. ˴ ˴ ˴ Ilectanea Hermetica," edited by W. Wynn Westcott, vol. v. (*Somnium Scipionis*, &c.), London, 1894.

† I refer here to the Kabalistic schools of Isaac de Loria and Moses of Cordova.

reached by all metaphysics; it is not necessary to suppose that it was derived from Babylonian initiations during the exile of seventy years, or from Greek speculation at Alexandria; it may be regarded more reasonably as a product of the unfinished exile of the Christian centuries. But in either case it is the ultimate point of theosophic speculation possible to the human mind, at which the mind always arrives. The doctrine of the *Sephiroth* is, in its turn, a very intelligible form of another widespread device of the world's thought when it seeks to bridge the gulf between finite and infinite, betweed absolute purity and that material world which, in one or other way, seems always to be regarded as unclean. The *Macroprosopus* and the *Microprosopus*, whether late or early in Jewish literature, are late at least in the history of human speculation. They are an attempt to distinguish between God as He is in Himself and in His relation with His children. As might be expected, they are the most characteristic of Jewry and, as such, offer the least connection with any external system. Yet they have some points of contact. As regards each and all, the first point to be fixed firmly in the mind is that they are the natural results of legitimate intellectual inquiry. Given the times and the circumstances, they are the kind of speculative doctrine which one might have expected *à priori*.

When we remember the persistence of tradition which has always characterised the most persistent of all races, when we remember that the Jew of the Christian dispensation may be said to have lived in the remembrance of his glory passed away, we can well believe that he was encompassed by an atmosphere of legend on which his fervid mind was at work continually, out of which he never stepped, and it would be unreasonable to suppose that all his literature, like all his thought, was not profoundly tinctured by this his intellectual environment.   But it is a wide and an unwarrantable step from the belief in such a natural and inevitable operation to a belief that Jewish tradition must or may be referred to any distinctive source in the past, from which it was perpetuated by some conventional initiation, as occult writers suppose, and some others also who have no such bias towards the mysterious to intervene in apology for their opinion. We have no ground for affirming with Basnage[*] that old Egypt is the true nursery of the Kabalah, though it is quite possible that Israel brought something from the Nile valley which does not appear in the Pentateuch.   Nor are we justified in agreeing with the illustrious Grand Master of the Ancient and Accepted Rite of Freemasonry, United States Southern Jurisdiction, when he suggests a direct communication of doctrine from the religion of Zoroaster[†] to Kabalism which must be referred to the period of the exile.[‡]   That the Jews derived

---

[*] L. iii. c. xiv.

[†] For some tables indicating "the harmony and identity of the Chaldean philosophy with the Hebrew Kabalah," see the "Chaldæan Oracles of Z'n . .i. edited by . ia.   l a   ndon, 1895, pp. 8-11. The true value of such parallels is shown by such frenzied developments .·: Archbishop Meurin's *Synagogue de Satan*, which will be noticed in Book vii. § 19.

[‡] "Morals and Dogma," Charleston, A.M. 5641, pp. 266, 267, and elsewhere throughout the compilation.   Compare Matter, *Histoire*

something from Babylon I have already noted, and amidst their chequered experience under Persian domination, after their final scattering, possibly the great body of Haggada may have received increment and colouring. More fantastic theorists have imagined that not only is there a Chinese Kabalah, but that it is the source of that which was in Israel. That the great unknown empire, in which all things from alchemy to the art of printing seem to have germinated, possessed, and still possesses, a vast body of traditional lore, of so-called secret teaching,* is mere commonplace on which there is no call to insist, and if occultists will be so unphilosophical as to term this Kabalah, there is as little need to dispute with them about the improper and confusing use of a mere word. That the book called "Yi-King,"† or Mutation, contains an esoteric religious tradition which has, as it is said, some analogies with Kabalistic doctrine, is neither surprising nor significant of anything except the irresistible tendency of the human mind to reflect after much the same manner, in all lands and times, upon mysteries that are everywhere the same, ever urgent, ever recurring. Such

---

Critique du Gnosticisime, who refers the Gnostic systems to the Zendavesta and the Kabalah.

* In conformity with which Bryant's "Analysis of Ancient Mythology" (vol. i. p. 94) and Oliver's "History of Initiation" (p. 79 *et seq.*) would have us believe that there were mysteries in China "similar to those of India," which again were more or less the same as those which subsequently flourished in Greece.

† For some information concerning this work and its Kabalistic analogies, see *L'Initiation, revue philosophique des Hautes Etudes,* tom. xxxvii. No. 3, Dec., 1897. Paris. *S.v. Y-King, Tao-see, Tao-te-King et la Numération,* p. 266 *et seq.* Also Eugène Nus, *A La Recherche des Destinés.* Paris, 1892.

analogies do not prove, as occultists would have us believe, the existence of a Wisdom-Religion, which, if they will suffer the interpretation, may be presumed to mean the secret science of the reintegration of the soul in God accumulated through the ages of initiation. In the natural order, the truly fundamental religion is the common ground of all, which stands in need of no formal perpetuation, as it is inborn in the heart and mind of humanity.* And yet the undoubted existence of the Mongolian race in Mesopotamia almost at the dawn of history may suggest that the Semite drew something from Mongolian Chaldea even in the days of Abraham,† as afterwards the Jew of Babylon may have had a certain contact with Confucianism in its earliest form. We may admit, readily and reasonably, that the Jew received everywhere and always retained the reception, provided that we leave him everywhere his own intellectual initiative, and bear in mind that the process was everywhere natural and informal, not arbitrary and conventional.

Passing over the regions of wild surmise in which Odin the Norse God becomes identified with the Kabalistic *Abba*, Frea with *Aima*, Thor with *Arik Anpin*, the Lesser Countenance, and the Supreme

---

* I refer here to sacramental and not to natural religion so-called.

† "The power of the Mongol rulers of Chaldea, about the time of Abraham, was far more extensive than that of the contemporary rulers of Thebes and of the Delta, and the victories of the great eighteenth dynasty in Egypt, extending over some three centuries at most, form only a passing episode in the story of Asiatic civilisation, which dates back probably earlier than the time of the Pyramids, which was native and original, and from which Egypt borrowed much in the days of its greatest rulers."—"Babylonian Discoveries," *Edinburgh Review*, April, 1898.

Being discerned behind the northern mythology with *Ain Soph*; passing over also certain Druidic correspondences into which it might be unwise to enter,* we may take much the same view as before regarding the alleged Gnostic connections of the Kabalah. We may concur cordially with King when he argues that whatever the date of the Zohar in its present form, its principles and traditions are similar to those taught in the schools of Babylon and Tiberias.† They are the same and they are also different, and the difference represents the growth of the intellectual thought of Israel, its proper native development under the various impulsions which it received between the period of Gnosticism and the period of the promulgation of the Zohar. We may acknowledge also that Marcus, as "a born Jew," devised something of the national heritage to the system which he produced. Yet Gnosticism is not Kabalism, though there are striking analogies between them, and something of common source is attributable to both. M. Amelineau is nearer the truth when he speaks of a coincident development of the two systems.‡ There are analogies in nature and

---

* Pike, following no doubt some unnamed authority, affirms that the Druids were true children of the Magi, whose initiation came from Egypt and Chaldea, "that is to say, from the true sources of the primitive Kabalah."—" Morals and Dogma," p. 103.

† "The Gnostics and their Remains." Second edition. London, 1897.

‡ *Essai sur le Gnosticisme Egyptien, ses développements et son origine Egyptienne. Par M. E. Amélineau*, published in *Annales du Musée Guimet*, tom. xiv. Paris, 1887, but written so far back as 1882, the date affixed to the preface. Compare Edersheim, who believed that "Gnosticism, like later Jewish mysticism, sprang from the contact of Judaism with the religious speculations of the farther East."

appearance between glass and rock-crystal, but glass is glass and a pebble is a pebble.*

It is unphilosophical because unneedful to go far back and far off when the explanation of given facts lies near in time and place. "That is best which lies the nearest," says the poet, and, artists or occultists, makers of verse or Kabalistic commentators, we should shape our work of art or interpretation without drawing needlessly from things remote. The prototype of Yetziratic and Zoharic theosophy is close to our hand in Jewry. The fusion of all systems which is a characteristic of the present day, has its parallel in that epoch of the past which witnessed the rise of Christianity. "At the time when John the Baptist made his appearance in the desert, near the shores of the Dead Sea, all the old philosophical and religious systems were approximating toward each other. A general lassitude inclined the minds of all toward the quietude of that amalgamation of doctrines for which the expeditions of Alexander and the more peaceful occurrences that followed, with the establishment in Asia and Africa of many Grecian colonies, had prepared the way. After the intermingling of different nations, which resulted from the wars of Alexander in three-quarters of the globe, the doctrines of Greece, of Egypt, of Persia, and of India met and intermingled everywhere. All the barriers that had formerly kept the

---

* The *Pistis Sophia* is the most valuable document for the analogies between Gnosticism and the Kabalah, but it is easy to exaggerate its evidence. Mr. C. W. King says that the doctrines are identical, and that it exhibits the leading principles of the Kabalah, but he does not seem to speak with a first-hand knowledge of Jewish theosophy.

nations apart were thrown down ; and while the
people of the West readily connected their faith with
those of the East, the latter hastened to learn the
traditions of Rome and Athens. . . . . The Jews
and Egyptians, then the most exclusive of all
peoples, yielded to that eclecticism which prevailed
among their masters, the Greeks and Romans."*
National ambition, however, rather than eclecticism
influenced the Jews, and though it was impossible,
having regard to their environment, that they should
not be largely tinctured, it was their object to tinge
other systems and not to modify their own, to show
that the ethnic philosophers owed everything to the
divine doctrine of Palestine. Philo the Greek of
Alexandria to some extent Hellenised the Hebrew
religion that he might the better Judaise the
philosophy of Hellas. From this fusion there arose
the nearest approach, if not in time and place at
least in form and subject, to Kabalistic theosophy
as regards its source in Jewry. There is no need
in this elementary study to refer to Aristobulus,
who a century before had received a similar vocation.
Philo, and the movement and mode of thought which
he represents, cannot reasonably have been without
an effect upon the literature of later ages in Jewry,†

---

* "Morals and Dogma," p. 247.

† I should observe here that Mr. Arthur Lillie, who has much
argued a process in the Buddhistic origin of Christianity, has discovered
in the Zohar not only the Trinity of Philo, but the Trinity of Buddhism,
and he holds that the Kabalah "was one of the secret books of the
Essenes."—*Modern Mystics and Modern Magic*, p. 14. He also says
that it was "written down from tradition by one Moses de Leon," thus
showing that he is not aware of the existence of Kabalistic books outside the Zohar.—*Ibid.*, p. 13. Finally, he says that it is "a book of
Magic."—"Madame Blavatsky and her Theosophy," p. 194. After this

though the history of that influence and the mode
of its transmission cannot be traced conclusively.
We must not, however, fall into the error of supposing
that the Kabalah is Platonism derived through Philo
and the Jewish school of Alexandria, or that it is
Jewish tradition modified by Philoism.   When we
find in the Sepher Yetzirah the alphabetical symbols
of the Logos made use of by God in the formation
of the universe, it is very easy to set it down to
Greek influence, but the fact remains that the
" Book of Formation " is essentially and charac-
teristically Hebrew, and this fact lifts it altogether
out of the category of Platonic succession.   Yet
we know where to look for the explanation of its
points of contact.   As regards the doctrine developed
by the commentators on the Sepher Yetzirah prior
to the appearance of the Zohar, as regards the
literature which makes contact with these, and as
regards the Zohar itself, saying nothing of the later
literature, which had recourse consciously and openly
to Greek sources, the case is much stronger.*   Philo

we shall not be surprised to find that St. Paul was a Kabalist.—*Ibid.*
So also was Jacob Bohme, whose three principles, one of which was the
" Kingdom of Hell," have something to do with the three supernal
Sephiroth.   For similar speculations, see " Buddhism in Christendom."
    * For example, the *Porta Cælorum* of R. Abraham Cohen Irira,
which forms the third part of Rosenroth's *Apparatus in Librum Sohar*,
was written expressly to exhibit the correspondences between Kabalistic
dogmas and the Platonic philosophy.   Later on the same theme was
taken up by Christian writers, some of whom connect the Kabalah with
Aristotle, and so we have works like Burgondo's *Podromus Scientiarum
Artiumve liberalium ad ipsos Peripateticæ Scholæ et Kabbalisticæ
doctrinæ purissimos fontes revocatus*, Venice, 1651.   So also at an
earlier period Thomas Campanella in his *De Sensu Rerum et Magia*,
Frankfort, 1620, joined Neoplatonism and Kabalism in his attempt to
explain the universe.

insists on the antithesis between God and the material world, the infinite and the finite; so, let us say, does the Zohar, which may be taken to stand for the whole literature. Philo affirms the absolute transcendency of God; so does Zoharic doctrine. Philo regards the divine nature as in itself escaping definition and in itself without quality; Kabalism denounces those who would attempt to describe God as He is in Himself even by the attributes which He manifests. Philo's descriptions of God are all negative; compare the *latens Deitas* of the Kabalah. Philo says that no name can be given Him; all Kabalism agrees. Philo regards the scriptural Deity as anthropomorphic, and allegorises upon all the descriptions, attributions and manifestations of Deity therein; compare the doctrine of the Two Countenances, designed to explain the same anthropomorphisms. Philo regards the letter of Scripture as a veil; so does the Zohar. Philo interprets it literally or mystically according to his purpose; so does Kabalistic exegesis. Philo regards the visible world as the gate of the world unseen, he believes in the possibility of an immediate contemplation of God, in the existence of an archetypal world, that things seen are a counterpart of things unseen,* in all of which we are enumerating express points of Kabalistic doctrine. These

---

* There is a twofold correspondence in Kabalism between superior and inferior things: one transcendental, being that of phenomena with their archetypes in the noumenal world, and one natural in the narrower sense of the term, being that which is summed up in the axiom: "There is no herb on earth to which a certain star does not correspond in the heaven." See Kircher, *Mundus Subterraneus*, ii. 401*b*. The whole theory of natural magic is contained in this maxim.

analogies are too numerous, too close, too consecutive, to leave any room for doubt that the heads
of Kabalistic teaching pre-existed in Jewry, and
we have further the explicit testimony of Philo as
to the existence of a mystic doctrine in Jewry.
Spontaneity, initiation, subsequent influences, all
remain unimpeded and are all necessary to explain
the existence of the Zohar and its connections, but
its source is not indeed Philo of necessity, much less
Philo exclusively, but that which produced Philo.
But more than all, it is hardy, independent specula
tion, wearing tradition like a veil which does not
conceal its essential individuality, and much nearer to
ourselves at times in its spirit than we should ever
suspect from its form. Yet we may suspect it on
philosophical grounds, for however concealed behind
the veil of symbolism, however much distorted in
strange glasses of vision, the sentiments and
aspirations of humanity have ever a common ground,
and through the vehicle of Kabalistic apparatus,
under many covers and tinctured by many fantastic
colourings of art and artifice, we see that our own
yearnings and longings find expression, after their
own manner, in this book of the words of the exile.
We acknowledge with the poet how truly all the lore
and the legend is

> " A part
> Of the hunger and thirst of the heart,
>   The frenzy and fire of the brain,
> Which yearns for the fruitage forbidden,
> The golden pomegranates of Eden,
>   To quiet its fever and pain."

When the "Faithful Shepherd" of the Zohar puts

these words into the mouth of the Father of universal Israel: "In this world my Name is written YHVH and read *Adonai*, but in the world to come the same will be read as it is written, so that Mercy shall be from all sides," * we see that at the beginning of the twentieth century we might have expressed differently the longing, the hope, the faith, for which this symbol stands, but it is still that which we all desire to express, and, furthermore, I do not know that our modern terms could have represented it better. Herein is the justification of the ways of God to man and herein the pious conviction of the believing heart that in the great day of the Lord there shall be no scandal to His children; that in spite of the darkness of our ways we have held rightly that He is light, that though we write Mercy in our hearts but read Law and its inflexible order in all around us, we shall one day know that it is Mercy on every side, the highest expression of the Law, or that Law is that order under which the Divine Charity is manifested. It is in messages like this that the abiding beauty and significance of the Kabalah are contained, not in the beard of *Microprosopus* or in the number of worlds suspended from the hair on the cranium of *Arikh Anpin. Gematria* and *Metathesis* may be pastimes fit only for children, but the voice of the Rabbis of the Zohar expressing the language of the heart of Israel needs no *Temurah* to expound its meaning, and it is by the ring of such utterances that the true believer of to-day is made conscious electrically that the Holy Synods were composed of men who are our brethren.

---

* Cremona edition, part ii. fol. 106*a*.

As this view disposes implicitly of the claim to a divine authorship, and places the theory of aboriginal tradition among fables, so also it forbids us to suppose that Kabalistic doctrines are the work of any single mind.

One feels instinctively, without any necessity of evidence, that these things are not and cannot be the unaided work of Moses de Leon.* They are a growth and a result. As, however, the Zohar assumed its present shape at a late period admittedly, it may credibly have taken part of it at the hands of this Spanish Jew. That his other works are inferior is no argument. Cervantes wrote many worthless romances before and after the sum of all chivalry. The "Galatea" did not make "Don Quixote" impossible. So also Beroalde de Verville wrote books on alchemy which are despised even by alchemists, but he wrote also the *Moyen de Parvenir*. Every *magnum opus* is antecedently improbable, and the intellectual distance between the "Sorrows of Werther" and the second part of "Faust" is like the void between *Ain Soph* and *Malkuth*, which it was the purpose of the *Sephiroth* to fill.

But if all masterpieces are antecedently improbable, it is true also that they are impossible without antecedents. There are certain dull old histories known to *literati* which were necessary to the plays of Shakespeare. So the formulation of the Zohar

---

* According to the Zohar itself, or more precisely, to a tract which it includes under the title of the "Faithful Shepherd," nine authors combined for the production of the work, but it is not necessary o attach any serious import to this statement.

must have been preceded by much raw material, both oral and written, parts of which were no doubt incorporated without any change in their formulation. For example, the " Book of Occultation " bears all the marks of antiquity, no less considerable than that of the " Book of Formation."

There is, of course, a point beyond which the reasonable critic will not pass. So far as it goes we are on safe ground with the meagre testimony of St. Agobard ; with R. Simeon Ben Jochai we are on purely traditional ground, and it is not to be supposed for a moment that more authenticity resides in the *dramatis personæ* of the Holy Synod than in those of the *Turba Philosophorum*. I do not mean that such names are entirely pretexts, for they may possess an honest basis in legend, but they are not literal or historical. They occupy a middle position between the script of a shorthand reporter and imaginary conversations like those of W. S. Landor.

VI. ISLAMIC CONNECTIONS OF THE KABALAH

When the Jew of the Exile sought a consolation in philosophy, and thus produced the higher part of Kabalism, compounded of his traditions, his speculations, his external receptions, his longings, the memories of his election and its glory, we must bear in mind that all exotics adjust themselves to their environment, not without certain changes even in the most persistent types. Now, the Jew is an anthropological exotic in all countries of the world and just because his persistence is so enormous that it is explained by a special law of Providence, we find that in all countries he has been modified sufficiently to guarantee his survival.   As in things physical, as in matters of daily life, so in the intellectual order, he lost nothing but he assumed much. The Jew of Salerno differed from that of France, and the Jew of Spain offered contrasts to both. Without attempting to add another hypothesis to the scores extant as to the origin of Kabalism, I propose to indicate that this literature is naturally, if partially, elucidated by the features of its partial birthplace.

Having made a reasonable allowance for spontaneity in Jewish thought, and having noted its observed connections and correspondences in distant times and places, it seems fitting that we should look now to that which lay the nearest.   Without disputing or defending the opinion that Israel may have possessed a tradition handed down by the oral way from early times, of which we have enough evidence to warrant the presumption that it existed but not enough to determine what it actually was, let us begin by considering where the Kabalistic books first began to circulate.   That was in Spain.   Now, what was the environment of the Jews in the Peninsula at the period in question—let us say, from the ninth century and onward?   It differed considerably from that which surrounded them in other countries of Western Europe.   Spain was for Israel not indeed a Garden of Paradise, but a species of oasis in the great wilderness of the Exile, for the simple reason that much of it was not then under Christian rule.* The Jew of Spain enjoyed comparative immunity; he possessed even political influence; he rose occasionally to high political power. It is not surprising, therefore, that Spain became a centre of Jewish literature and philosophy. Thence Jewish treatises passed into France and Italy under the Arabian equivalents of their authors' names, and were accepted as the speculations or teachings of the learned among the Moslems. Avicebron is a case in point. There can be no doubt whatever that the erudition of Mohammedanism exercised an influence on the Rabbins,† who reacted in their turn on the Moslem doctors.‡ The questions of priority and preponderance may be passed over, because they are here of no importance.

We have concluded already that the Zohar presents the mystic thought of preceding centuries in Israel under a certain aspect of transformation. The traditional knowledge, of which we have evidence as to its existence in Talmudic times, had received many developments from many sources and under the influence of many minds. There is ground for supposing that the nucleus in Christian times is first heard of in Palestine, which indeed follows from its connection, once admitted, with R. Simeon

---

* So also the necessities of the Christian princes in Spain till the thirteenth century led them usually to protect the Jews.

† The translation of the Talmud into Arabic by R. Joseph, disciple of Moses the sack-clothed, during the reign of Haschem II., King of Cordova, is the best evidence which can be cited on this point.

‡ Islamic mysticism is almost coincident with the mission of the great Islamic prophet. For example, the Ghoolat sect, famous for the "extravagance" of its doctrines, is referred to the time of Ali. See "Secret Societies of the Middle Ages," London, 1846, pp. 29, 31.

Ben Jochai. But despite the legend which represents
the Zohar as sent from Palestine by Nachmanides,
everything points to Spain and the South of France
as the chief scenes of the final developments of
the Kabalah, and it is not unreasonable to suppose
that it has been affected by the prevailing tone of
mystic thought in one or both of these places.
There is evidence to show that such influence was
at work outside the Zohar and prior perhaps to
its existence in the form that it now possesses.
It was then most probably a part of the very large
influence of Avicebron. In post-Zoharic mysticism,
and in the commentaries on the Zohar which are
the work of Spanish Jews, it may be traced more fully
and plainly. In no case does it justify the now
exploded criticism which would make the Zohar
merely a reproduction or echo of Arabian theosophy,
or would regard all Kabalism as referable to Islamic
mysticism for its sole source, plus the Greek influence
at work in Islam. This was the hypothesis of
Tholuck. We are concerned only with a question of
complexion and of tincture, and have other criteria by
which to judge the true significance of the points of
doctrinal resemblance between Sufi and Kabalist
concerning the latent state of Deity, the operation
of the Divine Will at the beginning of creation, the
emanation of the world, &c. The analogies are
interesting enough and the Orientalist who first
specified them had everything to justify him at his
period.* As it may not be uninteresting to cite a few

---

* See F. A. D. Tholuck: Sufismus Sive *Theosophia Persarum
Pantheistica*, Berlin, 1831, c.v. *passim*. Also *De Ortu Cabbalæ*,
Hamburg, 1837.

cases in point derived from other sources, let us take
a fact, one of many concerning which we possess
impregnable testimony. About the middle of the
fifteenth century, or, more exactly, from 1414 to 1492,
there flourished a Sufi poet named Nuruddin Abdur-
rahmann, known as Jami of Herat, among whose
works the "Seven Thrones" is most famous. One of
the poems in this collection is entitled "Salomon and
Absal," a mystic story of earthly and heavenly love.
In the epilogue to this poem, where the author
unfolds his meaning, the following lines occur:

> The Incomprehensible Creator, when this world
> He did create, created first of all
> The First Intelligence, First of a chain
> Of Ten Intelligences, of which the last
> Sole agent is in this our Universe,
> Active Intelligence so called.

It may at once be admitted that if we are to accept
the method and admit the quality of evidence which
has satisfied heretofore the several authorities who
have referrred Kabalism to definite sources in philosophy and religion, we are at liberty to infer from
this passage that somewhere about the year 1450 a
Sufic poet, so far away from Spain as Herat, was
adapting, with slight variations of a verbal kind, the
Sephirotic doctrine of the Kabalah a century before
the Book of Formation and the Zohar came into
circulation through the medium of print. I have
chosen this instance because it proves nothing of
itself on account of its lateness, but it gives a point
of departure backwards for tracing a possible connection between the mystical sects of Mohammedanism and the mystical sects of Israel.

With this let us compare for a moment the doctrine developed in the " Celestial Desatir," which has been described as " a very early attempt on the part of the ancient Persians to form a cosmological theory."* The *Desatir*, it should be observed, is a revelation addressed to the great prophet Abad, who is identified with Abraham. " The nature of God cannot be known. Who can dare to know it but He (Himself)? The entity and the oneness and the personality are ' His very nature and nothing beside Him.' " From this Being proceeded by free creation "him whose name is *Bahnam*, and called Prime Intellect and First Reason," and through him "*Asham*, the second intellect," who created in turn the intellect of the next lower heaven named "*Famesham*." From these proceeded the " Intellect of the heaven of *Kanian*" or Saturn ; of *Harmuzd*, or Jupiter ; of *Bahram*, or Mars ; of *Khurshad*, or the Sun ; of *Nahid*, or Venus ; of *Zir*, or Mercury ; and of *Mah*, or the Moon.

Here, again, we have the production of ten primary intelligences, recalling the Sephirotic emanations, which themselves have planetary attributions.

Let us now take another step. At the beginning of the twelfth century, or actually in the year 1100 A.D., Abu Bakr Ibn Al-Tufail, a noted Arabian physician, poet, mathematician and Sufi philosopher, was born at Guadix in Spain, and he died at Morocco in 1186. His chief work is a species of philosophical romance called " The Life of Hai Ebn Yokdan, the

---

* My knowledge is confined to the translation by Mirza Mohamed Hadi which appeared in successive issues of the " Platonist," vols. iii. and iv.

self-taught Philosopher." In this curious narrative we find Ibn Al-Tufail using a form of comparison which occurs almost verbatim in the Kabalistic books. " The Divine Essence is like the rays of the material sun, which expand over opaque bodies and appear to proceed from the eye, though they are only reflected from its surface." We find also substantially : (a) The *Ain Soph* of the Kabalists under the name of that One True One. (b) The reflection of that Being dwelling "in the highest sphere in and beyond which there is no body, a Being free from matter, which was not the Being of that One True One, nor the sphere itself, nor yet anything different from them both ; but was like the image of the sun as it appears in a well-polished mirror, which is neither one nor the other, and yet not distinct from them." (c) The immaterial essence of the sphere of the fixed stars. (d) The Sphere of Saturn—and so with the rest in harmony with the scheme of the *Desatir*, ending at this world, which is subject to generation and corruption, and comprehending all that is contained within the sphere of the Moon. None of the material essences were identical and yet none were different, either as regards the rest or in comparison with the One True One.*

The doctrine of the Divine Absorption is the very essence of Sufism and Sufism is contemporary with Mohammedanism itself. It is also mainly Pantheistic, as may be gathered from its proposed

---

* See the "Improvement of Human Reason exhibited in the Life of Hai Ebn Yokdhan. Written in Arabick above 500 years ago, by Abu Jaafar Ebn Tophail." . . . Newly translated from the original Arabick by Simon Ockley, A.M. London, 1711.

object. Some refer it to India, others to a Gnostic
origin, but the question does not concern us, for the
significant fact is that this form of Islamic mysticism
was one of the environments of the Kabalistic Jews
to whom we are indebted for part at least of the Zohar.
The influence of this environment was felt outside the
Kabalists, and was confessed even by the most
inflexible of the sects in Jewry—that of the Kairites,
or Literalists, who rejected all innovations in the
primeval doctrine of Israel, who set no store by
tradition, and were thus as much opposed to the
Talmud as to the Zoharic writings. The proof is
their analogies, indeed one might say their fusion,
with the Motozales, a sect of scholastic Arabs.* A
Kairite Jew of the period allows that his brethren
followed the doctrines of this sect, and they even
assumed its name.

The purpose of this section should not be misconstrued. Once more, it is by no means designed
to indicate that the mystic sects of Mohammedanism
are responsible for the peculiar scheme of the Kabalah,
or that the Sufi drew from the rabbin. Such devices
belong to a scheme of criticism which has fittingly
passed away. If we know anything concerning the
early connections of Sufism it is that they are
Neoplatonic, and that the Gnostics of the early
Shiite sects were attracted to it because of these
connections.† But to name Neoplatonism and Gnos-

---

* Munk : *La Philosophie chez les Juifs*, p. 10.

† On this point the reader may consult with advantage an
admirable account of Islamic mysticism in "A Year Among the
Persians," by E. G. Browne. London, 1893. It makes no references
to Kabalism, with which the author seems unacquainted, but it may be
gathered from what it tells us of Sufic commentaries on the Koran that

ticism is to cite analogies of Kabalism. To say that Sufism has been referred to a woman who died at Jerusalem in the first century of the Hegira is to say that Sufism began to live and move in an atmosphere of Jewish tradition. To say that Spain was the forcing-house of the Kabalists is to say that the mystic doctors of Jewry brushed arms with those of Islam, and to deny that there was any consequence of such contact is to deny nature. Sufism was Pantheistic and emanationist; Kabalistic emanationism was saved from Pantheism by the doctrine of divine immanence, and their literatures have no real likeness; but between the metaphysics of the Divine Love and the mystical absorption of Islam, and between the Kabalistic return of the soul to God or its union with the transcendent principle, which never departs from *Atziluth*, and the theory of ecstasy in Israel, it seems reasonable to suppose that there was not only the connecting link of the analogy between all mystics but a bond even in history.

VII. INFLUENCE OF THE KABALAH ON JEWRY

There is perhaps no one at the present day, certainly no Christian or occult student of the

---

these, although Pantheistic, have many points of contact with later Kabalism. We find not only the unmanifest state of Deity, but the attempt to explain why the contingent world (compare the *Liber Drushim*) was evolved from "the silent depths of the non-existent," the use of which term is so typical of the Ain Soph doctrine. See p. 129 for Mr. Browne's opinion that the early schools of Mohammedan philosophy in Persia were adaptations either of Aristotle or Plato, and were also the scholasticism of Islam.

subject, who is in a position to say exactly what kind of profit accrued to the mind of Jewry from the promulgation, let us say, of the Zohar.   From one point of view such an inquiry may be held to strike at the root of all occult science and philosophy, and for the rest it is one of those subjects which do not readily occur to the occultist.   I remember a conversation which I once had with a priest of the Anglican Church, who had passed through every school of initiation with which I am acquainted and through others which are outside my knowledge.   He assured me that the most profound student of occultism among all students whom he had met in his long experience was a Jew—I think of Poland. Let us make the most of this statement, since we know that there are initiations, and that the Jew is in most of them, concerned as he is in all interests, in evidence as he is in all lands, and, with due consideration to the late Sir Richard Burton and his posthumous treatise,* much better described by the famous passage in "Coningsby" than by a somewhat vexatious criticism pivoted on a monstrous charge. But it is quite certain that the adyta of the secret societies, though they are not closed to the Jew, are not in any sense possessed by the Jew, while as regards all such external signs of activity

---

' See "The Jew, the Gypsy and El Islam." London, 1898.   The charge is human sacrifice; its *p.* *tance* has been omitted by the editor on grounds that may be conjectured.   Cf. Desporte , *le Mystère du sang chez les Juifs de tous les temps*, Paris, 1890, the year of Burton's death.   Readers of Josephus will remember the curious story adduced by Apion concerning the Greek captive found in the Temple at Jersualem by Antiochus.   *Contra Apionem*, ii. 7.   Cf. Dr. H. Clay Trumbull, "The Blood Covenant," London, 1887, Appendix. p. 321.

as are manifested by current literature of occultism, any bibliography will show us how little he has done in this respect. What is much more important, however, is that, so far as it is possible to ascertain, the Kabalah has exercised only a very subsidiary influence upon the Children of the Exile. We can point to certain enthusiasms for which it is partially responsible, and they are those precisely which did their best to wreck Jewry and of which Jewry is now ashamed. The history of Abraham Abulafia, of Sabattaï Zevi and the founder of the Chassidim,* are typical cases in point, which warrant us in saying that the Kabalah gave spurious Messiahs to Israel.† It was perhaps the last instance of its activity before it ceased to exercise any powerful influence, and with this also it began, if we care to believe that Rabbi Akiba was the author of the "Book of Formation," in which case one of the supreme sources of Kabalism is connected with the bogus or at least the frenzied mission of Bar Cochba. When that false Messiah had been finally silenced by the sword, his disciple, or perhaps his instigator, and the inspirer also of R. Simeon ben Jochai, the head and crown of Kabalism, was barbarously martyred

---

* *I.e.*, the new order of the mysterious Baal Shem, which is still said to have its representatives in a number of Jewish communities and still holds the Zohar in high esteem. —"Israel among the Nations," pp. 61, 40, 345. The sect has its chief hold among Russian and Galician Jews; the name signifies "pious ones." In the time of Judas Maccabæus, it was the strict party among the Jews.—Edersheim, "History of the Jewish Nation." These are Scaliger's Order of the Knights of the Temple. The accounts of the original Chassidim are full of mythical elements.

† Mr. Zangwill in his "Dreamers of the Ghetto" has brought this notion recently to the knowledge of the external world.

for his share in the unhappy rebellion. If a literature may be judged by its influence, that of the Kabalah has been small ; it has encouraged false enthusiasm, and has been the warrant for direct imposture.*

So far as its operation was intellectual, there is very good ground for thinking that its field was the Christian rather than the Jewish mind.† And having established one useful point there is an opportunity here of making another. Kabalistic influence on Christendom has been of two kinds, but it has been much more of one kind than another. It has been an influence exercised by an occult claim upon the students and the acceptors of occult claims. But it has been much more the influence of possible missionary material on the missionary enterprise of the Christian Church. To begin at a late date— What gave the Kabalah of the Zohar to the Latin reading scholars of Europe? The *magnum opus* of Rosenroth. What impelled Rosenroth? The "splendid spectrum " of the conversion of Jewry *en masse*. And now, if we sweep backward to the very

---

* It has given also a few obscure sects to Jewry. A knowledge of Kabalistic mysteries was alleged to have imparted superhuman power to Lobele, chief Rabbi of Prague ; to Jacob Franck, the Polish distiller, of whose followers the so-called Christian Jews of Poland are still a small survival ; and to his contemporary, Israel of Podolia, who established the New Saints and had a recipe for miracles by means of the name Tetragrammaton.

† Mr. Zangwill is not of this opinion. Referring to the period which antedated immediately the mission of Sabbataï Zevi, he says : " The *Zohar*—the Book of Illumination, composed in the thirteenth century—printed now for the first time, shed its dazzling rays further and further over every ghetto." But perhaps he follows here the principle he has borrowed from Spinoza, " to see things *sub specie æternitatis*." I wish the same principle had inspired him to lay less stress on the exact date of the Zohar.

beginning of the Christian interest in Kabalism, almost coincident, in fact, with the appearance of the Zohar, and suppose that Raymond Lully was really, as it has been said that he was, the first Christian student of the Kabalah, what was the life-long labour of that amazing seneschal of Majorca, and for what did he renounce the world? To wrest, as it has been said, from reluctant Nature the elusive mastery of Nature, the Great Palingenesis of alchemy? The Hermetic treatises falsely ascribed to him may say Yes, but we know that they are the products of the school of forgery which produced the spurious Geber,* and that this was by no means the ambition of Raymond Lully. But was it the attainment of the religion behind all religions? Nothing of the sort; that is modern fantasy. The work of Raymond Lully was apostolical and missionary, and it closed with martyrdom at Bugia, in a feverish attempt to evangelise "Mahound." What prompted the fiery energy of Picus de Mirandola, that he filled the Papal Court with the rumour and the wonder of the Jewish tradition? The fact that he also regarded it as a certain mystic way by which the princes of the Exile might be brought to the gates of the Eternal City and the Ghetto might be transformed into a baptistry. Suppose, lastly, that Nicholas Flamel was really initiated by the "Book of Abraham the Jew," so that Kabalism connects integrally with alchemy, what prompted the unostentatious scrivener of old Paris to make precious metals by occult arts when his wants were few and his trade sufficient for a

---

* M. Berthelot, *La Chimie au Moyen Age, tome premier. Essai sur la transmission de la science antique au Moyen Age, passim.*

modest man? Why, he also had the missionary
spirit—witness his bequests, real or fabulous, for the
conversion of the heathen.

The inference is that the Kabalah was imported
out of Jewry to prove that Jewry might be
Christianised if it were handled wisely according to
the lights given in the Holy Synods.*

Now, I do not need to say that there are very
few occultists who would take any interest in the
Kabalah regarded from this point of view. They
are not, as a class, inspired by missionary zeal for
any form of official religion, and their literature, as
it stands, does not manifest more than sufficient
respect for the great orthodoxies of Christendom.
On the other hand, it is only in virtue of some
immense misapprehension that the esoteric tradition
of the Jews can be supposed to offer them the
religion behind all religions. What it does offer them
falls almost infinitely short. At its highest a bizarre
but truly strenuous attempt to unriddle the universe,
the most unaided of all metaphysics, the *systema
mundi* excogitated in a darkened synagogue with the
praying-shawl drawn over the eyes. What darkness
to be felt in the void! What strange lights flashing
in the darkness! In such a state Spanish Jew or
Spanish Mystic of the Latin Church, Moses de Leon,

One writer in modern times has even gone so far as to maintain
that "Christian doctrine, except the Trinity, which is Platonic, issues
wholly, with all its details, from the Talmud. Christianity is son and
brother of the Talmud."—Alexander Weill, *Moise, le Talmud et
l'Évangile*, ii. 92. The statement sounds perilous, but M. Weill is
not to be taken seriously. Compare *ibid.* ii. 91, "The Talmud is
itself the most violent adversary of Moses," *i.e.*, the Moses of M.
Weill. One paradox enables us to judge another.

if you will, or St. John of the Cross, exile of Babylon
or recluse of the Thebaid, must enjoy a certain
communication of the infinite. But to say more than
this is frenzy. And at its lowest, that is to say, on
that side upon which it makes contact no longer with
the infinite, but with the occult as it is understood
by occultism, finite of all things finite, what sombre
trifling unredeemed by the saving sense of triviality,
the physiognomy of the section *Yithroh*, the astrology
of the processes of Gaffarel, the star messages of the
Hebrew planisphere, the paper tubes of Eliphas
Levi ;* or, again, *notaricon, metathesis, gematria*,†
the arcana of the extended name, the virtues of
Agla and *Ararita* for conjuring heaven and earth.
It is here that occultism illustrates how it receives
only what it can give and how it comes to pass
that the interest of the occultist in the Kabalah is
less inspired by the occult theorems of the Zohar
than by the magic garters of the " Key of Solomon."
Hence even writers, like Papus in France, who have
exceptional claims on our consideration, find it
necessary to include in their scheme of Kabalism
the sorry literature of the Grimoires.‡ And they
and he have nothing to tell us of the Zohar. But
we do not find the Grimoires in Picus de Mirandola,
or in Raymond Lully ; we do not find much trace

---

* And the kind of Kabalah which A. Lelièvre undertook to defend
in his *Justification des Sciences Divinatoires* (Paris, 1847).

† Observe also the developments which these subjects received in
works like the *Caballa Anagrammatica* of Ranutius Longelus, *Placentiæ*,
1654—*ars mirabilis* indeed, as the author terms it.

‡ *La Kabbale*, pp. 10, 16, 26, the last especially, where the
reference to Molitor makes the author of the " Philosophy of Tradition "
apparently responsible for the identification of the *clavicula* and
" magical MSS." as a serious branch of Kabalism.

of magic in the *Kabbala Denudata*. The Lexicon of Rosenroth does not include the occult wonders of *Agla*, nor does it tell us after what manner the extended name is compounded, by a childcraft of acrostics, out of three verses in Exodus.   We do find all these in Agrippa, who wrote as a young man of things that he had heard and read, making a very dignified retractation of it all in his book of great excellence upon vanity.

There remains, of course, the mystic side of Kabalism, the return of the soul to God, and that path of ecstasy already mentioned, by which it was conceived that the soul might effect such reunion even in this life, but it is precisely this mystic side of which we see no effect in Jewry, and it is also this side which is neglected by modern occultism. For example, the present work is the first published in England which has any reference to the highest principle of the human soul in Kabalism and the instrument of unification with the Divine.

BOOK IV

THE WRITTEN WORD OF KABALISM:

FIRST PERIOD

ARGUMENT

The traces of Kabalistic literature outside the Sepher Yetzirah, and prior to the publication of the Zohar, are enumerated briefly to indicate that there was a gradual growth of the tradition and to correct exaggerated notions concerning it. There are several ancient treatises which connect with Kabalism, but are not regarded by modern scholarship as Kabalistic in the technical sense. This is the case with the Sepher Yetzirah itself; but there is no doubt that all these works pretend to embody an occult tradition, or that it was the elements of oral tradition which subsequently received development from the commentators on the Sepher Yetzirah, as well as from the Zohar, and, later still, from the expositors of Zoharic mysteries. The attention of early Kabalists was concentrated on the "Book of Formation," and numerous elucidations of that work appeared between the eleventh and thirteenth centuries.

I. EARLY KABALISTIC LITERATURE

IT is beyond controversy that there was a great body of mystic speculation and doctrine grown up in Jewry, of which the roots are to be found in the Talmud, while it is connected occasionally with brilliant and even with some great names. It is this transcendentalism which led ultimately to the Zohar, and should scholarship forbid us to confer on it the distinctive denomination of Kabalism,* we must defer to scholarship, though with the mental reservation that if the question be more than of words it is at most one of stages of growth, for that which was of mysticism in Israel between the period of the Talmud and the period of the promulgation of the Zohar is that which in the course of its evolution became the Kabalah and the Zohar.

The title of this section is to some extent tentative or speculative, but the modest conclusions of the previous book are a sufficient warrant for supposing that there are traces of Kabalism, outside the Sepher Yetzirah, prior to the promulgation of the Zohar, and possessing some literary remains. It is indeed essential to the natural history of the later work that it should have had its antecedents in literature. According to the most acceptable view these were certain *Midrashim* which, for the most part, are not now extant, and it is fair to suppose that, assuming such memorials, they must have exercised some influence.

So also the Sepher Yetzirah, whatever the date ascribed to it, was of high authority, and the veneration in which it was held was of the kind which creates literature. We must beware, however, of supposing that there was an unbroken line of Kabalists from the second to the twelfth century, as some occult writers have pretended. Supposing the Sephir Yetzirah in its present form to be later than the second century,

---

* There can be, I think, little doubt that the Kabalah was the "reception" of the *Bereshith* and *Mercabah* mysteries mentioned in the Talmud, or that this was the view always taken by Kabalistic Jev .

we must regard as its prototype a work already mentioned under the title of the Alphabet of Akiba, while the antithesis of " The Book of Occultation," one of the most important sections of the Zohar, must be sought in the anthropomorphic *Schiur Komah, i.e.,* " The Measure of the Height," in other words, the " Description of the Body of God," or development of the various Scriptural places in which the divine members are mentioned. The dates of these fragmentary works are conjectural, but there can be no doubt, as indeed there is no question, of their comparative antiquity. Connected with these are the Greater and the Lesser Palace, known also as the " Delineation of the Heavenly Temples,"* which, in common with the others, is not regarded by modern critics as Kabalistic, but it is allowed that all were instrumental in calling the Kabalah into existence.†

In accordance with the exigencies of his standpoint, Dr. Graetz, who may be taken to represent all that is most acrid and uncompromising in hostility to Jewish mysticism, fixes the origin of Kabalism, as to its date, in the tenth century, and thus by implication denies the claim of the Sepher Yetzirah to be included in its literature. He is followed, as we have seen, by

---

* Not to be confused with a work mentioned by Bartolocci under the name of R. Eliezer and dealing with the measurements of the earthly temple.

† " By the difficulty," says Ginsburg, " in which they placed the Jews in the South of France and in Catalonia, who believed in them almost as much as in the Bible, and who were driven to contrive this system whereby they could explain the gross descriptions of the Deity and of the plains of heaven, given in these Haggadic productions." It may indeed be affirmed that one spirit informed the chief works of mystical complexion which preceded the Zohar.

Ginsburg,* but it is not open to question that the work
is indispensable to the Kabalah, or that it is an
integral and fundamental part thereof. The tenth
century is, however, an important period in Jewish
history and Jewish letters, for at this epoch the
quickening of the Arabian mind was followed by that
of Israel† and was sometimes eclipsed thereby.
There was for a moment a lull in persecution ; the
academies in the East flourished, and in the West the
internecine struggle of Christians and Moslems in
Spain ensured a breathing space to the Children of the
Exile. Prior to that period, from the sixth century
and onward, there was a hiatus in the literature of
Israel. The canons of the Talmud were closed, by
the terror and peril of the time rather than inherent
necessity, and the history of Israel became one of
bitter struggle for existence. A certain hazardous
shelter was found under Persian dominion, and
ultimately the intellectual lamp of Israel shone forth
clearly and steadily during the Moslem domination of
Spain, which country from that period till the
beginning of the thirteenth century was like a second
Palestine to the Jew, and this land of refuge, under
the tolerant and enlightened sway of the Spanish
Khalifs, became almost as dear to his heart as the
Land of Promise. Montpellier in France and Salerno
in Italy were famous for their Jewish schools, but
that of Seville was, perhaps, more illustrous than
either. Spain also was a nursing-land of Kabalistic
literature, and the traces of the esoteric tradition

---

* Kitto's " Cyclopædia," third edition, 1864, s.v. Kabbalah
† Basnage, *Histoire des Juifs*, livre vii. c. 4, tom. v. p. 1503 *et seq.*

between the epoch which produced the "Book of Formation" and that of the "Book of Splendour" must be sought chiefly therein, though in the twelfth century something may be gleaned from Southern France and earlier still from Hay Gaon who flourished in the eleventh century, a Babylonian, on the borders of the Caspian Sea.*

There is neither space nor occasion here to produce a bibliographical list, and indeed the materials at our command can scarely be regarded as extensive, serving mainly to correct false and highly coloured impressions regarding the claims of Kabalistic tradition. The chief names of the period with which we are now concerned are:

I. Rabbi Eliezer, whose mystic system, as presented in the *Pirke*, connects on the one hand with the Sepher Yetzirah, and on the other with Zoharic teaching. We have, in the first place, God subsisting prior to the creation of the world alone with his Ineffable Name; next, the creation, prior to the visible world, of the *Thorah* or Law, together with the Throne of Glory, the Name of the Messiah, Paradise, Hell and the Temple of Jerusalem, *i.e.*, the archetype of the earthly temple; subsequently, the creation of the world by means of ten words. With this work may be connected the ancient *Midrash Conen*, which represents the *Thorah* as the foundation of the universe. It is a matter of con-

---

* Outside the dates and authorship ascribed by the old Kabalists to the Sepher Yetzirah and the Zohar there are other treatises attributed to the early days of the Exile. Thus tradition regards Eliezer Hagabite, son of Jose, a contemporary of Simeon ben Jochai, as a Kabalistic doctor and the author of a treatise on the thirty-two qualities of the Law. The antiquity of this work is doubtful.

jecture whether these works are slightly later or earlier than the Sepher Yetzirah.

II. The Gaon R. Saadiah, head of the Persian Academy of Sora, was the author of a commentary on the Sepher Yetzirah preserved in the Bodleian Library and only printed recently in France, as we shall see in the third section of this book.

III. The Gaon R. Shereerah, head of the academy of Pherruts Schibbur* in the neighbourhood of Babylon, was perhaps more distinguished for the violence with which he wrote against the Christians than for his Kabalistic knowledge. But Nachmanides† has preserved his observations on the " Delineation of the Heavenly Temples,"‡ or more correctly on the fragments which it embodies under the title of the " Proportion of the Height," otherwise called the " Description of the Body of God," which shows the Kabalistic leanings of Shereerah and creates the antithesis to the anthropomorphism of these early works which has been mentioned already as a key-note of Kabalism. " God forbid," he exclaims, " that man should speak of the Creator as if he had bodily members and dimensions!" This Rabbi was despoiled of his wealth and hanged by order of Cader, Khalif of the race of the Abassides.

IV. The Gaon R. Hay, son and successor of Shereerah as the head of the Babylonian School of Schibbur, is also credited with a commentary on the Sepher Yetzirah, which will be dealt with in its

* Or of Pumbaditha according to some authorities, including Graetz.
† In his commentary on the *Thorah.*
‡ Attributed to R. Ishmael, apparently the doctor of that name sentences are sometimes quoted in the Talmud.

proper place. The interpretation of dreams was one of the daily occupations of the Jewish academies, and their skill exhibited therein, or the credulity of the times, often purchased toleration and respect for the Rabbis at the hands of the Khalifs. To Rab Hay is attributed a treatise on this art, which was printed at Venice.* Outside his alleged commentary on the " Book of Formation " his voluminous works have many Kabalistic references, especially that entitled " The Voice of God in its Power." It will be sufficient to mention among these the doctrine of correspondences, of man as a microcosm and a peculiar theory of mystic contemplation. He possessed enormous influence and became subsequently the head of the academy of Pumbaditha in the neighbourhood of Bagdad. He died in 1038.

V. R. Chasdai† was a Prince of the Exile and temporal head of the Jews in Cordova. He was also a political minister under two Khalifs. He is said to connect the school of Hay Gaon with that of Gebirol.‡

VI. Solomon ben Yehudah Ibn Gebirol, the scholastic Avicebron and in all respects, Kabalistic and otherwise, a focus of intellectual and literary interest, was a contemporary of the famous Nagrila.

VII. R. Abraham ben David or Ben Dior Ha Levi, the great orthodox apologist of the twelfth century, has been included in the chain of Kabalism.

VIII. Moses Ibn Jacob ben Ezra,§ one of the

---

* Bartolocci, *Bibliotheca Rabbinica*, ii. 387.
† *I.e.*, Abu-Yussuf Chasdaï ben Isaac Ibn Shaprut.
‡ He died about the year 970.
§ See "Essays on the Writings of Ibn Ezra," in the Transactions of the Society of Hebrew Literature.

greatest Jews of his time, was of Granada, and
flourished in the earlier part of the twelfth century.
His work entitled the "Garden of Aromatics" shows
traces of the doctrine of Gebirol, but it appears by
his "Commentary on Isaiah" that he was in dis-
agreement with this doctor. Basnage says that he
did not reject the Kabalah, though he knew its
weakness, because he did not wish to be embroiled
with contemporary writers.* He wrote upon the
Divine Name and the mystic attributes of numbers
in connection therewith.

IX. The names of Juda Hallevi, who has some
references to the Sepher Yetzirah in his work entitled
Kusari, of Jacob Nazir, of Solomon Jarki, of R.
Abraham ben David, the younger, bring us to the
thirteenth century and to the period of (*a*) Maimonides,
who is reported, chiefly on the authority of R.
Chaiim, to have turned Kabalist at an advanced age
but in any case connects with mysticism, and was
acquainted at least with the existence of the twofold
mystic tradition distinguished as that of the Creation
and that of the Chariot ; (*b*) R. Azariel, of Valladolid,
famous commentator on the Sepher Yetzirah ; (*c*)
Shem Tob Ibn Falaquera, a disciple of Maimonides,
who connects with Gebirol ; (*d*) R. Abraham
Abulafia,† who wrote on the Tetragrammaton and

---

* Basnage quotes Skinner's letters and Usher in support of this
view, but he and they are in some confusion as to important dates in
Kabalistic history and literature. Graetz has a good account of Ibn
Ezra, but it is unnecessary to say that his analogies with Kabalism are
not mentioned.

† See Frankel, *Monatshrift f.   Weissenschaft
des Judenthums*, vol. v. p. 27, Leipsic, 1856. Graetz has also a long
account of Abulafia, designed to ridicule the mental condition to which
he refers the Kabalah.

the Mysteries of the Law, but his works have not been published.* He endeavoured to combine the theoretical and practical schools, but he was a quixotic adventurer and a Messianic enthusiast, to whose opinions it is unnecessary to give weight. It may be noted, however, that he exhibits some Christian tendencies.

Those who defend the authenticity of Kabalistic tradition find something to their purpose in all these writers and personalities, but they often proceed on a misconception. What, for example, is more likely to lead an unpractised student astray than the treatise of Abraham ben David Ha Levi, by the mere fact of its title? It is called *Seder Ha Kabalah*, the Order of the Tradition.† As a fact, it is the least mystical of all productions, and though I have termed its author a great orthodox apologist, he had a strong Aristotelian leaven. The occasion of his book was a Sadducean heresy prevalent in Castile and Leon, and represented by the work of Abu Alphrag, which maintained that the true synagogue was to be found among the Sadducees. The *Seder Ha Kabalah* vindicates the authority of the orthodox claim under the two heads of succession and universality, or community of doctrine among all the synagogues It embraces the entire history of the Jewish Church and the perpetuation of the Mosaic doctrine, which is the

---

* They include also the "The Fount of Living Waters," of which there is a Latin version in the Vatican. Graetz extends the number of his works to twenty ; Bartolocci knew only of three.

† It was the prototype of several later works, such as Ghedalia on the Chain of the Kabalah, the *Yuhasin* of Zakut, famous in connection with the Zohar, and the *Tsemach David*, already quoted.

tradition named in the title.* The work of Abraham
ben David Ha Levi is perhaps greater than was the
occasion which called it forth. The Jews were
divided among themselves upon many questions, of
which Sadducean pretensions were certainly not the
most important. The great distinction of the time
for the purpose of our own inquiry was between the
Jews who had adopted Aristotelian principles and the
Jews who opposed the innovation. The enlightenment and culture were incontrovertibly on the side of
the former; the fascination of mystic thought, in a
word, all that we connect with the ideal of rabbinical
Israel, went, however, into the opposite scale. There
were great names on both sides. Rabbi Abraham
and his *Sepher* exercised a large influence; his contemporary, Maimonides, who survived him by almost
a quarter of a century, was described by the
enthusiasts of his period as "the elect of the human
race," and by a play upon his name it was said of
him that "from Moses to Moses there was no one
like unto Moses."

The rival school was to some extent represented
by Avicebron, and some of those who assert that the
Zohar incorporated traditions belonging to preceding
centuries are content to rest their case on the writings
of this poet and philosopher. The evidence, however, is in a very confused state. On the one hand,
the system of Avicebron has many Aristotelian
traces; on the other hand, it has been asserted that
Maimonides has much to connect him with Avicebron,
though he was not acquainted with his works, while,

---

i, *Magna Bibliotheca Rabbinica*, i. p. 18 *et seq.*

M

further, the great masterpiece of the Talmudic Jew of Cordova, entitled "The Guide of the Perplexed," offers many indications of his sympathy with the speculative Kabalah.* In a general sense, however, those who wished to introduce Aristotelian principles into Jewish philosophy belonged to that school which subsequently opposed the Zohar,† as, for example, Abraham Ibn Wakkar of Toledo, at the beginning of the fourteenth century,‡ while those who accepted the Zohar belonged to that school which connects with Avicebron, among whom was Rabbi Abraham ben David of Posquiere, to whom one section of modern criticism attributes the invention of the Kabalah, and Isaac the Blind, with his disciples Azariel and Ezra, whose superior claim is favoured by Ginsburg.§ The Kabalistic interests of this school are outside all debate; it prized the Sepher Yetzirah, and one of

---

* There does not seem, however, the slightest ground for supposing, with Isaac Myer, that Maimonides was acquainted with the Zohar. On the contrary, there is more perhaps to be said for the conjecture of S. Munk that the Zohar quotes, or rather borrows, from Maimonides. See *Mélanges*, &c., p. 278. Among the Kabalistic correspondences of Maimonides are (1) His recognition of a secret sense in Scripture; (2) Of the inaccessible nature of God; (3) Of the universe as an organic whole. The student should also consult an interesting *Notice sur la Cabale des Hébreux*, prefixed by the Chevalier Drach to the second volume of his work already cited on the "Harmony between the Church and the Synagogue." He establishes (a) That where Buxtorf supposes the Talmud (Tract *Rosh Hashanah*) to allow the same authority to the Kabalah as to the text of Moses, the reference is really to the spiritual power of the Synagogue; and (b) that the alleged mention of the mystic Kabalah by Maimonides is a misconception (*L'Harmonie*, ii. xvi. xvii. xviii.). It is certain, however, that Maimonides mentions a lost tradition.

† In which, however, Munk traces Aristotelian influences. — *Mélanges*, pp. 278, 279.

‡ See the English translation of Steinschneider, p. 114.

§ Who follows Graetz literally.

the most important commentaries on that treatise
was produced within it.

When we investigate the claim made with regard
to Avicebron, we must not be discouraged at finding
that writers like Isaac Myer have much enhanced the
real strength of his Kabalistic connections. We find,
it is true, the doctrines of the Inaccessible God,
of the intermediaries between God and the
universe, of the emanation of the world, and even
of the universal knowledge attributed to the pre-
existent soul of man by all Jewish mysticism. But
what we should like to meet with in a mystic of the
eleventh century is a distinct trace of typical Zoharic
doctrine, let us say that of the Countenances, and not
Yetziratic references, Sephirotic correspondences and
so forth. The latter are to be expected at the middle
of the eleventh century, and in this case the former
are wanting. There remains, however, sufficient to
interest us, perhaps even to warrant the inclusion
of Gebirol among the precursors of Zoharic Kabalism,
and a short account of this author may be appended
as a conclusion to this section.

At that period when the influence of Arabian
imagination was infused into the romantic literature
of Western Europe, scholastic philosophy and
theology were receiving the tincture of Arabian
thought, but as, on the one hand, this tincture was
received sometimes without much consciousness of
its origin, so, on the other, influences were occasionally
referred to Arabian sources which were in reality
referable only to the Spanish Jews living under
the protection of the Khalifate during the Moslem
domination of the peninsula. A case in point was

the once renowned Avicebron, whose identity with
Solomon ben Yehudah Ibn Gebirol, a Jew of
Cordova, was first demonstrated by Munk in the
early part of the present century.* His chief
treatise, entitled the " Fountain of Life," in a Latin
version ascribed to the middle of the twelfth
century, became widely diffused ; Albertus Magnus,
St. Thomas of Aquin and Duns Scotus, all cited
it ; and it is said to sum the philosophy of the
thirteenth century. According to Renan, Avicebron
preceded the school of Arabian philosophy which
arose in Spain. He wrote philosophy in Arabic
and poetry in Hebrew ; the Jews valued his poetry,
but his metaphysics were not in repute among them ;
the Christian scholastics adopted his philosophical
ideas, and knew nothing whatever of his verses.
By both classes of his admirers he was respectively
celebrated as the greatest philosopher and the
greatest poet of his time. But the nominalists
denounced him ; realists like Duns Scotus entailed
on him their own condemnation ; while he is said
to have exercised an influence upon the mystics of
the Middle Ages, he was proscribed by the University
of Paris at the period of the publication of the
Zohar on the ground that he favoured Aristotle.
When the school of Averroes arose he was unknown
among it ; at a later period he was unknown to
Maimonides ; he was unknown also to the encyclo-
pædic learning of Picus de Mirandola ; and on the

---

* *Mélanges de Philosophie Juive et Arabe.* The hostile school of
Zoharic criticism has not done sufficient credit to Munk for his interesting
discovery, but he is not a *persona grata* on account of his theory that
the Zohar was founded on genuine ancient *Midrashim.*

threshold of the Reformation his memory may be said to have perished at the pyre of Giordano Bruno.

Avicebron was born about the year 1021 at Malaga; he was educated in the University of Saragossa, and he died at Valencia in 1070. He was patronised by Nagdilah—*i.e.*, Samuel-ha-Levi ben Josef Ibn Nagréla—a Prince of the Exile, who was also Prime Minister of Spain under the Kalifate of Habus. Nagdilah was the centre and mainspring of Jewish learning in that country, and it is thought that through him the sacred tradition of the Hebrews was communicated to Avicebron at a period when the Zohar and its connections were still in course of formation. It seems certain, in any case, that some of the conceptions and the system incorporated in these books may be found in his writings, more especially in the " Fountain of Life " and the " Crown of the Kingdom." The first is affirmed to be the earliest known exhibition of " the secrets of the speculative Kabalah."* The second, composed towards the end of his life, is a hymn " celebrating the only one and true God, and the marvels of His creation."

The existence of the Zoharic tradition some centuries previous to the time of Moses de Leon, the reputed forger of the Zohar, has been rested, among other supports, on the writings of this Spanish Jew, and he seems to have been acquainted indubitably with the Book of Formation. In the second book and twenty-second section of the

---

* There is some confusion here, as the Sepher Yetzirah is certainly speculative as contrasted with the so-called practical Kabalah, which was mainly the working of miracles by the use of the Divine Names.

"Fountain of Life" this passage occurs: "Hence it hath been said that the construction of the world was accomplished by the inscription of numbers and letters in the air," which is obviously the fundamental notion of the Kabalistic work in question. The table of the Thirty-Two Paths, which arises out of the Book of Formation, was the theme of one of his poems. Whether the later Kabalists derived from Avicebron or both from a common source cannot be conclusively determined, but having regard to the Jewish indifference for his philosophical writings, and to the probable existence of a vast mass of floating esoteric tradition, there can be no doubt as to the direction in which probability points.*

The connection between Avicebron and the Kabalah is not sufficiently explicit upon the surface of the "Fountain of Life" to have attracted the attention of critics like Ernest Renan; while Kabalistic critics refer the system which it develops to the ten *Sephiroth*, others suppose it to be based on the ten categories of Aristotle, a pantheism analogous to that of the early realists. "On the one hand," says Renan, "his application of Peripatetic principles to Mosaic doctrine alarmed the theologians; on the other hand, his concessions to orthodoxy concerning the creation and the free will of the Creator did not satisfy the extreme Peripatetic Jews." Of his alleged Kabalistic connections Renan was either unaware, as already suggested, or they were ignored by him.

---

* Graetz takes the opposite view, saying that the Kabalah borrowed many principles from Ibn Gebirol. He, of course, offers no reasoning on the subject.

An impartial examination of the " Fountain of Life " makes the pantheism of Avicebron less apparent than his Kabalistic correspondences. So far from identifying the universe with God, it establishes no uncertain contrast between them. In order to bridge the abyss, and to make it conceivable that one derived being from the other, he supposes nine intermediaries, *plus* the Divine Will, " through which the Absolutely Existing, who is above number," is " attached to its corporeal universe." The analogies which this conception offers to Yetziratic doctrine are self-evident and do not need enforcing, and yet our impartial judgment must pronounce the philosophy of Avicebron to be of Greek rather than Jewish complexion. It is at least clear that the *Fons Vitæ*, which is a dialogue after the manner of Plato, is tinctured deeply by Hellenic thought.

Modern scholarship has recognised three chief schools which led up to Zoharic Kabalism : (*a*) that of Isaac the Blind, to which belongs Azariel with his celebrated commentary on the Sepher Yetzirah ; (*b*) that of Eliezar of Worms, which is largely of the theurgic order ; and (*c*) that of Abulafia, which to some extent united the preceding and made use of the theurgic formulæ combined with contemplation to achieve union with God.

II. THE BOOK OF FORMATION

In developing the Kabalistic doctrine of the Instruments of Creation, in describing the Paths of Wisdom and in attempting to determine the date of the Book of Formation in connection with our investigation as to the authority of the Kabalah, we have nearly exhausted the subject of the tiny treatise which is regarded by most scholars and by every occultist as the nucleus of all Kabalism. It is difficult, however, to omit it in giving an account of the documents, and it will perhaps be best to begin this brief bibliographical notice by a summary of the points which have been determined previously concerning it.

The legend which attributes it to the patriarch Abraham, who transmitted it orally to his sons, by whom it was perpetuated in turn till the " sages of Jerusalem," committed it finally to writing, so that the tradition might not perish even when the chosen people seemed themselves on the eve of perishing—this, we have seen, is legend. It is interesting and respectable in its way. At the period when we first hear of the existence of such a tract it was possibly already old, and most old books have myths designed to explain them. Those who take the myths historically convert honest legend into something approaching farce. We must be content therefore to say that the Sepher Yetzirah is first mentioned probably in the ninth century ; there is some reason to suppose that it is quoted in the Talmud, but it is not wholly certain ;* it

* The treatise *Sanhedrim* contains the following passage : " By means of combining the letters of the ineffable names as recorded in SPR ITsIRH (*i.e*, the sealing names enumerated in the first chapter, being permutations of IHV), Rava once created a man and sent him to Rav Zeira. The man being unable to reply when spoken to, the Rabbi said to him, Thou art a creature of the company (initiated in the mysteries of necromancy) : return to thy dust."

may have antedated its first citation in literature by a generation, a century, or an age. Let us realise that we do not know, and that those who judge the question dogmatically on either side deserve to be classed as intemperate.

Let us now look a little more closely at the work itself. It is divided into five chapters, the first being concerned with the office of the *Sephiroth* in creation and the remaining four with what have been termed the Instruments—namely, the letters of the Hebrew alphabet. It was after the revelation of these mysteries to Abraham that he received the manifestation of God and that the covenant was instituted. According to the expression of the original, God "bound the twenty-two letters" on the tongue of the patriarch and discovered to him all their secrets.*

The symbolism of the Book of Formation having been sufficiently considered in the second part of our inquiry, there are only two points which require to be noted here. One is the absolute distinctness between God and the instruments of creation,† whether numbers or letters, which is

---

* *Sepher Yetzirah*, chap. vi.

† Hence Mr. C. G. Harrison is in error when he implies that pantheism is involved in the Sephirotic system, and thence proceeds to argue that, "It takes no account of the element of illusion which is necessarily implied in the theophanic doctrine."—See "The Transcendental Universe," London, 1894, pp. 86, 87. *Cf.* Alexander Weill, *Lois et Mystères de la Creation conformes a la Science la plus Absolue.* Paris, 1896. The writer refers to a work under a similar title which he issued forty years previously, purporting to be the translation of a Hebrew MS. by a master of Kabalah. "This writing is distinguished from all rabbinical and philosophical treatises by proclaiming the identity of the Creator with His creatures, based on the text of Genesis itself." Weill is a fantasiast who pretends to separate the frauds and contradictions which Esdras and his assistants introduced into the Pentateuch

established by this early Kabalistic work. Separated from all number and transcending all expression, He is represented as a faithful king sojourning in eternity and ruling the *Sephiroth* for ever from His holy seat. The second point concerns the emanation of the *Sephiroth*, to which, in preference to their creation, all later Kabalism inclines. There is little on the face of the Book of Formation to countenance this view; they appear as the instruments and servants of the King of Ages, informed by whose word they go forth "and returning, fall prostrate in adoration before the Throne."* It is said, however, that their end is joined to their beginning, as the flame is joined to the firebrand, and perhaps the principle of emanation is contained implicitly in this statement. We have no reason for rejecting a construction which has been adopted invariably, but it is just to draw attention to the fact that the first work which mentions the *Sephiroth* leaves this point in obscurity, while it certainly depicts God as the active architect of the universe, who graved, sculptured and builded.

The first *Sephira* is described as the Spirit of the Living God, the blessed and again blessed name of God living eternally. Voice, Spirit and Word—these are the Holy Spirit. TWO is the Breathing of the Spirit; the twenty-two tetters depend herefrom and each one of them is Spirit. THREE is the moisture

---

from the real work of Moses. *Cf.* the same author's *Moïse, le Talmud et l'Evangile.* Paris, 1875, tom. i. p. 99. According to Franck, the last word of the system developed by the Sepher Yetzirah is the substitution of absolute unity for every species of dualism.—*La Kabbale,* p. 159.

  * *Sepher Yetzirah,* chap. i.

which comes from the Breath; herewith God sculptured and engraved the first lifeless and void matter. He built TOHU, the line which circles snake-like about the world, and BOHU, the concealed rocks imbedded in the abyss whence the waters issue. This triad of the Spirit, the Breath and the Water corresponds to the conception subsequently formed of the Atzilutic or archetypal world. FOUR is the Fire which comes forth from the Water; with this God sculptured the Throne of Honour, the Ophanim or Celestial Wheels, the Holy Animals—*i.e.*, the four living creatures and the other serving Spirits. Within their dominion He established His habitation. This numeration seems to contain in itself the conceptions of *Briah* and *Yetzirah*, the archangelic and angelic worlds. It should be remembered, however, that the Book of Formation is concerned only with the sphere of operation tabulated subsequently as the third world of Kabalism. As each *Sephira* was supposed to contain all the *Sephiroth*, so there was a superincession of the four worlds which were all contained in each. The arrangement of the Sepher Yetzirah does not exhibit this clearly, but the numerations from five to ten inclusive must be held to represent Assiah. FIVE is the seal with which God sealed the Height when He contemplated it above Him. He sealed it with the name IEV. SIX is the seal with which He sealed the depth when He contemplated it beneath Him. He sealed it with the name IVE. SEVEN is the seal with which He sealed the East when He contemplated it before Him. He sealed it with the name EIV. EIGHT is the seal with which He sealed the West when He contemplated it behind Him. He sealed it with the name VEI. NINE is the seal with which He sealed the South when He contemplated it on His right. He sealed it with the name VIE. TEN is the seal with which He sealed the North when He contemplated it on His left. He sealed it with the name EVI. The ten numerations are finally classed together under the one title of "Ineffable Spirits of God." The sealing names are combinations of three letters, successively transposed, which enter into the name *Tetragrammaton.*

The Sepher Yetzirah was published at Mantua in 1592, but the Latin translation of Postel had preceded it by ten years.* The Mantua edition was accompanied by five commentaries.† Another Latin version will be found in the collection of Pistorius ; it is ascribed to Reuchlinus and Riccius. In 1642 a further edition was published at Amsterdam in Hebrew and Latin by Rittangelius. It was issued by Meyer at Leipsic in 1830, with a German translation and notes, and at Frankfort, 1849, with a German translation and commentary,‡ by L. Goldschmidt.

---

* The full title of this curious little volume is ABRAHAMI PATRIARCHÆ LIBER JEZIRAH, *sive Formationis Mundi, Patribus quidem Abrahami tempora præcedentibus revelatus, sed ab ipso etiam Abrahamo expositus Isaaco, et per Profetarum manus posteritati conservatus, ipsis autum 72 Mosis auditoribus in secundo divinæ veritatis loco, hoc est in ratione, quæ est posterior authoritate, habitus. Vertebat ex Hebræis et commentariis illustrabat* 1551, *ad Babylonis ruinam et corrupti mundi finem,* GULIELMUS POSTELLUS, *Restitutus. Parisiis,* 1552.

† It also contained two recensions of the text, the differences between which are regarded by some authorities as considerable and by others as unimportant variants.

‡ The "American Encyclopædia," iii. 521, 522, mentions the Amsterdam edition of 1642, with a Latin translation, but does not connect it with Rittangelius.

In 1887 Dr. Papus made a French translation to which he added the Thirty-two Paths of Wisdom and the Fifty Gates of Intelligence. With characteristic sincerity he admits that this was superseded by Mayer Lambert in 1891.

The one question which now remains for consideration is how we are to account for the importance attributed by occultism to such a work as the Sepher Yetzirah. Do its defenders believe that the combination of *Aleph* with all the other letters and all the rest with *Aleph*, *Beth* with all the others and all the rest with *Beth*, &c., &c., actually produced the universe? That seems an insupportable assumption. Do they regard the letters as symbols of forces and hold that the Sepher Yetzirah teaches that the universe originates in the orderly combination of certain forces? That is reasonable enough, but it is a commonplace which seems scarcely worth stating and certainly does not require a secret tradition to secure it. But do they consider that the letters represent occult forces, of a fixed, determinable character, and that initiation into the real meaning of Kabalistic tradition will discover their nature, explaining thus the secret behind the arbitrary doctrine of a virtue inherent in words and letters? This might indeed be valuable, but I have never met with an occultist who took such a view, or had anything to substantiate it if he did. In the absence of any light on this point we can only conclude that it is the arbitrary doctrine in question which accounts for the interest taken in the Sepher Yetzirah ; but the truly occult student, as I have defined him at the outset of this inquiry, can only be scandalised at the childish nature of Yetziratic tabulations.

III. CONNECTIONS AND DEPENDENCIES OF THE BOOK OF FORMATION

Were there evidence to warrant us in believing that Moses de Leon did actually, as his hostile relative is reported to have affirmed, write thc Zohar bodily "out of his own head," there would still be substantial evidence that the Kabalistic system which it contains was not his invention. The existence of the Sepher Yetzirah is part of this evidence, which appears, however, more fully and more strongly in the commentaries and developments of that work. We have seen already that when it came to be printed at Mantua, the Book of Formation was accompanied by five such connections, which at the same time do not exhaust the list that might be given in a full bibliography. The best known is unquestionably the *Sepher Sephiroth*, or "Commentary on the Ten *Sephiroth* by way of Questions and Answers," the work of R. Azariel ben Menahem ; that of Rabbi Abraham has been regarded as the most important from an occult standpoint, while the earliest in point of time is the work of Saadya Gaon in the tenth century. Another, which has been attributed to Hay Gaon in the early part of the eleventh century, would rank next in antiquity, but it has been usually rejected as spurious. Commentaries are also attributed to R. Moses

Botrel,* R. Moses ben Nahmann, R. Abraham ben
David Ha Levi the younger and R. Eliezer. With
the exception of the one last mentioned they are
all prior to the period when Moses de Leon is
supposed to have been at work on the Zohar, and
they have been used to show that the novelty of
that work " is of form rather than material."

The commentary of R. Saadya Gaon was
published in Hebrew at Mantua together with the
Sepher Yetzirah,† but it was written originally in
Arabic, and a copy is preserved in the Bodleian
Library. After remaining in MS. for over eight
hundred years this Arabic original was at length
printed at Paris, together with a French translation,
in 1892. In the introduction prefixed to his version,
M. Lambert observes that Saadya Gaon appears as
a theosophist in his commentary, which is equivalent
to saying that the first expository treatise on the
Sepher Yetzirah possesses a Kabalistic complexion,
though the author is frequently regarded as a purely
rationalistic writer. It must be confessed, however, that
Saadya offers little connection with Zoharic doctrine.
We have noted that the *Sephiroth* of the Sepher
Yetzirah show scarcely any trace of an emanational
system. For Saadya Gaon there is one intermediary
between God and the world, but this is the physical
air and not the transcendental numerations. In this
air God is everywhere present, and it penetrates
all bodies, even the most compact. Of the doctrine
of *Ain Soph* there is also no real trace. It is,

---

* He describes the Kabalah as a most pure and holy philosophy,
but exhibits no acquaintance with the Zohar.
† Bartolocci, iv. 267.

however, recognised, on the one hand, that we cannot have an adequate notion of the Divinity or His correspondences with the world, but, on the other, that some approximate idea may be obtained as to the latter and that they may be shown forth by means of figures and comparisons. One of these illustrations tells us that God is the life of the world as the soul is the life of the body, and as in man the soul is all-powerful, so God is omnipotent in the world. He is also its Supreme Reason, and as in man the rational faculty is the guide of life, so the Divine Power is directed by the Divine Reason. Above this elementary and commonplace form of natural theology the commentary never soars, and we may be indeed warranted in saying that the work, as a whole, has no inherent interest, though it is valuable as a historical document.

Unlike the Sepher Yetzirah, which makes no reference to pneumatology, Saadya Gaon devotes a certain space to the consideration of the soul in man ; and here, in a sense, he connects with Zoharic Kabalism, though he rejects metempsychosis, for he recognises its five aspects and calls them by their conventional names, which names, however, occur, as we have seen, in the Talmud.* Unfortunately, his classification is exceedingly clumsy, and he begins by following Plato in the recognition of three faculties—reason, concupiscence and anger. On account of reason the soul is called *Neshamah*, on

---

* Despite his hostility to reincarnation as understood by the Kabalah he accepts the pre-existence of souls and teaches that the resurrection of the body will take place when all souls destined for earthly life have passed through it.

account of concupiscence it is called *Nephesh*, and on account of anger it is called *Ruach*. The two other names, *Chaiah* (living) and *Jechidah* (unique), refer to the vitality of the soul and to the fact that no other creature resembles it.

The doctrine concerning divine and angelic names is also the subject of some references which are important to our inquiry because they establish the fact that Saadya Gaon did not ascribe to them any occult virtue. The names of the angels vary according to the events which they are commissioned to accomplish, and, in like manner, those referred to the Deity are descriptive of His operations. In the work of the creation He terms Himself *Elohim*; when ordaining the covenant of circumcision He is called *El Shaddai*; He is the I AM in connection with the wonders of the ten plagues; and He is *Jah* when producing the great miracle of the Red Sea.* As it is with the names of God and the angels, so is it with those of the stars, which vary according to their qualities—namely, their greater or lesser brilliance, their hot or cold natures, &c.

When explaining the object of the Sepher Yetzirah as representing the manner in which created things come into being, there is a reference to the ten categories—namely, substance, quantity, quality,

---

* The Zohar teaches that the name AHIH, which signifies I AM. indicates the unification and concealment of all things in such a manner that no distinction can be established between them. The name ASLR AHIR, I WHO AM, represents God on the point of manifesting all thin , including His Supreme Name. On the other hand the name Jehovah or AHIH AShR AHIH, I AM HE WHO IS, refers to the Deity, or is that name assumed by Him, on the occasion of the manifestation of the Cosmos.—Zohar iii. 65*b*, Mantua.

relation, place, time, powers, position, activity, passivity, and if these are to be regarded as referring to the numerations of the Sepher Yetzirah, it is clear that Saadya Gaon understood the latter as an Aristotelian philosopher. With these categories, the ten commandments are also forced to correspond in an arbitrary manner. For example, that against adultery answers to the category of position, for the act itself is a position and a contact.

Lastly, in his analysis of the Hebrew alphabet, the commentator seeks to account for its sequence. *Aleph* is the first sound pronounced—*i.e.*, it is vocalised at the back of the tongue. *Shin* is vocalised in the middle of the mouth and *Mem* on the lips. Unfortunately for the analogy, *Mem* precedes *Shin* in the alphabet, and indeed the design of the speculation seems past conjecture.

About the commentary ascribed to Hay Gaon there is considerable confusion, which Isaac Myer increases by representing that it deals with the "Book of Concealment," instead of that of Formation. There are no historic notices and no traces whatsoever of the former tract before the appearance of the Zohar, in which it was first made known. The work of Hay Gaon needs only to be mentioned in passing on account of its disputed authenticity. Other works attributed to him are not above suspicion, but it may be admitted in a general way that he had more distinct Kabalistic connections than Saadya. The condemned commentary deals largely with the mysteries of the Tetragrammaton and gives perhaps for the first time the curious quadrilateral method of writing it by means of letters and circles, to which so much importance was afterwards attributed by occult writers.* The commentary of Abraham ben David Ha Levi,† the younger of that name and a contemporary of Maimonides, whom he attacked bitterly, is also included in the Mantua edition of the Book of Formation, and was used largely by Rittangelius in that of Amsterdam, 1642‡ The intensest confusion prevails with regard to the personality of the author, who, on the one hand, is frequently identified with the writer of the *Seder Ha Kabalah*, and is, on the other, the subject of many contradictory myths prevailing in occult circles. Éliphas Lévi, who cites a passage from his treatise as a proof of the authenticity and reality of his own " discovery " of the *Magnum Opus*,§ makes a great deal of mystery concerning it and its rarity, but he has used evidently the edition

---

* By Éliphas Levi above all, who reproduces its diagram with additions which I regard as fanciful (*Dogme de la Haute Magie*, section dealing with the Kabalah), and elsewhere (*La Science des Esprits*) illustrates these additions by a Kabalistic document which I think also is one of his specimens of invention.

† Bartolocci, i. 15.

‡ *Liber Jesirah* (Hebrew and Latin) *qui Abrahamo patriarchæ adscribitur, una cum commentario Rabbi Abraham* F. D. (*i.e.*, Ben Dior) *super* 32 *Semitis Sapientiæ .. Translatus et Notis illustratus à Joanne Stephano Rittangelio...Amstelodami*, 1642. The thirty-two Paths referred to at the beginning of the Sepher Yetzirah are given in Latin and Hebrew, each followed immediately by the commentary of R. Abraham, likewise in Latin and Hebrew. Then comes the explanation of Rittangelius, which sometimes extends to many pages, quoting many authorities, including the Zohar and its Supplements. After the Paths, we have the Sepher Yetzirah itself, in Latin and Hebrew, with the editor's commentary, also in both languages. It should be added that the entire commentary of R. Abraham is not given by Rittangelius, who is content with presenting that part only which is devoted to the Paths of Wisdom.

§ *Rituel de la Haute Magie*, c. 12, where the Hebrew passage cited is completely unintelligible. *Cf. La Clef des Grands Mysteres,* pp. 233, 234.

of Rittangelius, which is perfectly well known and attainable in almost any national library.

We have admitted that the commentary of Saadya Gaon can scarcely be termed Kabalistic ; we have agreed to set aside another which abounds in Kabalistic material because its date and attribution have been challenged ; in the work of R. Abraham, however, there are Zoharic elements which admit of no question, and it is indeed to the school which he represents that Graetz and others have referred the authorship of the Book of Splendour. There is the peculiar distinction between upper and lower *Sephiroth* which is not only characteristic of the Zoharic period, but offers a connecting link between R Abraham and the late Kabalism of Isaac de Loria.* But more than this, there is the doctrine of the Unknowable God, of " the Cause of Causes which is not apprehended by any one outside Itself," being void of all distinction and all mode of existence. It has not assumed the final shape in which it is presented by the Zohar, and it appears to be something more concealed and latent than the conception of *Ain Soph*, the *Non Ens* or *Corona Summa*, which again is distinguished by R. Abraham from *Kether*, the Crown of Creation, on the ground that " the accident is not made from the essence nor the *Res* from the *Non Res* or *Non Ens*," thus occasioning an insoluble difficulty as to the emanation of the manifest universe. For the rest, the *Ain Soph* of our commentator is described in terms which are almost identical with

---

* There is no doubt that the ten *Sephiroth* were an evolved system in the time of the Yetziratic commentator.

Zoharic teaching. "Neither unity nor plurality can be attributed to It, because unity cannot be ascribed to that which is incomprehensible in its essence," the reason being that number is an accident belonging to the world of extension, place and time.

Among minor Zoharic correspondences, it may be noted that a peculiar importance is attributed to the letter *Aleph ;* it is the form of all the letters, and all the paths of wisdom are contained therein, but after the universal mode. There are also traces of the peculiar angelical system which was destined to receive so much elaborate extension from the commentators on the Book of Splendour.

Before dismissing this commentary we may note the alleged connection of its author with that Abraham the Jew* who belongs to the literature of alchemy. The testament of this mysterious personage transformed Nicholas Flamel from a simple scrivener into a seeker after the Great Work—a search, moreover, which legend represents as a success. The memorial in question was addressed to the nation of Israel dispersed by the wrath of God in France, by one who styled himself " priest, prince, Levite, astrologer and philosopher." The description which constitutes our sole knowledge concerning it is given in another testament, that of Nicholas Flamel, and it is very difficult to decide how far this can be regarded as authentic. Belonging as they do to alchemy, there is no ground here to discuss their respective claims,

---

* This title is used by Bartolocci in his bibliography to describe numerous writers who cannot be more closely identified.

but it is well to say that the attempt made by Éliphas Lévi to identify the Abraham of Flamel with the commentator on the Sepher Yetzirah not only institutes a connection between alchemy and Kabalism which is unwarrantable in itself but has no colourable evidence to cite in its own support, as there is no trace whatever of any alchemical meaning in the Hebrew commentator. Abraham the Kabalist belongs to the twelfth century. Flamel was two hundred years later, and the book which he mentions could scarcely have existed in Jewry, on the Levi hypothesis, for such a space of time without something transpiring concerning it.

As a literary and philosophical work the first place among the dependencies of the Sepher Yetzirah seems correctly assigned to the commentary of Azariel. Its author was born at Valladolid in or about the year 1160. According to some authorities he was a pupil of Isaac the Blind,* but others say that his teacher was R. Jehuda, son of Rabad. He became in turn the instructor of R. Moses Nachmanides, who also belongs to the chain of Yetziratic tradition.†

He is said to have travelled much in search of secret wisdom, but it was an age when men of learning were frequently wanderers, and it was perhaps less recondite motives which actuated him· He connects with the Kabalistic system which was expounded by the school of Gerona, and there are no

---

* A.D. 1190 to *circa* 1210. He taught the doctrine of metempsychosis and a few fragments of his writings are still extant.

† And brought, as Graetz admits, the influence of his great reputation to bear upon its fortunes.

real grounds for supposing that he acquired knowledge elsewhere, but he added the result of his own reflections. Many works have been attributed to him, of which some are lost and some have remained in MS. "The Explanation of the Ten *Sephiroth* by way of Questions and Answers" must have helped to shape the metaphysical speculations of the Kabalah and may well enough have originated more than it derived.

The teachings of Azariel aroused the opposition of the Aristotelian Jews, and it is thought by Isaac Myer that the logical form of his commentary was a concession to this school of thought. Whatever its motive, the fact, broadly taken, is of importance to our inquiry; it shows that the Sephirotic notion in its earliest development could not really have been that of the categories, since it had to be conformed to the principles espoused by the disciples of Aristotle. The Jewish *literati* followed various schools, and the influence attributed to the Stagirite has perhaps been exaggerated. The votaries of the so-called secret wisdom were a small minority. Platonism, as it is needless to say, was very little known in the West at the period in question, though it appears in the later Kabalism.

As regards both matter and form, Azariel's commentary has been the subject of high praise. It contains the doctrine of *Ain Soph*, which is not in the Sepher Yetzirah, and it has express views on the emanation of the *Sephiroth*, which are said to be contained in *Ain Soph* and of no effect when separated. Their emanation was possible because it must be within the omnipotence of the Deity to assume a limit. The essence and the real principle of all finite things is the Thought of the Supreme Being; if that were withdrawn, they would be left as empty shells, and this is true not only of the visible world but of the intermediaries between God and the creation. With his philosophical speculations the Kabalist mingles something from the fantastic region, attributing, for example, certain symbolic colours to the *Sephiroth.* * *Kether* is " like the Concealed Light," or the light which is veiled in darkness, the comparison intended being probably that of a luminous mist. *Binah* is sky-blue, because *Binah* is the great sea of Kabalism. *Chokmah* is yellow, *Chesed* white and *Geburah* red ; *Tiphereth* is white, red, or pink, *Netzach* is whitish-red and *Hod* reddish-white. *Jesod* is the combination of the previous triad, while *Malkuth* is like the light which reflects all colours. Azariel also countenances the Sephirotic division of the human body which is found in later Kabalism.

Moses ben Nahman, or Nachmanides, was born in 1194 at Gironne. Before he made acquaintance with the Kabalah he is said to have had a prejudice against it, but he was afterwards an enthusiastic student both of its speculative and practical parts, and both by his writings and influence contributed much to its development. His Kabalistic " Explanation of the Law " was completed in 1268, and among his many other works that called the " Garden of Delight," and another on the " Secrets of the *Thorah*,"

---

* According to the Zohar the colour attributions are as follows : *Kether*, black, white, or colourless ; *Tiphereth*, purple ; *Malkuth*, clear sapphire.

are full of theosophical speculations.*   He left
his native land to settle in Palestine, where he
died, apparently at a great age, but at what precise
time is not known.

The commentary on the Sepher Yetzirah which
passes under the name of R. Eliezer seems to have
been the work of a German Jew of Germesheim,†
author of the " Vestment of the Lord," one of the
greatest Kabalists of his period.   That he was the
instructor of Moses Nachmanides, as some authorities
have stated, is, however, a mistake, as Basnage has
indicated, for he belongs to a later date.   His works,
which are wholly Kabalistic, are (1) " The Vestment
of the Lord," but this has never been printed·
(2) " The Guide of Sinners," exhorting them to
repentance and amendment of life (Venice, 1543).
(3) A Treatise on the Soul, cited by Mirandola in
his thesis against the astrologers. (4) An explanation
of Psalm cxlv.   (5) A commentary on the Sepher
Yetzirah, appended to the Mantua edition of that
work.   The author flourished before and after the
middle of the fourteenth century.   Commentaries
on the Sepher Yetzirah are ascribed to R. Aaron

---

* His other works include an epistle on the use of matrimony in
exercising the fear of God ; a work on the nature of man from the text
of II. Samuel, vii. 19 ; a book of Faith and Confidence ; another on
War₃ ; and yet another on the Pomegranate.   These are not professedly
Kabalistic, like the " Treasure of Life," the " Treasure of the Lord,"
the " Garden of Pleasure" (mentioned in the text above), or the mystical
epistle on the thing desired.   As regards the practical part of the
Kabalah, he treated it with grave consideration, including its arts of
necromancy, the evocation of evil spirits and the methods of their
control.

† Basnage, *Histoire des Juifs*, c. vii. t. v. p. 1859.   See also
Bartolocci.

he Great,* under the title of "Book of the Points";
R. Judas Levi ;† Sabbatai Donolo ;‡ Juda ben
Barzillai ;§ and Isaac the Blind.

---

* Bartolocci, i. 15.
† *Ibid.*
‡ Edited by M. Castelli. Florence, 1880.
§ Edited by M. Halbertstamm. Berlin, 1885.

BOOK V

.

THE WRITTEN WORD OF KABALISM :

SECOND PERIOD

ARGUMENT

The divisions of the Zohar are set forth in successive sections so as to furnish a clear and comprehensive notion of the materials incorporated by this composite work. Its doctrinal content is established by means of copious quotations, selected with special reference to its importance from an occult standpoint.

I. THE BOOK OF SPLENDOUR : ITS CONTENT AND DIVISIONS

THE cycle of the Sepher Yetzirah lies within a manageable compass, and its most important dependencies are all available to the student by means of Latin translations. The *Sepher Ha Zohar*, on the other hand, is large in itself, it has considerable supplementary matter belonging to a later period and an extensive connected literature ; it has not been translated into Latin nor into any European language.* The consequence, especially

---

* The Italian reader may, however, be referred to an analysis of the Zohar by the Abbé de Rossi, which appeared in his *Dizionario storico degli Autori Ebrei*. The writer follows Morin as to the late date of the work.

to esoteric students, has been very unfortunate.*
Great confusion has obtained in regard, firstly,
to the content of the work and, secondly, to
the comparative importance of its various divisions.
Part of this must be undoubtedly attributed to the
ambitious design of Rosenroth's great collection. The
Kabbala Denudata, by attempting to cover much too
wide a field, gives no adequate idea of the work
which it is meant to elucidate. It attributes an
exaggerated, though not inexcusable, importance to
three tracts introduced into the body of the Zohar
and to late commentary on these; the apparatus in
the form of a lexicon which fills most of the first
volume, though it has a methodical appearance, is
little more than a chaos, in which late and early
expositors are bundled together after the uncritical
manner of the period; in a later section undue
prominence is given to some personal discussions and
correspondence between the Editor and Henry More,
the English platonist; finally, the second volume
includes an enormous treatise on the doctrine of the
Revolutions of Souls by a Kabalist of the seventeenth
century. With all its defects the *Kabbala Denudata*
remains of real value, but it would have been beyond
all price had a clearer genius governed its arrangement. As it is, the class of persons who are most

---

* Outside esoteric students the case of Basnage may be mentioned
as that of a well-informed writer, whose history of the Jewish people
from the time of Jesus Christ to his own date—the beginning of the
eighteenth century—is memorable in several respects, yet whose knowledge of the Zohar does not even extend so far as it might have been
taken by Rosenroth. He terms (*Livre* iii. p. 775) the Book of Concealment the first part of the work, and seems to regard it as comprised
simply in that and the two Synods. In a word, he had not read the
preface to the *Kabbala Denudata*, vol. ii.

concerned with the subject have been content to
follow the lead of Rosenroth, and to accept a little
tract known as the "Book of Concealment" as the
fundamental part of the whole Zohar, and the
developments of that tract as entitled to the next
highest consideration.   There are, of course, many
sources of information, for the most part not of an
occult kind, by which this false impression might
have been corrected—the work of Franck in France
and that of Ginsburg in England, to name two only
—but it has endured notwithstanding, and the latest
instance is found in the latest work published by Dr.
Papus.   There the bibliographical appendix states
that "the only complete translation" of the Zohar is
that of M. H. Chateau,* whereas the enterprise in
question is confined only to the tracts rendered into
Latin by Rosenroth, and these have been available
for years in the English version of Mathers.   The
Book of Occultation and its Zoharistic commentaries
are only accidents of the Zohar, and they furnish no
real notion of the scope of that work.   I should add
that from the occult standpoint the Zohar itself is
only an accident of the Kabalah—an accident in the
life of the alleged tradition, much as, from the standpoint of Latin Christianity, the New Testament is
not the exclusive foundation of the Church but an
event in her development.

   The Zohar proper, as I have stated in my

---

* *Le Zohar, Traduction française et Commentaire de* M. H.
Chateau. The bibliographical annotation accredits the translator with
minutieuse érudition and adds that he has carefully collated the
Hebrew texts, the Latin and the other versions. The work is poorly
produced, it bears no trace of the scholarship imputed to it and the
commentary is of slight value.

preface, purports to be a commentary on the Pentateuch, and to indicate its general scope I shall deserve
well of my readers if I depart from my general rule
of confining quotations from modern authors to footnotes and summarise the admirable observations of
Ginsburg : " The Zohar does not (apparently) pro-
pound a regular Kabalistic system, but dilates upon
the diverse doctrines of this theosophy, as indicated
in the forms and ornaments of the Hebrew alphabet,
in the vowel points and accents, in the Divine Names
and the letters of which they are composed, in the
narratives of the Bible and in the traditional and
national stories. The long conversations between its
author, R. Simeon ben Jochai, and Moses, which it
records ; the short and pathetic prayers inserted
therein ; the religious anecdotes ; the attractive
spiritual explanation of Scripture passages, appealing
to the hearts and wants of men ; the descriptions of
the Deity and the *Sephiroth* under the tender forms
of human relationship, comprehensible to the finite
mind, such as father, mother, primeval man, matron,
bride, white head, the great and small face, the
luminous mirror, the higher heaven, the higher earth,
&c., which it gives on every page, made the Zohar a
welcome text-book for the students of the Kabalah,
who, by its vivid descriptions of Divine Love,* could
lose themselves in rapturous embraces with the
Deity."

We are placed by this quotation in a position to
understand, firstly, after what manner the literature

---

* It is in this respect that the Zohar suggests analogies with
Arabian Sufism.

of Kabalism affected the fervid imagination of the
Jew and the kind of influence which it had on him,
well illustrated in the fascinating and terrible histories
of Messianic enthusiasm and illusion, as already
noted. We can understand, secondly, how much
there is to correct in the occult theory which has fixed
upon the Zohar as embodying the traditional knowledge of a religion behind all religions. No system
responds less readily to what is involved in such a
conception; no person could be less disposed than
the occultist to accept the full Kabalistic notion of
religion, were he really acquainted therewith. The
philosophical doctrines which I have sketched in the
early sections of the previous book do certainly
connect superficially with occult philosophy, which
itself seems to connect magnetically with everything
that is unsound in faith and unreasonable in doctrine.
The connection in the present instance can only show
that neither is of serious account in the last analysis.
That God is immanent in the material world is a
much simpler and more rational hypothesis than to
establish intermediaries between finite and infinite,
which create innumerable difficulties without resolving
any. Far more truly philosophical is the doctrine of
the Countenances, which I have described already as
the chief glory of Kabalism, but, so far as all effect is
concerned, it has passed away, like the Shekinah from
the Holy Place. At the present day we have other
and better means of excusing the anthropomorphisms
of the Bible, and, for the rest, no attempt to excuse
them has any connection, approximate or remote,
with the ground which occult philosophy assumes to
cover

The Zohar is divided by Rosenroth, after a somewhat artificial manner, into internal and external parts.*

I. The internal parts are those which are combined together in one scheme. They are :

(*a*) The text of the Zohar, properly so called. Apart from all its additions this is not of unmanageable dimensions.

(*b*) The *Sepher Dzenioutha*, or Book of Concealment.

(*c*) The *Idrah Rabbah*, or Greater Synod.

(*d*) The *Idrah Zuta*, or Lesser Synod.

(*e*) *Sabah D'Mishpatim*, the Discourse or Story of the Ancient One in section *Mishpatim*.

(*f*) *Midrash Ruth*, or Commentary on the Scriptural book of that name. There are fragments only.

(*g*) *Sepher Ha Bahir*, the Renowned or Illustrious Book, sometimes called Book of Brightness.

(*h*) *Tosephthoth, Addenda*, or Additions.

(*i*) *Rayah Mehemnah*, or the Faithful Shepherd.

(*j*) *Haikluth*, *i.e.*, Palaces, Mansions, or Abodes.

(*k*) *Sithrai Thorah*, or Mysteries of the *Thorah*, *i.e.*, the Law.

(*l*) *Midrash Hannelam*, or the Secret Commentary.

(*m*) *Razé Derazin*, or Secret of Secrets.

From this account are omitted the following tracts and fragments, on the ground that they do not

---

* *Kabbala Denudata*, vol. ii. p. 8.

appear in the Mantua edition of *circa* 1558, known as the Little Zohar : *

(*a*) *Midrash Hazeeth*, or Commentary on the Song of Solomon.

(*b*) *Pekoodah*, or Explanation of the Thorah.

(*c*) *Yenookah*, or the Discourse of the Youth.

(*d*) *Maamar To Hazee*, or the discourse beginning, Come and See.

(*e*) *Hibboorah Kadmaá*, or Primary Assembly.

(*f*) *Mathanithan*, or Traditional Receptions.

The ground on which these portions are set aside appears insufficient, as the sections *e, f, g, j,* and *m* in the first tabulation are also wanting in the Mantua edition.   The Great Zohar, the Cremona edition (1558-60), contains all the treatises enumerated in both the above lists.   I am not aware that any superior authority resides in the Mantua Zohar.†

II. As understood by Rosenroth, the external parts are those superadded to the earlier editions. These are :

(*a*) *Tikkunim H'Zohar*, or Supplements of the Book of Splendour, called also the Ancient Supplements, to distinguish them from further and later additions.

(*b*) *Zohar Chadash*—the New Zohar, containing matters omitted in the printed editions.   This has four parts.

---

* The Greater Zohar being that of Cremona.   Blunt's Dictionary of Doctrinal and Historical Theology makes a ludicrous confusion over this point, representing the Greater Zohar as the commentary on Genesis and the Lesser as the Book of Concealment.

† A Hebrew translation in MS. by Barachiel ben Korba is preserved in the Library of Oppenheimer.

(1)

(1) The text of the Zohar itself, scattered through which is the supplement of the tract *Midrash Hannelam*, part of which appears in the original work.

(2) *Tikkunim Chadashim*, or New Supplements.

(3) *Zohar Shir Hashirim*, or Exposition of the Canticle of Canticles appertaining to the Zohar.

(4) *Zohar Aike*, or Exposition of Lamentations, appertaining to the Zohar.

In the above tabulations are contained everything of the Zohar that has come down to us.[*] It will be unnecessary to say that its authenticity did not increase with its bulk.

For the better comprehension of the cycle Rosenroth recommends:

(a) Sepher Deruk Ameth, that is, the Way of Truth, being various readings in the Zohar arranged according to the Mantuan edition.

(b) Binah Amri, or Words of Understanding, being an elucidation of difficulties in the Zoharistic vocabulary.

(c) Zohar Chamah, or Splendours of the Sun, being a short commentary which follows the Mantua edition.

(d) Pardes Rimmonim, or Garden of Pomegranates, by R. Moses of Cordova, an explanation of numerous texts in the Zohar and *Tikkunim*.

(e) Mequr Chokmah, or Fount of Wisdom,

---

* *Kabbala Denudata*, ii. p. 9.

forming a continuation or new part of the Way of Truth.

(f) Marah Kohen, or the Vision of the Priest, a synoptic work, the greater part of which appears in the *Kabbala Denudata*, vol. ii. part i.

(g) Zar Zahab, or a Crown of Gold, used largely in the apparatus of Rosenroth.

(h) Pathach Ainim, or Gate of the Eyes, for the Biblical quotations in the Zohar and *Tikkunim*.

Rosenroth also highly recommends and largely reproduces the vast manuscript treatises of Isaac de Loria, compiled by R. Chaiim Vital, and further acknowledges his indebtedness to two other unprinted works, a Kabalistic commentary on the whole Law and a treatise entitled *Chesed* Abraham.

The Zohar proper, the conversations of Simeon ben Jochai with the prophets by whom he was visited, with the disciples by whom he was surrounded and of these, as we have seen, with each other, is not a work that is to be judged by the same standard as the purely allegorical portions which have been incorporated therewith, and to which Christian students of Kabalism have given so much prominence. It is, in the first place, far more natural and comprehensible, less distorted by monstrous symbolism, having occasionally a touch of nature to indicate its kinship with humanity, and condescending even at times to a Rabelaisian episode.* Finally, it does not betray much trace

---

   ... hundred rabbinical histories, fables and apologues are narrated in it, sometimes elucidating a knotty point of Scripture, as, for example, whether the destruction of animal life at the Deluge may indicate that the beasts also sinned, sometimes recounting the death of a just man, sometimes describing visions and narrating tales of wonder.

of that inner meaning which is loosely supposed of its entire content, for the most part, by those who would and do likewise discern a latent transscendentalism in Pantagruelism.* To determine whether the work, as a whole, is important from the standpoint of modern occultism, I shall now give a short synopsis of its doctrine on several vital questions of religion and philosophy. We have seen that in a certain manner—somewhat occasional and informal—it is a commentary on the Pentateuch, and it is understood and passed over that it is a forced, arbitrary commentary, which has nothing in harmony with the simple sense of Scripture. It would serve no purpose to enlarge upon this fact, which applies to all Kabalistic exegesis. The governing principle of its interpretation or treatment is the existence of several senses in the written word. These are differently enumerated, and there seems no reason why they should not be extended indefinitely, but they are reducible broadly under three heads, which are compared by the Zohar to the garment, the body which is within it and the soul which is within the body. "There are those unwise," it says, "who behold how a man is vested in a comely garment, but see no farther, and take the garment for the body, whereas there is something more precious [than either], namely, the soul. The Law has also its body. Some of the commandments may be called the body of the Law, and the ordinary

---

* Following the lead of Éliphas Lévi, especially in *Le Sorcier de Meudon*.

recitals mingled therein are the garments which clothe this body. Simple folk observe only these garments, *i.e.*, the narrations of the Law, perceiving not that which they hide. Others more instructed do not give heed to the vestment but to the body which it covers. And there are the Wise, the servants of the Great King, who dwell on the heights of Sinai and concern themselves only with the soul, which is the foundation of all and the true Law. These shall be ready in the coming time to contemplate the soul of that soul which breathes in the Law."*

This passage illustrates what I mean by the added depth and significance which the Kabalah reads into the Bible,† and it is, I think, also an instance of the intellectual humility of the great rabbins of the Exile who confessed to a sense in Scripture which exceeded their loving penetration,‡ so that after all subtleties of exegesis, all the symposiums of synods, the Word of God issued in a mystery, and the key of this mystery was the reward of the just and wise man in the world to come.

The necessity of the manifold sense followed from the insufficiency of the letter. Simple recitals and common words suggested only the human lawgiver ; if those only were the sum of the *Thorah*, it would be possible to equal, perhaps even to excel

---

* Zohar, part iii. fol. 152*b*, Mantua edition.

† I mean, of course, *ex hypothesi*. The extracted sense was too often a ridiculous illusion.

‡ Mr. Isaac Myer supposes that the higher soul of the *Thorah* signifies God Himself, but no doubt it is the divine sense of the Word which gives knowledge of the Word Itself.

it. Moreover, the sayings of Esau, Hagar, Laban, of Balaam and Balaam's ass, could not be "the Law of Truth, the Perfect Law, the faithful witness of God."* And hence the transcendental meaning, in which was the true Law, was supposed, to save Israel from scepticism, and it postponed rationalistic criticism for some centuries. It led of course into extravagance ; the second sense became in its turn inadequate and one more concealed was inferred. So also, besides a general latent meaning, there was that more particular triple significance attributed to each several word. As the possibilities suggested by such a method are infinite, it is unnecessary to say that these senses were never methodised, or that the Zohar does not unfold in a consecutive form either the allegorical or mystical meaning. It gives glimpses only, and it may be in this sense that the original Zohar is said to have been a camel's load. That original was a latency in the minds of Kabalistic rabbins, but it was never written with pen.

As the Zohar establishes the necessity of the concealed meaning on the insufficiency of the outward, and as the sense of such insufficiency is indubitably a late event in the history of sacred documents, we have full evidence for deciding the value of the claim which it elsewhere makes to a high antiquity for its interpretation. Had the Jew never come in contact with culture outside Judea he would never have conceived the "tradition," and the kind of culture which helped him to the sense

---

* Mantua edition, fol. 149*b*.

of insufficiency is not to be looked for in Egypt or in Babylon, but in the Hellenised thought of Rome.*

Having established the general principle of Zoharic exegesis, let us see next the kind of light which it cast upon the letter of Scripture and, in the first place, upon the creation of man. We know that, according to Genesis, he was made of the dust of the earth, that the breath of life passed over him and that he became a living soul. The Zohar is able to tell us what transpired before this event: " When it entered into the will of the Holy One to create man, He called before Him many hosts of the superior angels and said unto them, ' It is my will to create man.' They answered Him, ' Man will not continue one night in his dignity.'† Then the Holy One extended His finger and burned them. Thereafter He summoned other hosts into His presence, saying unto them, ' It is my will to create man.' They answered, ' What is man that Thou rememberest him ?'‡ He said unto them, ' But this man shall be in our image, so that his wisdom shall be greater than your wisdom.' When *Elohim* had created man, when man had fallen into sin, going forth as one guilty, there came Uzza and Azael, saying to the Holy One, ' We have an

---

* It does not follow that the Kabalah is Platonism. It was the consequence of a contact, but the growth and the increase was in the mind of Jewry.

† The reference is to Ps. xlix. 12, and the pleasing anachronism, by which the angels are made to quote David before the creation of man, is paralleled, if Poe may be trusted, by the Aristotelian phrases which Milton puts into the mouth of Lucifer.

‡ Quoting Ps. viii. 4.

accusation against Thee. Behold this son of man whom Thou hast made, how he hath sinned before Thee.' He answered them, 'If ye had been in like case, ye would have done worse than he has.' What then did the Holy One? He cast them down from their sacred station, even from heaven.* It must be confessed that this ridiculous fable has neither an inward sense nor an outward light. We know that Latin Christianity has a legend of the fall of the angels which connects that event in some misty manner with the scheme of redemption; it is sufficiently childish, but it speaks with the tongue of seraphs in comparison with this history, in which the superior good sense of the hierarchy is punished by burning and expulsion. There are, of course, many other passages in the Zohar which are explanatory of the creation of man. The breath of life is said to be the holy soul which has its origin from the Life Divine, and thus man started on his mundane course with a sanctified natural life (*Nephesh*) communicated from the heavenly *Chaiah*. And in this connection there is a suggestive and beautiful thought. "So long as that holy soul communicates with the son of man, he is the well-beloved of his Master. How many keepers watch and encompass him on all sides! He is the symbol of goodness both above and below, and the Holy Shekinah rests upon him. But when he turns aside from this path the Shekinah abandons him, the holy soul has no longer any intercourse with him, and from the side of the mighty evil spirit [Samael]

---

* Zohar, edition of Zolkiew, iii. 208*a*.

there is put in action a spirit which goes up and down in the world, resting only in those places from which sanctity has withdrawn, and thus the child of man is corrupted."* We learn also that the Throne of Glory had six steps,† and man was created on the sixth day "because he is worthy to sit on this throne."‡ There are again obscure references to the original physical condition of humanity. Adam and Eve were created side by side, not face to face; that is, seemingly, there was not a "desire of the female towards the male."§ It does not, however, appear that the awakening of this desire was the real cause of the lapse from perfection, a notion quite discordant with rabbinical views upon the sanctity and symbolism of sexual intercourse. The Kabalah and the mysticism which led up to it offer a very high ideal of the nuptial state. It is true that in the fragments of the *Bahir* the sin of Eve is presented as sexual, but if this is to be understood literally it was one of monstrous intercourse. According to Maimonides, however, the serpent represented the imaginative faculty.

Enough has been quoted to show that there is a curious theosophic lore in the Zohar concerning the creation of man, but there is nothing of any real occult significance; it is suggestive occasionally with the suggestion that is never wanting in fable and mythos, and it is most interesting within its own sphere, which is that of mythology and not certainly

---

* Cremona ed., part ii. fol. 21*a*.

† *Ex Hypothesi*. The prototype of Solomon's throne, as described in I. Kings x. 19. The Throne of Glory is in the Briatic world.

‡ Cremona ed., part ii. fol. 25*a*.

§ *Ibid.* fol. 26*a*.

of mystic religion. We may take the inquiry a step further and ascertain what the Zohar teaches concerning the state of Adam prior to his fall. We are told that he was clothed "in the garment of the Upper Splendour,"* for which Jehovah Elohim afterwards substituted the garment of skin, thus indicating that the fall was followed by a change of physical condition. There is no need to mention that this legend prevailed in many Eastern mythologies; it is not, on the one hand, the special inheritance of the Kabalah, nor can the latter show that it really came by it through an oral succession from early times. As often happens in the Zohar, there is a poetical inference from the fable which is better than the fable itself. "The good deeds which the son of man accomplishes in this world draw from the Light of Glory above, and he prepares for himself a garment against the day when he shall enter that world and appear before the Holy Blessed One."†

The Fall of man in the Zohar, as in its connections, insists upon the fact that it was the serpent Samaél who brought death into the world; but this serpent is to some extent allegorical, and the lapse was a lapse of the soul by the desire of the things below it. The death seems to be spiritual, for it is said that "the serpent takes away the higher souls [*Neshamoth*] of all flesh."‡ The tree of the trespass was banished from Paradise,§ which sounds fantastic; but the tree is allegorical and moves with man

---

* Fol. 103*b*. *Cf*. Mantua Edition, ii. 229*b*.
† *Ibid*. Cf. the parallel mythos of Talmudic times, which represents good deeds as creating good angels.
‡ Cremona ed., part i. fol. 28*a*.
§ *Ibid*. fol. 126*b*.

through his pilgrimage. Adam also was the cause of the eternal banishment of his descendants. In dealing with other sections of the Zohar we shall have occasion to refer again to the mythos of the Fall and shall observe that it is further involved by the introduction of monstrous elements.

If we turn now to the mystery of original sin, we shall find that it is intensified rather than explained. In Psalm xci. 11, it is said: "He shall give His angels charge over thee, to keep thee in all thy ways," which passage the New Testament applies in a special manner to Christ. The Zohar explains it as follows: "When man comes into the world there appears in him at that moment the evil spirit which always arraigns him. . . . This evil spirit never forsakes man from the day that he is born into the world. But the good spirit comes to the man from the day that he is made clean. When does a man become clean? At the age of thirteen years. Then he joins himself with both spirits, one on the right hand and one on the left, even the good to the right and the evil to the left, and these are the two spirits which are appointed ever to remain by man. If he strive after perfection the evil spirit is restrained, so that the right rules the left, and then both unite to secure him in all his ways."* It follows from this statement that the child is delivered over to iniquity in an especial manner, as it does not receive the good angel until it reaches the age of puberty.

Closely connected with the doctrines of the Fall of man and original sin is that of the Messiah, who,

* *Ibid.* fol. _.b.

for Jew and Christian alike, is a deliverer and an atonement, and much that we find in the Zohar recalls a host of Talmudic speculations on the same subject. In common with all souls, that of the Messiah is pre-existent. It was the spirit of the King Messiah which brooded over the waters at the creation.* He governs both above and below, gladdening the heart of Israel, but a judgment on idolatrous nations. When the souls in the Garden of Eden behold the just suffering for their Master they return and inform the Messiah. "When they inform Him of the afflictions of Israel in exile, and of sinners in Israel who reflect not that they may know their Lord, He lifts up His voice and weeps, as it is written, 'He was wounded for our transgressions'" [Is. liii. 5].† We read, again, of a Palace of Wicked Children in the Garden of Eden, to which the Messiah repairs, and there invokes upon Himself all the tribulations of Israel. "If He had not thus taken upon Himself the punishments for the transgressions of the law, no man would be able to endure them."‡ More curious and more significant is the passage which follows immediately. "Whilst the children of Israel abode in the Holy Land, they averted from the world all pain and suffering [? in the sense of punishment for trespass] by their prayers, worship and sacrifice, but now this is performed by the Messiah," yet so long only as man remains in the world, for he must receive his retribution afterwards. As it does not appear that Jews or Gentiles really escape the consequences of their mis-

---

* Cremona ed., part i. fol. 127*b*.   † *Ibid.* part ii. fol. 95*b*.
‡ *Ibid.*

deeds, this notion of vicarious atonement is quite of the fantastic order. Elsewhere, however, it is said that the righteous are the sacrifice and the atonement of the world. We must remember that the Zohar is a medley, and that medleys are not in correspondence at all points. I must be content to refer briefly to a very long passage which has been the subject of much controversy as to the date of the Zohar and is concerned with the appearance of the Messiah. It will be a time of woe and salvation, and of special affliction for Israel, but "he who is persistent in the faith shall attain the joy of the King." After this tribulation further distress shall follow from the combination of nations and kings, and then a pillar of fire extending from heaven to earth shall become visible to all men, at which time the Messiah shall come forth from the Garden of Eden and appear in Galilee, which was the first province to suffer destruction in the Holy Land and is the first, therefore, in which He must reveal himself. Thence He shall stir up war against the whole world. There will be many signs in the heavens, stars warring against the star of the East, after which the Messiah will be invisible for twelve months and at the expiration of that period will be taken up into heaven to receive the Crown of the Kingdom. He will again reveal Himself and wage war against the whole world, &c.*

It is idle to suppose that such a Messianic doctrine,† or, speaking generally, the scheme of

---

* Zohar, ii. fol. 7, Amsterdam edition.

† For very full information on the whole subject, see A. Hilgen- feld's *Messias Judæorum*, Leipsic, 1869, and Vincent H. Stanton's " Jewish and Christian Messiah," Edinburgh, 1885.

Kabalistic scriptural interpretation, can have the slightest occult importance ; it is essentially a Jewish scheme, supposing the exclusive claim of Jewry to the divine election, and the last source to which we can look for confirmation of the romantic notion that a transcendental doctrine of absolute religion has been perpetuated from the far past. Understood as it actually is, a thesaurus of Jewish theosophy, Jewish visionary doctrines, Jewish yearning and aspirations, which, because Jewry is part of humanity, is in contact at a thousand points with the aspiration and yearning of the whole heart of the world, it is a priceless memorial, but it loses all its significance in the attempt to misplace it. Because it is theosophical although Jewish, it has, of course, its points of connection with other occult systems, and not infrequently with matters which are beyond the range of that which is understood by occultism, in a word, with the things of mysticism, as, for example, in its transcendental speculations on the identity of subject and object in God and perhaps even in the mystic experience of the soul. It enters a good deal into that strange doctrine of correspondences which we meet everywhere in the domain which is embraced in the higher understanding of the term Magic. It might be described indeed as the extended mystery of correspondence. "Whatsoever is found on earth," says the Zohar, "has its spiritual counterpart on high and is dependent on it. When the inferior part is influenced, that which is set over it in the upper world is also affected, because all are united." From this doctrine the art of talismanic magic is the first logical consequence.

Elsewhere it is said : "That which is above is in the likeness of that which is below, and the likeness of that which is below is in the sea [regarded as the mirror of the inferior heaven], but all is one." * This is, of course, identical with the pseudo-Hermetic maxim, *Quod superius est sicut quod inferius et quod inferius est sicut quod superius*, &c., which may even have been formulated along the lines of the Zohar.

The peculiar philosophical system of the Kabalah of course receives a very full development in its chief literary memorial, but we are sufficiently acquainted with the heads of this system to make extensive quotation superfluous. The primordial manifestation of the unknown God was the production of a luminous point, which is Kether, and it seems certain that hereby the Zohar understands the Ego, for it says expressly that this was the light which Elohim created before everything. The nucleus of the luminous point is Thought, which is the beginning of all things. In its union with the Spirit † it is called Binah, and the diffusion of this Spirit brings forth a Voice, which in turn produces the Word, for the Zohar is a philosophy of the Word.⁺ In this Thought the forms of all things were evolved. The light of the Divine Consciousness is therefore the first matter of the manifested universe. " When *Elohim* willed to make the world, He produced a concealed light from which all the manifested lights were afterwards radiated, thus forming the superior

* Zohar, Cremona, part ii. fol. 9a.   *Cf.* part i. fol. 91a.   " As it is in all things below, so it is above."

† Kether is itself the Spirit, according to the Sepher Yetzirah.

⁺ Cremona ed., part i. fol. 131a.

world," or *Atziluth*, from which the other worlds were subsequently emanated.* It is said also, as we have elsewhere seen, that "in the beginning was the will of the King, prior to any existence which came into being through emanation from this will."† With this will is connected the notion of thought as the principle of all things, but unrealised in the primordial condition, and contained within itself. The expansion of thought produces spirit, which next assumes the title of intelligence, in which state the thought is no longer self-centred. The spirit in the course of its development produces a voice or word, but the thought, the understanding and the word are one alone, while the thought itself is bound up with *Ain Soph* and is never separated therefrom. This is the significance of the Scriptural statement that Jehovah is one and his Name is one.‡ Among the most suggestive and also the most recurrent teachings is the importance and universality of man in the scheme of things. For the Zohar, as for the poet, the world is "a disguised humanity," and "all that interests a man is man." It was the form of celestial man that God assumed at the beginning of his manifestation. This is the Shekinah, this the Mercabah or chariot, and this also is the sacred name of Jehovah. The form of man comprises all that is in heaven or on earth, and prior to its manifestation no form could subsist. It is the perfection of faith in all things and the absolute form of all. It is the summary and the most exalted term of creation. As soon as man appeared all was

---

* *Ibid.*, fol. 3*a*, 24*b*, 98*b*.   † Crémona ed., part i. fol. 56.
‡ Zohar, i. 246*b*, Mantua.

completed, both of the world above and the world below. Even those physical parts which he puts aside ultimately are conformed to the secrets of the Supreme Wisdom. So also in his threefold nature he is a faithful image of that which passes on high, and the souls of the just are above all the powers and all the servitors that are on high.* There is even a certain withdrawn and inconceivable sense in which man through Sephirotic mediation brings the *latens Deitas* into manifestation, and as all things exist and subsist for man, so the problem of evil in the universe is solved in his interest, as it is the condition of his development ; while with a Catholic comprehensiveness which has no parallel in any sacred literature the scheme of human existence is regarded by the Zohar with an optimism strange in its profundity, from man's pre-existence in the archetypal world to the beatific vision, the absorption and the eternal nuptials which await him.

The pneumatology of the Zohar is more fully developed in the connections of that work than in the commentary proper. The spiritual man is the highest degree of creation ; in him it was completed and he comprises everything. The soul originates in the Supreme Intelligence. "At the time when the Holy Blessed One desired to create the world . . . . ., He formed all the souls which should be given afterwards to the children of men."† It is also stated expressly that the soul enters the body when her time has come with protestations, grief and unwillingness.

---

* Zohar, Mantua edition, ii. fol. 42 ; iii. 114*b* ; iii. 144*a* ; iii. 48*a* ; 191*a* ; ii. 142*a* ; i. 91*b*.

† *Ibid.*, part ii. fol. 43*b*.

It is equally clear that it acquires nothing by the experience, unless it be the dignity of an ordeal which has been withstood successfully, for " all that souls learn in this world they knew already before they came into the world, which follows from the Talmudic doctrine that they were acquainted with the whole *Thorah*.* Their proper end is the return into Deity, but there are various abiding places and destinies for the higher spiritual principles, and even in this life they may depart from an unclean person.† It may be added that souls are created in pairs, but these pairs do not invariably come at the same time into the world.

In the excerpts which have been now given the Zohar appears at its best, but I may observe in conclusion that, again after the manner of a medley, it combines with things precious others that are of little value and not a few that are indescribably foolish. There are, for example, gross absurdities in the pneumatological portions. When the soul enters the body of the infant it cannot find room and has to await the growth of its envelope in considerable dis-comfort. Points of this kind might be multiplied indefinitely. They extend to all departments of the doctrine and obtain especially concerning the resur-rection of the dead, which, according to the Zohar, as there is no need to say, is the restitution of the physical body together with its proper soul. As this resurrection can take place only in Palestine the bones of Israel in exile will be transported thither.

---

* *Ibid.*, part iii. fol. 28a. Compare, however, Franck, *La Kabbale*, p. 236, where the very opposite teaching is ascribed to the Zohar.

† *Ibid.*, part i. fol. 37b.

It may be added that the Zohar took the Sepher Yetzirah into its heart of hearts, dwelt upon it, extended, magnified, almost transformed its symbolism. The Hebrew letters which figure in the earlier tract as the instruments of creation are for it the ciphers or vestures of the written law, the expression of the *Thorah*, and the *Thorah* is the archetype of all the worlds. Whether or not we are able to agree with Franck that the Sepher Yetzirah ends where the Zohar commences, and that they are the exact complements of each other, it is certain that the instinct of the early students who singled the "Book of Formation" from the rest of the pre-Zoharic *Midrashim* was not at fault in regarding it as the head and source of Kabalism.

But, in conclusion, as there was an occultism and mysticism in Israel prior to the *Sepher Raziel* and to the Zohar, so both were incorporated in the latter; both in the process underwent a species of transmutation, and as I venture to think the process, like that "sea-change" of the poet, produced something more strange and rich.. There are, at least, flights of mystic thought and aspiration in this great book of theosophy which are unknown to Gebirol and Ibn Ezra, and are more direct and strong in their appeal to the inner consciousness of man in this dawn of the twentieth century than in the famous commentary of Azariel or in the School of Isaac the Blind. And to confess this is to confess out of hand that the Zohar has still a message for the mystic. Perhaps all that is of value therein would be contained within a few leaves, but, as said of the choicest poems of Coleridge, it should be bound in pure gold.

II. THE BOOK OF CONCEALMENT

The *Sepher Dzenioutha*, the Book of Concealment or of Occultation, to which so much prominence has been given by occult writers, is not, therefore, as they occasionally seem to suppose, the beginning of the great cycle entitled the Zohar. In the Sulzbach edition, edited by Rosenroth, it begins at fol. 176*b* and ends at fol. 178*b* of the second volume. Most editions are either paged in correspondence with one another or refer readers to the pagination of the previous codices. Among early codices that of Lublinensis follows the Cremona edition, which, though used by Rosenroth for his references, was regarded by him as inferior to the simultaneous or slightly prior edition of Mantua. The latter he terms invariably *Codex correctus*. From the silence of occultists on the subject of the Zohar proper it might be judged that they do not regard it as of great occult importance; but there is a simpler explanation, which, as seen, is not far to seek. The " Book of Concealment," on the contrary, though small in its dimensions, is of the highest occult importance; it is regarded as the root and foundation of the Zohar,* as it is generally understood, and also as the most ancient portion of that collection, which is almost

---

* Mathers, "Kabbalah Unveiled," p. 14.

provably correct.*   It has been said further that it is
a theogony comprised in a few pages, but with
developments more numerous than the Talmud.†   In
a word, for occultists, the Book of Concealment and
the Book of Formation are the fountain heads of all
Kabalism. The Hebrew term which is rendered
Mystery, Concealment, or Modesty by Isaac Myers, is
given as Concealed Mystery by Mathers, without
pretending that the version is actually literal. For
Sepher Deznioutha Rosenroth gives *Liber Occultationis*.‡   The work is concerned with the manifestation
of the Divine Being as the term of His concealment
in the eternity which preceded manifestation. The
first chapter deals with the development of the Vast
Countenance, the image of the Father of all things,
the *Macroprosopus*, when equilibrium had been
established in the universe of unbalanced forces. This
Countenance, which is referred to Kether, or the
Crown, is compared by the Zoharistic commentators
to the tongue of a balance, *lingula examinis*. When
equilibrium obtained, the Countenance was manifested, the Ancient of Days appeared, God issued
from His concealment.§   This symbolism of the
balance depicting the harmony of the universal order

* Myers, "Qabbalah," p. 118.
† Eliphas Lévi, *Le Livre des Splendeurs*, preface, p. ii. ;
"Mysteries of Magic," 2nd ed., p. 97.
‡ Rabbi Loria says that it refers to things which are secret and
should be kept secretly, and compares Prov. xxv. 2, The Glory of God
is to conceal the word. But he also supposes an allusion to the circumstances under which the work is reported to have been composed—
namely, during the concealment of R. Simeon for twelve years in a
cave.
§ See *Commentarius Generalis Methodicus . . . è Libro
Emek Hammelech* in *Kabbala Denudata*, vol. ii. p. 47 *et seq.* of the
second part.

is the key-note of the treatise, which, in its own words, is the book describing "the libration of the balance." The balance is suspended in the place which is no place, that is to say, in the abyss of Deity, and it is said to be the body of *Macroprosopus*, referring to the *Sephiroth* Wisdom and Understanding,* which are the sides of the balance. The Countenance, which no man knoweth, is secret in secret, and the hair of the head is like fine wool hanging in the equilibrium. The eyes are ever open, and the nostrils of the Ancient One are as two doors whence the Spirit goes forth over all things. But the dignity of all dignities is the beard of the Countenance, which also is the ornament of all. It covers not only *Macroprosopus* as with a vestment, but also the *Sephiroth* Wisdom and Understanding, called here the Father and the Mother,† descending even unto *Microprosopus*, and it is divided into thirteen portions, flowing down as far as the heart, but leaving the lips free. Blessed is he, says the text, who receiveth their kisses! From the thirteen portions there descend as many drops of purest balm, and in the influence of all do all things exist and all are concealed.

---

* "For Wisdom is on the right upon the side of Benignity; Understanding is on the left upon the side of severity; and the Crown is the tongue in the centre which abideth above them."—*Ibid.*, p. 48. The meaning of the symbolism is that the equilibrium between Justice and Mercy must be assumed before the universe, having man for its object, could become possible, and the source of this notion must be sought in the *Bereshith Rabbah*. Compare also the teaching of the pre-Zoharic *Midrash Conen*, according to which the Grace of God prevents the opposing forces out of which the world was created from mutual destruction.

† *Ie., Abba* and *Aima.*

The "Book of Concealment," though small, as
I have said, in its compass, is full of digressions
which destroy its continuity and make the sense
difficult to extract. In addition to the manifestation
of *Macroprosopus*, it shows how the Most Ancient
One expanded into *Microprosopus*, to whom is
referred the name *Tetragrammaton*, whereas " I am "
is that of the first Ancient.* The letter I, which
is the first of the *Tetragrammaton*, corresponds to
the *Sephira* Wisdom, the supernal H to Understanding, of which *Microprosopus* is the issue,
corresponding to the six *Sephiroth* from Mercy to
the Foundation inclusive, and referred to the letter
V. It will be seen, therefore, that the primal
manifestation of Deity, which is connected with
the conception of the Crown, has no other name
than that which proclaims His self-existence, and
that the Hebrew Jehovah is in a sense a reflected
God. *Macroprosopus*, although manifesting in the
Crown, is still regarded as ever hidden and concealed,
by way of antithesis in respect of *Microprosopus*, who
is both manifest and unmanifest. When the life-
giving influx rushes forth from the Ancient One,
amid the intolerable refulgence of that great light
the likeness of a head appears. The distinction
between the two Countenances is the distinction of
the profile and the full face, for whereas the God of
reflection is manifested fully, the Great Countenance
is only declared partially, whence it is perhaps inexact

---

* Compare Bk. ii. § 4, where it is stated that AHIH is referred to
Kether, *i.e.*, as representing the world of *Ain Soph* ; and the *Tetragrammaton* to *Atziluth* generally.   There are various aspects of the
symbolism, but they are not really in contradiction.

to speak of *Microprosopus* as a reflection,* as He is rather a second manifestation, taking place in the archetypal world.

From the sides of the Lesser Countenance depend black locks, flowing down to the ears; the eyes have a three-fold hue, resplendent with shining light; and a three-fold flame issues from the nostrils. The beard, considered in itself, has nine portions, but when that of *Macroprosopus* sheds down its light and influence they are found to be thirteen. Though the Ineffable Name is referred to the Vast Countenance, it is also said that the manifestation of *Microprosopus* is represented by the ordinary letters of the Tetragram, his occultation by the transposition of the letters.

The Book of Concealment is described in its closing words as the withdrawn and involved mystery of the King, and as it is added that "blessed is he who cometh and goeth therein, knowing its paths and ways," there is urgent need for some explanation of its significance. This, as we shall see later on, was unfolded in many rabbinical commentaries, which are all confessedly posterior to the period of the public promulgation of the Zohar. There are, however, two works possessing the same authority as the Book of Concealment, for which also the same authorship is claimed, and constituting extensions of that work. The first of these will be the subject of some consideration in the next section.

---

* It is the device of Éliphas Lévi and connects with his method of interpretation.

III. THE GREATER HOLY SYNOD

The Book of Concealment has been simplified to the utmost in the preceding account. It may be now added that it is anonymous ; it quotes no rabbinical writers and has no references by which a clue to its date may be obtained. It has, however, two characteristics which give it the appearance of a much older document than those which follow it immediately, and are designed, as already said, to develop and expound it. These are its rudeness and the mutilations which it would appear to have undergone. The first translator, Rosenroth, supplies the gaps and omissions thus occasioned by conjectural words and passages placed within brackets, but even with these it is in an exceedingly faulty state. The treatise now under consideration is in most respects entirely different. It possesses almost a literary aspect, begins in narrative form, methodises the ensuing dialogues in a manner which is perfectly explicit and stands in need of few emendations. It deals, of course, with the barbarous symbolism of the preceding book and so far is admittedly repellent to modern taste, a fact which has been noted by at least one sympathetic critic who was himself an elegant and highly suggestive writer.* The first point which otherwise calls for notice is that the Greater Sacred Synod claims Rabbi Simeon Ben Jochai as the author of the " Book of Concealment," and itself contains the discourses of this Master in Israel, delivered in a

---

* Eliphas Levi, *La Clef des Grands Mystères.*

field beneath trees in the presence of his disciples, namely, Rabbi Eleazar, his son, Rabbi Abba, Rabbi Jehuda, Rabbi Josi, the son of Jacob, Rabbi Isaac, Rabbi Chiskiah, the son of Rav, Rabbi Chia, Rabbi Josi and Rabbi Jisa. These are historical names belonging to the period which succeeded the destruction of Jerusalem.

For an account of Rabbi Simeon himself we must have recourse to tract Sabbath of the Talmud, Babylonian recension, which contains the narrative which I will here give in its substance :

"On a certain occasion R. Jehudah, R. Josi and R. Shimeon were sitting together, and with them also was Jehudah, the son of proselytes. R. Jehudah opened the conversation, saying, ' How beautiful are the works of this nation (the Romans). They have established markets ; they have built bridges ; they have opened bathing-houses.' Whereupon R. Josi was silent. But R. Shimeon ben Jochai answered, saying : ' All these things have they instituted for their own sake. Their markets are gathering-places for harlots ; they have built baths for their own enjoyment, and bridges to collect tolls from those who cross them.' Jehudah, the son of proselytes, repeated this conversation, and it came to the ears of Cæsar, who proclaimed : ' Jehudah, who extols us, shall be extolled ; Josi, who said nothing, shall be exiled to Saphoris (*i.e.*, Cyprus) ; Shimeon, who has disparaged us, shall be put to death.' R. Shimeon and his son then went out and hid themselves in the lecture-hall, but afterwards in a cave, where a miracle took place, a date-tree and a spring of water being raised up for them. They laid aside their garments

and sat covered with sand up to their necks, studying
the whole time, and assuming their vestures only at
prayer-time, for fear that the same might wear out.
In this wise they spent twelve years in the cave, when
Elijah came to the opening, and said : 'Who will
inform the son of Jochai that Cæsar is dead and his
decree is annulled?' Hereupon they left the cave."*
The secret wisdom embodied in the Zohar is supposed
to have been the fruit of the long seclusion enforced
upon R. Simeon by the Roman decree.

The Talmud mentions expressly the learning
obtained during this period, but without specifying its
kind, According to the tradition of the Kabalists
the "Book of Concealment" was the first form in
which it was reduced to writing. The discourses of
the "Greater Sacred Synod" were recorded by Rabbi
Abba and so also in the case of the "Lesser Synod."
When the conversation was about to begin a voice
heard in the air showed that the Supernal Synod had
assembled in heaven to hearken, and the commentators add that the souls of the just gathered
round the speakers, coming from their rest in
Paradise, and the Holy Shekinah of the Divine
Presence.

The explanations and developments concern the
world in its void state before the manifestation of
the Supreme Countenance, the conformations of that
Countenance, or *Macroprosopus*, as also of *Microprosopus*, the Lesser Countenance, and after what
manner the inferior depends from the superior. It
must be said that the expounding and the extension

---

* Rodkinson, Babylonian Talmud, vol. i. pp. 57-59.

neither are nor assume to be explanatory in the sense that they unfold the real significance of the symbolism. As a fact, the treatise ends, like all treatises concerned with the mysteries of initiation, by saying that he is blessed who has known and beheld the concealed words and does not err therein. In an account like the present, which does not even pretend to be synoptic, it is impossible to attempt a tabulation of the singular typology with which the Greater Synod is concerned, and it should be noted in this connection that the few modern writers on Kabalism who claim to speak magisterially and from within an occult circle of knowledge, may have shown us glimpses in one or two rare instances of the system on which the typology is constructed, but have done nothing to elucidate and therefore to recommend it to our understanding. It is a question which it is hard to approach from the side of the literal sense, and to the occult student, in the absence of initiation, the esoteric aspects of the literature are chiefly a subject of curious speculation. Fortunately it has other aspects which make it deserving of consideration, or there would be no purpose in the present inquiry.

The unbalanced forces of the universe, the world in its void state, are considered under the symbolism of the kings who reigned in Edom before a king was raised up to rule over the children of Israel, that is to say, before the emanation of *Microprosopus.**

---

* The Kabalah represents the present universe as preceded by others which passed away quickly. According to Basnage, this notion also occurs in the Talmud, where it is said, with characteristic crassness, that when God was alone, in order to kill time, He diverted

At that time there was neither beginning nor end, and the Edomite kings were without subsistence. According to Rosenroth this signifies the fall of creatures partly into a state of rest, such as that of matter, and partly into one of inordinate activity, such as that of the evil spirits, in which case we are dealing not so much with cosmology as with the legends of souls. So also when the "Greater Synod" represents the Ancient of Ancients creating and producing the essence of light, the same interpreter, who speaks with the authority of immense knowledge, as regards at least the literature of Kabalism, observes that the reference is to the Law,* in other words, to the letters of the alphabet, by the transpositions of which the Law was recorded subsequently. For the rest, symbolism of this order is not simplified by its multiplication, and the record of Rabbi Simeon's discourses is only the "Book of Concealment" dilated in a glass of vision. Compare, for example, the description of *Macroprosopus* with the indications on the same subject contained in the previous section. "White are His garments as snow, and His aspect is as a face manifested. He is seated upon a throne of glittering brightness, that He may subdue them. The whiteness of his bald head is extended into forty thousand worlds, and from the

---

Himself by the formation of divers worlds which He destroyed forthwith. These were successive attempts at creation, by which Deity became experienced and at last produced the existing physical order. —*Histoire des Juifs*, t. ii. p. 712. Compare also the *Pirké* of R. Eliezer, according to which the basis of the existing universe is the repentance of God over His previous failures. This work is referred to an early period of the ninth century. For other Zoharic references to this subject see *Zohar* ii. 20*a*, Mantua.

* Understood as the essence of the light.

light of the whiteness thereof shall the just receive four hundred worlds in the world to come." The Vast Countenance itself is said to extend into three hundred and seventy myriads of worlds. The brain concealed within the skull is the Hidden Wisdom, and the influence of this Wisdom passes through a channel below and issues by two and thirty paths. The hair of *Macroprosopus* radiates into four hundred and ten worlds, which are known only to the Ancient One. The parting of the hair is described as a path shining into two hundred and seventy worlds, and therefrom another path diffuses its light, and in this shall the just shine in the world to come. When the forehead of *Macroprosopus*, which is the benevolence of benevolences, is uncovered, the prayers of the Israelites are received, and the time of its uncovering is at the offering of evening prayer on the Sabbath. The forehead extends into two hundred and seventy thousand lights of the lights of the supernal Eden. For there is an Eden which shines in Eden; it is withdrawn in concealment, and is unknown to all but the Ancient One. The eyes of the Vast Countenance differ from other eyes, having neither lids nor brows, because the guardian of the supernal Israel knows no sleep. The two eyes shine as a single eye, and were that eye to close even for one moment the things which are could subsist no longer. Hence it is called the open eye, ever smiling, ever glad. In the nose of *Macroprosopus* one of the nostrils is life, and the other is the life of life. With regard to the Beard of the Vast Countenance, called otherwise the decoration of all decorations, neither superiors nor inferiors, neither men nor prophets nor

saints, have beheld it, for it is the truth of all truths.
Its thirteen forms are represented as powerful to
subdue and to soften all the stern decrees of the judgments. Thirteen chapters of the "Greater Synod"
are devoted to the consideration of this subject,
including the number of the locks in each portion,
the number of hairs in each lock and the number
of worlds attributed to them. This ends the
discourse concerning *Macroprosopus*, and the treatise
proceeds thence to the consideration of the
Lesser Countenance. The conformations of *Microprosopus* are disposed from the forms of the Vast
Countenance, and His components are expanded
on either side under a human form. When
the Lesser Countenance gazes on the Greater, all
inferiors are restored in order, and the Lesser is
vaster for the time being. There is an emanation
from the Greater towards the skull of the Lesser, and
thence to numberless lower skulls, and all together
reflect the brilliance of the whiteness of this emanation
towards the Ancient of Days. From the brain of
Macroprosopus an influence descends, from the hair
an emanation of splendour, from the forehead a
benevolence, from the eyes a radiance, from the
nostrils a spirit and the spirit of life, from the
cheeks gladness, and all these fall upon the Lesser
Countenance. From the brain of *Microprosopus*
there are emanations of wisdom, emanations of
understanding, and emanations of knowledge ; in
each lock of the hair of *Microprosopus* there are a
thousand utterances ; his forehead is the inspection of
inspection, and when it is uncovered sinners are
visited with judgment. For the lesson of the

"Greater Synod" is that wrath may dwell with *Microprosopus*, but not in the Ancient of Days. So also the eyes of the Lesser Countenance possess lids ; when the lids are closed judgments subdue the Israelites and the Gentiles have dominion over them. But the eyes, when they are open, are beautiful as those of the dove, for they are then illuminated by the good eye. With one of those pathetic touches which soften occasionally for a moment the unyielding lines of Kabalistic symbolism, it is said that two tears dwell in the eyes of the Lesser Countenance, and the Holy of Holies, when He wills to have mercy on the Israelites, sends down these two tears to grow sweet in the great sea of wisdom, and they issue therefrom in mercy upon the chosen people. The special seat of severity in *Microprosopus* is the nose, and judgment goes forth therefrom, except when the forehead of the Vast Countenance is uncovered, when mercy is found in all things.

As in the case of the Ancient of Ancients, the discourse appertaining to the beard of *Microprosopus* fills many chapters, full of strange scholia on various passages of Scripture, and details minutely the conformations of its nine divisions, what it conceals of the Lesser Countenance, what it permits to be manifested with observations on the descent of a holy and magnificent oil from the beard of *Macroprosopus* and a general description of the correspondences and differences of the two adornments.

It should be observed that the body of *Microprosopus* is androgyne, and as at this point the symbolism is concerned very largely with the sexual organs, it will be obvious that it becomes still more discordant with modern feeling, and exceeds occasionally what it is considered permissible to express in English. A modern symbologist has said that nature is not ashamed of her emblems,* and there is no doubt that for the Kabalist the body of man was peculiarly sacred, whence for him there would be nothing repellent in dealing exhaustively with its typology. But it will be unnecessary in a descriptive summary to do more than allude to it. The student who desires to pursue the subject must be referred to the Latin version.

The sum of the whole treatise may be given in the words of the original. "The Ancient of Ancients is in Microprosopus; all things are one; He was all things; He is all things; He will be all things; He shall know no change; He knoweth no change; He hath known no change."† Thus God in manifestation is not really separable from God in concealment, and if the symbolism depict Him in the likeness of humanity, it is by way of similitude and analogy.

At the conclusion of the "Greater Synod," we are told that three of the company died during the deliberations, and their souls were beheld by the remainder carried by angels behind the "veil expanded above."‡

Amidst all its obscurity and uncouthness there are sublime touches in this treatise. The Kabalah is perhaps the first of all books which appeared in the

---

* Gerald Massey on phallic symbols, in a letter contributed to the *Spiritualist*.

† *Idra Rabba, seu Synodus Magna,* sectio xxxix. par. 920, in *Kabbala Denudata,* t. ii.

‡ *Ibid.,* § xlv. par. 1138.

U

western world reciting with no uncertain voice that
God is altogether without mutation and vicissitude—
that wrath and judgment are of man alone, placing
thus a new construction on the divine warning,
" Judge not, lest ye be judged"; and showing also
the higher significance of the not less divine promise,
" I will repay." Never for the true Kabalist could
this mean that God would repay the sinner in his own
spirit, outrage for outrage, hate for hate. The repay-
ment of God is the compensation of the everlasting
justice or the gratuity of the everlasting bounty. In
a sense the writers of the Zohar anticipated the most
liberal conclusions of modern eschatology.* Amidst
the firebrands of the Papal Church, it promulgated
for the first time the real meaning of the forgiveness
of sins.

IV. THE LESSER HOLY SYNOD

Similar in most of its characteristics to the more
extended discourse which preceded it, the " Lesser
Holy Synod," or *Idra Zuta*, is termed by Rosenroth
the Swan's song of Simeon ben Jochai, a supplement to the subjects not exhaustively treated in
the Greater Assembly. As the master's death is
recorded at the end of the treatise, the translator's
words must be understood of the instruction it
contains and not of its setting. The Synod consists

---

* Franck summarises the position as follows :—Nothing is
absolutely evil, nothing is accursed for ever, not even the archangel of
evil, for a time will come when his name and angelic nature will be
restored to him. *La Kabbale*, p. 217.

of the survivors from the former conclave, with the addition of Rabbi Isaac. Simeon begins by affirming that it is a time of grace; he is conscious of his approaching end; he desires to enter without confusion into the world to come; and he designs to reveal those sacred things in the presence of the Shekinah which hitherto have been kept secret. Rabbi Abba is appointed as scribe, and Simeon is the sole speaker. The discourse still concerns *Macroprosopus* and *Microprosopus*, with the correspondences between them, but it sketches only the subject of the concealed Deity and deals at great length with the manifestation of the Lower Countenance. In both cases, as would indeed be expected, it repeats, substantially and verbally, much of the preceding Synod; but it gives some additional symbolism, as, for example, concerning the three heads of *Macroprosopus*, "one within the other and the other above the other," and at a later stage a very considerable extension of symbolism regarding the first manifestation of the Ancient One under the form of male and female, which is, in fact, the emanation or " forming forth " of the supernal *Sephiroth—Chokmah*, or Wisdom, and *Binah*, or Understanding. So also the instruction concerning *Microprosopus*, when it is not a close reflection of the "Greater Synod," deals with His androgyne nature and His union with the Bride, who cleaveth to the side of the male until she is separated, *et accedat ut copuletur cum eo*, face to face. Out of this comes the great Kabalistic doctrine of the sexes, so much in advance of its time, in whatever Christian century we may elect to place the literature, namely, that male and female separated are but mutilated humanity, or, as it expresses the idea, are but half the body, that no blessing can rest on what is mutilated and defective, that no divided being can subsist for ever, nor receive an eternal blessing, " for the beauty of the female is completed by the beauty of the male."* The conjunction of the supernal male and female is said to be in the place called Zion and Jerusalem, which further on are explained to signify Mercy and Justice. " When the Bride is united to the King in the excellence of the Sabbath, then are all things made one body. And then the most Holy God sitteth on His throne, then are all things called the complete name, the Holy Name. When this Mother is united to the King, all the worlds receive blessing and are found in the joy of the universe."†

About this point the discourse of Simeon ceases and Rabbi Abba, the scribe, still in the act of writing and expecting that more should follow, heard nothing. But afterwards a voice cried, " Length of Days and Years of Life," and yet another, " He seeketh Life from Thee." A fire abode in the house the whole day ; when it was taken away Rabbi Abba saw that the holy light, the holy of the holy ones, had been wrapped away from the world ; he lay upon his right side and a smile shone upon his face. Rabbi Eleazar, the son of Simeon, rose up and taking his hands, kissed them. " But I," says Abba, " licked the dust under his feet." It is added that during

---

* *Idra Zuta, seu Synodus Minor*, § viii. *passim.* The foundation of this mysticism concerning the nuptial state must be sought in Talmudic literature.

† *Ibid.*, § xxii. par. 746 *et seq.*

his obsequies the bier of the deceased saint was raised in the air, and fire shone about it, while a voice cried, "Enter in unto the nuptial joys of R. Simeon."

It will be seen that in spite of a somewhat monstrous symbolism the Kabalistic narratives have at times the touch of nature which gives them kinship with this world of ours.

V. THE DISCOURSE OF THE AGED MAN

The prominence given by Rosenroth to the Book of Concealment and its sequels was not without its warrant, as they are certainly the most arresting, I might almost say sensational, of all the tracts imbedded in the Zohar. Those which remain to be examined will now be taken in the order in which they are placed in the *Kabbala Denudata*, and their inferior, or at least more sober, interest will appear by the short analyses which will accompany their tabulation. The first to be enumerated is that entitled *Sabah D'Mishpatim* (*Historia de sene quodam in sectione Mishpatim*). The term *Sabah* signifies ancient man and Mishpat is judgment, referring to Exodus, from the beginning of c. xxi.—"Now these are the judgments"—to the conclusion of c. xxiv. The discourse occurs in the Cremona edition, pt. ii. fol. 43, col. 169; in the Mantua, vol. ii. fol. 94; in the Sulzbach, vol. ii. 94*a*. It narrates a conversation between the prophet Elias and Rabbi Simeon ben Jochai on the subject of the ordeals and metempsychosis of the soul, to which there are allusions at some length in the *Bereshith* section of the Zohar proper. Isaac de Loria's elaborate doctrine concerning the "Revolutions of Souls" is drawn from this discourse of Elias with the mystic light of Kabalism. We shall have again to consider this doctrine in connection with later Kabalism, in order to disabuse occultists of the idea that any reasonable view of reincarnation is contained in the Kabalistic writings. A specimen of the original text may, however, be given in this place, separated from many technicalities which would be burdensome to the beginner.

" All souls go up with the revolutions or windings [that is, are subjected to the law of transmigration], but the children of man do not know the ways of the Holy One ; they know not how He judges the children of man every day in all time, how the spirits (*Neshamoth*, the higher soul, *anima animæ* of Christian theology) ascend to be judged before they descend into this world, or again how they go up to judgment after that they have departed from this world ; to how many revolutions and mysterious ordeals they (or their essential substances) are subjected by the Holy Blessed One ; how many naked souls and how many naked spirits enter the other world, yet not through the King's curtain ; how many worlds revolve with them and how the world itself turns about in many concealed wonders. And the children of men do not know, neither do they comprehend, how souls revolve like a stone which is cast from a sling, even as it is written : 'And the souls of thine enemies them shall He sling out, as out of the middle of a sling.' But while it is permitted to reveal, now is the time to make known all these mysteries, and how all the spirits go out from that great tree and from that mighty river which flows from Eden, but the lesser spirits (*Ruachin, Ruach,* the *anima* or *pysche*) issue from the small tree. The higher spirit comes from above, the lesser from below, and they are united as male and female."*

The Kabalistic division of the soul into five parts has been given in Book II. of the present work with the necessary elucidations. The basis of the doctrine is set forth as follows in the "Discourse of the Ancient One":

"When the child of man is born into this world there is appointed to him animated life (*Nephesh*) from the side of the animals, the clean side, from the side of the Holy. Wheels (the *Auphanim,* a Kabalistic order of angels, assigned by some attributions to *Chokmah*). Should he deserve more there is appointed to him a rational spirit (*Ruach*) from the side of the Holy Living Creatures (*Chaioth Ha Kadosh,* another order of angels, commonly attributed to *Kether,* which seems, however, inconsistent with this tabulation). Should he still deserve more there is appointed to him a higher spirit, even from the side of the Thrones (*i.e., Aralim,* the order of angels ascribed to *Binah,* whence come the higher souls, according to the *Bereshith* section of the Zohar proper). These three are the mother, the male servant and the handmaid, even the Daughter of the King. Should he deserve yet more there is appointed to him an animal soul (*Nephesh*) in the

---

* Zohar, Cremona ed. part ii. fol. 45*a.*

way of *Atziluth* (that is, the lowest essence of the supernal portions of the soul), from the side of the Daughter, *Jechida*, the only one (*Jechida* is the quintessence, the highest nature of the soul), and the same is called Daughter of the King. If he still deserve more, there is appointed to him the rational spirit (*Ruach*) of *Atziluth*, from the side of the Central Pillar (that is, Benignity, the middle pillar of the Sephirotic Tree), and he is called the Son of the Holy Blessed One, whence it is written : 'Ye are the children of the Lord your God (Deut. xiv. 1). And if he deserve even more there is appointed to him a higher spirit (*Neshamah*) from the side of *Abbah* (the supernal Father, attributed to *Chokmah* in the Atzilutic world) and of the Supernal Mother (*Aimah*, attributed to *Binah* in the same world), whence it is also written : 'And He breathed into his nostrils the breath of life' (literally, souls of life, Gen. ii. 7). What is life? It is *Jah* (the Divine Name attributed to *Chokmah*), whence we have heard : 'Let everything that hath breath (*i.e.*, life, *i.e.*, all souls) praise the Lord' (*i.e.*, *Jah*), (Ps. cl. 6). And in it is Tetragrammaton (*i.e.*, J.D.V.D., *i.e.*, JHVH) perfected. But if he deserve still more there is appointed to him JDVD, in its full completeness, the letters of which are Jod, He, Vau, He: Heh, Vau, Heh, Jod, which is man in the path of *Atziluth*, and he is then said to be in the likeness (*simulacrum*) of his Lord, whence also it is said : 'And have dominion over the fish of the sea' (Gen. i. 28)), that is, he shall rule over all the heavens and over all the *Auphanim* and *Seraphim*, over all the Hosts and Powers, above and below. When, therefore, the child of man deserves the *Nephesh* from the side of the daughter *Jechida*, this is to say: 'She shall not go out as the men-servants do'" (meaning probably that he shall serve God in His house for ever, Exod. xxi. 7).*

This passage is worth quoting not only as an illustration of the discourse in which it occurs, but because it gives a clue to the probable meaning of occultists when they speak of a concealed sense in the Zohar. It is not to be supposed that when Kabalism divides and subdivides the soul it means anything else than to distinguish certain essences and qualities therein; in a word, it means what it says, just as modern theosophy does at the present day when it affirms seven principles in man. The concealed sense of the Zohar, as before indicated, is simply the extraction of some method from its vast and confused mass, which at first sight appears altogether delirious. In the present instance it will be seen that the animistic nature of man has a sevenfold aspect, whereas other Kabalistic dicta really extend it to ten. When these discrepancies are harmonised we have the concealed sense of the Zohar as to the inner nature of man.

Perhaps we might reach it by supposing that the discourse of Elias really describes the development of mystic experiences in seven stages, ending, as it states literally, in the communication of the divine to man.

---

* Zohar, ii. 94*b*, Brody ed.

VI. THE ILLUSTRIOUS BOOK

Excerpts of considerable length, purporting to come from a work entitled *Sepher Ha Bahir*, or *Liber Illustris*, are given in the Cremona edition of the Zohar at the places which here follow. Part I., col. 76, 79, 82, 86, 88, 104, 110, 112, 122, 125, 127, 130, 137, 138, 185, 241, 462. Part II., col. 145 and 259. Part III., col. 151, 176, 301, and 333. They are omitted in the so-called "Little Zohar" of Mantua, but reappear in Rosenroth's Sulzbach edition and in those of later date which are based thereon. In 1651 these excerpts were brought together into a volume and published at Amsterdam, which was at that period a great stronghold of Jewry. A reprint of this volume appeared at Berlin in 1706. Some interesting but complex questions are involved in the consideration of this work, which is thus known to us only by quotations. It is alleged on the one hand to be of higher antiquity than any Kabalistic book and hence of superior importance to the Sepher Yetzirah itself; on the other it is affirmed to be a manifest forgery, included in the condemnation of the Zohar, and by implication also the fruit of the inventive faculty of Moses de Leon. Between these extreme views there is placed that which considers the extant extracts unauthentic but believes in the existence of an old Kabalistic treatise, under the same title, which is now lost. An examination of the ascertainable facts does not, I think, compel our respect for any one of these opinions, and a more modest, indeterminate conclusion will perhaps be the safest to form. In other words, there is evidence that the *Sepher Ha Bahir* was in existence prior to the promulgation of the Zohar,* but there is no evidence that it preceded it by a considerable period, and there are no means of knowing whether or not the extracts which occur in the Zohar represent in some sense the original work.

It is to be regretted that occult students have passed over the fragments of the *Sepher Ha Bahir* as they have passed over the Zohar proper, and for the same reason, namely, because it is not available by translation. It would have been interesting to know whether they would have accepted the Kabalistic legend which has gone abroad concerning it. Of that legend one aspect appears in the bibliography of Papus, which, however, indicates no first-hand research, and simply reproduces information of which Molitor is the avowed source. In the "Methodised Summary of the Kabalah" the president of all Martinism ascribes the *Sepher Ha Bahir*, which he renders "Light in the Darkness," to R. Nechoniah ben Hakannah, the master of R. Ismaelis ben Eliezer, the high-priest, who flourished during the half-century preceding the birth of Christ. Such is the Kabalistic legend concerning the authorship of the work. Some notable sayings of Nechoniah are preserved in the Talmudic collections, and other works are also ascribed to him, namely :

(*a*) Letter on Mysteries or Secrets concerning

---

* Because it was denounced as a forgery by Rabbi Meir ben Simon in the first half of the thirteenth century, thus antedating the period at which hostile criticism places the public appearances of the Zohar. Graetz ascribes the forgery to Azariel himself, on what grounds may be gathered from the general warrant of his Kabalistic criticism.

the advent of Messiah, His divinity, incarnation and resurrection. This epistle was addressed to his son, who is said to have embraced Christianity. It betrays the hand of a Christian, and there can at least be no question that it is a late imposture. Paulus de Heredia Hispanus translated it into Latin and dedicated it to Henry of Mendoza, legate of the King of Spain.

(*b*) *Sepher Kanah*, the Book of the Fragments of the Temple, but this is also attributed to Ismael (Samuel) ben Eliezer. It is in any case another forgery, which deals with the generation of Christ, embodying apocryphal narratives taken from the Talmud.

(*c*) A Kabalistic Prayer, to be recited by pupils on entering or leaving the gymnasium. It is included among the *Mishnayoth*, a fact which shows that it is not Kabalistic in the proper sense of the term.

(*d*) *Sepher Happeliah.*

(*e*) *Sepher Haminchad*, concerning the mystery of the name of God, a work akin to the *Bahir.*

The other aspect of Kabalistic legend concerning the " Illustrious Book " may be used to colour the pretension that the Zoharistic quotations do not represent the original. It is said to be of such profound occult significance that it has been preserved among the hidden treasures of Israel, *in Manus Cabbalistorum Gennanorum*, says Wolf,* quoting Shem Tob. Buxtorf,† Bartolocci‡ and Buddæus,§

---

* *Bibliotheca Hebræa.*
† *Bibliotheca Hebræa Rabbinica.*
‡ *Bibliotheca Magna Rabbinica.*
§ *Introductio ad Historiam Philosophiæ Hebræorum.*

relate the same story, but none of them challenge the excerpts found in the Zohar, receiving them explicitly as genuine, while all likewise agree that the *Bahir* was regarded by Kabalists as their oldest document. The question of authenticity was in recent times first raised by Simon, who, speaking of the book printed in Holland, observes : " It does not appear that this is the ancient *Bahir* of the Jews, which is much more extended and has not yet been printed."* It is obvious that this is neither the language of criticism nor of knowledge ; we may infer that Simon was unacquainted with the fact that the Amsterdam publication only collected the Zoharic extracts, and that he might not have impeached the extracts had he been aware of that circumstance. Bartolocci mentions a general opinion that manuscript copies of the *Bahir* were to be found in many Continental libraries and particularises one such MS. in the Vatican collection.

The impeachment of the Zoharic excerpts naturally became part of the general charge against the Zohar itself ; the theory which ascribed that work to Moses de Leon was exceedingly comprehensive and made a clean sweep of everything included therein. It finds an almost exact parallel in the consistent application of those principles which are held to prove the Baconian authorship of the Shakespeare plays ; serving equally well for Marlowe, Massinger and all Elizabethan literature, that literature directly or indirectly is attributed to Bacon. Legend says as we have seen, that the complete Zohar was origin-

* *Histoire Critique du Vieux Testament.*

ally a camel's load ; were the whole of it now extant
no doubt the Jew of Leon would still have been its
exclusive author. Raymond Lully is said to have
written five hundred separate treatises ; the list
may be seen in the first volume of an unfinished and
impossible attempt to collect them into a folio edition,
the editor supplying not only the precise years but
the months in which they were composed. What
Raymond did, as they say, could not have been impossible to Moses. But, as a fact, the *doctor illuminatus*
wrote only a low percentage out of all that gorgeous
list, and reasonable criticism regards the spendthrift
Israelite as a possible compiler and polisher who
may have played a little at "writing out of his own
head," and that is all, not, however, because it regards
the Zohar as the work of Simeon ben Jochai, or even
of R Abba, but because it regards R. Moses as
human.

Graetz, the German historian of Jewry, whose
distinctive criticism of Kabalistic literature has
obtained much vogue, lays down a principle of criticism which ought to be written in capitals at the head
of most impeachments of the Zohar, namely that it is
not compulsory for a hostile critic to be more careful
in his arguments than those who plead in defence.
Without seeking to determine what is compulsory in
criticism, it may be observed that there is also no
binding law to enforce serious consideration for a
scholar who adopts that principle. What Graetz did
openly has been done tacitly or unconsciously by
others. Taking the case now under notice, I do not
know of one instance in which the challenge of
authenticity has been accompanied by an assigned

reason ; it is simply part of the programme to get rid anyhow of anything which goes to show that the whole Zohar was not written at the end of the thirteenth century. The reason is not far to seek ; the excerpts from the *Bahir*, if genuine, involve the existence not merely of purely Kabalistic but of typically Zoharic teaching prior to that date ; as this proves too much for the imposture theory, they are set down as part of the imposture. One critic who espouses the antiquity of the Zohar has, however, rejected the *Bahir*. He says : " The *Sepher Ha Bahir*, attributed to Nechonia ben Hakana, contemporary of Hillel the Elder and Herod the Great, is often cited. Various fragments, manifestly unauthentic, still pass for extracts from this book."* Perhaps so ; but why, if so ? It is for some determinate and material reason that one looks and waits in vain, failing which the identity of the Zohar quotations with the original must be accepted as a tolerable hypothesis, because no reason has been given to the contrary. It is quite another thing to affirm that they are the work of Nechoniah, or that they are older than the Sepher Yetzirah. Placing this cosmogony somewhere about the ninth century, because it was then almost indubitably quoted and it is not worth while to dispute as to how long it antedates the first reference made to it ; regarding the Zohar itself as, at least, a gradual growth between that period and the date of its publication, there seems no objection to considering the *Bahir* a

* Adolphe Franck, *La Kabbale, ou la Philosophie Religieuse des Hébreux.* Paris. 1843. If the unauthentic nature follows from the fact that it is falsely attributed, then the Sepher Yetzirah belongs to the same category.

production of the formative age of the work which is made to quote it. When the extracts were inserted therein we do not know; absent from the Mantua edition, which was simultaneous with that of the Cremona codex which contains them, it is possible that they were first added when the Zohar was prepared for press under the supervision of R. Isaac Delates, that unknown but "highly learned Jew unsurpassable in all the branches of knowledge required," whom the publisher describes. In this case, they have no connection with Moses de Leon.

There is, of course, little unanimity in hostile or indeed any Kabalistic criticism. As, on the one hand, a defender of the Zohar challenges the *Bahir* excerpts, so the latter have been exalted as the prototype and actual inspirer of the former work. This view, though in any case of little moment, involves the existence of the *Bahir* prior to the alleged date about which the Zohar was produced out of the head of Moses de Leon, like Minerva out of the head of Jupiter, ready made and at one leap. Morinus, who has left perhaps the most sensible review of the subject, founds his opinion that the *Bahir* was a product of the thirteenth century, on the silence of writers prior to that date, and especially of Moses Nachmanides, a Kabalistic Jew of Jerusalem, whose literary labours belong to the period before and after 1250. According to Wolf the first reference to the *Bahir* is made by R. Shem Tob, who was a contemporary of Moses de Leon, but belonging to a younger generation. This, however, is a mistake, because R. Azariel, the author of the great treatise on the Sephirotic system, and born, as we have seen, about 1160, in his commentary on the Canticle of

Canticles, sometimes ascribed to Nachmanides, quotes
the *Bahir*, not under its own name but under that of
Yerushalmi. The proof is that the Italian Jew
Recanati, contemporary of Moses de Leon, used these
quotations, and, misled by the name, inferred that
they were from the Jerusalem Talmud, but afterwards
discovered them in the *Bahir*, to which a Palestinian
origin is ascribed. By how much the lost treatise
antedated Azariel we have no ground for conjecturing,
but the position of Wolf and Morinus is destroyed by
the fact here recorded, which leaves the *Bahir* where
we should be disposed to place it, between the date
when the Sepher Yetzirah is first mentioned and the
publication of the Zohar.

The name *Bahir* is referred to Job xxxvii. 21 :
" And now men see not the bright light which is in
the clouds," according to the Authorised Version, or
according to Dr. Durell's amended rendering, " And
now men see not the light which is above (or
within) the clouds, &c." Hence " light in darkness,"
is a good equivalent of the Hebrew word. The
subject-matter of the book, which is in the form of a
dialogue between certain illuminated doctors, is the
mystery inherent in the divine names, and it contains
a very full exposition of the celebrated *Shemaham-
phoras*, the expounded name of deity. It belongs
therefore to the least philosophical part of Kabalism,
and we can understand and sympathise with the
instinctive dislike of Franck to accept the excerpts
by which it is known to us. Facts, however, must
have precedence of predilections, and though the
later history of the doctrine of divine names may well
make an admirer of the higher Kabalism ashamed of

k

the connection, it is far older than that of the *Sephiroth* or the two Countenances. Some other matters are also discussed, including a single reference to *Ain Soph*, and the two quotations which here follow exhibit a close connection between the *Bahir* and the " Discourse of the Ancient Man." The first concerns *Jechidah*, the fifth principle of the human soul.

" It is written : The silver is mine and the gold is mine, saith the Lord of Hosts. What does this mean ? It is like unto a king having two treasures, one of silver and one of gold. The first he put to his right and the second to his left, saying : This is prepared so that it is easy to spend it. He has done everything in an easy way. Hence it is said : Thy right hand, O Lord, is become glorious in power. (Ex. xv. 6). If a man may rejoice in his inheritance, it is good, but if not, it is said : Thy right hand, O Lord, hath dashed in pieces the enemy. (*Ibid.*) What does this signify ? Surely this is the gold. It is written : The silver is mine and the gold is mine. Why do they call it gold ? Because three measures are included in it. [That is to say, the word consists of three letters, Z H B, *Dzain, He, Beth*]. The *Dzain* is seven measures [*i.e.*, this letter represents the number 7] ; the *He* is Unity [*i.e.*, A Ch D V Th, Unity=419=5 according to Kabalistic addition, and 5 is the number of *He*] ; the *Beth* [representing the number 2] signifies *Chokmah* and *Binah*, and they are called *Neshamah* because of the last five *Sephiroth*. The *Neshamah* has five names : *Nephesh, Ruach, Neshamah, Chaiah* and *Jechidah*." *

---

* Zohar, Cremona ed., part i. fol. 116*b* and 117*a*.

The second excerpt concerns the Fall of Man, and its quotation is of some importance for the purpose of this study.

" It is written : Now the serpent was more subtle than any beast of the field (Gen. iii. i.). R. Isaac said : That [the serpent] is the evil inclination. R. Judah said : It is a real serpent. When they came to R. Simeon, he said unto them : Surely it is all one ; This is Samael, and he has been seen upon a serpent, but his shadow and the serpent are Satan, yet all are one. When Samael descended from heaven, riding on this serpent, and his shadow was seen, all creatures fled from him, but coming to the woman with soft words he brought death to the whole world. Surely with wiles he invoked curses on the world and despoiled the first tree which the Holy Blessed One created in the world. [The reference here is apparently to the Sephirotic tree and, by implication, to the primordial Adam. Compare the Kabalistic thesis of Picus de Mirandola · *Peccatum Adæ fuit truncatio Malkuth ab arbore Sephirotico.*] The *Neshamah* of the male comes from male, and of the female from female [*i.e.*, from the male and female sides of the Sephirotic tree]. This is why the serpent had recourse to Chavah. He said unto himself : Because her soul is from the North I can persuade her quickly. [The North, says Myer, is the left side, facing eastward in worship ; it is therefore the side of wrath and severity, connected by the Kabalists with the idea of the female. But the *Tikkune Ha Zohar* terms *Netzach* and *Hod* the *latera Aquilonis*. There is no con sistency in these attributions.] And the persuasion has been because he came on her. The disciples

asked : How did he that? He said unto them :
He, Samaël, the wicked one, intrigued with all the
hosts above against his Master, because the Holy
Blessed One had said unto Adam : Thou shalt have
dominion over the fish of the sea and over the fowl
of the air [understood of the evil spirits and the
angels]. Samaël asked : How therefore can I make
Adam sin before Him, so that he shall be driven
away from His sight? So he descended with all
his hosts, and he sought upon the earth a companion
like unto himself, but it had an appearance even
as a camel. [This curious comparison is based on
the fact that the Hebrew G M L means camel when
certain vowel points are added to these consonants,
and reward or recompense with others. The significance of this is developed in the *Pekude* section
of the Zohar, commenting on Gen. xxiv. 64 : And
Rebekah lifted up her eyes, and when she saw Isaac,
she lighted off her camel. The camel is here said
to signify the mystery of death, referred to in
Prov. xix. 17 : That which he hath given will He
pay him again. The connecting idea is, firstly, that
reward, in the sense of retribution, came into the
world by the serpent, and, secondly, that the peculiar
nature of the Fall is indicated by the alleged hidden
sense of the term camel which represents the *pudenda*.
Compare Cazotte's *Diable Amoureux*, where the
impure demon is revealed at last with the head of
that animal.] So he rode upon it and came to
the woman and said unto her : Did not *Elohim*
forbid thee to partake of any of the trees in the
garden? She answered : We have been forbidden
only the tree of knowledge which is in the garden ;

of that only did *Elohim* say, Ye shall not partake thereof, neither touch it, lest ye die. What, then, did Samael the wicked one? He touched the tree, and the tree cried out. Then said Samael: Lo, I have touched the tree, yet I have not died. Do thou touch it, and thou also shalt not die. Whereupon the woman laid hold of the tree, and beholding the angel of death approach her, she said: Surely I shall now die, and the Holy Blessed one will form another woman and will give her to Adam. But I will do thus; I will cause him to eat with me, so that if we die we shall die together, and if we live we shall live together. . . . Then the Holy Blessed One said unto her: Is it not enough that thou hast sinned but thou must also bring sin unto Adam? Then answered she: Lord of the world, the serpent induced me that I should sin before Thee. So the Holy Blessed One caused all three to come before Him and condemned them with nine curses and with death. He also cast Samael and his followers down from the place of their holiness in heaven; He cut the feet off the serpent and cursed him, yea, more than all beasts, and commanded that he should lose his skin after seven years."[*]

I have said that this passage is of importance to our subject, because it shows the kind of light which Kabalistic literature casts upon the first and greatest event in the spiritual history of man as it is presented by Scripture. Literal or mystical, the story of the Fall is not elucidated by the addition of monstrous elements, and the occult student in

---

[*] Zohar, Cremona ed., part i. fol. 28*a*, *b*.

particular will feel that the *Sepher Ha Bahir* exhibits in this place neither depth nor dignity. Like the Zohar itself, and most other tracts which it embodies, it has occasionally a suggestive passage. For example, it affirms that the world to come is a world that has come to pass already, because six out of the seven portions of the primordial light which was produced by God for the creation of the universe are reserved as the portion of the just in the life which is beyond.

It remains to say that William Postel is reported to have rendered the *Bahir* into Latin, but, if so, I can find no record that the translation was ever printed.

VII. THE FAITHFUL SHEPHERD

The Zoharistic treatise bearing this title records conversations between Simeon ben Jochai and Moses, who appeared to the great light of Kabalism and gave him many instructions and revelations. Elias took part in the conference, and the witnesses included not only Abraham, Isaac, Jacob, Aaron, David and Solomon, but God Himself. This indicates that in spite of the transcendental doctrine of *Ain Soph* and the Two Countenances, the Zohar recurs occasionally to the same anthropomorphic conceptions that are found in the Talmud. Ginsburg says: " The chief object of this portion is to show the twofold and allegorical import of the Mosaic commandments and prohibitions, as well as of the Rabinical injunctions and religious practices which obtained in the course

of time." The extant excerpts from these discourses
are dispersed through the Cremona edition in the
following order : Part I., col. 104, 126, 207, 211, 214,
247, 322, 343, 346, 378, 483 ; Part II., col. 72, 165,
203, 281, 328 ; Part III., col. 1, 26, 32, 42, 45, 47, 56, 57,
79, 122, 144, 147, 171, 187, 209, 214, 233, 235, 277, 289,
329, 332, 339, 343, 394, 400, 404, 408, 41'3, 422, 429,
430, 431, 432, 433, 434, 447, 451, 456, 457, 458, 459,
460, 461, 466, 468, 472, 519, 534. As regards their
authenticity, Franck classes these excerpts along with
those of the *Bahir*, but, as in that instance so in this,
he gives no account of his suspicions, which may be
taken, however, to follow from his conviction that
much of the Zohar is really attributable to the period
of Simeon ben Jochai and the disciples that came
after him. In either case, the "Discourse of the
Faithful Shepherd" contains much that is important
to our purpose. Its views on vicarious atonement
and on the Messiah to come will enable us to appreciate further the value of the occult standpoint ; some
of its moral teachings will illustrate its ethical
position ; its references to the Shekinah will cast light
on this curious feature of Kabalism ; and its speculations on angels and demons will show the Zoharistic
foundation for the later system of pneumatology
which was developed by Isaac de Loria.

The discourse introduces two phases of vicarious
atonement. the one effected through the sufferings of just men and the other by means of the
Messiah.

"When the righteous are afflicted by disease or
other sufferings in atonement for the sins of the
world, it is so ordered that all the sinners of their

generation may obtain redemption. How is this demonstrated? By every member of the physical body. When all these are suffering through some evil disease, one of them is afflicted [*i.e.*, by the instrument of the leech] so that the others may recover. Which member? The arm. It is chastised by the blood being drawn from it, which ensures healing in all the other members of the body. It is in like manner with the children of the world; the members are in relation with each other even as those of the body. When the Holy Blessed One willeth the health of the world, He afflicts a just man therein with pain and sickness and heals the rest through him. How is this shown? It is written: But He was wounded for our transgressions, He was bruised for our iniquities: the chastisement of our peace was upon Him, and with His stripes we are healed (Isa. liii. 5). ' By his stripes,' as by the bruises [incisions] made in bleeding the arm, are we healed, that is, recovery is insured to us as members of one body."*

Here, it will be said, the Kabalah recognises the great and fruitful doctrine of the solidarity of humanity. That is quite true, and it is one of those instances wherein Jewish theosophy has forestalled modern ideas. But if we take the illustration which it gives, we shall see that it is fantastic in character; the affliction of a diseased rabbi does not as a fact benefit his neighbour physically, and only on the most arbitrary hypothesis can we suppose that the patience with which he may suffer will reflect credit

---

* Zohar, Cremona ed., part iii. fol. 101a.

on any one but himself. It would be barely reasonable to dispute about such a position were it not necessary to show occultists the real messages of the Kabalah on points with which they are concerned. Now the modern students of occult philosophy everywhere reject with disdain the doctrine of vicarious atonement. Let us pass thence to the question of Messianic atonement, concerning which it is said in the Vision of the Faithful Shepherd :

"This is also exemplified in the history of Job. For the Holy Blessed One, seeing that the entire foundation was sinful, and how Satan appeared to accuse them, said unto Him, ' Hast thou considered my servant Job, that there is none like him in the earth' (Job i. 8), to save his generation through him ? " This may be illustrated by the parable of a shepherd who beheld a wolf approaching to rend his sheep and destroy them. What did this shepherd ? Being wise, he gave unto the wolf the strongest and stoutest bell-wether, even that which the flock was accustomed to follow, and while the wolf was bearing it away, the shepherd hurried with his sheep to a place of safety, and then returning rescued the bell-wether from the wolf. So does the Holy Blessed One deal with a generation : He surrenders a righteous man into the power of the accuser for the salvation of the generation through him. But when such an one is strong like Jacob, it is said, A man wrestled with him (Gen. xxxii. 24). But he (Satan) will be unable to prevail, and in the end he will supplicate the righteous man to release him *Ibid.* 26), for the righteous man, chosen by the Holy Blessed One, is too strong for the evil one and bears the most cruel afflictions willingly for the redemption of his generation; whence also he is held as their saviour, and the Holy Blessed One constitutes him shepherd over all the flock, to feed them in this world and to rule over them in the world to come."*

The clumsy and inadequate parable which thus represents the Almighty flying from Satan as the shepherd flies from a wolf, and in accordance with which the just man is at first compared to a bell-wether and afterwards to the shepherd of the flock, is something more than a literary failure. Theologians have, I believe, found some trouble in locating the accuser of Job, and it is perhaps most accurate to say with the poet that "He, too, is God's minister," but the Zoharic commentary on Job makes him in most respects a match for the Almighty, who must have recourse to a stratagem in order to save his people. The Kabalah on the problem of evil is therefore, in this place, neither illuminating nor reassuring; it is, in fact, crass and childish. "The ancient pillars of the world [the intellectual luminaries of Israel] differ," says the same disquisition, as to the nationality of Job. One affirms that he was a righteous Gentile who was chastised for the atonement of the world. At a certain time R. Hammarumnah met the prophet Elijah and said to him: How is it to be understood that the righteous man suffers while the wicked one has joy of his life? He answered, saying, The just man of few sins receives his punishment for these in this world, and hence it is that he suffers here; but the man whose sins are many, while his good deeds

---

* Zohar, Cremona ed., part ii. fol. 100b.

are few, receives recompense for the latter in this
world and hence has the joy of life."*

In this instance the Kabalah offers an explanation
which, shallow though it be, is identical with that
accepted by some sections of Christian theology, by
which, however, it is applied more mischievously.
Thus, not only the sporadic good actions of those
who are wicked habitually but all natural goodness
can find their reward only in this world. The
Kabalah is not disfigured by methodised enormities
of this kind. There are times also in which it loses
its grotesqueness for a moment, and by some not
unhappy reference to Scripture illustrates an elementary spiritual truth, as, for example, concerning the
change necessary to sinners.

" Those who are oppressed with sin need a change
of place, a change of name and a change in their
actions, even as it was said unto Abraham : Get thee
out of thy country (Gen. xii. 1). Here is a change
of place. And : Neither shall thy name any more
be called Abram, but thy name shall be Abraham
(Gen. xvii. 5). Here is a change of name. A change
of deeds : he changed from his former evil actions to
good actions."† The Christian mystic might develop
the significance of this quotation in connection with
the new name of the Apocalypse, the new name
received in confirmation, ordination and the monastic
and conventual life. Such analogies, though suggestive,
are of slender value ; the change mentioned in the

---

* Zohar, Cremona ed., part ii. fol. 106b. Compare the Mantua
edition, 1, 6, 8, where it is said that the pure man is in himself a true
sacrifice and that the just are the expiation of the universe.

† Zohar, Cremona ed., part ii. fol. 98b.

Zohar has indeed no special mystical importance; it concerns only the initial fact of spiritual life.

We have seen in the fragments of the *Bahir* that the scriptural history of the Fall of man is disfigured rather than elucidated by Zoharic commentary. The consequences of the first sin are thus described in the Faithful Shepherd.

"Come, see! Had Adam not sinned man would have known not the taste of death before he ascended to the superior world, but having sinned he became acquainted with the taste of death before ascending to the world above. Through the sin of Adam the rational spirit (*Ruach*) is separated from the body which remains in this world. It has to cleanse itself in the river of fire (Dan. vii. 10), to receive punishment, after which it goes up to the Garden of Eden, which is above the earth, and there are prepared for it other garments of light, in conformity with the appearance of the body in the present world; it is clothed therein and therein is its habitation for ever."*

This passage is important because it shows that Jewish theosophy has nothing better to offer us than the old Biblical instruction that sin "brought death into the world and all our woes." It is not our purpose here to question that doctrine, but simply to demonstrate that the Zohar, where it is intelligible, does not improve on accepted religious instruction.

Let us now select an instance from one of those portions which are more peculiarly Kabalistic in their

---

* *Ibid.*, part iii. fol. 79*b*. According to the *Idra Zuta* the Upper or true Eden is the principle of life and understanding.

subject. The Zoharistic speculations on the Shekinah
have an air of mystic symbolism which would be
perhaps naturally wanting in commentary upon
ordinary doctrinal matters. It is said that the
relation of the Shekinah to the other lights of creation
is like that of the soul to the body, but she—for the
divine manifestation is presented under a feminine
aspect—"stands to the Holy Blessed One as the body
stands to the soul." In this, of course, there is nothing
profound ; the Shekinah is the vestment of the
Almighty. But the discourse of the Faithful Shepherd
adds that all are one, that is, God is one with His
manifestation. This may be illustrated by the much
more interesting and spiritual doctrine of the
Eucharist ; the bread is the vestment of Christ, the
mode of His manifestation in His Church, but Christ,
by the hypothesis of the doctrine, is one with the veil
which He assumes. It is otherwise in man, says the
Zohar. "His body is earth, but the soul is called
reason. The one is death, the other is life." This is
the ascetic notion which modern occultism has agreed
to reject. "But the Holy Blessed One is life, and the
Shekinah also is life. Whence it is written : She
[meaning the Shekinah, but the Scriptual reference
is to Wisdom] is a tree of life to them that can lay
hold upon her" (Prov. iii. 18). The Shekinah of
Kabalism is not, however, merely the visible splendour
which shone in the Holy of Holies. The Faithful
Shepherd affirms that the Holy Blessed One is con
cealed in the mysteries of the *Thorah* and is known
or manifested by the commandments, for these are
His Shekinah and this is His image. This is a very
beautiful, spiritual and poetic conception, and it does

not need the gift of the mystic to understand and
appreciate it. It is one of those instances in which
we feel that a depth is added to the sacred tales of
Jewry. We may not at this day feel disposed to
accept literally and, so to speak, physically the alleged
manifestation in the Temple ; here the Zohar helps
us to something truer and profounder than the letter
of the legend, and we acknowledge gladly that the
little people of Palestine, encompassed by the
idolatrous nations, had truly something of the divine
in the law which was given them. The passage
continues : " As He is humble, so is the Shekinah
humility ; as He is benevolent, so is she benevolence ;
as He is strong, so is she the strength of all the
nations of the world ; as He is the truth, so is she
the truth ; as He is the prophet, so is she the
prophetess ; as He is righteous, so is she righteousness ; as He is King, so is she Queen ; as He is
wise, so is she wisdom ; as He is intelligent, so is
she His intelligence ; as He is the crown, so is she
His diadem, the diadem of glory. Therefore the
masters have decided that all those whose inward
part is not like unto the outward semblance shall
have no admission to the house of the doctrine.
As the image of the Holy Blessed One, whose
interior He is, whose outward splendour is the
Shekinah ; He, his interior internally, she his exterior
externally, so that no difference subsists between
her the outward and Him the inward, as she is an
outflow from Him, and hence all difference is removed
between external and internal, and as, further, the
inner nature of YHVH is concealed, therefore is
He only named with the name of the Shekinah,

Adonai ; hence the masters say, Not as I am written [YHVH] am I read."*

The connection between the Shekinah and *Malkuth*, in the light of the alleged unity of God and the vestment which conceals Him, suggests the identity of the divine and the universe, but it is only in the sense of immanence. The Kabalah, as we have seen many times, is in some respects the very opposite of pantheism.

Our quotations must close with a few references to the pneumatology of the Faithful Shepherd. They concern, firstly, the great Presence Angel Metatron, who is the sole occupant of the Briatic world, as the supernal Adam is of that of *Atziluth*. He is the garment of Shaddai. According to some his form is that of a boy, while others ascribe to this angel a female aspect. This shows a connection with the Shekinah, and indeed Metatron, with the difference of an added letter, signifies the cohabiting glory.† There is, secondly, some information con cerning Samaël, or Satan, and his wife Lilith. The first was once a servant of the Holy Blessed One and the second a maid of Matroncetha.‡ Their ultimate destruction is hinted, but meanwhile Lilith is the devastation of the world and the lash in the hands of the Holy Blessed One to strike the guilty. So she, too, is God's minister.

---

* Zohar, Cremona ed., part ii. fol. 106a, Myer, " Philosophy of Ibn Gebirol," p. 341.

† *Ibid.*, part iii. fol. 106b.

‡ Zohar, Cremona ed., part iii. fol. 134b.

VIII. THE HIDDEN THINGS OF THE LAW

The extant morsels of this work are located by Rosenroth as follows in the Cremona edition: Part I., col. 221, 258, 262, 370. Part II., col. 250. Dr. Ginsburg has discovered others in the Amsterdam edition, to which his references are made. They traverse ground covered by other sections of the Zohar, such as the evolution of the *Sephiroth*, the emanation of the primordial light and so forth. In a word, the contents show nothing which need detain us long. As an example of the puerility and pretensions of its exegesis, let us take the following passage :

"It is written, If thou faint in the day of adversity, thy strength is small (Prov. xxiv. 10). 'Thy strength'; this means, if his grasp on the *Thorah* become languid. 'In the day of adversity'; this means, when he so weakens his strength becomes small [thus changing the simple statement of Scripture into a foolish platitude.] What is meant by 'thy strength becomes small'? It means *Ko-a'h* [the initials of words signifying the Throne of Glory]. Then the evil is expelled, so that it cannot come near man and cannot accuse him [the meaning seems to be that when a man does not weaken in adversity, his strength is like that of the right hand, the Throne of Glory being on the right of God]. But when man deviates from the *Thorah* [or has a weak hold thereon], then the strength is the strength of the left hand, because that evil which is the left side rules over man and sets aside the Throne of

Glory." * On the whole, we shall most of us prefer
to conclude simply with Solomon that giving way in
the day of adversity is a sign of weakness. Those
who prefer the Mysteries of the *Thorah* have full
opportunities for entering more deeply into the
significance of Solomon's homely aphorism, for they
have only to remember that the Throne of Glory is
a title of *Tiphereth*, and of *Malkuth* occasionally,
because it is the seat of *Tiphereth*.

In a more notable passage, which is supposed by
Myer to distinguish certain stages of mystic vision, it
is said that the will of the King is discovered in three
colours. The first is above and so far away that no
eye can perceive it in its purity, but it is distinguished
(dimly) by contracting the range of vision [*i.e.*, by the
closing of the eyelids, as in blinking]. The second
colour is seen with one eye shut, and cannot be
seen by the other eye except when that eye is shut
so that it can see little, as in blinking. The clearness
of the light could not be endured otherwise. Of this
it is written, What seest thou? [Jer. i. 11. The
prophet, however, did not see the will of God but a
branch of an almond-tree]. The third colour is that
bright luminous mirror which cannot be looked into
at all, except between the rolling of the eyes when
the lids are altogether closed and they move in their
sockets. There can then be seen in that rolling the
light of the luminous mirror, and the colour thereof
can be comprehended only by him who beholds the
shining with eyes shut, whence it is written, The hand
of the Lord was upon me (Ezek. xxxvii. 1), and The

* * *

* *Ibid.*, part i. fol. 89a.

hand of the Lord was upon me in the evening (*Ibid.* xxxii. 22).* No doubt the Kabalists had visions and means of inducing visions, as also had Boehme, St. John of the Cross and all the seers and mystics, but this clumsy process confuses cause and effect, while it offers no intelligible result.

As another example, let us see what the Mysteries of the *Thorah* can tell us of the three angels who appeared to Abraham.

"It is written, And lo, three men stood by him (Gen. xviii. 2). These are three angels, clothed in ether, which came down to this world, and were seen in appearance even as a child of man. And they were three like that above, because the rainbow is only seen in three colours [this point should interest ethnologists]. Surely this is so. And these are three men ; three colours, white, red and green. The white is Michael, because he is the right side ; the red is Gabriel, because he is the left side ; and the green is Raphael. And these three colours are those of the rainbow, because it is never seen otherwise than with them. Hence it is written, And the Lord appeared unto him [Abraham] in the plains of Mamre (Gen. xviii. 1), that is, the Shekinah revealed itself in these three colours. It is also written, And they that be wise shall shine as the brightness of the firmament (Dan. xii. 3). They shall shine with a light which is enkindled by igniting a splendour. That brilliant light which is hidden, the spark of all sparks, of all lights, is therein invisible and hidden, concealed and made known, seen and not beheld. This shining

---

* Zohar, Cremona ed., part i. fol. 66*a*.

light came out from the supreme fountain of enlightenment, shown in the day and hidden at night. And this is the only thing seen, wherein all colours are concealed, and it is called by the name YHVH."*

The account in Genesis, upon which this pretends to be a commentary, is exceedingly perplexing, and to say that the three men are three angels clothed in the light of the Shekinah scarcely removes the difficulties. The explanations of Christian interpreters may not be wholly satisfactory, but they are much better than the Zohar in any instance, and more especially in that section which dissolves the mysteries of the *Thorah* by a process of multiplication.

As a specimen of the demonology in the *Sithrai Thorah* one quotation may be appended :

" When man joins himself with the truth, that is, the *Thorah*, he requires proving in the same place where his father was put to the proof ; so shall he ascend perfect and shall return perfect. Adam went up, but, not watching over himself, he was enticed by that harlot, even the first serpent, and sinned with her [*i.e.*, Lilith]. It is written, And Jacob passed out from Beersheba, and went toward Haran (Gen. xxviii. 10). 'And went toward Haran,' that is, the side of the harlot, which is a mystery. 'From the strength of Isaac,' that is, from the strength of judgment, from the lees of old wine, went out a spark which comprised male and female, and it spread itself out to many sides and into many paths. The male is called Samael, and the female is always comprised

* Zohar, Cremona ed., part i. fol. 89*b*.

in him ; as it is on the holy, so is it on the evil side, male and female are merged one in the other. The female of Samael, which is the serpent, is called the harlot." *

IX. THE SECRET COMMENTARY

We know that Scott provided headings to very many chapters of his romances by pretended quotations from old plays which existed only in his imagination, and it occasionally happened that these mythical excerpts contained stronger lines than much of his acknowledged versecraft. Those who believe that Moses de Leon wrote the Zohar out of his own head will account in a similar manner for the manifold fragments of unknown treatises which are found only in that work. Of some of these it may also be said that they are more interesting than the Zohar proper. As we have seen, the whole world of Kabalism has agreed to exalt the "Book of Concealment" over all the other discourses attributed to Simeon ben Jochai, but for the purposes of our present inquiry it must be confessed that considerable interest attaches to the "Secret Commentary." The extant fragments of this work are found in the Cremona edition at the following places: Part I., col. 257, 260, 261, 264, 265, 268, 269, 272, 273, 276, 296, 370. The field which they cover is chiefly that of the destiny of souls, future punishments and rewards, the resurrection of the body and the doctrine

---

* Zohar, Cremona ed., part i. fol. 86a.

concerning angels and demons. The connection of
the soul with the body and the perfection which
is to come for both are the subjects of the following
passage :

" R. Abbah the Ancient rose up upon his feet
and said : Rest and peace shall be thine, R. Simeon
ben Jochai, for thou hast brought back the crown,
that is, the *Thorah*. We have learned in the
Mathnuthah Kadmoah that because the higher soul
[*Neshamah*] dwells in its perfection in the upper
place [*i.e.*, prior to birth], it has no desire towards
the body except to create from it other similar souls
[*Neshamoth*]. These come out of her, but she abides
in her place. Thereupon R. Simeon ben Jochai
stood up and explained : If in this world which is
vanity, into this body which is a fetid particle, the
Neshamah yet enters, verily, in the time to come,
when all are made clean, when the body will be
in the fulness of its perfection, the perfect *Neshamah*
will enter therein, in the world above. R. Acha also
said : This very soul and this very body the Holy
Blessed One is prepared in the time to come to
establish in eternal continuance, but both will be
perfect in the perfection of knowledge, attaining to
that which cannot be reached in this world." *

Occultists are accustomed to regard the re-
assumption of the same physical body by the
progressed and glorified spirit as an unphilosophical
and material doctrine, not at all of that kind which
we should expect to meet with in the Zohar ; but
it is there all the same, and we shall find it more

---

* Zohar, Cremona ed., part i. fol. 76*a*.

fully developed in other passages. Before proceeding to these, let us see what happens to the soul at death.

" R. Isaac said : At that time when the *Neshamah*, having deserved it, ascends to her superior place, the body lies peacefully at rest in its bed, as it is written, He shall enter into peace ; they shall rest in their beds, each one walking in his uprightness (Isa. lvii. 2). What does this mean? 'Walking in uprightness.' R. Isaac said : The *Neshamah* goes straight to the place prepared for it in Paradise." *

In another part of his discourse the same Rabbi distinguishes two Edens and two places of perdition :

" The Holy Blessed One not only created a paradise on earth and a *Gehennon* on earth, but a garden of Eden above, and a *Gehennon* above. He created a garden of Eden on the earth below, as it is written, And the Lord God planted a garden eastward in Eden (Gen. ii. 8). He created also a *Gehennon* on the earth, as it is written, A land of darkness, as darkness itself (Job x. 22). In like manner he created a garden of Eden above, as it is written, But the soul of my lord shall be bound in the bundle of life with the Lord thy God (I. Sam. xxv. 29). And it is again written, The Spirit shall return unto God who gave it (Eccles. xii. 7). He created also the *Gehennon* above, as it is written, And the soul [*Nephesh*—animal soul] of thine enemies them shall be sling out as out of the middle of a sling (I. Sam. xxv. 29)." † In this exceedingly interesting passage, as need scarcely

---

* Zohar, Cremona ed., part i. fol. 75*a*.   † *Ibid.* 67*b*.

be observed, the citation from Job does not at all refer to any earthly *Gehennon*, nor does any such consequence as a superior place of perdition follow from the text in Samuel. The Zohar unfortunately abounds in this kind of unreason.

The next point upon which we may seek information from the occult commentary is that of retributive justice in the world to come :

" R. Judah said, The time of a man's departure from this life is the day of the great judgment, for then the *Neshamah* separates from the body. But man does not depart from this world until he has beheld the Shekinah. Hence it is written, There shall no man see me and live (Ex. xxiii. 20). Three angels come with the Shekinah to receive the *Neshamah* of the righteous. Hence also it is written, And the Lord appeared unto him in the plains of Mamre : as he sat in the tent-door in the heat of the day (Gen. xviii. 1). That is, the day of judgment, which burns even as an oven for the separation of the *Neshamah* from the body. 'And he lift up his eyes and looked, and lo, three men stood by him,' who search the deeds which he has done, and through whom he confesses, yea, even with his mouth. When the *Neshamah* sees this, it parts from the body as far as the opening of the gullet and there tarries until it has confessed all things whatsoever which the body has committed with her in this world. Then the *Nashamah* of the righteous man rejoices over her deeds [the higher soul is presented by the Kabalists under a feminine aspect] and because she has been so faithfully preserved." R. Isaac adds, " The soul of the just man longs for the hour when it shall depart from this vain world so as to rejoice in the world of the future."*

Setting aside such grotesque details as the pausing of the soul in the gullet, and the mere confusion occasioned by the mention of an oral statement, what is described in the passage above is almost identical with the Catholic notion of the particular judgment. According to this the Christian soul, whatever sentence is about to be pronounced upon it, sees Christ, as the soul of the Jewish Kabalist sees the glory of the presence. We find, therefore, that the Zohar at its best has no richer gift to offer us than a variation upon all that which the occultist has agreed to set aside as belonging to the letter and the convention. It is, perhaps, superfluous, as to the Kabalist it is certainly useless, to point out that the apparition of the angels to Abraham in the plains of Mamre can by no natural process of exegesis bear the construction placed on it. It is understood, of course, that the Kabalah has no such processes.

Having seen how the soul is judged, another quotation will afford us some vague notion of the future happiness of the righteous :

" R. Joseph said : At that time the just man shall attain full knowledge ; namely, in the day when the Holy Blessed One shall rejoice over His works, the just shall know Him in their hearts, and their understanding shall be as great as if they had seen Him with the eyes, for it is written : And it shall be said in that day, Lo, this is our God (Isa. xxv. 9). The joy of the soul when dwelling in the body surpasses

---

* Zohar, Cremona ed., part i. fol. 75a.

all, because they are both constant, knowing and
comprehending their Creator, and rejoicing in the
splendour of the Shekinah. This is what is meant
by the good which is preserved for the just in the
world to come. Hence it is written : These are the
generations of Isaac, Abraham's son (Gen. xxv. 19).
This refers to the *Neshamah* which deserves such
joy and is perfect in her elevation. ' Abraham begat
Isaac, *(Ibid.)*, that is, the soul brought forth this
rejoicing and cheerfulness in the world. R. Yehudah
said unto R. Cheyah : This have we learned that there
is a feast which the Holy Blessed One will prepare
for the righteous in the coming time. What is this
feast ? He answered him : When I came before those
holy angels, even the lords of learning, I knew only
this which ye have heard, but afterwards I received
the explanation through R. Eleazar, who said : The
feast for the righteous in the coming time will be
thus, as it is written : They saw God and did eat and
drink (Ex. xxiv. 11). Now these are the foods, even
as we have been taught. And R. Eleazar said again,
We have learned in one place, ' We have rejoiced,'
and in another, ' We have been fed.' What is the
difference ? Thus spake R. Simeon ben Jochai :
' Those of the just who deserve so much only, the
same shall only rejoice in the reflection, because they
cannot comprehend all, but the truly righteous shall
be satiated till they attain the fulness of understanding.' This, therefore, is to be understood by
eating and drinking, and the same is the feast and
this also is the partaking thereof. Whence have we
this ? From Moses, for it is written : And he was
there with the Lord forty days and forty nights : he

did neither eat bread nor drink water (Ex. xxxiv. 28). For what reason did he neither eat bread nor drink water? It was because he was fed by another feast, even the celestial splendour which is from above. And such shall be the feast of the just in the coming time. R. Judah said: The feast of the just in the coming time shall consist of rejoicing in his joy, for it is written: The humble shall hear and rejoice (Ps. xxxiv. 2). Thereupon R. Hunnah said: All shall rejoice who trust in Thee, eternally shall they sing. R. Isaac said: The one and the other shall be fulfilled in the time which is to come. R. Joseph said: We have learned that wine which is guarded and kept in the grapes from the first six days signifies the ancient and mighty words which have not been revealed to man since the creation of the world, but they will be made known to the righteous in the time which is to come. And thus it is eating and drinking, yea, surely this is so."*

It must be acknowledged that in this very interesting passage the Zoharic doctrine is a great advance upon the monstrous allegory of the salted leviathan in the Talmud, and yet the point reached with so much circumlocution in the rabbinical discourse is summed up in a single sentence by the Christian apostle, who says that "it hath not entered into the heart of man to conceive what God hath prepared for those who love Him." Nor is the mystical significance greater, though Isaac Myer has increased it by pointing out that the term wine signifies Kabalistically "the mysterious vitality and

---

* Zohar, Cremona ed., part i. fol. 80.

spiritual energy of created things," an opinion based on its investigation by *notaricon*, for wine $= 70 =$ God or secret.*

As to the future condition of the wicked, the Secret Commentary gives the following statement by R. Samuel speaking on the authority of R. Jacob: "The souls of the wicked are given into the hands of the angel Dumah [the Angel of Silence who, according to the Talmud, has charge of disembodied spirits], who conducts them to Gehennon for judgment."† As to the duration of punishment, the opinions expressed in the Zohar are confused if not conflicting, but it does not seem to be everlasting.‡

Two other passages in the Secret Commentary refer to the resurrection of the dead :

"R. Isaac spake and said : The mandrakes give forth a smell (Song of Solomon vii. 13). Our rabbis have learned : In the time which is to come the Holy Blessed One will quicken the dead and will awaken them from the dust, that they be no more an earthly habitation. Formerly they were created from the dust of the earth, which hath no permanence, as it is written : And the Lord God formed man of the dust of the ground (Gen. ii. 7). But in that time they shall be sifted from the dust of that building and shall stand a firm building, and the same shall be unto them a lasting habitation. Thus it is written : Shake thyself from the dust ; arise . . . . O captive daughter of Zion (Isa. lii. 2).

---

* " Philosophy of Ibn Gebirol," p. 358.

† Zohar, Cremona ed., part i. fol. 80*b*.

‡ Though this also is taught here and there in the medley. It may be added that a quotation furnished by Jellinek from the *Beth Hammadresh* represents that the Divine Compassion, touched by the sufferings in hell, ordains the release of all in bondage therein.

They shall stand firm, they shall rise up from under the earth and receive their *Neshamoth* in the land of Israel. For at that time the Holy Blessed One shall diffuse over them all kinds of odours from the garden of Eden, as it is written : The mandrakes give forth a smell. R. Isaac added ; Do not call it mandrakes [*Dudaim*] but friendship [*Dodim*], meaning that body and soul are friends and companions to each other. R. Na'hman said : This word truly means *Dudaim*, for the *Dudaim* [understood as the love-apple] bring forth love in the world. What does this mean ? 'They give a pleasant smell.' It describes the rectitude of their deeds, through which their Creator becomes known and comprehended by their generation. 'And at our gates are all manner of pleasant fruits, new and old' (Song of Solomon vii. 13). 'Our gates,' that is, the gates of heaven, which are open and through which the *Neshamoth* shall descend into the bodies. 'All manner of pleasant fruits' ; these are the *Neshamoth.* 'New and old,' that is, those whose souls have departed from them for many years and those which have left them for a few days past, yet deserve, through the probity of their actions, to enter the world to come."*

Hence it seems to follow indubitably that the Kabalistic world to come is the millennial earth of Christianity, and hence the destiny of the righteous is substantially identical in the Zohar and in the Apocalypse. The theory of the risen body in the "Secret Commentary" recalls also that which was much better expressed by St. Paul when he said : "It is sown a natural body, it is raised a spiritual body."

---

* Zohar, Cremona ed., part i. fol. 80.

The other passage is as follows:—"While the *Neshamah* has its nourishment from the supernal splendour, the Holy Blessed One says to the angel *Dumah:* Go and proclaim to that body that I am prepared to quicken it at the time when I shall raise up the just in the age which is to come. But the body answers: Shall I have pleasure when I have decayed? [Referring to Gen. xviii. 12 where Sarah says: After I have waxed old, shall I have pleasure?] Even when I have decayed in the dust, and have dwelt in the earth where worms and moles have eaten my flesh, shall it be possible for me to be renewed? Then the Holy Blessed One says unto *Neshamah:* It is therefore written: And the Lord said unto Abraham . . . is anything too hard for the Lord? (Gen. xviii. 13, 24). At a time which is known to me for raising the dead, I shall bring back to thee that body, made wholly new, even as it was formerly, that it may be like unto the holy angels. And that day is set apart for me to rejoice with them, as it is written: The glory of the Lord shall endure for ever: the Lord shall rejoice in His works (Ps. civ. 31)."*

We see, therefore, that on the most important of all subjects, namely, the destiny of the soul, the Kabalah has nothing to offer us but that which Jew and Christian possess independently of any secret doctrine. We have not to consider here whether this common doctrine is insufficient, but to remember only that it is so held by occultists. That the risen body is transfigured we learn from the following passage, which is also a specimen of Kabalistic angelology.

* *Ibid.* fol. 66.

" When it is said : His servant (Gen. xxiv. 2), this means the servant of Elohim. ' The oldest servant of his house' (*Ibid.*). Who is this? It is Metatron, who is appointed to glorify the body in the grave. Hence it is written : And Abraham said unto his eldest servant (*Ibid.*), namely, to Metatron, the eldest of his house, for he is the first of the creatures of Elohim, governing all that belongs to Him. The Holy Blessed One hath given him dominion over all His hosts. And we have learned, said R. Simeon, that R. Joseph said on the authority of Rab that all the hosts of the servant take delight and felicity in the pureness of the soul. We have learned also that the light of the soul in the world to come is greater than the light of the Throne and that the soul takes the light from the Throne." *

The last statement seems to mean that the glory of God is essential to the Godhead, but the soul must acquire her lustre.

We must leave these interesting fragments at this point. Much as we may despise the imbecile theory which would attribute them to the inventive genius of Moses de Leon, it seems quite clear that they afford no support to the occult estimate of the Zohar.

X. THE LESSER SECTIONS OF THE BOOK OF SPLENDOUR

We have now passed in review the chief tracts and fragments which constitute the Zohar. Beyond

---

* Zohar, Cremona ed., part i. fol. 76*b*.

these there are various lesser sections which may be noticed for the sake of completeness. They fall under two heads :

a. Certain fragments, not of considerable importance, which are common to the two *editiones principes*, namely, 1, "Additional Pieces"; 2, Excerpts from a commentary on Ruth; 3, Excerpts from a work entitled "Mansions or Abodes"; 4, One portion of a treatise on the Secret of Secrets.

b. Other fragments which are peculiar to the Cremona edition and are therefore wanting in that of Mantua, namely, 1, The quaint history and dis course of a Young Man; 2, Excerpts from an Explanation of the Law; 3, Excerpts from a Com mentary on the Song of Solomon; a discourse beginning "Come and See!" 4, Some pieces entitled "Traditional Receptions."

A. THE ADDITIONS

The small additional pieces which pass under the generic name of Tosephtha, *i.e.*, *additamenta*, or accessions, are scattered through the Cremona folio as follows :—Part I. col. 83, 87, 145, 176, 188, 189, 203, 222, 259, 265, 295, 303, 318, 367, 371, 487, 513; Part II. col. 48, 107, 120, 163, 238, 358, 426; Part III. col. 50, 82, 97, 98, 117, 149, 155, 163, 177, 184, 186, 191, 274, 331, 441. Some of these fragments are addressed more particularly to proficients in the secret things of Kabalistic doctrine. Perhaps the most curious of all concerns the Treasury of Souls situated in the supernal Eden.

" Before the world was created all the spirits of the just [*i.e.*, the rational spirits, the *Ruachin*] were hidden before Him in thought, each in his likeness [*i.e.*, they existed in the divine thought, possessing characteristic individuality]. But when He formed the world, then were they manifested,* remaining before Him, in their own likenesses, yea, even in the highest place. He then gathered them into a treasury in the supernal garden of Eden, and that treasury is never filled, but cries out for ever: 'Behold, the former things are come to pass, and new things do I declare' (Isa. xlii. 9). What does this mean? It means, I show forth all by their name, and this treasury hath neither desire nor appetite, save only to accumulate souls therein [the word here used signifies the higher soul, or third principle of the Kabalists], even as *Gehennon*, which hath neither desire nor lust, save only to take souls and to purify them, calling daily, Give! Give! What does this mean? It means, Burn! Burn! And that treasury receives all souls till the time they are clothed and come down to this world. Through the sin of *Adam Kadmon* [not the supernal Adam of the Atziluthic world], which brought on the evil side to the world, the soul [*Neshamah*] must be clothed in these garments, which are the other garments" [*i.e.*, not the original vestments of unfallen man, but a coarser material envelope].†

---

* Compare Zohar ii. 20*a*, Mantua, where it is said that all things and all creatures before they were associated with the universe, and whatever the time of their existence, appeared in their true forms before God at the beginning of the present creation.

† Brody edition of the Zohar, iii. 303*b*. See also Mantua edition, ii. 97*a*, concerning the profound mysteries of that Palace of Love wherein are assembled all the well-beloved souls of the Celestial King, who is joined to them by kisses of love.

From this it follows that the sin of Adam did not take place on earth, but in a higher region, which is indeed a recurrent legend of mysticism. The involution and confusion of Kabalistic psychology is well illustrated by another passage:

"It is written: Let the earth bring forth the living creature (Gen. i. 24). This means the animal nature [*Nephesh*] which is the higher life [*i.e.*, *Chaiah*, meaning possibly the *Nephesh* of *Chaiah*, the fourth principle of the Kabalists; according to one classification, *Chaiah* is referable to *Chokmah* in the Sephirotic system]. And because this life of the animal nature [*Nephesh Chaiah*] is holiness from above, so when the holy earth draws up through her, and is comprised in her, then is she called the higher soul [*Neshamah*]. And come, see! Whensoever the child of man walketh in the true way, when his mouth and tongue utter forth holy words, this higher soul [*Neshamah*] cleaveth unto him, and he is the friend of his Lord, having many watchers protecting him on all sides. He is designated for good above and below, and the holy Shekinah rests upon him."*

B. The Commentary on Ruth

The few fragments of the unknown *Midrash Ruth* which occur in the Zohar will be found in the Cremona edition, Part I., col. 61, 86, and Part III., col. 114, 124, 130, 174, 181, 184, 332, 530. It should be noted that a *Midrash Ruth* is attributed to Rab, the last master of the Tanaites, who died in A.D. 243,

* *Ibid.* 301a, *b.*

and as I believe that this work has never been printed, it is possible that it is the source of these quotations. There is also extant an allegorical commentary* which has been twice printed, and yet another, attributed to the fourth century.

C. THE MANSIONS OR ABODES

We have already made acquaintance with a work anterior to the appearance of the Zohar in which there is a methodical description of heaven. It must not be confused with the excerpts which, under the above title, termed in the original HIKLVTh, rendered Palaces by Rosenroth, give account of the structure of Paradise and the infernal region. Their places in the Cremona edition will be found in Part I., col. 116 *et seq.*; Part II., col 358 *et seq.*, and col. 438. The mansions are seven in number and were the original habitations of the earthly Adam. After the fall of man they were reconstituted and became the abode of the saints. The term which signifies Mansion, Temple or Palace, is applied to *Malkuth*, in which *Tiphereth* is said to be concealed as in a palace. So also the name Adonai [ADNI], Lord, is the Palace of Tetragrammaton, because it is the same number as HIKL=*Palatium*=65. This name is attributed to *Binah*, and in an especial manner to *Kether*, on the authority of the Zohar proper, for HIKL, Palace, is the place in which HKL, that is, the

---

* *Commentatio Allegorica super quinque parvos Libellos, videlicet, Canticus Canticorum, Liber Ruth,* &c. See Bartolocci, *Bib. Rab.* These commentaries, with "allegorical expositions of the Ancient Rabbins," were printed at Venice in 1545 and again in 1550.

all, is contained, seeing that *Kether* includes the whole world of *Atziluth*. In a sense also the term is applied to all the *Sephiroth*. In the plural, HIKLVTh = Palaces, are the branches of the *Sephiroth* in the inferior worlds. The palace of the Holy of Holies corresponds, says Rosenroth, to the three supernals.

The Zohar proper has also a good deal to tell us concerning the seven heavens, one above the other, like the layers of an onion. "Each heaven trembles with fear of its Lord, through whom they all exist and all are taken away. Over all the Holy Blessed One holds all in His power." There are also seven earths below, arranged after the same manner. "These earths are disposed according to their names, and between them is the Garden of Eden and Gehenna." They are inhabited by creatures of whom some have four faces, some two, while others are single visaged, like humanity. They are not the children of Adam ; some of them are clothed in skins and others in shells, "like the worms which are found in the earth." It would serve no purpose to enlarge upon monstrous inventions of this kind. The concealed meaning which some occultists suppose them to possess is again evidently the plan upon which they are based, and to understand them is to know the method by which they can be calculated out, so to speak. In neither case are they justified to reason. For example, we have just seen that ADNI is the mansion of JHVH ; by counting the numbers of these names we see why the Kabalists said this, but we do not see that it served any reasonable purpose to say it. It is entertaining and curious, but at the same time it is assuredly theosophical fantasia.

D. THE SECRET OF SECRETS

The single fragment which is extant of this treatise is found in Part II. of the Cremona edition, beginning at col. 134. It treats, firstly, of the connection between the soul and the body, of which a sufficient idea has been conveyed by previous quotations ; and, secondly, of physiognomy, which, no doubt, in a certain manner connects with the lower divisions of occult science, but is not of much importance to our inquiry. It may, however, be worth while to say that Kabalistic physiognomy proves, as might be expected, to have no connection whatsoever with any accepted principles to which this empirical art may be supposed to have attained, and is, indeed, purely arbitrary and conventional. Lavater was something of a mystic, but fortunately for his subject, he borrowed nothing, as probably he knew nothing, of the Zohar and its connections. Four general types of the human countenance are distinguished, and these are referred to the faces of the four living creatures in Ezekiel's vision. We have thus the leonine, the bovine and the aquiline types, and another, less easy to characterise, but corresponding to the " living creature " which " had the likeness of a man." The approximation of any individual to a given type depends upon his intellectual and moral rank. Physiognomy, however, according to the Secret of Secrets, " does not consist in the external lineaments, but in the features which are mysteriously drawn within us. The features of the face vary, following the form which is impressed on the inward face of the spirit. The spirit only produces all those physiognomical peculiarities which are known to the wise, and it is through the spirit only that the features possess meaning. When spirits and souls pass out of Eden [*i.e.*, the Supreme Wisdom] they possess a certain form which is afterwards reflected in the face." M. Gabriel Delanne, the latest and perhaps most accomplished writer on the French theory of reincarnation, would say that the Zoharic fragment here refers undoubtedly to the perisprit of the Kardec school of spiritism, which he holds to be the plan or type upon which the body of the man is fashioned. The "Secret of Secrets" also pretends that every feature in a given countenance indicates to those who can read therein whether it is possible or not for the possessor to be initiated into divine mysteries.* It is, perhaps, unnecessary to say that the fragment does not disclose the rules which governed the sages in their discernment, so that the Kabalah is not likely to be of much practical use to the few occultists who may be inclined to include physiognomy within the charmed circle of the secret wisdom.

E. The Discourse of the Young Man

The little history which has passed under this name will be found in the Cremona edition of the Zohar, Part. II., comprised in a few columns, 91 *et*

---

* In the writings of the Gaon R. Shereerah and other literature preceding the appearance of the Zohar we meet with notions of physiognomy and chiromancy of a parallel kind. They recur in the supplements of the Zohar.

seq., which follow shortly after the " Book of Concealment." It is the childish account of an impossible or certainly an extremely uninteresting rabbinical prodigy, the son of R. Hammnuna, but living at the period in question with his widowed mother in a certain village. One day two disciples of R. Simeon ben Jochai, namely, R. Isaac and R. Judah, passed through this village on a journey and paid a visit to the widow. When her son returned from school she wished to present him to the rabbis to receive their blessing, but he declined to approach them, after the unamiable manner of prodigies. The reason assigned by the narrative is that he discerned by the odour of their garments that they had not recited the requisite " Hear, O Israel!" in honour of the unity of God. He did not, however, disdain to converse at the table, delivering sundry discourses (1) On the symbolism of washing the hands, a function of some mystery, because it is written, So they shall wash their hands and their feet, that they die not (Ex. xxx. 21), that is, Aaron and his sons, when entering the tabernacle of the congregation; (2) On grace before meat; (3) On the Shekinah; (4) On the utterance of Jacob, " The Angel which redeemed me from all evil, bless the lads" (Gen. xlviii. 16); and on other matters. The cautious critic will not be prepared to deny that the invention of this history was beyond the genius of R. Moses de Leon. However, the discourses convinced the disciples of Simeon ben Jochai that such a precocious youth could not be the child of human parents, and the great light of Kabalism, when the remarks were repeated to him, coincided with this opinion.

Our analysis of the Zohar, regarded as a literary
document, has reached its utmost limit, and this
specimen of the matters not included in the Mantua
recension must be held to serve for the whole.
Though he regarded the Mantua edition as *Codex
correctus*, Rosenroth ingarnered all the tracts and
fragments embraced by that of Cremona when he
produced his own careful codex; but it must be
remembered that the Zohar had in all probability
grown under the hands of transcribers and makers of
glosses during the space, approaching three centuries,
which elapsed between its first promulgation and the
date when it was first printed. We have no means
of knowing how much of it was actually contained in
the script of Moses de Leon. The suspicion under
which it has remained may be partly accounted for
by its frequent quotation of unknown works which
have been considered fictitious; but the Zohar was
edited prior to the persecution of the Jews inaugurated
by the atrocious edict of Ferdinand and Isabella, and
many documents existing in Spain may have been
destroyed during that fiery epoch. Again, it is
impossible to say that Continental libraries contain
no MSS. by which ths excerpts of the Zohar might
be justified. The unprinted literature of Jewry has
been catalogued by various bibliographers, but no
critical knowledge of its contents is possible by
recourse to bibliographies. Let us take, for example,
the passages from a commentary on the Canticle of
Canticles, which is peculiar, as we have seen, to the
Cremona *editio princeps*. These excerpts have not,
I believe, been identified, but there is a MS. in the
Vatican Library which is mentioned by Buxtorf

under the very same title, namely, *Midrash Chazeeth* *
It is the work, as he tells us, of an unkown author, but
a uniform tradition assigns it to a Tanaite commentator *circa* A.D. 100. The existence of such a
work, of course, predicates nothing; but why
should a commentary on the Song of Solomon
be called MDRSh ChDzITh, which is understood as
a reference to Proverbs xxii. 29? I speak under
correction, but I know of no ground except in the
idiosyncrasy of the author, and I am inclined to infer
therefore that the same catchword would not have
been used by two writers, but that the editor of the
Zohar quoted the alleged Tanaite treatise.

XI. THE ANCIENT AND LATER SUPPLEMENTS

The sudden appearance in public of a work which
either has or purports to have remained in concealment
for several centuries may be expected to lead to the
discovery or manufacture of continuations or connections thereof, and thus we have two series of
Zoharic writings subsequent to the Book of Splendour
and distinguished as its ancient and later supplements.
As productions of this kind multiply their authenticity
does not tend to assume a stronger guise, and the
documents with which we shall deal in this section
the reader will do well to regard as without determined

---

* Among later MS. commentaries, also in the Vatican, Bartolocci
mentions that of R. Abraham ben Isaac Tze'mach Levi, the physician,
and that of R. Immanuel ben Solomon written towards the end of the
fifteenth century.

claims. I should add, however, that considerable importance and authority have been always ascribed by Kabalists to the Ancient Supplements, and according to Franck they have been known as long as the Zohar itself. They contain explanations of the term BRAShITh by R. Simeon ben Jochai after seventy different ways, and hence the work is divided into seventy chapters, with eleven further chapters added at the end. It was printed by Jacob ben Napthali at Mantua in 1557 under the editorship of Immanuele di Benevento, and appeared again at Cracovia.

Among notable matters in these Ancient Supplements we find the attribution of the members of the human body to the *Sephiroth*, whence the practical magic of the West may have obtained later on its notion of divine and angelic names ruling those members.* The apex of the head and brain is referred to *Kether*, the brain as a whole to *Chokmah*, the heart to *Binah*, the back and breast are attributed to *Tiphereth*, the arms to *Chesed* and *Geburah*, the legs to *Netzach* and *Hod*, the generative organs to *Jesod*, the feet to *Malkuth*. Later Kabalism recognises other correspondences, the arbitary nature of which is obscured sometimes by an appearance of methodical precision.

There are better things than this in the supplements to the Zoharic books, and it may be well supposed that some out of all the seventy ways of interpreting the much-debated word which is rendered " beginning " in Genesis should be

---

* According to the Zohar itself the erect figure of humanity exhibits the letters of the *Tetragram* superposed one upon the other. ii. 42a, Mantua.

suggestive as well as curious. A single instance must, however, suffice. "'In the beginning God created.' This is the soul when it emerges from the bosom of its mother and is taught thereof. 'And the earth was without form, and void, and darkness was upon the face of the deep' (Gen. i. 2), because the eyes of the soul were closed. Hath it opened its eyes? 'And God said : Let there be light.' Hereafter man is gathered in from this world, and this then is written about the soul. 'And God said, Let the waters under the heaven be gathered unto one place, and let the dry land appear.' When the soul is removed from a man his body remains even as 'dry land.'"

That French school of occultism which is just beginning to recognise in the plays of Shakespeare a veiled scheme of initiation has, it must be admitted, an influential mystic precedent in the biblical exegesis of the Zohar, of which the above passage seems to be a very neat instance, arbitrary beyond all words, and yet not without a certain grace of notion.

One of the most celebrated quotations from the Ancient Supplements is, however, the Prayer of Elijah, though it belongs only to the prefatory part.[*]

"Lord of the universe, one alone art Thou, but not according to number. Thou art the most sublime of all that is sublime, the most withdrawn of all things concealed, and conception cannot attain Thee. Thou hast produced ten forms which we call *Sephiroth*, and Thou guidest by means of these the unknown and invisible as well as the visible worlds. In

---

[*] Namely, the beginning of the second preface.

them Thou dost veil Thyself and, permeated by Thy presence, their harmony remains undisturbed. Whosoever shall depict them as separated, it shall be accounted unto him as if he dismembered Thy unity. These ten *Sephiroth* are developed in successive gradations, so that one is long, another short and the third intermediate between them; but Thou art He who guideth them, and whether from above or below art guided Thyself by none. Thou hast provided the *Sephiroth* with garments which serve human souls as intermediate phases; Thou hast muffled them in bodies, so-called in comparison with the vestments surrounding them, and the totality corresponds to the members of the human form. . . . Thou art the Lord of the worlds, the Foundation of all foundations, the Cause of all causes; Thou dost water the Tree from that source which spreads life everywhere, as the soul spreads it through the body. But Thou hast Thyself neither image nor form in all that is within or without. Thou didst emanate heaven and earth, that which is above and that which is below, with the celestial and terrestrial hosts. All this didst Thou do that the worlds might know Thee. . . . Yet no one can conceive Thee in Thy reality; we know only that apart from Thee, whether above or below, there can be no unity, and that Thou art Lord of all. Each *Sephira* possesses a prescribed name, after which the angels are called, but Thou hast no determinate name, for all names are informed by Thee, and Thou only givest them force and reality. If Thou shouldst withdraw [from the vestments], they would be left like bodies devoid of souls. Thou art wise, yet not with positive wisdom; thou art intelligent, but not with a definitive intelligence, nor hast Thou a fixed place ; yet all these things are attributed to Thee, so that man may conceive Thine omnipotence and may be shown how the universe is guided by means of severity and mercy. If therefore a right or left side or any centre be named, it is only to exhibit Thy government of the entire universe by comparison with human actions, but not because any attribute can be really imputed to Thee corresponding either to law or to grace."

The distinction between God and His attributes, and hence between God and the *Sephiroth*, which in a manner are His attributes emanated, is insisted on elsewhere in the Supplements by the help of a striking illustration:

" Woe unto those whose hearts are so hardened, whose eyes so blinded, that they regard God as the totality of His attributes ; they are like unto a madman who should describe the King as the totality of his insignia. Behold a king wears his insignia only that he may be known through them, and verily, the King of Kings, the Concealed of all the hidden, the Cause of all causes, is disguised in a splendid garment so only that He may be known thereby, and thereby may impart to the dwellers on this earth a conception of His sacred nature."*

This distinction has at first sight an appearance of considerable profundity, but perhaps in the last analysis it is rather childish than otherwise, for it is obvious that even in our finite humanity there is a latent and unseen nature behind all its manifested

---

* Supplement, 21.

characteristics. Man is not exhausted by any description of his attributes, and to insist that this is true also of God seems scarcely necessary.

From what has been quoted above it will be seen that the Ancient Supplements are identical in their teachings with the Zohar itself, and some affirm that the original work had existed from time immemorial at Fez in Africa.* We have no means of checking this statement, nor is there any authority for supposing with Isaac Myer that it was brought thither by disciples of Rab Hay, the Gaon of the Sages of Chirvan on the Caspian Sea.† There is, on the other hand, no need to say that hostile critics make use of weak points in the Ancient Supplements as if there were no distinction between these and the Zohar proper.

In the section on the bibliographical content of the Book of Splendour we have seen what is broadly embraced by the New Zohar, namely, a sequel to the "Hidden Commentary," certain additional supplements, a commentary on the Canticle of Canticles, and another on the Book of Lamentations. This enumeration conveys no idea of importance, and perhaps it will be unnecessary to say that occultists are for the most part unaware that these tracts are in existence. I should add that they have not been translated, nor am I acquainted with the existence of any printed copy beyond that of Cracow, though it has been termed the *editio princeps*. This appeared in 1703, or subsequently to the *Kabbala Denudata*. Its history seems

---

* Compare the statement which rests on the authority of the Supplements, that the full publication of the Zohar is reserved for the end of time.

† " Philosophy of Ibn Gebirol," p. 47.

entirely unknown, and it would be preposterous to make any claim concerning it. It may also be noted that later still Isaac ben Moses of Satanow, though otherwise of some literary repute, wrote a forged Zohar which may have deceived a few persons, but it was speedily unmasked.

BOOK VI

THE WRITTEN WORD OF KABALISM :

THIRD PERIOD

ARGUMENT

The growth of Kabalistic literature is sketched, firstly, in the commentaries on the Zohar and, secondly, in some independent treatises which connect with the general tradition. Two works are chosen for separate consideration, one on the Mysteries of Love, because of its general diffusion, and one on the application of the Kabalah to Alchemy, because of the importance of its design and the credit which it has obtained in the modern school of occultism.

I. EXPOSITORS OF THE BOOK OF SPLENDOUR

THE works which are recommended by Rosenroth as assisting to a better comprehension of the Zohar fall under two heads—namely, those which are designed to elucidate technical matters and those which may claim to be original expository treatises. In the first are included the " Words of Understanding," which is actually a Zoharic lexicon or vocabulary ; the "Gate of the Eyes," which is concerned with the Scriptural passages in the Zohar and Ancient Supplements and the *Zar Zahab*. The second section contains the famous "Garden of Pomegranates," the "Way of Truth," with its sequel the "Fount of Wisdom," and the masterly digest of the Zohar proper, entitled the "Vision of the Priest." Outside these there are a few works which may be regarded as extensions or developments of Zoharic doctrine, but more especially of that part which is concerned with spiritual essences. The scope of our inquiry is too simple and elementary for the discussion of technical matters or the pretensions of word-books and other collections which deal with these. Except in so far as they have been utilised in the *Apparatus* of Rosenroth, they will be available to, as they concern only, the Hebrew and Aramaic scholar who has a first-hand acquaintance with the Zohar. To mention them in this place will be therefore sufficient, and we may proceed at once to the consideration of the commentaries and developments to which that work gave rise, and to the names, illustrious in later Kabalism, which are connected with these.

A. MOSES OF CORDOVA

Assuming that the Zohar first became known in Spain towards the end of the thirteenth century, there was a lapse of two hundred and fifty years, according to the dates fixed by modern scholarship, before any literature followed from it. Hence this literature may be largely regarded as a consequence of the Cremona and Mantua editions. Franck says* that two Zoharic schools were founded about the same

---

* *La Kabbale,* p. 4.

time in Palestine, namely, the middle of the sixteenth century, the first by Moses of Cordova, and
the second by Isaac de Loria. On the other hand,
Bartolocci* and Basnage† agree in assigning Moses
of Cordova to the fourteenth century. The earlier
date is of importance to the history of Kabalism,
because certain side issues of documentary criticism,
untouched in this study, depend upon it. Here I
need only say that Franck does not state his
authority or indeed his reason for accepting the
later period. In either case Moses of Cordova is
the first commentator on the Zohar, for, assuming
that Bartolocci was mistaken and that Basnage
reproduced his error, Joseph Gigatella, called the
divine Kabalist and thaumaturge, who was of the
time of Ferdinand and Isabella, was a writer on
the *Sephiroth*, and connects with the Sepher Yetzirah
rather than the Zohar, though he refers to the
Kabalistic Work of the Chariot.

As his name indicates, Moses of Cordova was
a Spaniard, but he travelled to Palestine, and it is
conjectured that he was instrumental in founding
the Academy of Sapeth in Upper Galilee, nine miles
from Bethsaida. In either case he was one of i
teachers and helped to make it illustrious, for he
was regarded by his fellow theosophists as the
greatest light of Kabalism since Simeon ben Jochai.
Franck says that he adhered to the real significance
of the original monuments of Kabalism, but, although
this appears worthy of praise, he seems to complain
that R. Moses was wanting in originality. Howe

---

* *Bibliotheca Magna Rabbinica*, t. iv. p.
| *Histoire des Juifs*, livre vii. c. 24, t. v. p. 1942.

this may be, the work by which he is known is of high authority in Kabalism. It is entitled the "Garden of Pomegranates" (*Pardes Rimmonim*), referring to the versicle in the Canticle of Canticles, iv. 13 : "Thy plants are an orchard of pomegranates." Basnage says that, after the manner of Kabalists, he discovers whatsoever he pleases in that single sentence.* The pomegranate, with its innumerable seeds, is a favourite object for symbolism, and the garden, orchard, or paradise has deep lessons for all mysticism. Here, in a general sense, it is the treasury of Scriptural meanings, and the word by which it is described having four consonants, these meanings are classified as four : PRDS ; the P signifies the literal sense, R the mystic sense, D the enigmatic sense, and S the secret and concealed sense.

Dwelling upon these involved meanings, as may be well imagined, the "Garden of Pomegranates" is an obscure and difficult treatise, and the attempt made by Rosenroth to dismember it for the purpose of his *Apparatus*, while it gives no idea of its contents, creates a lively image of its complexity. The attribution of the letters of the Tetragrammaton to the *Sephiroth*, the mystic meaning of words deprived of their context, the names applied to the *Sephiroth*, their superincession and their union with *Ain-Soph*, the mystery of the Throne and the Shekinah, primeval *Tohu* and *Bohu*, the unknown darkness, these are specimens here and there of the subject matter. But as the heart of the Kabalist, in opposition to the ascribed character of his nation, was fixed with peculiar in-

---

* *Histoire des Juifs*, l. vii. c. 24, vol. v. p. 1943.

tentness on the eternal destinies of man and not on
temporal concerns, so his chief interest was the soul,
ever recurring in his writings, as if it were impossible
to atone sufficiently for the silence of his sacred books.
There is therefore no need to say that a special tract
in the "Garden of Pomegranates"* is dedicated to the
subject of the soul, discussing the region from which
it emanates, its purpose in the world, the profit of its
creation, its union with matter, its superiority over the
angels, its chief divisions, their relation one with
another, the *Sephiroth* to which they are referred, the
places to which they resort after death, the absence of
one or both of the higher divisions in many individuals,
and the good and evil angels accompanying each
human being. The tract also devotes a very curious
chapter to the *simulacrum* which presides at generation,
a phantasmal image of humanity which descends on
the male head *cum copula maritalis exercetur inferius.*
It is affirmed to be sent from the Lord, and no pro-
creation can take place without its presence. It is
not, of course, visible, yet might be seen if licence
were given to the eye. This phantom or *imago* is
prepared for each man before he enters the world,
and he grows in the likeness thereof. With the
Israelites this simulacrum is holy, and it comes to
them from the Holy Place. To those of another
religion it descends from the side of impurity, and
hence the chosen people must not mingle their
simulacrum with that of the Gentile.†

* Namely, Tract xxxi., translated in the *Kabbala Denudata
Apparatus in Librum Sohar pars secunda,* i. 100 *et seq.*

† This fantasy rests on the authority of the Zohar, which states
t.. t is an emanation of the celestial form of each man, *i.e., Jech 'zh*
—Mantua edition, iii. 107.

Another curious speculation is founded on a text of the Zohar which says that the good works performed by a person in this world become for him vestments of price in the world to come. Here was a poetic sentiment which had to be methodised and made literal inevitably by a late Kabalist. When a man who has performed many good works finally falls away from righteousness and is lost, what becomes of his earlier works? Though the sinner may perish, they, says R. Moses, remain. If, therefore, there be a just man walking in the ways of the Supernal King, yet wanting something of his vestments, God will supply the deficiency from the good works of the impious one. The preference is given to those who, taken in their youth, have been unable to fulfil all the precepts of the Law.

B. ISAAC DE LORIA

Of this Kabalist Bartolocci and Basnage have very little to tell us, and it is not necessary to say that he is ignored by writers like Graetz. He is referred by Basnage to the seventeenth century * and by Franck, as aiready seen, to that which preceded it. He has been regarded as the greatest rabbinical doctor at his period in Germany. However, he died at Sapheth or Separth, having published nothing himself, though some suspected treatises are attributed to him. The substantial authenticity of the great body of his doctrines collected by his disciple, R. Chaïm Vital, has not, however, been challenged, and Franck bases thereon his hostile judgment of Loria,

---

* *Histoire des Juifs*, l. vii. c. 31, p. 2089, vol. v.

on the ground, firstly, that he was, like Moses of
Cordova, not original ; and, secondly, that he departed
from Zoharic Kabalism to indulge in his own reveries,
a criticism which stultifies itself. It is certain, how
ever, that Loria did innovate or extend, and that this
is also his title to interest. He is not a mere echo or
reflection, and he makes good reading because he is
a wild fantasiast. Rosenroth terms him the eagle of
the Kabalists. It is, of course, impossible to say how
far his scribe and disciple, R. Chaim, may have developed his developments and elaborated his fantasies.
The vast thesaurus which represents both seems
never to have been printed, except in so far as it is
given in the *Kabbala Denudata*, where the excerpts,
embodying whole treatises, fill some three hundred
quarto pages of close print. They include :

I. The first tract, so called, of the *Liber Drushim*,*
i.e., Book of Dissertations, forming the second volume
of the collection. It occasioned an interesting correspondence between Rosenroth and Henry More, who
was surprised, as he expresses it, by the unexpected-
ness of its doctrine, but found much with which he
could sympathise, as we shall learn later on in the
book devoted to the Christian students of the
Kabalah.

II. A commentary on the "Book of Concealment,"† forming the second tract in the sixth volume
of the collection. It is not given in its absolute
integrity—*cujus maximam partem infra exhibemus*,
says Rosenroth.‡

---

* *Kabbala Denudata, Apparatus* . . . . *pars secunda*, i. 28 *et seq.*
† *Ibid.* ii. *pars secunda, tractatus quartus*, p. 3 *et seq.*
‡ In the *Præfatio ad Lectorem*, p. 16, vol. ii.

III. The "Book of the Revolutions of Souls,"* forming the first tract in the fifth volume of the collection, which seems to have been even larger than the Zohar itself—in fact, almost the camel's load of the legend. A portion of this tract seems to have been printed, or another under a similar title and attribution, namely, *De percussione Sepulchri*, at Venice in 1620, together with *De Precibus*, recalling another subject treated in the collection.

The *Liber Drushim* is a metaphysical introduction to the Kabalah, which discusses a variety of subtle and abstruse questions much after the manner of the scholastic philosophy, and there is no doubt that Isaac de Loria would have diffused a great light of reasoning at Salamanca had he been a Christian Doctor instead of a Jewish Rabbi. His first point, as he tells us, is one over which the Kabalists, late and early, had already outwearied themselves, namely, for what reason were the worlds created and was their creation of necessity? Assuredly from the period of the Angel of the Schools, the halls of Salamanca, of Padua, of Louvain and the other seats of scholastic learning, had echoed with this debate. Perhaps the Kabalists owed something to the Scholastics, perhaps they drew both from one another. In the early centuries of Christianity the so-called Areopagite offers curious points of contact with the system of Sephirotic emanation in the angelical world, and the Wisdom of the Exile was encompassed on all sides by the great debate of Christian speculation. It would

---

* *Kab. Den.* ii., *partis tertiæ tractatus secundus pneumaticus*, p. 234 *et seq.*

be interesting to discriminate the extent of the tincture and to ascertain whether the plummet of Kabalism sounded lower depths than the schoolmen, but I doubt whether the dimensions of the present volume would suffice for this one excursion. Let me indicate therefore the answer of Isaac de Loria, and perhaps some student at large among scholastic quartos will find illuminating parallels in the Scholastics.* The answer is that God cannot fail of perfection in all the works and names of His magnificence, His excellence and His glory; but unless those works were brought from potentiality into act they could not have been termed perfect, as regards either the works or the names. The name *Tetragrammaton* signifies perpetual existence, past, present and future, in the condition of creation before the creation, and thereafter in the immutability of things. But if the worlds had not been created, with all that is in them, it could not have thus signified the continuity of existences in every instant of time, and *Tetragrammaton* would have been an empty name. How very curious is the treachery of this reasoning, which ascribes to a name of the Deity an existence independent of the intelligent creatures whose convention it is! But we should probably find many parallel treacheries among scholastic reasoners, were there any one at hand to disinter them. So also the name of *Adonai*, or the Lord, involves the idea of ministers or servants, and if there were no ministers God could not be called by this name. But after the creation of the worlds and the production of the

---

* He must go further, however, than B. Hareau in his treatise *De la Philosophie Scholastique*. Paris. 1880.

divine works from potentiality into accomplishment, God has fulfilled His perfection in every operation of His powers, and in all His names without any exception.

The next point discussed by the *Liber Drushim* is why the world was created at the time and moment that it was. and not at an earlier, or, for that matter, at a later epoch. The answer is that the supreme and most excellent Light is infinite, exceeding comprehension and speculation, and that its concealed foundation is far from all understanding. Before anything was produced by emanation therefrom, there was no time or beginning therein. This is the solution of the difficulty which is offered by all official theology, and it could have no aspect of novelty at the late period of Isaac de Loria. It may be affirmed in a general way that when the Kabalists touch the common ground of speculation they seldom surpass their epoch in profundity or subtlety, I might add also in the adequacy of their views, though philosophical sufficiency was not, of course, to be expected on any side.

But it is not often and it is not for long that works like the *Liber Drushim* confine themselves to the common ground of speculation, and the Kabalist in this instance passes speedily into the transcendental region of the *Sephiroth* and the manner of their emanation, another question, as he tells us, which has involved all Kabalists in controversy. Do they proceed from one another in the simplicity of a successive series, or is their emanation in columns? There is authority for both views and also for a third, which represents them as a series of homocentric circles. These questions, says R. Isaac, are hard and difficult to resolve, but he offers a solution on the authority of the Zohar, namely, that before the order of things was instituted, they were disposed one over the other, but after that time in three pillars, those of Mercy and Severity, with the central column of which *Kether* is the summit and *Malchuth* the base.

In subsequent chapters the *Sephiroth* are considered under a dual aspect, namely, as regards the portion of the Divine Light contained in each and as regards the containing vessel, while these are again distinguished into an ambient and an inward Light, and an external and internal vessel. The existence of many worlds prior to the Sephirotic emanations is affirmed, herein following, as we have seen, both Talmudic and Zoharic tradition. Finally, several classifications of the *Sephiroth* are considered in the last chapter.

The study of the *Liber Drushim* may be especially recommended to those occultists who have been taught to regard the Kabalah as a doctrine of certitude, whereas it is largely empirical, its leading theorems giving rise to as much disputation regarding their proper meaning as the principles of any other speculative philosophy.

The commentary on the "Book of Concealment," as might be expected, is written somewhat on the *lucus a non lucendo* principle. It does not yield itself readily to an analysis of contents, as it takes various paragraphs of the text and exposes their meaning consecutively, with the help of the *Idra Rabba* and the *Idra Zuta*. The peculiar designation of the treatise is explained by Proverbs xxv. 2 : " It is the glory of God to conceal a thing," and *Ibid.* xi. 2 : "With the lowly is wisdom." The second reference explains why it is termed both the Book of Conceal-ment and that of Modesty. On the authority of the Zohar, section *Pekude*, the balance symbol, which has made this treatise so famous in Kabalism, is explained to represent the Male and Female principles, which indeed follows from the developments of the "Lesser Holy Synod." The male denotes Mercy, the right hand pillar of the *Sephiroth*, and the female Severity, the pillar on the left hand. These principles are termed the Father and the Mother, and in the Hebrew Alphabet are referable to *Jod* and *Nun*. The Father is perfect love and the Mother perfect severity. The latter had seven sons, namely, the Edomite kings, who had no foundation in the Holy Ancient One. These are empty lights dispelled by the source of lights concealed within the Mother. Male and female are conformations of the Holy Ancient One, corresponding to *Kether*, and repre-sented mystically by three heads signifying : *a*, the Unmanifested Wisdom, which is so withdrawn that it is as though it were not, in contradiction to that which is manifested in the thirty-two paths ; *b*, the Supreme Crown, which is the Holy Ancient One ; and *c*, the Head which neither knows nor is known, namely, the *Ain Soph*. Thus on the one side of *Kether* is *Chokmah*, and on the other is the *latens Deitas*, and *Chokmah*, or Wisdom, is the Father, while the Mother is the increment of Understanding, *i.e.*, *Binah*.

These instances of Loria's skill in developing

the symbolism of the three supernal *Sephiroth* must suffice as a specimen of the whole commentary, which, it may be added, does not proceed beyond the first chapter of the " Book of Concealment." He concludes that the sum of the whole mystery is that man in his prayers should fix his mind upon the foundation of all foundations, that he may derive to himself a certain influence and benediction from the depths of that source. In this manner the obscurities of Kabalism are at times redeemed by the simplicity of the lesson which is extracted from them.

" The Book of the Revolutions of Souls" is no doubt a more fascinating treatise than an obscure exposition of so obscure a work as the *Sepher Dzenioutha*, but it is also difficult to give account of it in a small space because the system which it develops is much involved, even for a Kabalistic work. The greatest importance has been attached to it by occultists like Eliphas Levi, who made no distinction between Zoharic and later doctrine. It will be therefore useful to see what is really involved in the famous treatise of Isaac de Loria.

The basis of its scheme is the doctrine of the " Book of Concealment" and its expository synods, concerning the seven Edomite kings who emanated and passed away prior to the production of the present universe. In these kings there was good as well as evil, and a separation was therefore made, that which was good being used for the material of the four Kabalistic worlds as they are now constituted. Each of these worlds, according to Isaac de Loria, has its *Macroprosopus*, Supernal Father, Supernal Mother,

Microprospus and Bride, all derived from the seven kings. A like origin is attributed to souls, and they are disposed similarly in the four worlds, some corresponding to the Bride, some to *Microprospus*, some to the Father Supernal, some to the Supernal Mother, and some again to the *Microprospus* in the world of *Assiah*. The totality of these souls constitutes Psyche in *Assiah*, which in reference to the supernal personalities of that world has therefore five parts : the Psyche in the Psyche, or *Nephesh* of *Assiah*, the *mundus factivus;* the medial spirit, or Ruach of the *Psyche factiva ;* the *mens,* or *Neshamah ;* the *vitalita*s, or *Chaiah ;* and the *singularitas*, individuality, or *Jechidah*, all belonging to the *Psyche factiva*, or *Nephesh* of *Assiah*. There is a similar distribution through the three superior worlds, *Ruach* and its five-fold division being referred to *Yetzirah, Neshamah* to *Briah, Chiah* to *Atziluth*, and *Jechida*, possibly to the world of unmanifest Deity which is beyond *Atziluth*. Loria's system proceeds, however, upon a five-fold division of four principles only. Each of the five divisions are again attributed as follows in the Sephirotic scheme :

    I. *Nephesh* to *Malkuth*, the Kingdom, *i.e.*, the Bride.

    II. *Ruach* to the *Sephiroth* of *Microprosopus.*

    III. *Neshamah* to the Mother, *i.e.*, *Binah*.

    IV. *Chiah* to the Father, *i.e.*, *Chokmah*.

    V. *Jechidah* to *Kether*, *i.e.*, the Crown.

We are now in a position to appreciate the standpoint of Franck when he observes that Loria added his own reveries to Zoharic teaching. The

developments have at the same time been considerably
simplified in this digest.

All these souls were contained in the proto
plastic Adam at the time he was formed, some
corresponding to the head, others to the ···
and so with all the members. Now these souls
are those of the Israelites, who are the .
unica in terram. We must look elsewhere
for the origin of the nations of the world. The
recrements, the evil and rejected parts of the
Edomite kings are the *cortices* or shells which
compose the averse Adam Belial. But when the
protoplasts partook of the forbidden fruit, their fall
confounded the good with the evil of the *cortices*, that
of Adam with the male shells of Samael or Adam
Belial, and that of Eve with the evil of his bride
Lilith, the *spurcities* of the serpent; for the serpent
had commerce with Eve according to Isaac de Loria,
which does not seem to be the consistent doctrine
of the Zohar. It was after this fall that the nations
of the world were produced from the shells. This
is the doctrine which occultists accept by implication
when they speak, as they do speak, of the connection
between later Kabalism and the secret traditions
on which their devotion is fixed. To put the
position tersely, the souls of the Israelites are
distributed in the members of the protoplastic
Adam, regarded in his mystical extension through
the four worlds, and the souls of the Gentiles in
the members of Adam Belial. Liberation from the
foulness and venom of the serpent is by generation
and death only, whereby the good is separated from
the evil, until all the nations of the world shall have

been brought forth from the evil and the Israelites from the good kind.

From the time when the good and evil were thus confounded two things have been necessary— (1) That the good man should be separated from the evil; (2) That the portion of the good should be restored. The first is accomplished by the observation of the prohibitive precepts of the law, and the second by that of the affirmative. Both classes must be accomplished in all their number, and in thought, word and deed, by every soul, whose revolutions must therefore continue until the whole law has been fulfilled. This law must also be studied in each of its four senses, failing which the revolutions of the deficient soul will again be prolonged. This scheme seems to apply exclusively to the Israelites, as the nations of the world can only be destined to return whence they came, and Adam Belial is obviously not under the law. The scheme, however, is subject to a certain mitigation, as revolution proper is sometimes replaced by *status embryonatus*. Revolution is the entrance of a soul into the body of an infant at birth to experience the pain and trial prepared for that body. The alternative condition is the entrance of a soul into the body of a grown man, who must be at least thirty years old,* *i.e.*, when he is obliged to fulfil the precepts. The *status embryonatus* is entered either (*a*) Because the soul in question has something to fulfil which was neglected in the preceding revolution; or (*b*) For the benefit of the man who is

---

* The Jewish age of reason.

impregnated, *i.e.*, to justify and direct him. Revolution occurs (1) For the cleansing of sin; (2) For the fulfilment of a neglected precept; (3) For the leading of others into the right way, in which case the returning soul is perfect in justice; (4) To receive the true spouse who was not deserved by the soul in the prior revolution. Four souls may revolve in one body, but not more. while the *status embryonatus* may associate three alien souls with a single man, but again no more. The object of all revolutions and all Kabalistic embryology is the return of the Israelites into the stature of the first Adam, all having been involved in his fall since he included all.

Such is the Kabalistic doctrine of revolution according to Isaac de Loria. It is not pure Zoharic doctrine, nor is it any scheme of reincarnation peculiar to any school of occultism at the present day. In so far as it differs from the Zohar, it would be unreasonable to regard it as a fuller light of an old tradition; it is very interesting and very curious, yet fitly described as a reverie, written by R. Chaïm Vital out of the head of Isaac de Loria, and perhaps owing something to the scribe.

C.—Napthali Hii 1/

This German Kabalist belongs to the seven teenth century, but I find no biographical particulars concerning him. His work, entitled "The Valley of the King," was made great use of by Rosenroth, who gave, firstly, a compendium of its entire content in the form of one hundred and

thirty "Kabalistic Theses,"* arranged with considerable perspicuity ; in the second place, the first
six sections of the treatise, designed as an introduction
to the Zohar for the better comprehension thereof ;†
and, thirdly, all that part of it which is concerned
with the " Book of Concealment" and the two Synods
as a commentary on these works.‡ The greater part
of the " Royal Valley" is therefore included in the
Kabbala Denudata, the excerpts extending over several
hundred pages. Its author belonged to the school of
Isaac de Loria, and appears to have traversed a portion
of the ground covered by the Lorian MSS. of R.
Chaïm Vital. We know these only, as we have seen,
by the excerpts of Rosenroth, which are concerned so
largely with the doctrine of spiritual essences. After
the same manner that these develop and exaggerate
Zoharic pneumatic teaching, so the " Royal Valley"
extends Kabalistic cosmology, but not with as much
extravagance. The *mundus prior* of Kabalism, *i.e.*, the
emanation of the seven Edomite kings, is termed the
world of *Nephesh*, and it was destroyed with the souls
belorging to it because evil prevailed therein. The
actual world is that of *Ruach*, in which good and evil
are confused, but good comes out of the evil and at
last all shall be good. Then a new world shall suc-
ceed that of *Neshamah*, and this will be the Sabbath
of grace. It follows, therefore, that the present order
must pass away, and this is symbolised by the death
of the second Hadad, the eighth Edomite king, as

---

* *Kabbala Denudata, Apparatus in Librum Sohar pars secunad*,
i. 150 *et seq.*
  † *Ibid.* ii. 152 *et seq.*
  ‡ *Ibid.* ii. *partis secundæ tractatus quartus*, p. 47 *et seq.*

recorded in I. Chron. i. 50, 51. In the day of this
destruction the spirits of impurity, namely, the shells,
shall be entirely destroyed and burnt up, God will
establish a new creation and will bring forth from
His glorious light the mystery of the *Neshamah* of
His great name. The dominion of this *Neshamah* is
the king who shall reign over Israel, and in that day
the Lord shall be one, and His name one.

The hypothesis of the creation of the world
begins with the contraction of the Divine Presence,
producing that space which is termed primeval air.
" Before the emanations issued forth and the things
which are were created, the supreme light was infinitely
extended. When it came into the Supreme Mind to
will the fabrication of worlds, the issue of emanations
and the emission as light of the perfection of His
active powers, aspects and attributes, then that light
was in some measure compressed, receding in every
direction from a particular central point, and thus a
certain vacuum was left in mid-infinite, wherein
emanations might be manifested."

It is to this treatise that Kabalism owes the
curious conception of the evolution of the *Sephiroth*
by a process of explosion through the excess of
light which distended them. From the fragments of
the broken vessels originated the Four Worlds, the
shells both good and evil, and myriads of souls. This
notion is fundamentally similar to that of Isaac de
Loria, and becomes identical in its developments.
As it is impossible to compress the scheme of the
treatise within the limits that are here possible, I will
add only that the " Royal Valley " regards *Kether* as
containing in potence all the remaining *Sephiroth*, so

that they were not distinguishable therefrom. "Precisely as in man there exist the four elements in potence but undistinguishable specifically, so in this Crown there were all the remaining numerations." It is added that in the second world, called that of the restoration, *Kether* became the Cause of Causes and the Ancient of the Ancients. We see, therefore, that, according to the late school of Kabalism, the first attempt at manifestation by the *latens Deitas* went utterly astray, and that the evil of the whole world is the result of the failure of God. This peculiar instruction is also found in the Talmud.

D.—ABRAHAM COHEN IRIRA

This Portuguese Jew was another follower of the school of de Loria, but tinctured with the Platonic philosophy, which he sought to harmonise with Kabalism in his "Gate of the Heavens,"* as we have already seen. His other treatise is *Beth Elohim*, the "House of God," containing three dissertations in exposition of the doctrines of Loria, but directly founded upon and citing at considerable length the pneumatological portions of the "Faithful Shepherd," the *Pekude* section in the Zohar, and the "Ancient Supplements" of that work.† So much space has been given to Kabalistic psychology that it will be permissible to dismiss this writer in a few words. The first dissertation in the "House of God" rests chiefly on the utterances attributed to R. Simeon ben Jochai, who is termed the mouthpiece of holiness and the

---

* *Kabbala Denudata, Apparatus . . . . pars tertia*, t. i.
† *Ibid.* ii. *partis tertiæ tractatus I.*, p. 188 *et seq.*

angel of the Lord ; it recites the emanation of the *Sephiroth* according to the received doctrine, develops the system of the hierarchy of evil spirits, who are still termed *cortices*, or shells, and of the ten sinister or impure numbers. It examines also in a special chapter the opinion of R. Isaac de Loria concerning eleven classes of shells, and of R. Moses of Cordova concerning the connection of the angels with the celestial bodies, and concerning their physical vestments. The second dissertation treats of the different angelical orders and the seven heavens, while the third deals with elementary spirits and the nature of the soul.

The House of God has been included unaccountably by some occult writers* among the books which constitute the Zohar, but it is simply a commentary or development, of considerable importance in its own sphere, yet neither possessing nor claiming any pretension to antiquity.

E.—R. Issachar ben Naptiiali

This expositor of Kabalism seems to have been a contemporary of Loria, and, like him, was a German. His chief work, the " Vision of the Priest " was printed at Cracovia in 1559.† It is a synopsis of the entire Zohar, or, more properly, a methodised analysis of its contents, distributed under a number of titles, each of which is sub-divided according to the Mosaic books. It has been found almost

---

* As for example, Mr. S. L. MacGregor Mathers in the introduction to his " Kabbalah Unveiled."

†   in the *Kabbala Denudata*, ii. *pars prima en ne tractatus primus*, p. i. *et seq.*

impossible to make use of it for the purposes of this study, and it is indeed designed only for the assistance of the scholar who may desire to consult the Zohar on a given subject. The other works of R. Issachar are of similar character, and are, in fact, those technical treatises mentioned at the beginning of the present section as outside the scope of the present inquiry.

II. THE BOOK OF PURIFYING FIRE

When a given order of mystic symbolism, possessing distinct objects and a sphere of application more or less defined, is applied to the purposes of another order, we may expect to derive some curious results from the analogy thus instituted if we can get to understand the method, though, as I have already indicated, this superincession of typology is usually somewhat dazing in its results. The treatise entitled *Æsh Metzareph*, which signifies Purifying Fire, is an instance of the application of Kabalistic apparatus to the purposes of alchemy, and is, so far as I am aware, the sole instance of its kind. In this connection we shall, however, do well to remember that Hermetic and Kabalistic philosophy are ascribed by the majority of authorities in occultism to a common source,* while the rabbicinical influence in alchemy is well illustrated by such legends as that

---

* Thus Thomas Vaughan (Eugenius Philalethes), see Book vii. § 11, affirms in his *Magia Adamica* that the learning of the Jews, *i.e.*, their Kabalah, was chemical, and that Flamel's "Book of Abraham the Jew" is the best proof thereof. See A. E. Waite, "Magical Writings of Thomas Vaughan," London, 1888, p. 112.

of Rabbi Abraham and Flamel. It is true that a work under the title of "The Philosophical Stone" is attributed to Saadiah by Moses Botrel, but we know it only by a single quotation, and we are not in a position to say whether or not it is concerned with metallic transmutation. A few alchemical allusions are to be found in the Zohar, which recognises the existence of an archetypal gold, and regards the metals generally as composite substances. But these references are almost less than incidental, and it is needless to say that there is no occult chemistry, seriously speaking, in the great theosophical storehouse.

The treatise on Purifying Fire is written in Aramaic Chaldee, which is the language of the Talmud and the Zohar. It was made use of so largely by Rosenroth in his Lexicon that practically the whole work is found rendered into Latin in the pages of the *Kabbala Denudata.** It was reconstructed from this source in the early part of the eighteenth century by an occultist styling himself A Lover of Philalethes, and was by him put into an English vesture.† In the year 1894 this translation was included in a series of Hermetic reprints under the editorship of Dr. Wynn Westcott.‡ The preface and notes which accompany this edition appear under the pseudonym of *Sapere Aude*, and are of considerable value. No information is, however, given as to the

---

I make this statement on Dr. Westcott's authority, but no one has ever seen the original since Rosenroth.

† *Æsh Metzareph*, or Purifying Fire. A Chymico-Kabalistic treatise collected from the *Kabbala Denudata* of Knorr von Rosenroth, London, 1714.

‡ *Collectanea Hermetica*, vol. iv. London, 1894.

Chaldee original, and the gaps occurring in the reconstruction have not been filled.

There is no evidence available by which we can fix with any degree of precision the period at which this treatise was composed.* It is subsequent, of course, to the promulgation of the Zohar, which it quotes frequently. It is subsequent to the Garden of Pomegranates by R. Moses of Cordova, a treatise possibly belonging to the middle of the sixteenth century, which it also quotes. It borrows processes from R. Mordechai, a Kabalistic alchemist, whose date I have failed to discover,† and it refers to the forged Latin treatises of Geber. We may therefore conclude that it does not antedate Rosenroth by any considerable period, and may be placed conjecturally at the beginning of the seventeenth century. Finally, it contains expressions which are common to most of the Latin alchemists, and were by them derived from the Greeks, such as, "He that is wise may correct natures." It does not therefore possess the interest or importance which would attach to a chemico-Kabalistic treatise of the Zohar period, and I have not been able to find any evidence as to the authority ascribed to it.

In the supplement to his "Key of the Great Mysteries," Eliphas Levi gives, firstly, what he terms

---

* It is mentioned by Claverus in a treatise entitled "Observations on the most useful things in the world," 1706, p. 72 *et seq*. He gives an account of it designed to show that the Jews accommodated the Kabalistic *Sephiroth* to *Chrysopœia*, *i.e.*, the art of Alchemy. He states also that the Jews hold the *Æsh Metzareph* in such high esteem that they consider no Christian worthy of reading it.

† A number of writers, mostly Kabalistic, are classed under this name in the bibliography of Bartolocci.

the fragments of the _Æsh Metzareph_, terming it one
of the most important books of Hermetic science ;
secondly, the complements of its eight chapters, being
further fragments which he claims to have discovered ;
thirdly, the hypothetical restitution of the original.*
The methods of the brilliant French occultist are well
illustrated in each case. It should be observed that the
fragments are designed to exhibit the difficulties and
the weariness which his researches have spared to his
readers, and to illustrate the conscientious and serious
nature of his studies. The first section proves when
examined not to be the fragments of the _Æsh
Metzareph_, but a loose paraphrase which has a very
slender correspondence with the original. The second
section, which is similarly paraphrase, is substantially
to be found in Rosenroth and the English version.
The hypothetical reconstruction serves only to show
that Levi, like every one else, never saw the original
which some have said is still extant, or he would
not have so misplaced his ingenuity. Lastly, he
attributes the work to Rabbi Abraham of the Flamel
legend, thus investing it with an antiquity which is
contradicted by its own references.†

Before indicating, howerer briefly, the heads of
its contents, it is necessary to observe that the _Æsh
Metzareph_ must be for the ordinary student only a
curious memorial of the connections instituted

---

* See _Renseignements sur les grands mysteres de la philosophie
/ .   'ique_, p. 405 _et seq._

† Firstly, in the title, which reads, _Fragments de L'.1sh .Mézareph
du Juif Abraham ;_ secondly, in the hypothetical recomposition of the
treatise which connects it with the mystic book   · by Flamel.
The _Æsh Metzareph_ is entirely anonymous, and is included as such
in the bibliography of Wolf, ii. 1265.

between two orders of mystic symbolism. It is described by its latest editor as "suggestive rather than explanatory," and he adds that its alchemical processes are not set out "in such a way that they could be carried out by a neophyte ; any attempt to do so would discover that something vital was missing at one stage or other." The statement is true of all alchemical literature, and the *Æsh Metzareph* has the common difficulties of purely Hermetic books further complicated by the system of Gematria and the Sephirotic correspondences of the metals.

On the correspondences here indicated the treatise is mainly based, and it is in this sense that the mysteries of alchemical transmutation are said to " differ not from the superior mysteries of the Kabalah." The *Sephiroth* of the material world are identical with those of the archetypal, and they are the same in the mineral kingdom. The alchemical root of the metals corresponds to *Kether ;* all metals originate therefrom, as the other *Sephiroth* are all emanations from the Crown. The Crown is concealed ; so also is the metallic root. Lead is referred to *Chokmah*, which proceeds immediately from *Kether*, as Saturn from the metallic root. Tin has the place of *Binah*, Silver that of *Chesed*, and these three are the white metallic natures. Among the red, Gold is in correspondence with *Geburah*, Iron with *Tiphereth*, and the hermaphroditic Brass with *Netzach* and *Hod*. Quicksilver is referred to *Jesod*, and "the true Medicine of Metals" to *Malkuth*. The attribution will appear in some cases a little conventional, and it depends upon a curious use of Scriptural

authority. However, the writer adds : " If any one
hath placed these things in another order, I shall not
contend with him, inasmuch as all systems tend to
the one truth." In illustration of this, he gives
another attribution, as follows :

" The three Supernals," namely, *Kether*, *Chokmah*
and *Binah* are the three fountains of metallic things.
" The thick water," that is, Mercury, " is *Kether*, Salt
is *Chokmah* and Sulphur is *Binah*" These are the
three principles of the alchemists. This attribution,
says the treatise, is " for known reasons." *Chesed*,
Geburah and *Tiphereth* correspond as before to
Silver, Gold and Iron ; *Netzach* is Tin, *Hod* is Copper,
Jesod is Lead, while *Malkuth* is the " Metallic
Woman," the " Luna of the Wise " and the " Field
into which the seeds of secret minerals ought to be
cast, that is, the Water of Gold." The attribution in
either case has a concealed sense which " no tongue
may be permitted to utter." The superficial explanations offered here and there should not therefore be taken seriously, as, for example, that Silver
is referred to *Chesed* " on account of its whiteness,
which denotes Mercy and Pity." The Kamea or
Magical Squares of the planets are given in connection with each of the seven metals, but not always
correctly.

The peculiar genius of the work is well illustrated
in the third chapter, where Daniel's vision of the
beast with ten horns is interpreted alchemically by
the help of *gematria*.

III. THE MYSTERIES OF LOVE

With the sole exception of Abraham Cohen Irira, the succession of Kabalistic writers whom we have thus passed in review never descended to the use of a vulgar tongue. To that exception we must now add the case of R. Juda, son of Isaac Abravanel, better known under the designation of Leo the Hebrew. I must confess that there is no reason of a necessary kind for his inclusion in an account of the chief documents of Kabalism; he is exceedingly late, having been born in the kingdom of Castile shortly after the middle of the fifteenth century, and it is even stated that he broke away from all Jewish tradition by becoming a Christian. At the same time there are two points by which he is forced upon our notice; in the first place, he is a favourite subject of allusion with occult writers, and cannot therefore be overlooked in a work which deals expressly with the occult interest in Kabalism; in the second place, his dialogues on love have been more popular than any Kabalistic treatise. According to the best opinion, they were written originally in Italian and first appeared at Rome in the year 1535. They were reprinted at Venice in 1541. Then they were translated into Latin by Sarrazin, being published, according to Wolf, in 1564 at Vienna. This version, which has been praised for its elegance, was next included by Pistorius in his famous *Artis Cabalisticæ Scriptores*, Basle, 1587. They were rendered twice into Spanish, the first version, and the only one of my acquaintance, being that of Juan Costa, in 1584. Lastly, there have been at least three French translations, namely, by Pontus de Thiard, 1580; the Seigneur du Parc Champerrois; and Alexander Weill, 1875.

Though he wrote, as it is said, in Italian, Abravanel was Spanish by birth, but was driven from his native country through the edict of Ferdinand and Isabella. This was in 1492. His first refuge was Naples, where he entered the king's service, but the king died and his realm fell into the hands of Charles VIII., after which the Spanish Jew again became a wanderer. Some say that he retired to Sicily, afterwards to Corfu and Ponilles, and, finally, to Venice, where he died in 1508. Others relate that he fixed his abode at Genoa, and there practised medicine with honour for a long period. As to the change, real or pretended, in his religious opinions there is also serious confusion. Basnage says that he was a man of a mild nature who mixed familiarly with Christians, but inveighed against them in his writings, especially against the priests and the Pope.* Pistorius, on the other hand, represents him as a converted Jew.† He is the subject of high praise, based on intimate knowledge, in the bibliography of Bartolocci.‡

It must be confessed that the occult interest in Leo the Hebrew is not of an intelligible kind, and it is past speculation why he was included by

---

* *Hist. des Juifs*, l. vii. t. v. pp. 1898, 1899.

† So also does Drach in his notice of the Kabalah in *L'Harmonie entre l'Eglise et la Synagogue*.

‡ *Bibliotheca Rabbinica*, iii. 86. There is no mention of his conversion in the notice, but the original edition of the "Dialogues" describes their author as *di natione Hebreo et di poi fatto Christiano*.

Pistorius in his ambitious and unfinished attempt to engarner the signal treatises of Kabalism. We look in vain for the essential doctrines of the Jewish theosophy, as we have learned them from the Zohar; we look in vain even for the reveries of the school of Loria; we have in their place the elegant sentimentalism which characterised Italian literature at the period; we are reminded now of Boccalini, and now of the declamatory Latin exercises of Palingenius. The machinery of the dialogues, if they can be said to possess machinery, belongs to classical mythology; the allusions, the illustrations, the images are echoes of the Greek and Latin poets; when the philosophical authority is not Aristotle, it is Plato; there is only one direct reference to the Kabalah in the whole three hundred folio pages which the dialogues occupy in Pistorius, and it is then a slender allusion to successive renewals of the world, which suggests that the author had misconceived the "restoration" of the "Book of Concealment." As against this there is not one trace of Hebrew thought or influence; there is nothing which would lead us to suspect a Jewish authorship except such negative evidence as the similarly entire absence of any Christian reference. If the work can be said to recall anything outside the unwise literature of the sixteenth century in Italy, it is certain Sufic poets adapted to the understanding of Venetian ladies in the days of the Doges. And here, indeed, is the true secret of its popularity. It is not only so pleasing, so educated according to the lights of its period, so correct in its sentiment and breathing so little but sentiment, so refined in its

amorous passion and so much above reproach, that it
does not contain a single obscenity or a single
recondite thought.   One of its French translators has
thought it worth while to append a glossary of its
difficult words, but it has no difficulties and its words
are simplicity itself.   It has many passages which
even at the present day may be called delightful
reading, and it is redeemed from the commonplaces
of sentiment by tender suggestions of shallow allegory.
The Philo and Sophia of the dialogue are enough by
their mere names to suggest transcendentalism to an
occult student, and more than one criticism has
supposed it to be concerned wholly with the love of
God.   As a fact it discerns in all things the activity,
the influence and the power of the master passion,
and another of the secrets of its popularity in the
warm-blooded world of the South, is that however
much love is transcendentalised in the dialogues, it is
always sexual.   So also the philosophy of this love is
the doctrine of delectation and felicity.   Delectation
is union with the beloved, and the good and the
beautiful are identified in words that recall the light
metaphysics of Cousin and the blessed life of Fichte.

The general definition of love is that it is a
vivifying spirit which permeates all the world, and a
bond uniting the entire universe.   But the proper
definition of the perfect love of man and woman is
the concurrence of the loving with the beloved to this
end, that the beloved shall be converted into the
lover.   When such love is equal between the partakers
it is described as the conversion of the one into the
other being   Below this human love there is not
only that which subsists among mere animals, but in

things insensible, in the first matter, in the elements and in the heavenly bodies, which are drawn one to the other and move in regular order by the harmonious impulse and interaction of a reciprocal affection.

Even the knowledge of God seems to be presented, as regards language and images, under a sexual aspect. God is loved in proportion as He is known, and as He cannot be known entirely by men, nor His wisdom by the human race, so He cannot be loved as he deserves, for such an exalted sentiment transcends the power of our will. The mind, therefore, must be content to know God according to the measure of its possibility and not that of His excellence. The knowledge and love of God are both necessary to beatitude, for He is the true intellectual agent with Whom consists felicity, which is not to be found in the knowledge of all things, but in the One alone who is Himself all others. This felicity does not consist in the act cognoscitive of God, which leads to love, nor in the love which succeeds such knowledge, but in the copulation of the most interior and united divine knowledge, for this is the sovereign perfection of the created intellect, the last act and happy end in which it finds itself rather divine than human. Such copulative felicity with God cannot, however, be continuous during our present life, because our intellect is here joined to the matter of our fragile body.

It may be added that Leo the Hebrew, like Raymond Lully, accounts for the self-sufficiency of the divine nature on the ground that the love, the lover and the beloved are all one in God ; that God alone is the end of all love in the universe ; and that

His love towards His creatures is the stimulation
of a desire of good for their sake and not for His
own. It may be inferred also that a transcendental
meaning is not improbably contained in such speculations as that of the sleep of love, of amorous
contemplation, of the graving of the image of the
beloved in the thought of the lover, and of the ravish-
ment of this state.

IV. MINOR LITERATURE OF KABALISM

We have now completed our study of all
Kabalistic writings to which any currency has been
given in connection with the claims of occultism, but
we have by no means exhausted the literature either
before or after the appearance of the Zohar. It has
been classified in chronological order in a special list
by Bartolocci at the beginning of his great work, and
those who desire to pursue the subject further will
there see how impossible it is to deal with in this
place. It is, moreover, outside the purpose of our
inquiry. A few names, however, may just be
mentioned which are to some extent typical of the
minor literature of Kabalism.

When the Zohar was on the verge of the
historical horizon, in the reign of Alphonso X., we
find at Toledo Rabbi Mevi, the son of Theodore,
Prince of the Levites of Burgos. Though a
Kabalist and a light of Kabalism, he opposed
Nachmanides, thus showing that at a comparatively
early period there was little unanimity among the
doctors of theosophy and the voices of tradition on

the subject of theosophy or tradition. His book is entitled "Before and Behind," which is supposed to indicate that he had approached the Kabalah from every point of view.*

Side by side with philosophical Kabalism the spurious practical part, the *Ars Kabalistica*, never wanted its professors. As neither worse nor better than the rest we may mention R. Chamai of Arragon, in the early part of the fifteenth century. One of his practical secrets was the determination of the sex of an unborn child by placing the nuptial couch from north to south, thus indicating respect for the majesty of God, which resided between east and west, and might suffer dishonour by marital intercourse taking place in the same direction.

Such consideration, it was deemed, would not go without its reward in the birth of male children.†

In the reign of Ferdinand and Isabella, and a victim of their edict of expulsion, flourished Joseph Gikatella, called the divine Kabalist and the Thaumaturge, who wrote on the attributes of God, the Divine names, and the *Sephiroth*.‡

At the period of Picus de Mirandola Kabalists abounded in Italy, many of whom were refugees from persecution in Spain and Portugal. Picus in his *Apologia* affirms that his demonstrations of Christian dogma in Jewish theosophy effected the conversion of a Kabalist named Dattilius. As it is one of few instances on record the sincerity of the change may

---

* Bartolocci, *Bibliotheca Magna Rabbinica*, iv. 18; Basnage, *Histoire des Juifs*, v. 1773.

† Bartolocci, *Bibliotheca Magna Rabbinica*, ii. 840: Basnage, *Histoire des Juifs*, v. 1895.

‡ *Ibid.* v. 1899.

be allowed to pass unchallenged.* Long afterwards, that is to say, in 1613, Samuel Nachunias, a Jew of Thessalonica, but residing at Venice, also abjured Judaism and wrote the " Path of Faith." So also, about 1672, Mordekai Kerkos composed a treatise specially against the Kabalah, but it has not been printed. Basnage hints that such an action at that period seemed scarcely less subversive in Israel than to embrace Christianity. On the other hand, Judas Azael, about the same period, contributed to the literature of the tradition by his " Thrones of the House of David," a treatise dealing with the Fifty Gates of Understanding, while in Germany Nathan of Spire, better known, however, for a treatise in praise of the Holy Land, produced a Kabalistic commentary on Deuteronomy iii. 13, under the title of *Megillah Hamneoth.* In Holland, a few years previously, the famous Manasses composed his work on the resurrection of the body, which connects with Jewish esoteric theology by its defence of metempsy-chosis ; and Isaac About, a Brazilian settled in the Low Countries, translated the *Porta Cælorum* of Abraham Cohen Irira from the original Spanish into Hebrew.

In the sixteenth century Paul Elhananan became a convert to Christianity, and in his *Mysterium Novum* sought to prove from the Kabalah that Jesus of Nazareth was the true Messiah. Petrus Galatinus also abjured Judaism ; so did Johannes Fortius, who wrote on the mystical meanings of the Hebrew letters. Paul de Heredia was a convert of the fifteenth century. Bartolocci (iv. 420) mentions Louis Carret, a Frenchman of the sixteenth century, who in his " Visions of God " defended the truth of the Catholic faith by means of the Kabalah. Later names are Aaron Margalita, whose many works attempted to Christianise the Kabalah ; Rittangelius, the editor of the Sepher Yetzirah, who turned Protestant ; and Prosper Ruggieri.

Y

These meagre memoranda, which do not pretend to represent a serious study, may close with the name of Spinoza, who also connects with Kabalism, though it must be confessed that the tincture which he exhibits is little more than the memory of early reading.

BOOK VII

SOME CHRISTIAN STUDENTS OF
THE KABALAH

ARGUMENT

The opinion of modern occultists that the Kabalah is a vehicle of
the secret doctrine of absolute religion was never held by occultists
in the past ; even those who ascribed it to a Divine source were
actuated only by the notion that it was a disguised Christianity,
and in most cases their real interest was the conversion of the Jews
by its means. The chief Christian students of the Kabalah are
cited successively to prove these points. The modern opinion
began with Eliphas Levi, and it is shown that his authority is
unreliable. Some minor misconceptions are corrected and some
extrinsic points of interest are developed in the course of the
sketches.

I. INTRODUCTORY

So far as our inquiry has proceeded no system of
philosophy would seem less connected with what is
known conventionally as magic than is the Kabalah
to all outward appearance. That there was, however, a systematic connection, by which I mean a
connection permitting the philosophical doctrine to
emerge as fairly distinct, there can be no doubt. We
owe our mediæval withchcraft chiefly to this source ;
we owe also our mediæval demonology ; and the
Jew, hounded out of Spain by the iniquitous edict of

Ferdinand and Isabella, left to the Inquisition and its devildom another pretext for extermination, more fuel for the burning—in a word, the tremendous legacy of sorcery. The Jew was avenged in the magician.

When enumerating the alleged branches of esoteric tradition in Israel I endeavoured to distinguish that of magic from philosophy. While the traces of the philosophical tradition are nowhere met with in antiquity, that of magic abounds. It was to be expected that the newer order of ideas should become interfused with the older. But the Sepher Yetzirah and the Zohar are not magic, and that which drew the Christian students of the literature and made them seek to fathom the Kabalistic mystery was assuredly its philosophical, transcendental indeed, but not its thaumaturgic part.

We are on the track here of another great misconception which prevails among the class of thinkers who have most reason to concern themselves with the claims of the Kabalah. It is useless for occult writers and their too easy disciples to continue, as they have done in the past, appealing to Christian authorities as to great names supporting their view of the subject. Those who accepted and those who vindicated the authenticity of the secret tradition had never dreamed of the religion behind all religions, nor did they look to the sanctuaries of Egypt for any light but that which perchance was carried into it by the descendants of Abraham. The occult writers make two errors. In the first place, they cite among Christian Kabalists many authorities, within and without the mystic circle, who have no claim to the title; in the second place, they misconstrue entirely the position of those whose title itself may be beyond any challenge. Over and above these points, many names, great and otherwise, which it looks well to engross on the deeds of a brief for the defence, bear witness only to the prevailing ignorance.

The purpose of the brief studies which follow is to demonstrate these facts, which possess considerable importance for those whom I address, and are therefore an integral part of my scheme. They are not biographical sketches, and they are not bibliographical notes. They are designed to exhibit that among the names commonly cited in connection with Kabalism, some should no longer be mentioned, some belong only to a Quixotic attempt at discovering an *eirenicon* for Christendom and Jewry, some are not worth citing, because, despite their imputed authority, they have nothing of moment to tell us, and some, a bare residuum, with a handful of recent writers, may be left on the otherwise vacated benches.

II. RAYMOND LULLY

The name of Raymond Lully has been usually cited as that of a considerable authority on the Kabalah, as upon several other departments of the secret knowledge. It is time to affirm that few ascriptions seem to possess less foundation in fact. It must be said, first of all, that there is substantial ground for supposing that there were two distinct persons bearing this name, or that it was assumed for

a second time at a later date. The original Raymond
Lully was that seneschal of Majorca whose legend I
narrated some twelve years ago in the "Lives of
Alchemystical Philosophers." He was born during
the first half of the thirteenth century.* The second
Raymond Lully was an alchemist. His legend,
enshrined in the deceitful memorial of a so-called
Abbot of Westminster,† was unknown, so
far as I can trace, till the beginning of the
seventeenth century,‡ but the works by which he is
distinguished from his prototype are certainly
much earlier, possibly by two centuries. There is a
third and modern legend, which bears all the marks
of invention by its narrator, Eliphas Levi, and this
identifies the two personages by prolonging the life of
the first through the instrumentality of the great
elixir.§ It is described as a popular legend, but
Raymond Lully and his namesake were never of
enough importance to impress the imagination of the
people. . The first was a philosophical reformer and a

---

* The dates attributed to some of his works, if accurate, would show
that he was separated from his predecessor by more than a century, but
they are in a sad state of confusion, and all popular sources of information
are misleading. See, for example, Blackie's "Popular Encyclopœdia,"
s.v. Alchymy.

† *Testamentum Cremeri, Abbatis Westmonasteriensis, Angli,
Ordinis Benedictini.*

‡ It was published at Frankfort in 1618, by Michael Maier, being
the third tract of the *Tripus Aureus, hoc est tres tractatus chymici
selectissimi.* In 1678 it reappeared in the *Museum Hermeticum
Reformatum et Amplificatum,* and is known in English by a translation
of that collection, edited by myself, 2 vols. London. 1893.

§ With material derived from Eliphas Levi, and a pyrotechnic
terminology from M. Huysman, a bizarre work entitled *Le Satanisme et
la Magie,* by Jules Bois, compresses all the legends into one small
pellet of fable which, published in 1895, is, I suppose, the last
misconstruction on the subject of Raymond Lully.

Christian evangelist, martyred for an ill-judged attempt at the propagation of the faith among the Mussulmen of Africa. The second has been described, but on what grounds I am unable to state, as a "Jewish neophyte" or proselyte of the gate. This is therefore the personality which would naturally connect with Kabalism. The second Raymond Lully connects, however, exclusively with alchemy, and his works are evidence that he did not renounce the Christian faith.* It is to him must be attributed those keys, compendiums, testaments and codicils of alchemy which are found in all the great collections of Hermetic treatises. He was so far imbued with the apostolic spirit of his predecessor that his great ambition was to engage some Catholic monarch in another barren crusade for the recovery of the Holy Sepulchre. According to his legend he transmuted into gold sufficient base metal for the minting of six million nobles, for the benefit of an Edward, King of England, on condition that he assumed the Red Cross. The king did not keep his promise, and the adept escaped as he could from the extortion of further projections.

The confusion of the two Raymonds is perhaps more excusable among occultists than for ordinary biographers. That alchemy connects with Kabalism, or that Kabalism became identified with alchemy, the

---

* Witness the address to the Deity at the head of the *Testamentum Nova ri Raymundi Lullii* (Mangetus : *Bibliotheca Chemica Curiosa*, i. 707, 708) ; the last words of its theoretical division—*Laus honor* et *gloria Jesu* (*ibid.* 762) ; the *Testamentum Novissimum*, addressed to King Charles (*Ideo, mi Carole dilecte, te in filium sapientiæ dilectissimum ut fidei catholicæ ampliatorem eligam* ; and again : . ' ' *itur in nomine sanctæ Trinitatis et æternæ Unitatis*, &c. (*ibid.* p. 790).

treatise on Purifying Fire sufficiently testifies, but the
alchemist *per se* is not, as we have seen, a Kabalist,
and there is no single word of Kabalism in the
Hermetic treatises of Raymond Lully the second.
The doctor of Majorca does connect artificially with
the esoteric tradition of the Jews, by the arbitrary use
of certain words and methods, though he was not
a proselyte of the gate, but his system is a
mechanical introduction to the sciences, and has no
title to the name, having nothing to do with a
tradition, exoteric or esoteric, Jewish or Gentile. It
has, moreover, no mystical foundation, and is concerned wholly with an educational method. It is,
therefore, untrue to say that Raymond Lully was one
of the grand and sublime masters of transcendent
science, as Eliphas Levi describes him. In the *Ars
Magna Sciendi* and the *Ars Notoria* there is as much
occult significance as in the scholastic jest concerning
chimæra bombinans in vacuo. The Notary Art of
Solomon, which Robert Turner first printed in
English, connects remotely with Kabalism, and the
Ars Notoria of Raymond Lully has a verbal connection, and no more, with this enchiridion of Jewry.
It is the same with the treatise entitled *De Auditu
Kabalistico*, an *opusculum Raymundinum*, or particular
application of the method of Lully, which has been
ignorantly included among his works. The name
alone is occult, and its selection is beyond
conjecture.* The work proves on examination to be

---

* It is fair to say that Franck takes the opposite view, but with
what qualification for judgment may be gathered from the fact that he
accepts the attribution to Lully of the work mentioned above. He
says that Lully was the first to reveal the name and existence of the

a late offshoot of the great vacant pretentious system which enabled those who mastered it to dispute on all subjects with success, though perhaps without knowledge of any. Some great minds were captivated by it, but such captivities are among the weaknesses of great minds. The best that can be said for the *Ars Magna* is that it was discoursed upon by Cornelius Agrippa and that it was tolerated by Picus de Mirandola. And of these facts, at the present day, neither possesses a consequence. The chief philosophical mission of the first Raymond Lully was to protest against the school of Averroes ; his chief practical work was the exhortation of prelates and princes to found schools for the study of languages so as to facilitate the conversion of

---

Kabalah to Christian Europe, for which there is no ground in fact ; he thinks that it would be difficult to determine how far Lully was "an initiate of this mystic science" or the precise influence which it exercised on his doctrine. "I refrain from saying with a historian of philosophy (Tennemann) that he borrowed thence his belief in the identity of God and Nature" (I think that Tennemann has here misconstrued his author), "but it is certain that he had a very high idea of it, considering it a divine science, a veritable revelation addressed to the rational soul, and it may perhaps be permissible to suppose that the artificial pro. .. used by Kabalists to connect their opinions with the words of Scripture, such as the substitution of numbers or letters for ideas or words, may have contributed in no small degree to the invention of the Great Art. It is worthy of remark that more than two centuries and a half before the existence of the rival schools of Loria and Cordova, at the very time when some modern critics have sought to place the origin of the Kabalah, Raymond Lully makes already a distinction between ancient and modern Kabalists." The passage on which Franck seems to depend for his general view is as follows : *Dicitur hæc doctrina Kabbala quod, idem est secundum . . . Hebræos ut receptio veritatis cujuslu ' ; .t divinitus revelatæ animæ rationali . . . . Est igitur Kabbala habitus animæ rationalis ex rectâ ratione divinarum rerum cognitivus. Propter quod apparet quod est de maximo etiam divino consequvtivè divina scientia vocari debet.* This extract is derived from the *Opus Raymundinum* already mentioned.

the heathen ; but there were few who heard or heeded him. It was only after his death that his system obtained for a time a certain vogue. The collapse of the process of his beatification is one of the great escapes of the Latin Church, because it would have helped to accredit a system which began and ended in words. It was not, as it has been described erroneously, a universal science, or a synthesis of knowledge ; it was chaffer and noise ; its egregious tabulations are a mockery for the modern understanding. Even the martyrdom of this eccentric Spanish enthusiast had a strain of the folly of suicide, if the martyrologists have told it truly. It had, however, its defenders, and it had in time its miraculous legend. So also, and for the space of some centuries, there was a quiet and intelligible cultus of Raymond Lully in the Balearic Islands, which, like some other local sanctities, has become perhaps scarcely a memory.

I should add, in conclusion, that there are works by or attributed to the original Raymond Lully which have no connection with his *Ars Magna Sciendi*, as they have none with occult science, and belong to a higher category. When we turn over the vast, uncompleted collection of his *Opera Omnia*, and dwell, as the devout student will gratefully do, on certain passages concerning the eternal subsistence of the lover and the beloved in God, concerning contemplation in God—*quomodo omnis nostra perfectio sit in perfectione nostri Domini Dei*—and the deep things of divine union, we begin to discern the existence, so to speak, of a third Lully, who has qualities which recommend him to our admiration which are wanting in the

Doctor illuminatus, though he invented the *Ars Magna,* and in the *Doctor alchemisticus,* even if he transmuted metals.

III. PICUS DE MIRANDOLA

Magical legend has availed itself of the name of Mirandola, and on the warrant of his Kabalistic enthusiasm has accredited him with the possession of a familiar demon.* His was the demon of Socrates which a late Cardinal Archbishop has brought within the limits of natural and clerical orthodoxy.† His marvellous precocity has furnished a thesis to the ingenuity of M. Gabriel Delanne, for, as with the music of Mozart and as with the mathematics of Pascal, it remains a ground of speculation how this Italian Crichton acquired his enormous erudition. M. Delanne would assure us‡ that he brought it with him at his birth, that it was an inheritance from a previous life, and that Picus de Mirandola Kabalised in a college of Babylon. On the other hand, Catholic writers, for whom his studies are unsavoury, affirm that he was swindled by an impostor who sold him sixty bogus MSS. on the assurance that they had been composed by the order of Esdras. "They contained only ridiculous Kabalistic reveries." These MSS. have been enumerated and

---

* Migne's *Dictionnaire des Sciences Occultes,* t. ii. col. 308. |

† See Manning's brochure, *s.v.* "The Daimon of Soci .. London, 1874.

+ See in particular *Etude sur les Vies Successives, Mémoire présenté au Congrès Spirite International de Londres* (1898), *par Gabriel Delanne,* p. 61, where Mirandola is a case in point.

described by Gaffarel, and his monograph on the subject will be found, among other places, in the great bibliography of Wolf. We are not concerned with these nor yet with the apocryphal stories of their original authorship and eventual sale. But as Mirandola, who was born on February 24, 1463, and died mentally exhausted in 1494, is the first true Christian student of the Kabalah, it is important to know what he derived from his studies in this respect. Now, unfortunately, we are met at the outset with a difficulty only too common in such inquiries. Of the Kabalistic conclusions arrived at by Picus de Mirandola, and actually bearing this name, there are two absolutely different versions extant; there is that which we find in the collected editions of his works, both late and early, reproduced in the collection of Pistorius with a voluminous commentary by Archangelus de Burgo Nuovo, and there is that which we find with another commentary, though curiously by the same writer, in a little volume, published at Bologna in 1564, and again at Basle in 1600.* The evidence is in favour of the first version, though I have so far failed to meet with an alleged original edition said to have been published at Rome in 1486, and therefore in the lifetime of the author. We may accept either version without prejudice to the point which it is here designed to establish, and that is the nature of the enthusiasm which prompted Picus de Mirandola. In the first place, though he speaks of magic in terms which may be held to indicate that he possessed a

---

* *Archangelus de Burgo Nuovo agri Placentini* : *Apologia pro defensione doctrinæ Cabalæ*, &c. Ostensibly a reply to an impeachment of Mirandola by Peter Garzia.

tolerant and open mind as to some of its claims, and, like a learned man as he was, did not regard it after the vulgar manner, he cannot be considered as, in any real sense, an occult philosopher. The only department of occult science which he has treated at any length is astrology, and to this he devoted a long, savage and undermining criticism, which in some of its salient parts is as good reading as Agrippa's " Vanity of the Sciences," and on its special subject takes much the same point of view. We should not therefore expect that he betook himself to the esoteric speculations of Jewry because he was attracted by the transcendental powers attributed to the Divine Names, because he intended to compose talismans, or because he desired to evoke. I must not speak so confidently as to possible fascinations in the direction of *Gematria* and *Themurah*, for his was a subtle and curious intelligence which found green spots or rather enchanted cities of mirage in many deserts of the mind, and he might perhaps have discovered mysteries in beheaded words and achroamatica in acrostics. There is, however, no proof that he did. The bibliographical legend which represents him purchasing MSS. on the assurance that the prophet Esdras had a hand in their production will disclose his probable views as to the antiquity of Kabalistic literature. He took it, we may suppose, at its word, and the legend also indicates that he was persuaded easily ; it was a common weakness in men of learning and enthusiasm at the period. On the other hand, it is more than certain that he did not regard this antiquity as a presumption that the Kabalah was superior to Latin Christianity ; the wisdom which he found in the Kabalah was the wisdom of Christian doctrine;* when he hung up his famous theses in Rome and offered to defray the expenses of every scholar who would dispute with him, those theses included his Kabalistic Conclusions, but that which he sought to establish was a *via media* between Jewry and Christendom. When he turned the head of Pope Julius with the secret mysteries of the *Thorah*, the enthusiasm which was communicated for a moment to the chair of Peter was, like Lully's, that of the evangelist. The *servus servorum Dei* found other zeal for his ministry, and the comet of the schools blazed itself out. The Kabalistic Conclusions alone remain to tell that Rome had a strange dream in the evening of the fifteenth century. They lie in a small compass and, as I believe it will be of interest to show what Picus de Mirandola extracted from his sixty MSS., I will here translate them for the reader. I ought perhaps to premise that Eliphas Lévi translated some of them in his own loose fashion and published them with a suggestive commentary, in *La Science des Esprits*,† ascribing them to the collection of Pistorius but without mentioning the name of Mirandola. He also gave what purports to be the Latin originals, but these he has polished and pointed. To do justice to his genius they are much better than the quintessential Kabalism of Picus, but as they are neither Picus nor the Kabalah, I shall not have recourse to them for the purposes of the

---

* The existence of Christian elements, or at least of materials which might be held to bear a Christian construction, is admitted by several Jewish writers of the post-Zoharic period.

† Part II. c. iv. p. 147, *et seq.*

following version, except by some references in the footnotes.

Kabalistic Conclusions:

I.

As man and the priest of inferior things sacrifices to God the souls of unreasoning animals, so Michael, the higher priest, sacrifices the souls of rational animals.

II.

There are nine hierarchies, and their names are *Cherubim, Seraphim, Chasmalim, Aralim, Tarsisim, Ophanim, Ishim, Malachim,* and *Elohim.*

III.

Although the ineffable name is the quality of clemency, it is not to be denied that it combines also the quality of judgment.*

IV.

The sin of Adam was the separation of the kingdom from the other branches.

V.

God created the world with the tree of the knowledge of good and evil, whereby the first man sinned.†

VI.

The great north wind is the fountain of all souls simply, as other days are of some and not all.‡

---

* As Lévi tersely puts it, *Schema misericordiam dicit sed et judicium.* He utilises it to denounce the doctrine of everlasting punishment.

† Hence Levi infers that the sin of Adam was educational.

‡ I have given this literally without pretending that it has much meaning. Levi reduces it to *Magnus aquilo fons est animarum,* explaining that souls enter this world to escape idleness.

VII.

When Solomon said in his prayer, as recorded in the Book of Kings, " Hear, O Heaven." we must understand by heaven the green line which encircles all things.*

VIII.

Souls descend from the third light to the fourth day, and thence issuing, they enter the night of the body.†

IX.

By the six days of Genesis we must understand the six extremities of the building proceeding from Brashith as the cedars come forth out of Lebanon.

X.

Paradise is more correctly said to be the whole building than the tenth part. And in the centre thereof is placed the Great Adam, who is *Tiphereth.*

XI.

A river is said to flow out from Eden and to be parted into four heads signifying that the third numeration proceeds from the second, and is divided into the fourth, fifth, sixth, and tenth.‡

XII.

It is true that all things depend on fate, if we understand thereby the Supreme Arbiter.§

---

* Lévi renders this *Cœlum est Kether*, which does not, at first sight, seem to represent it. See, however, Conclusion, 48, and note thereto.

† This is mangled by Lévi, who seems to have misunderstood its meaning. For the night of the body he substitutes the night of death.

‡ Conclusions 9, 10, 11 signify, according to Levi, that the history of the earthly paradise is an allegory of truth on earth.

§ Levi gives, *Factum fatum quia fatum verbum est,* an admirable specimen of polishing.

XIII.

He who shall know the mystery of the Gates of Understanding in the Kabalah shall know also the mystery of the Great Jubilee.*

XIV.

He who shall know the meridional property in dextral co-ordination shall know why every journey of Abraham was always to the south.†

XV.

Unless the letter *He* had been added to the name of Abram, Abraham would not have begotten.‡

XVI.

Before Moses all prophesied by the stag with one horn (*i.e.*, the unicorn).§

XVII.

Wheresoever the love of male and female is mentioned in Scripture, there is exhibited mystically the conjunction of *Tiphereth* and *Chienset* (or *Cheneceth*) *Israel*, or *Beth* and *Tiphereth*.‖

---

* The significance evaporates in Lévi's shortened recension, *Portæ jubilæum sunt.* He explains the Jubilee as the joy of true knowledge.

† Levi's explanation is feeble, namely, that the south is the rainy quarter, and that "the doctrines of Abraham, *i.e.*, of the Kabalah, are always fruitful."

‡ *Per additionem He Abraham genuit*, this being "the feminine letter of the Tetragram."

§ *I.e.*, says Lévi, they saw only one side of truth; Moses is represented bearing two horns. Lévi adds that the unicorn is the ideal.

‖ Levi substitutes *Mas et fæmina sunt Tiphereth et Malkuth*, and gives a sentimental explanation which has no connection with Kabalism

XVIII.

Whosoever shall have intercourse with *Tiphereth* in the middle night shall flourish in every generation.*

XIX.

The letters of the name of the evil demon who is the prince of this world are the same as those of the name of God— *Tetragrammaton* — and he who knows how to effect their transposition can extract one from the other.†

XX.

When the light of the mirror which shines not shall be like the light of the shining mirror, the day shall become as the night, as David says.‡

XXI.

Whosoever shall know the quality which is the secret of darkness shall know why the evil demons are more hurtful in the night than in the day.

XXII.

Granting that the co-ordination of the chariots is manifold, nevertheless, in so far as concerns the mystery of the *Philaterios*, two chariots are prepared, so that one chariot is formed from the second, third, fourth, and fifth, and these are the four philateria which *Vau* assumes, and from the sixth, seventh,

---

* Lévi interprets by distinguishing the marriage of mere animals, human or otherwise, from the true human and divine marriage of souls, spirits and bodies.

† Levi substitutes *Dæmon est Deus inversus* and argues with characteristic logic that, could the former be said to exist, then God as his opposite could certainly have no existence.

‡ This apparently puzzled the commentator, so he invented a substitute which partly reproduces an apocryphal saying of Christ.

eighth, and ninth a second chariot is made, and these are the philateria which the *He* final assumes.*

XXIII.

More than the quality of penitence is not to be understood (or applied) in the word (which signifies) " He said."†

XXIV.

When Job said : "Who maketh peace in his highest places," he signified the austral water and boreal fire, and their leader, concerning which things there must be nothing said further.‡

XXV.

Brashith—i.e., in the beginning He created, is the same as if it were said : "In Wisdom He created."§

---

* That is to say, *Chokmah, Binah, Chesed* and *Geburah* form the chariot, seat, or throne of the third letter of the Tetragram ; while *Tiphereth, Netzach, Hod* and *Jesod* constitute the chariot of the fourth letter. For other classifications of the *Sephiroth* according to the symbols of a superior and inferior chariot, see *Kabbala Denudata*, 1. 535, 536.

† This is the best rendering which I can offer of the obscure original—*Supra proprietatem pænitentiæ non est utendum verbo dixit.* It is quite certain that its intention is not represented by Levi's substi tuted aphorism *Pænitentia non est verbum*, which he translates, " To repent is not to act." According to Archangelus de Burgonuovo, the meaning is that he who seeks the forgiveness of sins must not have recourse to the Son nor to the Holy Spirit. The proof offered is that the word rendered *dixit* belongs to the Son, and that which stands for *dicens* to the Holy Ghost. This refers to certain sayings of Christ. Forgiveness is to be sought from the Father. The Kabalah is not, however, a commentary on the New Testament.

‡ Levi substitutes : *excelsi sunt aqua australis et ignis septen-trionalis et præfecti eorum. Sile.*

§ Pointed by Levi, this appears as *In principio, id est in Chokmah.*

XXVI.

When Onkelos the Chaldean said : "*Buadmin*"
—*i.e.*, with or by the Eternals, he understood the
Thirty-two Paths of Wisdom.*

XXVII.

As the first man is the congregation of the
waters, so the sea, to which all rivers run, is the
Divinity.†

XXVIII.

By the flying thing which was created on the
fifth day we must understand angels of this world,
which appear to men, and not those which do not
appear, save in the spirit.‡

XXIX.

The name of God, composed of four letters,
Mem, *Tsade*, *Pe*, and final *Tsade*, must be referred
to the Kingdom of David.§

XXX.

No angel with six wings is ever transformed.‖

---

* This is given boldly by Lévi as *Viæ æternitatis sunt triginta duo.*

† Levi sums the idea by writing *Justi aquæ, Deus mare*, and
shows in his annotation how God becomes man and man God after
his familiar Voltairean fashion.

‡ Lévi gives, *Angeli apparentium sunt volatiles cæli et animantia*,
which exceeds the Kabalistic idea. I do not think it was intended
to say that birds are angels of the outer form, but that the flying things
created on the fifth day are symbols of the angels who have appeared to
men, wearing the likeness of humanity, as to Abraham and to Lot,
not those seen in the interior state and in vision.

§ Lévi reads Daniel.

‖ Meaning, says Lévi, that there is no change for the mind
which is equilibrated perfectly ; but this is mere ingenuity.

XXXI.

Circumcision was ordained for deliverance from the impure powers wandering round about.

XXXII.

Hence circumcision was performed on the eighth day, because it is above the universal bride.

XXXIII.

There are no letters in the entire Law which do not show forth the secrets of the ten numerations in their forms, conjunctions, and separations, in their twisting and direction, their deficiency and superfluity, in their comparative smallness and largeness, in their crowning, and their enclosed or open form.*

XXXIV.

He who comprehends why Moses hid his face and why Ezechias turned his countenance to the wall, the same understands the fitting attitude and posture of prayer.†

XXXV.

No spiritual things descending below can operate without a garment.‡

XXXVI.

The sin of Sodom was the separation of the final branch.

---

* *Literæ sunt hieroglyphicæ in omnibus*, according to the shorter recension of Lévi,

† *Absconde faciem tuam et ora*, writes Levi, connecting the praying shawl in his comment with the veil of Isis !

‡ *L'esprit se revetent pour descendre et se dépouille pour monter*, says Lévi elsewhere in his writings. Here in his annotation he reasons that, as we cannot live under water, so spirits without bodies are unable to exist in our atmosphere.

XXXVII.

By the secret of the prayer before the daylight we must understand the quality of piety.

XXXVIII.

As fear is outwardly inferior to love, so love is inwardly inferior to fear.

XXXIX.

From the preceding conclusion it may be understood why Abraham was praised in Genesis for his fear, albeit we know by the quality of piety that all things were made from love.

XL.

Whensoever we are ignorant of the quality whence the influx comes down upon the petition which we put up, we must have recourse to the House of Judgment.*

XLI.

Every good soul is a new soul coming from the East.†

XLII.

Therefore Joseph was buried in the bones only and not in the body, because his bones were virtues and the hosts of the supernal tree, called *Zadith*, descending on the supernal earth.

---

* Literally, *Domum Naris;* and hence Lévi's abridgment is *Nasus discernit proprietates*, which he defends from the "Book of Concealment."

† The distinction between new souls and old is developed at some length by Isaac de Loria. Eliphas Levi overlooks this point and has recourse to a sentimental explanation. He takes occasion also to deny that reincarnation was taught by the best Kabalists, but he is not quite correct as to his facts.

XLIII.

Therefore also Moses knew no sepulchre, being taken up into the supernal jubilee and setting his roots above the jubilee.

XLIV.

When the soul shall comprehend all that is within its comprehension, and shall be joined with the supernal soul, it shall put off from itself its earthly garment and shall be rooted out from its place and united with Divinity.*

XLV.

When prophecy by the spirit ceased, the wise men of Israel prophesied by the Daughter of the Voice.

XLVI.

A king of the earth is not manifested on the earth until the heavenly host is humbled in heaven.†

XLVII.

By the word "ath," which twice occurs in the text, "In the beginning God created the heaven and the earth," I believe that Moses signified the creation of the intellectual and animal natures, which in the natural order preceded that of the heaven and the earth.

XLVIII.

That which is said by the Kabalist, namely, that the green line encircles the universe, may be said also

---

* Levi gives *Anima plena superiori conjungitur*, and understands this to mean that a complete soul is united with a superior soul, whereas the reference is undoubtedly to the divine soul.

† The version of Levi is an entirely different aphorism, namely, *Post deos rex ver... r terram.*

appropriately at the final conclusion which we draw from Porphyry.*

XLIX.

Amen is the influence of numbers.†

We have seen that a rival series of Kabalistic Conclusions has been referred to Picus, and so also the number of the above series is occasionally extended to seventy. The collection of Pistorius contains only those which have been cited, and they are possibly intended to connect with the Fifty Gates of Understanding, less the one gate which was not entered by Moses. To develop any system from these aphorisms would appear almost impossible, and this difficulty has occurred to earlier critics. Their source is also uncertain like their meaning, despite the labours of their commentator, Archangelus de Burgo-Nuovo, who was himself a Christian Kabalist, but disputatious, verbose, and with predetermined theological motives.

IV. Cornelius Agrippa

The untimely death of Picus de Mirandola took place in the early childhood of another Christian

---

* According to Lévi, the Kabalists represent Kether as a green line encompassing all the other *Sephiroth*. I do not know his authority, but Azariel, in his commentary on the Sepher Yetzirah, says, as we have seen, that it is the colour of light seen through a mist. I assume that this is not green, though Zoharic observations on the rainbow seem to indicate that some Kabalists at least were colour-blind. It should be noted that Norrelius in his *Phosphorus Orthodoxæ Fidei*, 4, Amsterdam 1720, translating from an elegy on R. Simeon ben Jochai, given in the *Sepher Imre Binah*, explains that the *linea viridis* is the new moon.

† An affirmation of the mind, an adhesion of the heart, a kind of mental signature, says Levi.

Kabalist, Cornelius Agrippa of Nettersheim, born at Cologne in 1486. It is to him that we owe the first methodical description of the whole Kabalistic system, considered under the three heads of Natural Philosophy, Mathematical Philosophy and Theology. Agrippa is therefore of very great importance to our inquiry, and his three books, entitled *De Occulta Philosophia*, are the starting-point of Kabalistic knowledge among the Latin-reading scholars of Europe. It is needless to say that his treatise enjoyed immense repute and authority. We must remember, however, that it is professedly a magical work, by which I do not mean that it is a ritual for the evocation of spirits, but it unfolds the philosophical principles upon which all forms of magic were supposed to proceed, and this is so true that the forged " Fourth Book," which was added to it soon after the death of Agrippa, and does provide a species of magical ritual, is so much in consonance with the genuine work that it might well have been by the same hand. We must therefore expect that the magical side of Kabalism, that which deals with the properties and the virtues of Divine Names and so forth, is much more fully developed than the cosmology of the Sepher Yetzirah or the Divine Mysteries of the Zohar. We have also to remember that, although Agrippa was the first writer who elucidated the Kabalistic system, he was far more learned in the occult philosophy of Greece and Rome than in that of the later Hebrews. He was sufficiently acquainted with Hebrew to be able to understand and expound the mysteries of the Divine Names and the *Notaricon* connected therewith. Of the literature itself he gives no information from which we could infer his knowledge ; he does not mention the Sepher Yetzirah or the Zohar, both of which were then only accessible in manuscript, and I am inclined to think that his acquaintance with Kabalistic subjects was formed chiefly through the *Conclusiones Cabalisticæ* of Mirandola, which, as we have seen, appeared at Rome in the year of Agrippa's birth. It should be added also that there are serious errors in his division of the Hebrew alphabet which would not have been made by one who was acquainted with any authoritative source of knowledge, as, for example, the " Book of Formation," and mistakes without number in his lettering of the Divine Names ; but the latter point cannot be justly pressed, as the faults may have rested with the printer.

It is noticeable in this connection that the doctrine of the occult virtues residing in words and names is expounded from the authority of the Platonists.* It is only in the scales of the twelve numbers, dealt with somewhat minutely in the second book, that the Kabalistic system is developed, but this has remained the chief source of information among occult students up to this day.† The most important information is, however, in the third book, devoted to theology and the doctrines, mainly Kabalistic, concerning angels, demons and the souls of men, but creating correspondences with classical

---

* It should be noted, however, that he preceded the chief Hellenising schools of later Kabalism.

† On the general question of Agrippa's connection with Kabalism, see Frederich Barth : " Die Cabbala des Heinrich Cornelius Agrippa von Nettersheim," Stuttgard, 1855.

mythology wherever possible. Thus, *Ain Soph* is identified with the Night of Orpheus and the Kabalistic Samael with Typhon. The ten *Sephiroth* are described as the vestments, instruments, or exemplars of the Archetype, having an influence on all created things through high to low, following a defined order.

It would serve no purpose to repeat all the points of the instruction, because much of it has been already given, while the tables of commutations showing the extraction of angelical names would require elaborate diagrams. My object is to note rather than illustrate exhaustively the character of Agrippa's exposition, which is concerned largely with the so-called practical Kabalah, and very slightly with the more important philosophical literature. It brought him no satisfaction, and before his troubled life drew to its disastrous close he recorded his opinion that the Kabalistic art, which he had "diligently and laboriously sought after," was merely a "rhapsody of superstition," that its mysteries were "wrested from the Holy Scriptures," a play with allegory proving nothing. As to the alleged miracles wrought by its practical operations, he supposes that there is no one so foolish as to believe it has any such powers. In a word, "the Kabalah of the Jews is nothing but a pernicious superstition by which at their pleasure they gather, divide and transfer words, names and letters in Scripture ; and by making one thing out of another dissolve the connections of the truth." What was done by the Jews for the literature of the Ancient Covenant was performed, he goes on to say, for the Greek documents of Christianity by the Ophites, Gnostics, and Valentinians, who produced a Greek Kabalah, as Rabanus, the monk, later on attempted with the Latin characters.

I do not know that a modern writer could have put the position more clearly. I do not think that any one at the present day can regard transpositions and extractions seriously, but the question is whether these things were not after all a subterfuge, or if not exactly a subterfuge, a corruption of an older system. Agrippa adds another argument which also, from its own standpoint, could not be better expressed : " If Kabalistic art proceed from God, as the Jews boast, and if it conduce to the perfection of life, the health of men and the worship of God, as also to the truth of understanding, surely that Spirit of Truth which has left their synagogue and has come to teach us all truth, would not have concealed it from His Church even until these last times, and this the more seeing that the Church knows all things which are of God, while His mysteries of salvation are revealed in every tongue, for every tongue has the same power, if there be the same equal piety ; neither is there any name, in heaven or on earth, by which we can be saved, whereby we can work miracles, but the one name Jesus, wherein all things are recapitulated and contained."

Of course, in the last analysis this argument proves too much. There is either a peculiar virtue in Divine Names or there is not. If there be, the Christian cannot well deny it to Jehovah ; and if there be not, the doctrine of the Great Name in Christianity is a sublety no less idle than the Tetragrammaton or the Schemahamphorash. We know, however, that, in so far as names represent ideas, they are moving powers of the intellectual world ; when they are used without inspiration and without knowledge they are dead and inert, like other empty vehicles. The Kabalistic Jews believed that they could dissect the name without losing the vital essence which informs it, and they erred therein. The name of Jesus spells grace and salvation to millions, but it spells nothing when lettered separately and nothing when it is transposed. To say otherwise is to rave.

V. PARACELSUS

Among the great names of occultism which are cited in support of the influence exerted by the Kabalah and the authority which it possessed, that of Paracelsus is mentioned. We are given to understand, for example, by Isaac Myer, that it is to be traced distinctly in the system of the great German adept.* Statements like these are themselves a kind of Kabalah, which are received by one writer from another without any inquiry or any attempt at verification. In this way we obtain lists of authorities, references and testimonials which seem at first sight to carry great weight, but they will bear no examination and defeat their own purpose when they come into the hands of a student who has sufficient patience to investigate them. In the present instance we have to remember that Paracelsus occupies an exceptional position among occult

* " Philosophy of Ibn Gebirol," p. 171.

philosophers ; he was not a man who respected or quoted authorities ; he owed very little to tradition, very little to what is understood commonly by erudition.* If we take his alchemical treatises and compare them with Hermetic literature, we shall find that they are quite unlike it, and that he was, in fact, his own alchemist. When he concerns himself with magic, he has few correspondences which will enable him to be illustrated by other writers on this subject : again, he was his own magician. And to come to the question of the Kabalah, if we discover, on examination, that he has anything to say concerning it, we should expect that it would be quite unlike anything that went before him, and quite foreign to the known lines of Kabalism. Once more, we should find that he would prove to be his own Kabalist. In every department of thought he illustrated his own maxim : *Alterius non sit qui suus esse potest.* It must be added also that any contributions which he offers are seldom helpful. They do nothing to elucidate what is obscure in previous authorities, and they constitute new departures which are themselves much in need of explanation.

Nearly two centuries elapsed between the death of Moses de Leon, the •first publisher of the Zohar, and the birth of Theophrastus of Hohenheim, and though no attempt to print it took place till some forty years after his turbulent life closed so sadly at Strasburg, or wherever it actually occurred, there

* He is said, indeed, to have boasted that his library would not amount to six folio volumes.—Gould's " History of Freemasonry," vol. ii. p. 77.

can be no doubt that it was quite accessible in manuscript, or that Paracelsus, had he chosen, could have made himself acquainted with its contents. It seems fairly certain, however, that he never acquired the language from which it had not been translated, and that his knowledge of the Kabalah would in any case be limited to what he could gather from authors who wrote in Latin or some current tongue ; but his own works show that he was at very little pains of this kind. As to this, it is only necessary to collect the few references on the subject which they contain.

The study of Magic and the Kabalah is enjoined several times on the physician, and old medical authorities are scouted on the ground that they were unacquainted with either.* The "Cabala" is in one place identified with Magical Astronomy,† which, I presume, refers to the Paraselsic theory concerning the stars in man and the stars of disease, and connects with the contextual statement that all operations of the stars in all animals centre at the heart. It is identified also with Magic itself, of which it forms a part.‡ But from indications given in another place, Kabalistic Magic seems to have signified some obscure operations with the faculties of the astral body.§ Subsequently this point is exposed more plainly, when the Kabalistic art is said to have been built up on the basis of the

---

* *De Causis et Origine Luis Gallicæ*, Lib. iv. c. 9, *Opera Omnia*, Geneva, 1658, vol. iii. p. 193, *b.* Also *De Peste*, Lib. ii., *pr. ibid.*, vol. i. p. 408.

† *De Pestilitate*, Tract. i., *ib., ib.*, p. 371, *b*

‡ *De Peste*, Lib. i., *ib., ib.*, p. 405, *b.*

§ *De Vita Longa*, Lib. i. c. 6, *ib.*, vol. ii. p. 56, *b.*

doctrines concerning the sacramental body, which appears after the death of the corruptible, and explains spectres, visions, apparitions of a super- natural character, &c.* The art of judging what is concealed by certain outward signs—in a word, the theory of signatures—is said to be the Kabalistic art, " once called ' caballa,' afterwards ' caballia' " It has also been falsely termed Galamala, from its author, and is of Ethnic origin, having been transmitted to the Chaldæans and the Jews, by whom it was corrupted, " for the Jews were exceedingly ignorant in all ages."† Finally, the use of certain prayers and *signacula*—*i.e.*, talismans, in the cure of diseases is connected with the Kabalah.‡

These meagre instances exhaust the three folio volumes which constitute the Geneva collection of the works of Paracelsus. I should add, however, that there is a short section entitled " Caballa," which forms part of a treatise on the plague, but it is concerned with the official elements of early science and with the alchemical elements, Salt, Sulphur and Mercury. There is also a reference in one place to some " books of the Caballa," apparently the work of Paracelsus and in this case no longer extant. By the student of Paracelsus that loss may be regretted, but it is not of moment so far as the Kabalah is concerned, for it is evident that this term, like many others, was made use of in a sense which either differs widely from its wonted meaning, or is the lowest form

---

* *De Natura Rerum*, Lib. viii., *ib.*, *ib.*, p. 101, *b*.
† *Philosophia Sagax*, Lib. i., *ib.*, vol. ii. p. 565, *b*.
‡ *De Vulneribus*, Lib. v. in *Chirurgia Magna*, Pars. iii., *ib.*, vol. iii., p. 91 *b*.

of that meaning. The Kabalah for Paracelsus, when it is not something quite fantastic and unimaginable, is a species of practical magic, and here we shall do well to remember that the adept of Hohenheim flourished at a period when, as we have seen, the spurious literature of clavicles and grimoires was fast multiplying.

It is very difficult to judge Paracelsus, and many false statements have been made concerning him by friends and enemies. But it is well to know that he was not a student of the Kabalah in any sense that we should care to associate therewith.

VI. JOHN REUCHLIN

As these sketches are not constructed biographically, there will be no difficulty in regarding the subject of the present notice as the representative of a group, which group illustrates most effectively the standpoint and purpose of our inquiry as regards the Christian students of the Kabalah. The missionary enthusiasm which may be said to have begun with Mirandola, which, if Lully had been a Kabalist, would have been already at fever heat in the *doctor illuminatus* of Majorca, which ceased only in the early part of the eighteenth century, assumed almost the aspect of a movement between the period of Reuchlin and that of Rosenroth. It was not a concerted movement; it was not the activity of a secret society or a learned body ; it was not actuated by any occult interests, and perhaps still less by those of an academic kind. The shape which it assumed in its literature was

z

that of a deliberate and successive attempt to read Christian dogma into the written word of Kabalism. It does not appear so strenuously in the work of Rosenroth as it does in the collection of Pistorius,* because in the days of the *Kabbala Denudata* there was, perhaps, more reason to hinder such intellectual excesses. Nor is it so strong in the writings of Reuchlin as in those of Archangelus de Burgo Nuovo. It is impossible to survey the vast treatises, extending in some cases to hundreds of folio pages, by which the enthusiasm is represented, and it is fortunately not necessary. We have only to establish their proper connection with Kabalism and to show that it has been so far misconceived by occultists.

We are justified in regarding Eliphas Levi as to some extent the mouthpiece of modern occult thought; it is to him more than to any one that such thought owes its impulse towards the Jewish tradition as to the absolute of philosophy and religion, " the alliance of the universal reason and the Divine Word."† It was he first who told us that " all truly dogmatic religions have issued from the Kabalah and return therein," that it has " the keys of the past, the present and the future."‡ In order to receive initiation into this great tradition he has counselled us, among other books, to have recourse to the "Hebrew writers in the collection of Pistorius."§

---

* *Artis Cabalisticæ, hoc est, reconditæ theologiæ et philosophiæ Scriptorum*, Tomus I., Basiliæ, 1587.

† *Dogme de la Haute Magic*, p. 95, 2me édition, Paris, 1861 ; "Transcendental Magic," p. 20; "Mysteries of Magic," second edition, p. 502.　　　‡ *Ibid.*

§ *Ibid.* Students who know the collection of Pistorius will be aware that a large part of it is Christian in authorship, and that, with the exception of the *Porta Lucis*, none of its treatises were written originally in Hebrew.

Following this direction, occultists have been taught
to regard the famous Basle folio as a storehouse of
genuine Jewish tradition.   No impression could well
be more erroneous.   The works engarnered by
Pistorius are neither the Jewish tradition nor
commentary of authority thereon.   It is well also to
add that they are not the work of occultists or
of persons who believed that " Catholic doctrine,"
or Lutheran, is " wholly derived " from the Kabalah.
The writers are of three types : I. The Jew who had
abjured Israel and directed his polemics against it.
He is represented by Riccius, and his presence is
fatal to Levi's standpoint.   Lévi recommended the
Christian to become a Kabalist ; Riccius thought it
logical for the Kabalist to turn Christian.*   II. The
born Christian, who believed that the Jew was in the
wrong for continuing in Judaism when the Kabalah
taught the doctrine of the Trinity, the Divine Word
and so forth.   He also is in opposition to Lévi, who
thought the Jew was in the right because the germ
of all dogmas could be found in the traditions of
Israel.   This type is represented by Reuchlin,† who
is learned, laborious and moderate, but also by
Archangelus de Burgo Nuovo, who does frequent
outrage to good sense, and seems to regard the
Kabalah as a note-book to the New Testament.
Reuchlin toyed with Lutheranism ; Archangelus was

After his conversion this German repaired to Padua, where he
taught philosophy with great credit.   He was invited back to Germany
by the Emperor Maximilian.   He belongs to the sixteenth century.
His chief work treats of " Celestial Agriculture."

ful politician, diplomatist and man of the world.
He also belongs to the sixteenth century.   Some account of his life
will be found in Basnage, t. v. pp. 2059 *et seq.*

a Catholic prelate. III. The purely natural mystic'
who might be either Jew or Gentile, who has no
Kabalistic connections worth reciting, and to whom
Christianity does not seem even a name. He is
represented by a writer who, as a fact, was born a
Jew and seems to have been included by Pistorius
because of his supposed conversion. I refer to
Abravanel, whose " Philosophy of Love " is the subject
of special mention by Eliphas Levi as if it were a
text-book of Kabalism. The " Dialogues " have been
already dealt with, and here it is enough to say that
their citation annihilates Levi, because a student of
the Kabalah might as well be referred to the " Art "
of Ovid.

As regards Pistorius himself, the only point at
which he makes contact with occultism is in the
fact that his enterprise was undertaken, among other
reasons, as a counterblast to the superstitions which
the Kabalah had promoted in Christendom ; a
reference, we may presume, to the unfortunate
budget of Agrippa and to the increasing grimoire
literature. The Kabalistic studies of the editor
began in his boyhood, but, so far from leading
him to the boasted certitude of Levi, he passed
under their escort into Protestantism, and there
was conferred upon him the august distinction of
figuring as one of the deputies charged to present
the Lutheran Confession of Faith to the Diet of
Augsbourg. Having registered the fact itself as
an illustration of the quality of his progress towards
the Absolute, it is of course permissible to regard
his sympathies with the attempted purgation of the
Church in a spirit of clemency, perhaps even of

interest, or to confess, at least, that they were excusable on the ground of natural infirmity, seeing that he was for long subjected to persecution, fostered by a monkish inquisitor, because he had saved the books of Jewry from confiscation and burning throughout all Germany. In place of them, as opportunity afforded, they burnt *De Verbo Mirifico* and *De Arte Cabbalistica*, the contributions of Reuchlin to the right understanding of the secret tradition in Israel. The treatises remain all the same as witnesses of the standpoint of Christian students in the sixteenth century, and they help to warrant us in affirming that the chief Latin collection of Kabalistic writers, outside the *Kabbala Denudata*, contains no evidence in support of the occult hypothesis.

I must by no means leave this brief and confessedly inadequate notice of Reuchlin and his connections without a word of reference to his learned pupil, J. A. Widmanstadt, whose collection of Hebrew manuscripts, for the most part Kabalistic, is one of the great treasures of the Library of Munich. In the course of his life-long studies he gave special attention to the Zohar and to the theurgic side of the Jewish tradition.

VII. WILLIAM POSTEL

A philosophical, or rather an occult, legend has gathered in an unaccountable manner round the name of William Postel, and it is supplemented by a popular legend which has depicted this peaceable, though perhaps somewhat puerile, monk in a vestment of thaumaturgic splendour. The philosophical legend we owe almost exclusively to Eliphas Lévi, and to a few later writers in France who have accepted his leading, and, with him, appear to be impressed honestly by Postel's well-intended but too often inane writings, among which is included the " Key of Things Kept Secret from the Foundation of the World." Postel was the son of a poor Normandy peasant; by his perseverance and self-denial he contrived to obtain an education, and became, on the authority of his chief admirer, the most learned man of his time. " Ever full of resignation and sweetness, he worked like a labouring man to ensure himself a crust of bread, and then returned to his studies. Poverty accompanied him always, and want at times compelled him to part with his books; but he acquired all the known languages and all the sciences of his day; he discovered rare and valuable manuscripts, among others the apocryphal Gospels and the Sepher Yetzirah; he initiated himself into the mysteries of the transcendent Kabalah, and his frank admiration for this absolute truth, for this supreme reason of all philosophies and all dogmas, tempted him to make it known to the world."*

So far Éliphas Lévi, whose undeniable influence upon all modern occultism has done more than anything to exaggerate the true philosophical position of the Jewish secret literature. The redeeming point of Postel is his exalted piety, by which he is connected with the mystics; the points

---

* *Histoire de la Magic.* Paris, 1860, liv. v. c. 4, p. 347.

to be regretted are his extravagance, his transcendental devotion to a religious and homely nun of
mature years, and his belief that he underwent a
process of physical regeneration by the infusion of her
spiritual substance two years after her death.* To
the Council of Trent, convened for the condemnation
of the heresies connected with the Reformation, he
addressed a benevolent but unpractical epistle,
inviting it to bless the whole world, which seems
outside the purpose of a deliberative assembly
considering doctrinal questions. The result of these
errors of enthusiasm was that Postel was shut up in
some convent, a course dictated possibly as much by
a feeling of consideration, and even of mercy, towards
a learned man unfitted for contact with the world, as
by the sentiment of intolerance. The seclusion, in
any case, offered him the kind of advantages that he
most needed, and he died in peace, having retracted,
it is said, everything that was disapproved by his
superiors.

As already seen, Postel connects with Kabalism
by the great fact that he discovered and made known
in the West that celebrated " Book of Formation "
which contains some of its fundamental doctrine.†
He also expounded its principles in a species of
commentary to which I shall recur shortly.‡ His

---

* *Ibid.*, p. 250.

† " Postel was the first, to my knowledge, who translated into
Latin the most ancient and, it must be confessed, the most obscure,
monument of the Kabalah ; I refer to the ' Book of Creation.' "—A.
V. Franck, *La Kabbale*, p. 16. He adds : " So far as I am in a
position to judge of this translation, which at least equals the text in
obscurity, it appears faithful in a general way."

‡ Tradition also refers to him a Latin translation of the Zohar,
or which Franck sought vainly in the public libraries of Paris. About

own doctrine has also some points of contact with Zoharistic tradition, though its summary by Eliphas Levi is loose and inexact, like all literary and historical studies undertaken by this modern adept.

"The Trinity," his interpretation begins, "made man in Its image and after Its likeness. The human body is dual, and its triadic unity is constituted by the union of its two halves ; it is *animus* and *anima ;* it is mind and tenderness ; so also it has two sexes —the masculine situated in the head, and the feminine in the heart. The fulfilment of redemption must therefore be dual in humanity ; mind by its purity must rectify the errors of the heart, and the heart by its generosity must correct the egoistic barrenness of the head. Christianity has been heretofore comprehended only by the reasoning heads ; it has not penetrated the hearts. The Word has indeed become man, but not till the Word has become woman will the world be saved. The maternal genius of religion must instruct men in the sublime grandeurs of the spirit of charity ; then will reason be conciliated with faith, because it will understand, explain and govern the sacred excesses of devotion."*

The particular excess of Postel was that he recognised the incarnation of this maternal spirit in the person of the pious nun before mentioned.

1890, M. le Baron Vitta, of Lyons, is said to have purchased a MS. copy of a Latin version for 25,000 francs. Stanislas de Guaita, who mentions the circumstance, suggests that it may be the missing work of Postel. The French *Biographie Universelle* also ascribes a Latin version to Gui de Viterbi (s. v. Simeon b. Jochai), but does not indicate the whereabouts of the MS.

* *Hist. de la Magic*, liv. v. c. 4, p. 348.

Éliphas Lévi, who took no illuminations and no
enthusiasms seriously, terms this spiritual ardour
a lyrical puerility and a celestial hallucination, but
there is no lyrical element in the Latin of Postellus,
and, whatever the source of the hallucination,
the lady died making no sign.   Into the question of their subsequent reunion after a manner
which recalls the *status embryonnatus* of Kabalistic Pneumatics, it would be imprudent here to
enter.   From the period of its occurrence the mystic
always termed himself *Postellus Restitutus*; it is
reported that his white hair became again black,
the furrows disappeared from his brow, and his
cheeks reassumed the hues of youth.   Derisive
biographers explain these marvels as derisive biographers might be expected, as if, Levi well observes,
" it being insufficient to represent him as a fool, it was
necessary also to exhibit this man, of a nature so
noble and so generous, in the light of a juggler and
charlatan.   There is one thing more astounding than
the eloquent unreason of enthusiastic hearts, and that
is the stupidity or bad faith of the frigid and sceptical
minds which presume to judge them."*

A less unsympathetic historian than those confounded by Levi reduces the doctrines of Postel
under two heads, (1) "That the evangelical reign of
Jesus Christ, established by the apostles, could not
be sustained among Christians or propagated among
infidels except by the lights of reason," which appears
wholly plausible. (2) That a future King of France
was destined to universal monarchy, and "that his

* *Ibid.*

way must be prepared by the conquest of hearts and
the convincing of minds, so that thenceforth the
world shall hold but one belief and Jesus Christ
shall reign there by one King, one law and one
faith." Given universal monarchy as a possibility
of the future, no Frenchman who is true to his
traditions would conceivably assign it otherwise than
to a King of France. However, one or both of these
propositions led the biographer in question to infer
that Postel was mad, and I cite this conclusion less on
account of its essential merit than because it afforded
Lévi the opportunity for a rejoinder of characteristic
suggestiveness. "Mad, for having dreamed that
religion should govern minds by the supreme reason
of its doctrine, and that the monarchy, to be strong
and lasting, must bind hearts by the conquests of the
public prosperity of peace! Mad, for having believed
in the advent of His Kingdom, to whom we daily cry,
Thy Kingdom come! Mad, because he believed in
reason and justice on earth! Alas, it is too true, poor
Postel was mad!" He wrote little books at intervals
which, I must frankly admit, are almost impossible to
read, and in the case of the *Sepher Yetzirah* the
printer has done his best to make the difficulties
absolute; but as I have promised to speak of the
commentary which accompanies the translation, I
must at least say that it should be described rather as
a collection of separate notes. Franck recommends
no one to be guided by the views which it expresses,
but they scarcely suggest leading, as they contain
nothing of real importance, and some of them are
almost childish. Among the points which may be
noted are :—(*a*) Defence of the lawfulness and

necessity of the concealment of sacred things ; (*b*) A pertinent and useful distinction between the terms creation, formation and making, as used in the Sepher Yetzirah ; (*c*) The antiquity of the belief in ten spheres of the heavens ; (*d*) The recourse to numerical mysticism to show why the *Sephiroth* are, in the words of the Sepher Yetzirah, " ten and not nine," the necessity of the number ten being shown by the progression from the unit to the quaternary, as follows :—$1 + 2 + 3 + 4 = 10$. And this, according to the mystical mode of calculating, brings us back to the unit, even as the external universe brings back the soul to God ; (*e*) The attribution of the angelic choirs to the *Sephiroth*, thus showing that Postel's study of the Kabalah was not confined to the one document which he is known to have translated.

Of Postel's original writings, that entitled *De Rationibus Spiritus Sancti Libri Duo*, 1543, seems on the whole the most soberly reasoned ; if, unfortunately, it has no connections with the Kabalah, it has at least some with good sense. It is useful also for occultists who are disposed to be influenced by Levi, and hence to regard Postel as a very great adept of their mysteries. While it is quite true that he was excessively fanciful in his notions, which are extravagant in the philological as well as the conventional sense of that term, it is not at all true that he had set aside or exceeded the accepted doctrinal views of his period, nor does he appear to have possessed a specific light on given points of teaching which can be regarded as considerable for his period. He upheld, for example, the doctrine of eternal damnation, and justifies it in such a manner that no room is left for the conjecture that he was not saying what he meant. Now this doctrine is not only intolerable to the occultist, but it makes void his scheme of the universe. For the rest, Postel was a good and single-minded Christian, who, in spite of his *Clavis Absconditorum a Constitutione Mundi*, and in spite of the panegyrics of Éliphas Lévi, had no knowledge whatsoever of the so-called Book of Thoth, and had never dreamed of looking for a doctrine of absolute religion beyond the seat of Peter.

VIII. THE ROSICRUCIANS

Among many adventurous statements advanced concerning this mystic fraternity, we are not infrequently told that it gave a great impetus to the study of the Kabalah. This assertion is so far from being founded in any accessible fact, that one is tempted to rejoin that it gave no impetus to anything except a short-lived curiosity and a certain pleasant fantasia in romantic fiction. The truth is that no statement should be hazarded on either side. In the first place, the historical evidence for the existence of the order, though it points to certain conclusions, is in a very unsatisfactory state,* and any knowledge of another kind which may be still in existence is in the custody of those who do not commit themselves. I have

---

* It is open therefore to numerous singular constructions, one of the most remarkable being that placed on it by Mrs. Henry Pott, in "Francis Bacon and his Secret Society," London, 1891. See c. xii. especially, and compare Clifford Harrison, "Notes on the Margins," London, 1897, p. 49: "There is every good reason to suppose that the founder of Inductive Philosophy was a Rosicrucian."

never met in literature with an express statement designed to indicate knowledge and to represent authority which could bear investigation. On the contrary, I have found invariably those which most assumed the complexion of assurance were only the private impressions of persons who had no title to conviction, nor even a sufficient warrant for an estimable opinion by their acquaintance with the exoteric facts. I have therefore to say that there is no known student of the Kabalah,* with possibly one exception, whom it is possible to fix at all as the member of a Rosicrucian Fraternity, laying any claim to antiquity, for it is well known that there have been, as there still are, several corporate societies, some semi - Masonic, as in England, some mystic, as in France, which have indicated their occult interests and purposes by adopting the name. There is no mischief in such adoption, provided the limits of the pretension are clear, and, with the exception of one or two which have appeared in America, this has, I think, been the case.

The few great names of the past which connect with Rosicrucianism and at the same time with Kabalism are not to be identified with the Fraternity, except by a common ground of sympathy.† Such were Fludd and Vaughan. More-

---

* The term is sometimes used loosely in connection with the Rosicrucians, as if meaning a tradition of any kind. Thus, Mr. W. F. C. Wigston speaks of "German philosophers and writers . . . who each and all held up Freemasonry as a branch of their own Rosicrucian Kabalah."—The Columbus of Literature, p. 203, Chicago, 1892. The Rosicrucian Kabalah, understood in this sense, was the Divine Magia.

† In an interesting paper read before the Quatuor Coronati Lodge, and published in its transactions, Dr. Wynn Westcott, Supreme

over, the few memorials which we possess of it, especially those belonging to the eighteenth century, indicate that it was mainly engrossed by alchemical processes. The possible exception I have mentioned, namely, the one case in which a well-known student of the Kabalah, or rather a well-known expositor of Kabalistic subjects, may have received initiation into a Rosicrucian order going back through the last century, is Eliphas Levi. It seems almost certain that he received initiation of some kind, and it has been recently stated by a French occultist who has access to some important sources of information that the scattered groups of Rosicrucian societies were reorganised by Eliphas Levi, presumably about the year 1850. But this solitary instance does not really save the situation, more especially as I shall establish later on that Eliphas Levi, though he has obtained a great reputation among occultists as a Kabalist, was not entitled to it by any profound or even tolerable acquaintance with the literature which contains the Kabalah.

IX. ROBERT FLUDD

The name of Robert Fludd stands high among the occult philosophers of England ; he was a man of wide learning, of great intellectual ambition, of exalted spiritual faith. He was also an experimental scientist of no mean order. If we add to this that he

Magus of the English Rosicrucian Society, describes Rosicrucianism as a new presentation of Gnostic, Kabalistic, Hermetic and Neo-Platonic doctrines.

is an accessible figure, not too remote in time, and that a short pilgrimage in Kent will lead us to the lovely country house in which he lived and died,* it will not be difficult to understand the fascination which he has exercised on many who, for the rest, have never dared to stir the dust from his folios. I have already had occasion in more than one work to account for this Kentish transcendentalist, and as there is only a single mystery in his life, to which no one is likely to bring light, I shall not need here to retrace ground that has been travelled. The one mystery is whether he did ultimately enter the Fraternity of the Rose-Cross. It is clear from the tracts which he wrote in defence of this order that he had not then been initiated into its mysteries.† Perhaps so much energy and devotion earned that reward in the end, as there is ground for supposing was the case with his friend Michael Maier, who espoused the same cause in Germany. But we do not know, and the modern occult writers who pretend that he was a Rosicrucian are either misled or are romancing.

His connection with Kabalism is, however, the only point with which we are here concerned, and as to this there is no doubt of his proficiency, for he occupied himself a great deal with vast cosmological hypotheses, which were drawn to some extent from this source. He was forty years of age when the

---

* See "Haunts of the English Mystics," No. 1, in "The Unknown World," Vol. i. p. 130, *et seq.*

† Perhaps the *Valete Nostrique Memores estote* of the *Epilogus Autori ad Fratres de Rosea Cruce* may create a different impression in the minds of some readers. See *Apologia Compendiaria*, Leyden, 1616.

Rosicrucian controversy first gave opportunity to his pen, and the "Compendious Apology," which he then published in reply to Libavius, a German hostile critic, exhibits his Kabalistic studies. I must add also that it gives evidence of his besetting intellectual weakness, an inordinate passion for the marvellous, which leads him to dwell unduly on the thaumaturgic side of the Jewish secret knowledge. Having given the usual legend of the tradition, its reception by Moses from God, and its oral perpetuation till the time of Esdras, he divides the Kabalah into two parts, that of Cosmology, dealing with the forces operating in created things, both sublunary and celestial, and expounding on philosophical grounds the arcana of the written law. This division, he observes, does not differ materially from the Natural Magic in which Solomon is recorded to have excelled, and he adds that the magical powers of natural things, concealed in their centre, can be brought forth by this species of Kabalah. The second division is entitled *Mercavah*, which contemplates things Divine, angelical powers, sacred names and *signacula*. It is sub-divided into *Notaricon* and *Theomantica*. *Notaricon* treats of the angelical virtues and names, of demoniacal natures and of human souls; *Theomantica* investigates the mysteries of the Divine Majesty, of sacred names and pentacles. Those who are proficient therein are invested with wonderful powers, can foretell future things, command entire Nature, compel angels and demons, and perform miracles. By this art Moses worked his various signs and wonders, Joshua caused the sun to stand still, Elijah brought fire from heaven and raised the dead to life. But it is a gift of God, through His Holy Spirit, which is granted only to the elect.

It will be seen that this classification presents not the exalted if bizarre traditions of the Zohar, but the debased and superstitious apparatus of the *Sepher Raziel* and of later Kabalism, ignored if not unknown by writers like Rosenroth. In the vast folios which followed the " Compendious Apology " the Kabalistic connections of Fludd's philosophy are implicit and suggestive rather than patent and elaborated, and I think are positive proof that he had no acquaintance with the Zohar. In his Cosmology of the Macrocosmos* which deals with its metaphysical and physical origin, he has recourse chiefly to the Platonic and Hermetic writings, and although many other authorities are cited, nothing is borrowed from the Kabalists, except indeed the Tetragrammaton, which figures within a triangle in one of the illustrations. The complementary treatise on the Microcosm recalls Kabalism in its doctrine of angels and demons. Slight correspondences may be traced in his other writings, but they indicate no real knowledge. In discussing the properties of numbers† (*i.e.*, the *Sephiroth*) and the Divine Names attributed to them, the diagram which accompanies the remarks shows that he misconstrued totally the Kabalistic scheme of emanation. So also some later observa-

---

Cosmi Majoris scilicet et Minoris Metaphysica, Physica atque Technica Historia, 2 vols., Frankfort, 1617 and 1629.

† *Philosophia Sacra et vere Christiana, seu Meteorologica Cosmica*, 1626.

A A

tions concerning *Metatron* and the positive and
negative sides of the Sephirotic Tree* suggest no
special knowledge. When replying to Father
Mersenne, Fludd defends what he terms his Kabalah,
but the term is used loosely and has certainly very
little to do with the Kabalah of Jewry.† It may
be observed, in conclusion, that the Kentish mystic
was pre-eminently a Christian philosopher, and, like
other subjects, that of the esoteric tradition in Israel
was approached by him from the Christian standpoint.

X. HENRY MORE

The Cambridge Platonic philosopher is regarded
by Basnage as a great Kabalist and his contributions
to the *Kabbala Denudata* as in some sense discovering
the sentiment and spirit of Jewish theosophy.‡
Franck, on the contrary, regrets their inclusion by
Rosenroth on the ground that they are personal
speculations which are not at all in harmony with
Kabalistic teaching.§ While there can be no question
that the just view belongs to the later critic, More is
interesting because of his enthusiasm and earnest-
ness. His point of view is also of importance to our
inquiry, because his name belongs undeniably to the
literature of English mysticism. Let us begin therefore by stating that he approached the subject as a

---

* *Medicina Catholica, seu Mysticum Artis Medicandi Sacrarium*,
2 vols., Frankfort, 1629, 1631.
† *De Sophiæ cum Moria Certamine*, 1629.
‡ *Histoire des Juifs*, Livre iii. c. 10, tom. ii., p. 786.
§ Ad. Franck : *La Kabbale*, p. 22.

Christian who desired the conversion of the Jews, who regarded the Kabalah as a fitting instrument to effect it, and not in the case of the Jews only, but even of Pagans. He came, therefore, to its study and elucidation not as an occultist, not as a seeker for an absolute doctrine of religion, nor even for a higher sense of Christianity, but like Picus and Postel and Reuchlin, or like his correspondent and editor Rosenroth, as one imbued with an evangelical spirit.*

The introduction of More to the Kabalah was brought about, as it has been supposed, by means of Isaac de Loria's *Liber Drushim*. There is no reason to believe that he undertook an independent study of the Zohar, and hence as his contributions to the subject are all prior to the appearance of the *Kabbala Denudata*, it follows that his acquaintance was not exhaustive, nor was it perhaps very good of its kind. At the same time, his study of the *Liber Drushim* called forth a well-reasoned letter from his pen, addressed to Rosenroth,† in which the description of the *Sephiroth* under the form of spheres is condemned as a fiction of the later rabbis and their relation to the denary is affirmed. The critical position of the writer is, however, conclusively established by the attribution of the Pythagorean denary to a Kabalistic origin. This letter was accompanied by a number of questions and considerations in development of the debated point and other difficulties,

---

* And desiring the *Ecclesiæ emolumentum*, as the same corre spondence shows.

† *Epistola ad Compilatorem, Apparatus in Librum Sohar, Par secunda*, p. 52, *et seq. Kab. Den. t. i.*

all which are duly printed by Rosenroth, to whom space seemed no object, together with his *Amica responsio*, which cites the authority of the Zohar in support of the circular form of the *Sephiroth*.* More replied with an *Ulterior Disquisitio* and an accompanying letter, in which he announces his belief that he has hit upon the true Kabalah of the Jewish *Bereshith*. This epistle is in English and quaintly worded. The conclusion entreats Rosenroth to intimate to his readers "how beneficiall this may prove for the preparing of the Jews to receive Christianity, the difficultyes and obstacles being cleared and removed by the right understanding of their own Cabbala."

There is no need to follow this friendly discussion, which, it must be confessed, becomes exceedingly tedious in the *Ulterior Disquisitio*. More, however, contributed another thesis in exposition of the Vision of Ezekiel, *i.e.*, the Kabalistic work of the Chariot, together with a Kabalistic catechism and a refutation of the doctrine that the material world is not the product of creation *ex nihilo*, in which last the Platonist seems to have scarcely understood the Kabalah.

Of all these the most interesting is the *Mercavæ Expositio*, which contains nineteen postulates, fifty-two questions arising out of the text of Ezekiel and the replies thereto. It affirms, (*a*) That all souls, angelical and human, with that of the Messiah included, were created at the beginning of the world ;† (*b*) That the material world in its first estate was diaphanous, or

---

* In *Caput* ii., *Consideratio tertia, ibid.*, p. 91.
† For this there is Talmudic as well as Zoharic authority.

lucid ; (c) That it had two chief elements, the Spirit
of Nature and the vehicle of the Holy Spirit ; (d)
That it was divided into four parts, which are the
four worlds of the Kabalists ; (e) That all souls were
at first enclosed in *Atziluth*, but were subject to
revolution in the other worlds ; (f) That souls which
the Divine decree has sent into *Assiah*, but are free
from willing sin, are sustained by Divine virtue,
and will assuredly return to *Atziluth* ; (g) That in
Atziluth the souls and the angels are absorbed wholly
in the Beatific Vision, but that in *Briah* they have
a tendency to external things ; (h) That the soul of
the Messiah in *Atziluth* made such progress in the
Divine Love that it became united with the Eternal
Word in a Hyper-Atzilutic or Hypostatic manner,
and was thus constituted Chief of all souls and
King of the four worlds, which took place at the
beginning of the Briatic world, the special heritage
of the Messiah.   At this point the Christian Kabalist
introduces the compact of the cross and dissolves all connection with the scheme of Jewish
theosophy.

The *Mercavæ Expositio* contains numerous
references to another work of More, entitled
*Conjectura Cabbalistica.** which preceded his correspondence with Rosenroth.   It is a presentation of the
literal, philosophical and mystical, or divinely moral
sense of the three initial chapters of Genesis.   It
was received, so the author assures us, neither from

---

* "A Conjectural Essay of interpreting the Mind of Moses
according to a threefold Cabbala, viz., Literal, Philosophical, Mystical
or Divinely Moral," London, 1662.   The attempt was dedicated to
Cudworth.

men nor angels, and as a fact the "conjecture" illustrates the criticism of Franck, for it has very little in common with any ancient or modern Kabalah ever received in Jewry. The literal section is a bald paraphrase of the scriptural account of the creation and fall of man. The "Philosophic Cabala" is established on the denary after the following fantastic manner :—

The Archetypal World = Monad, 1.
The First Matter = Duad, 2.
The Habitable Order = Triad, 3.
The Making of the Starry Heavens = Tetrad, 4.
The Making of Fish and Fowls, or Union of the Passive and Active Principle = Pentad, 5.
The Making of Beasts and Cattle, but chiefly of Man = Hexad, 6.

What becomes of the rest of the denary does not appear. In his first estate Adam was wholly ethereal, and his soul was the ground which was blessed by God, whereby it brought forth every pleasant tree and every goodly growth of the heavenly Father's own planting. The Tree of Life in the garden of man's soul was the essential will of God, while the Tree of Knowledge was the will of man himself. We have here the keynote of the allegory, which is merely pleasing and altogether unsubstantial. It may, however, be noted that the sleep which fell upon Adam was a lassitude of Divine contemplation. The "Moral Cabala" recognises two principles in man, namely, spirit and flesh. It gives apparently a synopsis of the work of regeneration, depicting, firstly, the spiritual chaos, when man is under the

dominion of the flesh; next, the dawning of the
heavenly principle, corresponding to the *Fiat Lux*,
but the analogy in most instances seems at once weak
and laboured. For example, the fruit-bearing trees
are good works, the manifestation of the sun is the
love of God and our neighbour, and so forth. On
the whole, it may be concluded that More's connection
with the Kabalah is an interesting episode in the life
of an amiable scholar, but it was without real
increment to either.

XI. THOMAS VAUGHAN

With the questionings, difficulties and tentative
expositions of Henry More it will be useful to
contrast what is said on the subject of Kabalism
by his contemporary Eugenius Philalethes, otherwise Thomas Vaughan. It will not be forgotten
by students of the byways of literature in the
seventeenth century that the two writers came into
collision in pamphlets. When Vaughan began his
philosophical labours by the publication of two
tracts on the nature of man and on the universal
Spirit of Nature, More, who was after all more
Platonist than mystic, and had scant tolerance for
mystic terminology, published some observations
concerning them, to which the Welsh mystic replied
in satires with the polemical virulence of his period.
The dispute itself deserves nothing less than oblivion,
but Thomas Vaughan has been regarded, and not,
I think, with exaggeration, as the greatest mystic,
theosopher and alchemist, with one exception in

the last respect,* produced by his century in England ; and as he died nearly twenty-five years before the appearance of the *Kabbala Denudata*, the source and extent of his Kabalistic knowledge will help us to fix the state of scholarship in England on the subject before the formation of the group of Cambridge Platonists. Vaughan, in his early works, confesses himself a disciple of Agrippa, and the " Three Books of Occult Philosophy "† represent the general measure of his knowledge concerning the esoteric tradition of the Jews, while the opinion which he had formed thereon must be referred to the " Retractation " of his master, that admirable work on the " Vanity of the Sciences and the excellence of the Word of God." I must not say that he shows no independent reading ; he quotes on one occasion a passage in the *Porta Lucis*‡ which is not to be found in Agrippa, and there are one or two other instances,§ but for the most part he is content to represent his model and his first inspirer. If my readers accept this judgment, they must interpret his own statement that he spent some

---

* The exception is Eirenæus Philalethes, that truly " Unknown Philosopher," with whom Eugenius has been so often identified, and from whom of late years so often and carefully distinguished by myself and other writers, that it is unnecessary in this connection to say anything concerning him, except that his numerous works have no points of contact, at least explicitly, with Kabalism.

† Translated into English one year after the appearance of Vaughan's first treatises.

‡ Concerning the restraint of the superior influences occasioned by the sin of Adam.

§ Of which some are sufficiently erroneous, as, for example, in *Magia Adamica*, when he states that Malkuth is the invisible, archetypal moon. I speak under correction, but I know of no authority for the Lunar attribution of the tenth Sephira.

years in the search and contemplation of the Kabalah reflectively and not bibliographically, which further will assist them to see how the peculiar mysticism of Thomas Vaughan can offer distinct points of contact with the Zohar without that text-book of Kabalism, then wholly untranslated, having been read by the mystic.

In his discourse on the antiquity of magic we find him alive, like the students who had preceded him, to the distinction between the true and the false Kabalah. The latter, described after the picturesque manner of his period, as the invention of dispersed and wandering rabbis "whose brains had more of distraction than their fortunes," consists altogether "in alphabetical knacks, ends always in the letter where it begins and the vanities of it are grown voluminous." But in respect of the "more ancient and physical traditions of the Kabalah," Thomas Vaughan tells us that he embraces them for so many sacred truths.* He recognises also a metaphysical tradition in which the greatest mystery is the symbolism of Jacob's Ladder. "Here we find two extremes—Jacob is one, at the foot of the ladder, and God is the other, who stands above it, *emittens formas et influxus in Jacob, sive subjectum hominem.* The rounds or steps in the ladder signify the middle nature, by which Jacob is united to God."† With this symbolism he contrasts the "false grammatical Kabala" which "consists only in rotations of the alphabet and a metathesis of letters in the text, by

---

* "Magical Writings of Thomas Vaughan," edited by A. E. Waite, London, 1888, pp. 109, 110.

† *Ibid.*, p. 111.

which means the scripture hath suffered many racks and excoriations." The true Kabalah only uses the letters for artifice, that is, with a view to concealment.* Of the physical side of the genuine tradition he gives an unfinished presentation in alchemical language, which is, however, transfigured, for Thomas Vaughan regarded alchemy as a spiritual and physical science, having its operations in the infinite as well as in the mineral kingdom. For him the *Sephiroth* are ten secret principles, of which the first is a spirit *in retrecesso suo fontano,* while the second is the Voice of that Spirit, the third is another Spirit which proceeds from the Spirit and the Voice, and the fourth is "a certain water" proceeding from the third Spirit, and emanating Fire and Air.† It will be seen that the reflections of the Welsh mystic on the apparatus of Kabalism are not elucidating, and while recording the Sephirotic attributions of the Sepher Yetzirah are not fully in consonance therewith.

We shall be inclined, on the whole, to confess that Vaughan's connection with the Kabalistic writers is like his communications with the brethren of the Rosicrucian Order. He knew nothing of the latter "as to their persons," so he tells us in his preface to a certain rare translation of the *Fama* and *Confessio* of the Fraternity, and it was merely by report and consideration on things heard at second hand that he was aware of the mysticism in Jewry. As time went on and he outgrew the simple leadingstrings of Cornelius Agrippa, so he strayed further

---

* *Ibid.*   † *Ibid.,*   110.

from Kabalistic interests, and though he never lost
the fascination betrayed in his earlier works, he passed
far away over the fields of spiritual alchemy, where no
Æsh Mezareph could help him.   When he published
"Euphrates, or the Waters of the East," in 1655, he
shows no longer any trace of the tradition in Israel.
In *Lumen de Lumine,* which appeared some four years
earlier, there are, however, a few references to the
subject, and one indeed constitutes an adumbration
of the Christian Kabalah as impressed on the curious
mind of the transcendental royalist.   The pretext by
which it is introduced is a speculation concerning the
"Fire-Soul," or informing spirit of the earth, which is
described as an influence from the Almighty derived
through the mediation of the *terra viventium.*   The
mediating being thus darkly described, is said to be
the Second Person, and that which "the Kabalists
style the Supernatural East."   To explain this
symbolism Vaughan adds : "As the Natural Light of
the sun is first manifested to us in the East, so the
Supernatural Light was first manifested in the second
person, for he is *Principium alterationis,* the Beginning
of the ways of God, or the first manifestation of
his Father's Light in the Supernatural generation.
From this *Terra Viventium* or Land of the Living
comes all Life or Spirit."*   The Kabalistic warrant
of this notion is the axiom : *Omnis anima bona
anima nova filia Orientis.*†   The East in question
is *Chokmah,* which is contrary to Kabalistic statements, and *Chokmah* is the Son of God.   This also is

---

* *Lumen De Lemine*, London, 1651, pp. 80-82.

† Vaughan also cites the obscure eighth conclusion of Mirandola,
and says that the third light is *Binah*, the Holy Ghost.—*Ibid.*, p. 83.

opposed to the Sephirotic attributions with which we are familiar, but there is some trace in early Kabalistic writers of an attribution of the Three Supernals to Father, Son, Bride, with which the later rabbins are said to have tampered so as to elude its Christian inferences. In either case Vaughan is interesting as a strange light of Christian mysticism and not as an expositor of the Kabalah.

XII. KNORR VON ROSENROTH.

From the occult standpoint it is, perhaps, more interesting to ascertain the motives which led the editor of the *Kabbala Denudata* to the consideration of Jewish theosophy than those of any other student of the subject. To Christian Knorr von Rosenroth the occultist owes nearly all his knowledge of the Zohar, for the bibliographical writers who preceded him give only meagre notices of the Kabalistic *magnum opus*, and it is not even mentioned by Mirandola, Agrippa, or Postel. Now Rosenroth occupies a somewhat curious position which occultists for the most part have failed to remark, because they know very little about their chief illuminator in the mysticism of Israel. I propose to show that he was actuated by the same missionary enthusiasm which characterised all the Christian neophytes who preceded him,* but I shall begin by enumerating one

---

* It was indeed, both before and after, the conventional *raison d'être* of almost every work on the subject. See, for example, Beyers' *Cabbalismus Judaico - Christianus Detectus Breviterque Delineatus.* Wittemberg. 1707.

or two points which indicate that he had occult connections. Born in the year 1636, a German noble bearing the title of baron, he appears on the scene of history shortly after public curiosity had died out on the subject of the Rosicrucian mystery. Joachim Junge, Johann Valentin Andreæ and Ægidius Guthmann, three persons to whom rival theories have attributed the invention of that mystery,* were still alive ; Robert Fludd, the English apologist of the Fraternity, was on the threshold of death, but had not yet passed away ; Thomas Vaughan was a schoolboy ; Eirenæus Philalethes had just written his *Introitus Apertus* to show the adepts of alchemy that he was their brother and their peer ;† Sendivogius had exhausted his projecting powder and was living in seclusion, an aged man, on the frontiers of Silesia ;‡ John Baptist van Helmont, who long before had testified that he had seen and touched the philosopher's stone—of a colour like saffron in powder, but heavy and shining like pounded glass§—had christened his son Mercurius ; and Mercurius van Helmont, the contemporary and friend of Rosenroth, divided his laborious existence between a tireless search after the secret of trans muting metals and the study of the Kabalah, Rosenroth, Kabalist like Helmont, was, like Helmont, probably a chemist, and on the crowded title-page

---

* "Real History of the Rosicrucians," by A. E. Waite, c. viii., especially pp. 220—222.

† See *Præfatio Authoris*, which appears in all editions of the *Introitus apertus ad Occlusum Regis Palatium*.

‡ A. E. Waite : "Lives of Alchemysticall Philosophers," London, 1888, p. 179.

§ In his treatise *De Vita Eterna*.

of his great work, we find it described as *Scriptum omnibus philologis, philosophis, Theologis omnium religionum, atque philochymicis quam utilissimum.* The justification is that the *Loci communes Cabbalistici* include a *Compendium Libri Cabbalistico-Chymici, Æsch Mezareph dicti, de Lapide Philosophico.* I have had occasion in the sixth book to give some account of this curious treatise.

We have reason therefore to suppose that Rosenroth was infected with the alchemical zeal of his friend, the second generation of an alchemical family. We may suspect, however, that he was more mystic than Hermetist; we are told that he loved meditating on the Holy Scriptures and that he knew them by heart. Like his countryman Khunrath, he was a Lutheran, and Eliphas Levi would have said of him, as of the author of the *Amphitheatrum*, "herein he was a German of his period rather than a mystic citizen of the eternal kingdom."* In matters of religion his peculiar bent is determined by the fact that he wrote an "Explanation of the Apocalypse," about which I will forbear from wearying my readers. More to our purpose is a dialogue on evangelical history, in which a Kabalistic catechumen proposes questions on the four Gospels and a Christian replies. With this also we may connect a treatise entitled *Messias Purus*, in which the life of Jesus Christ, from his conception to his baptism, is explained according to the doctrines of the Kabalah. In a word, the motto of his correspondent Henry More was that also of Rosenroth : "May the glory of our

---

* *Histoire de la Magie*, Introduction, p. 33. Paris, 1860.

God and his Christ be the end of all our writings!"
In conformity with this he begins his enumeration of
the reasons which justify the appearance of a Latin
version of the Zohar* by affirming that at a period
when the divisions of Christendom are traceable to
diversity of philosophical opinions and metaphysical
definitions it must be important to investigate a
philosophical system which flourished during the age
of Christ and his apostles, and from which fountain
the sacred oracles have themselves drawn largely. In
the preface to the translation of the Zohar he
expressly founds his opinion that Kabalistic dogmas
may be of Divine revelation on the ground of their
sanctity and sublimity, as well as their great use
in explaining the books of the Old and New
Testaments. He also notes that, unlike the
later Jewish writings, the Zohar does not contain
a single utterance against Christ. Finally, after
enumerating twenty-four reasons why the Jews
should enjoy toleration at Christian hands, he
mentions the chief things which will assist their
conversion. They include of course the ordinary
common places of piety and the ordinary devices of
proselytism, but there is stress laid upon the promotion of the study of Hebrew and Chaldaic, and
on the translation of the New Testament into those
languages.† The disquisition is conventional enough,

* *Apparatus in Librum Sohar, Pars Secunda*, p. 3 *et seq.*, Kab.
Den., Tom. i.
† With this description the reader may compare a little t
which belongs to the *Kabbala Denudata*, though unfortunately it is
met with very rarely in extant copie , *i.e.*, *Adumbratio Kabbalæ
Christianæ, id est Syncatabasis Hebraizans, sive Explicitio ad dogmata
Novi Foederis, pro formanda hypothesis, ad conversionem Judæorum*

but it is important, because it indicates, firstly, the
project which was ever near to the heart of Rosenroth, and, secondly, how little he dreamed either of
an esoteric Christianity or of a withdrawn Wisdom-
Religion, how little he looked to find in Kabalistic
doctrine a deeper sense of Christian doctrines, or
indeed anything but their consecration in the eyes of
Jewry, by demonstrating that they were to be found
in the Zohar. He did not wish the Christian to
become a Kabalist, but he longed very much for the
Kabalistic Jew to become a Lutheran. He is said to
have endured great sacrifices, outside the vast labour
involved, over the publication of the *Kabbala Denudata*,
but there is no need to add that it entirely missed its
aim ; it has enabled a few students to get a confused
notion of the Zohar, and it has in this way done
immense service to occultists : it is outside probability
that it ever brought a single Jew into the Church of
Christ, and as Rosenroth failed in his public aim, so
at the close of his life he had the misfortune to see
his daughter depart from the reformed religion and
embrace, under the influence of her husband, the faith
of the Catholic Church. Taken altogether the story
of Christian Rosenroth has a touch of heroism and
tragedy, and with all its faults his gift to scholarship
is one of permanent value, and it is, I think, a useful
task to indicate the circumstances under which he
gave it and the motives by which he was prompted.*

---

proficientis. It is an addendum to the second volume, separately paged,
and is in the form of a dialogue between a Kabalist and a Christian
philosopher. It has been translated quite recently into French.

At a later date the same motives inspired two small treatises
which are interesting in their way, and are worth mentioning for the
benefit of students who may wish to pursue the subject. (1) *Phosphorus*

I should add that over the antiquity of Kabalistic
doctrine and literature he was by no means credulous
for his period, seeming indeed to admit that there
may have been an admixture of late material with
the ancient fragments of the Zohar.   He evidently
regarded the Book of Concealment as the oldest and
most important of its treatises, and this is the only
one which he was inclined to ascribe to the direct

*Orthodoxæ Fidei Veterum Cabbalistarum, seu Testimonia de Sacro-
Sancta Trinitate et Messia Deo et Homine, ex pervetusto Libro Sohar
deprompta, qua nunc primum Latiné reddita, suisque et R. Johannis
Kemperi Judæo-Christiani animadversionibus concinné explicata,
Judæis æque ac Christianis speciminis loco edidit Andreas Norrelius
Suecus, qui item commentarios Kemperianos suis illustravit notis.
Amstelodami,* 1720.   The prolegomena are concerned with the praise
of R. Simeon ben Jochai, showing the authority of the Zohar, and its
superiority to the Talmud on the ground that its author flour
before Judah the Prince.   The Talmud is quoted (p. 10), to
that R. Simeon studied the Kabalah in the cave, and that he and his
son wrote the Zohar therein, or that part of it which is in the Jerusalem
dialect.   The Hebrew portions are referred to other authorships (p. 16).
The translated matter is chiefly from the " Faithful Shepherd," and
follows the Mantua edition of the Zohar.   (2) *Lux in Tenebris, quam
Zohar Antiquum Judæorum Monumentum, genti suæ occoccatæ præbet,
in denissimis rerum divinarum tenebris, ad mysterium SS. Trinitatis
eo facilius appræhendendum, et Majestatem Christi Divinam non
pertinaciter oppugnandam, et Honorem Spiritus Sancti Recentiorum
more non fœdandum . . . Studio M. Nicolai Lütkens* (without place
or date, but about the same period as the treatise of Norrelius).   In the
first two chapters there is an attempt to prove that th   f the
Trinity is concealed in Leviticus xvi. 18, and Deut. vi. 5.   The third
chapter investigates Gen. xix., 24—*De Domino qui a Domino pluit*, in
the same interest.   The fourth chapter treats of the Lord God of II
I   3; and the fifth of the Lord God, ib. xlviii., 16.   The sixth
chapter seeks to prove that the three supernal *Sephiroth* w
and characters under which the pre-Christian I   nished the
Three Persons of the One Divin   (3) Compare with
Diatribe Philologica de R. Simeone Filio Jochai auctore Libri Soh. ,
*qua viri celeberrimi Christiani Schoettgenii Dissertatio docens R.
Simeonum Filium Jochai Religionum fuisse Christianum modiste
examinatur et contrarium potius evincitur, auctore Justo Martino
Glæsenero, Hildesiæ,* 1736.   A pamphlet of twenty-two pages.

authorship of R. Simeon ben Jochai. Of the rest, some may have been the work of R. Abba and some of the school which succeeded these masters.

XIII. RALPH CUDWORTH

The honoured name of Ralph Cudworth, perhaps the greatest theosophist of his age, is still a precious memory in English theological literature of the higher type, though, except among rare students, the "True Intellectual System of the Universe" is now unknown. It is a mine of Platonism, learning and sapience, and more than this, it is a deeply reasoned treatise of its period in opposition to the atheism of that period ; its points are established victoriously, and turning over the leaves of the colossal folio one almost regrets that the difficulties of the seventeenth century disturb us no longer and that their solution no longer helps us. It must be confessed that Cudworth connects somewhat superficially with Kabalism, and the connection, such as it is, need not detain us long. The chief thesis of the " Intellectual System " is that behind all the tapestries and embroideries of pagan mythology there is the doctrine of monotheism, and that civilised man in reality has never worshipped but one God, whose threefold nature was a " Divine Cabbala" or revelation, successively depraved and adulterated till it almost disappears for Cudworth among the " particular unities " of Proclus and the later Platonists.* Among

* For the purposes of this notice I have used the original edition of the "True Intellectual System of the Universe," London, 1668.

the cloud of witnesses who are convened in support
of this view are included the later Rabbinical writers,
the *Halacoth* of Maimonides, the *Gnolath Tamid*
of Moses Albelda, the *Ikkarim* of Joseph Albo,
the commentaries of R. David Kimchi, the book
Nitzachon and the glosses of Rabbi Solomon,
references and citings which at least serve to show
that this Christian divine had attempted some
curious exploration in the unknown world of
Hebrew literature.   His conclusion was " that the
Hebrew Doctors and Rabbins have been generally of
this persuasion, that the Pagan Nations anciently, at
least the intelligent amongst them, acknowledged
One Supreme God of the whole world, and that all
their other Gods were but Creatures and Inferior
Ministers, which were worshipped by them upon these
two accounts, either as thinking that the honour done
to them redounded to the Supreme, or else that they
might be their Mediators and Intercessors, Orators
and Negotiators with Him, which inferior Gods of
the Pagans were supposed by these Hebrews to be
chiefly of two kinds, Angels and Stars or Spheres,
the latter of which the Jews as well as Pagans
concluded to be animated and intellectual."   The
question at the present day is chiefly archaic or
fantastic, but it has its interest, for it serves to
illustrate the strange contrast which exists between
the Hebrew mind at the period of Maimonides and at
that far distant epoch when the song of the Psalmist
described the idols of the Gentiles as " silver and
gold, the work of the hands of men."

In addition to the " True Intellectual System of
the Universe" Cudworth published some sermons and

a discourse on the "True Notion of· the Lord's Supper,"* afterwards translated into Latin by Mosheim, with a confutation representing the consubstantial doctrine of Lutheran theology,† and yet again enlarged upon by Edward Pelling in his "Discourse on the Sacrament." The drift of the thesis is represented sufficiently by the summary of the first chapter: "That it was a custom of the Jews and Heathens to feast upon things sacrificed, and that the custom of the Christians in partaking of the Body and Blood of Christ once sacrificed upon the Cross, in the Lord's Supper, is analogous thereto." It is outside my province to pronounce upon this view, but as a Christian Mystic who holds that sacramentalism is the law of Nature and the law of Grace, it may just be remarked in passing that no theory which reduces the Eucharist to a memorial or a religious banquet can be mystically acceptable. Cudworth was by no means a mystic, and the most that his subject afforded was an opportunity to give further evidence of his unusual erudition, and it may be added of no inconsiderable skill in its management. The thesis is mentioned here because it has recourse so frequently to the Rabbinical writers, to the glosses of Nachmanides, the writings of Isaac Abravanel, the *Mishna*, the commentary on that work by Rabbi Obadiah, the scholiasts on Judges, rare MSS. of Karaite Jews and so forth. The Zoharic writings are not quoted, but it was because they contained nothing bearing on the matter in hand; had occasion arisen, no doubt Ralph Cudworth

---

* London, 1676.   † This translation appeared in 1733.

would have given evidence of equal familiarity with that cycle of Kabalistic literature.

XIV. THOMAS BURNET

With the Cambridge school of Platonists the name of Thomas Burnet, some time master of the Charterhouse, connects by association rather than the similarity of intellectual pursuits. He entered Christ's College in 1654, when Ralph Cudworth was master, while Henry More was just in his fortieth year. It was probably to the last-named divine that he owed his slight knowledge of the subject which entitles him to mention in this place. The amicable discussion between More and the editor of the *Kabbala Denudata* appeared, as we have seen, in that work in the year 1677, but the "Interpretation of the mind of Moses" had preceded it by a number of years. When Burnet published his *Telluris Theoria Sacra*, he gave no evidence of his interest in Platonic or Kabalistic subjects; it has been described by Brewster as a beautiful geological romance. It is, of course, concerned largely with the Mosaic scheme of creation, and the more important work which followed it, dealing as it does with the ancient doctrine concerning the origin of things, is really its extension or sequel.* In this interesting volume, written elegantly in Latin of the period, *tout un grand chapitre*, as the bibliography of Dr. Papus describes it, is devoted to the Kabalah.

* *Archæologiæ Philosophicæ sive Doctrina Antiqua de Rerum Originibus, Libri duo, editio secunda* (the best), London 1728.

As already hinted, it bears no evidence of original
research, or indeed of any first-hand knowledge, but
it is justifiable by our purpose to ascertain how a
literature which fascinated, though it did not
altogether convince, the Cambridge Platonists,
impressed the liberal mind of a bold and not
unlearned thinker belonging to the next generation.
We find, as might be anticipated, that Burnet raises
no question as to the wisdom of Moses, by which
he understood what all other Kabalistic students
have understood also, a knowledge of natural
mysteries derived from the Egyptian education of
the Jewish lawgiver. He differs, however, from the
Kabalists by questioning seriously how much of
this wisdom came down to the Israelites. Assuming
some tradition of the kind, there could be no doubt
that it was depraved in the lapse of time.* In
particular, the Kabalah, as we now possess it,
abounds in figments of imagination and in nugatory
methods. From this statement of the general
position, which may be regarded as the common
ground of all criticism, he proceeds to a more
detailed examination, with the specific results of
which no sympathetic inquirer at the present day
can reasonably quarrel. The debased character
of the Jewish tradition is indeed, as already seen,
admitted by those who most earnestly maintain its
mystical and theosophical importance.

If we attempt, says Burnet, to separate anything
which may remain uncorrupted in the Kabalah, to
divide the genuine from the spurious, we must first of

---

* *Fædissime licet à Neotericis corrupta et adulterata.*

all purge away that numerical, literal, grammatical part which seeks to extract arcane meanings from the alphabet, the Divine Names and the word-book of the Scriptures. The magical and superstitious element must also be purged away. We must further bear in mind, and this, I think, is the most sensible and necessary of all the secondary points raised in the criticism, that the enunciation of common notions in uncommon language cannot be accepted as the true Kabalah. The warning which it implies is not less needed at the present moment than in the days of Thomas Burnet. The delight in unintelligible language because it is unintelligible is as characteristic of some occult writers at the present day, even as of gloom-wrapped Hades according to the Ritual of the Dead, and it is a tendency which has an inscrutable foundation in the entire subject. It would seem indeed that the sphinx who propounds the arcana in terms as monstrous as herself needs only a commonplace to overwhelm her, as in the case of Œdipus.

In accordance with his intention Burnet proceeds to divide the Kabalah into the Nominal and Real. The first is that which he has specified as worthless— *Gematria, Temurah, Notaricon, Vocabula*. Its devices, he says, are the diversions of our children, and in truth it would seem hard to decide whether intellectual superiority and philosophical seriousness should be ascribed to rabbinical anagrams or to the apparatus of " Tit: Tat: To." In any case, " they do not belong to sane literature, much less to wisdom."

So far we can accept very readily the judgment

of Burnet, but destructive criticism is always comparatively easy, and there was no novelty in the line
taken even so far back as the second half of the
seventeenth century. When he comes, however, to
consider what he has agreed to regard as the real
Kabalah, his insufficiency is quite evident, and his
slender knowledge, drawn only from the *Kabbala
Denudata*, when it does not arrest his judgment, leads
him into manifest error. Thus, he tells us that the
real Kabalah contains two things which are important
for our consideration, the doctrine of the *Sephiroth*
and that of the Four Worlds, but he complains that the
conception which underlies the former does not appear
clearly. With the help of the Lexicon of Rosenroth
he decides finally that they are emanations from God.*
He sets forth what he can glean from that source concerning *Kether* and *Chokmah*, and then surrenders the
inquiry in the hope of finding more intelligible statements concerning the Four Worlds.† He concludes,
however, that the condemnation of all the pseudo-
mystics of Kabalism, Theosophy and Hermetics is
that of the unbelievers who continued to love the darkness rather than the light when the light was come
already into the world.‡ He assumes, as might be
expected, that the " Book of Occultation " is the most
important part of the Zohar, and glancing at the

---

* Elsewhere, he attempts to consider their significance in
connection with the axiom—*ex nihilo nihil fit.*

† He mentions in addition to the *Sephiroth* and the Four Worlds,
the thirty-two Paths of Wisdom, from the Sepher Yetzirah and its
commentary, and the Fifty Gates of Providence " through which Moses
attained his marvellous science, and concealed the same in the
Pentateuch," *i.e.*, according to the Kabalists.

‡ John, iii. 19-21.

commentaries of Isaac de Loria and of Hirtz on the tract in question and its developments, confesses his inability to understand either from text or interpreters what is meant by the symbolism of the Vast and the Lesser Countenance. "We are all of us liable some time or other to be distracted by reasoning, but it is a common complaint of the mind among Orientals to be distracted by allegories."

To sum the general position : We know from Maimonides that the Hebrews once possessed many mysteries concerning things divine, but that they have perished.* It is at the same time scarcely possible that all foundation should be wanting to the Kabalah, yet if its doctrines were openly and clearly set forth, it is hard to say whether they would move us to laughter or astonishment.

Thomas Burnet has higher claims to consideration than his ability as a critic of Kabalism. He had perhaps few qualifications from which he might be expected to understand or sympathise with the aspirations embraced by theosophy. He was one of the rare precursors of liberal theology, and he is said to have closed the path of his promotion by venturing to express the opinion that the story of the Garden of Eden should not be understood literally. In a later treatise on the "Faith and Duties of Christians,"† he is also stated to have excluded so much that seemed to him doubtful or unimportant in accepted doctrine that it is questionable whether even Christianity remained. A posthumous work on eschatology and the resur-

---

* "The Guide of the Perplexed." Part i., c. 71.
† *De Fide et officiis Christianorum.*

rection* maintained that the punishment of the wicked would terminate ultimately in their salvation. I should add that some pretended English versions of the Archæological Philosophy do not represent the original, and in particular omit altogether the Kabalistic section.

XV. SAINT-MARTIN

The life and doctrine of Louis Claude de Saint-Martin, the Unknown Philosopher, who at the end of the eighteenth century and amidst the torch lights of the Revolution diffused in France the higher spirit of mysticism, having been the subject of a special study,† I shall refer to him here only very briefly, for his Kabalistic connections are discussed at some length therein. He was the recipient of an esoteric tradition through Martines de Pasqually, the genesis of which remains undetermined, though it was termed Rosicrucian by his initiator, and is now termed Swedenborgian by his present interpreters in France. It is a tradition which differs very considerably from other presentations of occult doctrine, and in particular it has little in common with what we know or may infer concerning Rosicrucian teaching. In the writings of Pasqually, with which we are acquainted only through some excerpts published by one of Saint-Martin's biographers‡ and in the cate-

---

* *De Statu Mortuorum et Resurgentium.*

† See A. E. Waite :—"The Life of Louis Claude de Saint-Martin, the Unknown Philosopher, and the Substance of his Transcendental Doctrine," London, Philip Wellby, 1901.

‡ It is right to say that Kenneth Mackenzie, in his "Cyclopœdia of Freemasonry," attributes to him three published works which, so far

chisms of the Masonic Rite propagated by him, which are also most probably his work, the tradition is presented in a very crude manner. It was much developed by Saint-Martin, who indeed brought to it a gift of genius which was wanting in his instructor. Now, Saint-Martin was a man who cared very little, and does not scruple to say so, for purely traditional doctrines, at least as traditional, nor did he show much deference towards doctors of authority therein. He considered books at best a makeshift method of instruction, though he wrote many; he preferred learning at first hand from God, Man and the Universe. Till he came under the influence of Jacob Bohme he neither quoted nor possessed "authorities," with the exception of the Scriptures. He drew, of course, from the source of his initiation, but he never mentions it in any clear manner, except in his correspondence and his life-notes, both published posthumously. There is nothing to indicate that he had ever read Kabalistic literature; there is every presumption that he did not. Some of his lesser doctrines possess a Kabalistic complexion. There is that in particular concerning the Great Name which I have developed at some length in the study to which I have referred, but it has lost all touch with Kabalism in the hands of Saint-Martin. So also he has a complex system of mystic numbers which suggests the Rabbinical *Notaricon*, but it is entirely out of line with all other numerical mysticism,

---

as I am aware, are unknown, and I must add that personally I regard them as mythical. It may be noted further that while this volume was passing through the press the fragmentary treatise referred to in the text has been published in Paris.

and makes the question of its origin one of the most attractive problems in later occult history. I conclude that Pasqually, whom I take to have been a sincere and perhaps even a saintly man, as his Masonic school was almost a seminary of sanctity, derived from a source which retained some filtrations of Kabalism, and that they were brought over by Saint-Martin without any historical associations whatever.* He has therefore little title to be included among the defenders and expounders of Kabalistic doctrine, which would have come as a surprise to himself. This is done, however, by French occult writers at this day,† who seem anxious to annex anyone, from Shakespeare to the author of " Supernatural Religion," and I regret that I must add by one among the rest who from his position in the modern rite of Martinism has the opportunity to know differently and the gifts which make use of opportunity.

XVI. ÉLIPHAS LÉVI

Between the period of Saint Martin and that of Alphonse Louis Constant, the subject of the present notice, the French literature of Kabalism may be more correctly said to have been initiated rather than

---

* That man is superior to the angels, and may even instruct them, is, I think, the most convincing instance in Saint-Martin of such a filtration. This notion is found in the Zohar, and in some of its commentators.

† More especially in the case of the so-called facetious allegory *Le Crocodile*, in which it may be safely said that there is not a single trace of Kabalism.

to have received a new impetus by the publication of Adolphe Franck, to whose views on the subject of post-Christian religious philosophy among the Jews, I have already made frequent reference.* I have also indicated that much of its value remains unimpaired after the lapse of nearly sixty years, and indeed modern criticism has in certain definite respects inclined to return to his standpoint, as regards not only the antiquity of Zoharic tradition but of much of the body of the Zohar. Franck's work has, of course, its limitations, and it is well known to scholars that his excerpts from the Kabalistic books were early subjected to severe strictures in Germany; but for an accomplished and luminous review of the whole subject nothing of later date can be said to have superseded it. Its analyses of the Sepher Yetzirah and of the Zohar, together with its delineations of the correspondences between the philosophical school of Kabalism and the schools of Plato, of Alexandria, of Philo, created French knowledge on the subject, and together with the researches of Munk, published some few years subsequently, have been practically the only source of that knowledge down to recent times, with the exception of such light as may be held to have been diffused by the writings of Eliphas Levi. As regards both methods and motives, Franck and Levi are located at opposite poles. The first was an academic writer having no occult interests; the second claimed not only initiation but adeptship, not only the ordinary resources of scholarship focussed on a

---

' *Kabbale ou la Philosophie Religieuse des Hébreux.* Par. A·l. Franck, Paris, 1843.

literary and historical problem, but all the advantages which could be derived from the exclusive possession of its master key.

Among the lesser difficulties of Kabalistic criticism the proper allocation of Alphonse Louis Constant in the throng of students and expositors is not without its gravity. Whether in France or in England few have approached the subject with sympathies in the direction of occult science and philosophy who do not owe their introduction to Eliphas Lévi. I speak, of course, of the period subsequent to 1850,* and I may add that few persons thus initiated have done anything but read the interpretations of their first leader into the obscure body of dogma which comprises the esoteric tradition of

---

* Although the elegant treatise of Franck had, as we have seen, preceded Levi's interpretatations by several years, appearing in 1843. So far as I can recollect the professed adept never referred to the sympathetic criticism and defence of the more academic writer. Prior to 1843 the most extraordinary ignorance must have prevailed upon the subject in France, since it was possible for a distinguished philosopher to write as follows :—" When Christian philosophy made its appearance in the world it crushed Paganism and Theurgy, and in the second century humanity was made subject to a severe regime, which set aside mysticism. It did not reappear till the fourteenth and fifteenth centuries in certain schools of Italy and Germany. This new mysticism, called Kabalah, from a name known already in the schools of Alexandria, but since entirely disappeared, and signifying oral tradition, issued from the bosom of the scholastic, and acted with the instruments of the scholastic, as formerly the neoplatonist Porphyry evoked with Platonic words. The Cabbala *(sic)* of the fifteenth century put in operation bizarre formulæ, magic squares and circles, mysterious numbers, by the power of which the demons of hell and the divinities of heaven were compelled, as it was pretended, to appear in obedience to the wand ; hence the mystic ecstasies of Raymond Lully, who attracted such zealous partisans and furious enemies, causing blood to flow ; hence the delirium which brought Bruno to the stake." Victor Cousin : *Cours de Philosophie*, Paris, 1836. It would seem impossible to record a greater number of inaccuracies, or to display more signal ignorance, within the dimensions of a paragraph.

the Jews. If it be necessary, therefore, to reduce very largely the authority attributed to Eliphas Lévi, I must expect to alienate the sympathy of his many admirers, but this is only a question of the moment, and so far as it is possible to take a plain course in the matter there can be no real need for hesitation. But the question, which looks so simple in its first aspect, is no sooner raised than it is complicated by several kinds of considerations and indeed by incompatible facts. When I published a few years ago my English version of Levi's " Transcendental Magic," I stated that it was the work of a writer who had received initiation into a school of traditional knowledge, nor must I deny that this school possesses the respect of its partici-pants. A certain proportion of its tradition was made public for the first time in Levi's treatise and under circumstances which seem then to have been regarded as inopportune. I do not think that I shall be making an unpermissible statement if I now add that the course pursued by the author brought him, as it is alleged, into conflict with his superiors, and that it barred his progress through the higher grades of that initiation.* On the one hand, therefore, the possibilities of his communication ceased at the limit of his knowledge, while, on the other, it can be shown abundantly that he was not in any solid sense of the word a first hand student of the literature of occult philosophy. I do not think that he ever made an independent statement upon any historical fact to which the

---

* On this point see my letter in " Light : a Journal of Psychical, Occult and Mystical Research," July 4, 1896.

least confidence could be given with prudence.
He never presented the sense of an author whom
he was reviewing in a way which could be said to
reproduce that author faithfully. As in the one
case he embroidered history by the help of what
Mr. Arthur Machen would term a decorative imagination, so it occurred frequently that he attributed to
an old author the kind of sense which it would be
very interesting to find in old authors, but is not
met with except by the mediation of a magician
with the transmuting power of Abbe Constant.
He takes, for example, a perfectly worthless little
book by Abbot Trithemius, which does not reflect
the opinions of that learned Benedictine, but is
simply a trifle addressed to a German prince
explaining how some persons in antiquity distributed
the government of the world among certain planetary
intelligences ruling successively and reassuming rule
in rotation. He invests it with the importance of
a grand and sublime achievement of prophetic
science, whereas it does not show half the acumen
of our empirical friend Nostradamus, and is equalled
in any year of grace by the almanacks of Raphael
and Zadkiel. Here is an instance of what Levi
reads into an author. Nor do we need to depart
from this unhappy little treatise to test his reliability
over an express matter of fact. He tells us that the
forecast of Trithemius closes with a proclamation
of universal monarchy in the year 1879. Trithemius
says nothing of the kind, but only modestly remarks
that the gift of prophecy so generously attributed to
him by his reviewer would be required to discern
anything beyond that period. I mention this matter,

:o which I have drawn attention previously in the revised edition of the "Mysteries of Magic," not because I wish to accentuate charges against a writer whose brilliance and literary beauty we all admire, but because it is necessary to exhibit the quality of mind which was brought by Eliphas Levi to the illumination of Kabalistic literature. I wish to prepare my readers, more especially those who admire him, as I also admire him, though not as critic, not as expositor, not as historian, only as a literary thaumaturgist working great wonders with the magic of words—I wish to prepare them, I say, for the fact that the deliberations of the Holy Synods will be found to have suffered many changes and transfigurations through the medium of their inter-preter, and that any matter of sharp fact in the hands of this unaccountable juggler seems to become pyrotechnic and to detonate, if I may speak so roughly, into the most twisted squibs and crackers.

I will not dwell upon the miserable plight of every Hebrew quotation in those works which he may be supposed to have passed for press. No ordinary carelessness would account for such blunders, nor could they be explained by supposing that he was ignorant of their language. His acquaintance must have been slender enough, but it is not necessary to be proficient in Hebrew or indeed in Chinese to ensur: the accuracy of a few excerpts. The excerpts in Eliphas Levi "no one can speak and no one can spell." But even in simpler matters his blunders are incredible. He gives the three mother-letters of the Hebrew alphabet inaccurately,* which for an accredited

---

* *La Clef des Grands Mystères*, Paris, 1861, pp. 199, 200.

student of the Sepher Yetzirah is almost as inexcusable as if an English author erred in enumerating the vowels of our own language.

The instance, however, to which I wish to draw particular attention, because it seems to me impressive and even final, occurs in the posthumous work entitled the "Book of Splendours."* Of this the first part is intended as a compressed translation of the "Greater Holy Synod." Now, Levi says that the deliberations of this conclave are contained in a Hebrew treatise entitled *Idra Suta*, and these words appear accordingly at the head of his version. But the *Idra Suta*, or more correctly *Zuta*, is the name of the Lesser Synod, as will appear by referring to the fourth section of the fifth book of the present volume, while *Idrah Rabba* is that appertaining to the record of the Greater Assembly. What should we think of the qualifications of a commentator on the books of the Old Testament who informed us that the word *Bereshith* was applied to Deuteronomy? It will be observed that I do not make this criticism to show that Levi was unqualified because he was ignorant of Hebrew, but to prove that he was guilty of egregious errors the indication of which neither supposes nor requires any knowledge of the kind.

That in spite of his slipshod criticism, his careless reading and his malpractices in historical matters the works of Eliphas Levi do contain valuable material may, of course, be explained by saying that he drew from his initiation and verified his knowledge badly by the ordinary channels. This is true up to a

---

* *Le Livre des Splendeurs, contenant le Soleil Judaïque* . . . *Etudes sur les Origines de la Kabbale,* &c. Paris, 1894.

certain point, and yet it does not do justice to the entire position, omitting indeed one of its essential features. What seems to me to distinguish Lévi from all other occult writers is not his knowledge as an initiate, but the peculiar genius of interpretation which he applied to that knowledge, the surprising results which he could obtain from an old doctrine, even as from an old author. They were certainly not reliable results, they were certainly not in harmony with any secret knowledge, they represented the standpoint of the agnostic rather than the transcendentalist, and they afflicted the transcendental standpoint in consequence, but they wore the guise and they spoke the language of occultism, and it is they which have fascinated his students, they which have multiplied his admirers, they also which have undeniably imparted a new impulse to the study of occult philosophy. This is equivalent to saying that the influence of Eliphas Lévi does not make for a proper understanding of occult doctrines, and as concerns the Kabalah that it reads a meaning into the esoteric tradition of Israel which is not fully in harmony therewith.

Let us take, for example, his inverted text of the first chapter of Genesis, for which he claims a Kabalistic foundation.* It is needless to say that it neither has nor could have any rabbinical authority and that it first occurred to the mind of a Frenchman in the second half of the nineteenth century. As it exceeds quotation in this place I must refer the reader to the work in which I have rendered it at

* _La Clef des Grands Mystères_, p. 334 _et seq._ "Mysteries of Magic, second edition, London, 1897, p. 108 _et seq._

length.* It may be, however, shortly described as
replacing the history of creation by God with that of
God's creation by man. It is, if you prefer it, the
evolution of the God-idea in humanity, though I
much fear that Mr. Grant Allen must have been
hindered by the limits of his erudition from utilising
it. As an exercise of ingenuity it is admirable, but
the point at which the sober critic must diverge from
the interpreter is that "this occult Genesis was
thought out by Moses before writing his own."

Let us take another case which, though it brings
us to the same question, is more perhaps to our
purpose, because it is a construction placed upon
Zoharic symbolism. For Eliphas Levi the Great
Countenance of the Zohar is the evolution of the
idea of God from the shadow divinities represented
by the Kings of Edom. *Microprosopus* is the grand
night of faith. The one is the God of the wise, the
other the idol of the vulgar. The one is the great
creative hypothesis, the other the dark figure, the
restricted hypothesis. As it is to the Lesser Countenance that the name of *Tetragrammaton* is
attributed, it follows that the secret of the Zohar is
the mystic utterance of the adept to the recipiendary
of the Egyptian mysteries : "Osiris is a black god."
Microprosopus is, however, "neither the Ahriman of
the Persians nor the evil principle of the Manichæans,
but a more exalted concept, a mediating shadow
between the infinite light and the feeble eyes of
humanity ; a veil made in the likeness of humanity
with which God Himself deigns to cover His glory ;

* *I.e.*: "The Mysteries of Magic," first and second edition,
London, 1886, 1897.

a shadow which contains the reason of all mysteries, explaining the terrible Deity of the prophets, who threatens and inspires fear. It is the God of the priests, the God who exacts sacrifices, the God who sleeps frequently and is awakened by the trumpets of the temple, the God who repents having made man, but, conquered by prayers and offerings, is appeased when on the point of punishing."*

That this interpretation has fascinated many students can be no cause for surprise ; one is amazed and delighted irresistibly at discovering an esoteric tradition in which all theological difficulties seem to dissolve together. If it seem at first sight incredible that the Kabalah should conceal so reasonable and elegant a doctrine, the symbolism is so plausibly accounted for that it seems to enforce acceptance. When we come, however, to a close analysis of text and construction we find that the one does not warrant the other and that the evolution of the God-idea in humanity had no more occurred to the authors of the Zohar than it would have occurred recently to Mr. Grant Allen to write a " Book of Occultation." It is not a case in which it is necessary to tax space and patience by the demonstration of a negative exhaustively, which has always technical difficulties. The validity of the construction is seen by the text with which it is connected. We all know how much Fitzgerald is supposed to have imparted into Omar Khayyam, but his graceful verses are literal and line upon line compared with the high fantasy of Lévi's Zoharistic analysis. As an example of this

---

* *Le Livre des Splendeurs*, pp. 69, 70.

it is sufficient to refer the student who may desire an express case for comparison to the forty-third section of the *Idra Rabba* as it stands in the Latin version of Rosenroth with the excursus on Justice in the "Book of Splendeurs" which follows, says Eliphas Levi, the text of Rabbi Schimeon. It is mere brilliant illusion and mockery.*

Another extreme instance is the inversion of the *Sephiroth* which gives despotism an absolute power as the dark side of the supreme power of *Kether*; blind faith as the shadow of eternal wisdom in *Chokmah*; so-called immutable dogma which is at the same time inevitably progressive as the antithesis of active intelligence in *Binah*; blind faith again as the inversion of spiritual beauty in *Tiphereth*; divine vengeance as opposed to eternal justice in *Geburah*; willing sacrifice as the shadow of infinite mercy in *Chesed*; abnegation and voluntary renunciation as opposed to the eternal victory of goodness in *Netzach*; eternal hell as opposed to the eternity of goodness, presumably in *Hod*; celibacy and sterility as opposed to the fecundity of goodness, presumably in *Jesod*; while *Malkuth*, corresponding to the number of creation, is said to have no negative aspect, because celibacy and sterility produce nothing.†
Without dwelling on the carelessness of the arrangement, in part sephirotic and in part transposing and abandoning the sephirotic series, or on the failing ingenuity which repeats the same contrasts, I may point out that advanced views on despotism, on the transfiguration of dogmas and on vicarious atone-

---

* *Ibid.*, p. 86 *et seq.*   † *Ibid.*, p. 74 *et seq.*

ment are not likely to have been held even by the most illuminated rabbins and that since arbitrary tabulations and artificial contrasts are easy exercises, and can be varied to infinity, we may appreciate the contrasts here created by the evidence which supports them and that is simply the magisterial affirmation of the interpreter.

Eliphas Levi represents, however, the inauguration of a new epoch in the study of the Kabalah, undertaken not as a mere object of research or as a part of the history of philosophy. The students whom we have considered heretofore have been either Christian propagandists or writers by the way whose connection with the subject is unsubstantial ; but the standpoint of Levi is that there is a religion behind all religions and that it is the veiled mystery of Kabalism, from which all have issued and into which all return. Christian doctrine, in particular, is unintelligible, apart from the light cast on it by the deliberations of the Holy Assemblies. Now it is precisely this standpoint, its derivatives and connections, that have created modern occultism. In the past the magician was content to evoke spirits, the alchemist to produce gold when he could, the astrologer to spell the dubious message of the stars, the Kabalist of sorts to be wise in anagrams and word-puzzles, but these things are now regarded only as parts of a greater mystery, and in a very true sense Eliphas Lévi has been the supreme magus who has revealed the horizon of this mystery. He had his antecedents and he drew suggestions from there and here, but he wrote it all up and he coloured it. It is true that later on his own scepticism did its best to

spoil the splendid illusion, but this is not observed by
his disciples.

XVII. TWO ACADEMICAL CRITICS

Having regard to the fact that, as already stated,
there has been always in England a certain number
of persons who have been interested, mostly through
sympathy with occultism, in the study of the
Kabalah, it will appear almost incredible that there
are no memorials of their interest between the period
of Thomas Vaughan and the year 1865, a space of
two centuries. There is a similar hiatus in the
merely academical interest represented by Burnet.
I do not say that there have been nowhere any
references to Kabalism ; they have made up in
number what they wanted in learning and authority ;
and a few valuable gleanings might be gathered from
early editions of the larger cyclopædias, but as
there has been no occult student who wrote anything
of real moment concerning it, so there has been no
scholar apart from occult interests who has treated
the subject seriously. The work of Dr. Ginsburgh,
so well known that it scarcely needs describing, was
epoch-making, because it was the first clear, simple
and methodised account of Kabalistic doctrine and
literature. It leaves naturally much to be desired,
as it arose in an informal manner out of a meeting
of some literary society in Liverpool, and the nucleus
of the short paper produced for the occasion in
question was afterwards expanded into a slender
volume. It is a meagre measure to allot to so large
a subject, but it was as much as could be warranted

by the existing interest, which is sharply determined by the fact that a second edition was never needed. There is good reason to believe that it did not represent Dr. Ginsburgh's knowledge at the period, yet it went much further than cyclopædic or theological notices. Dr. Ginsburgh is therefore entitled to a place among the Christian students of the Kabalah, and I purpose in this brief notice, which is mainly concerned with a standpoint, to connect him with the name of a writer who recalls him in France of to-day. Both, I believe, are accomplished Hebrew scholars; both of Jewish origin. Dr. Ginsburgh is, however, a Christian, and has done work in connection with the Trinitarian Bible Society, while M. Isidore Loeb, so far as I am aware, has remained in the faith of Jewry, and it is therefore only by way of contrast with his English prototype that I am warranted in referring to him in this place. There is a period of a quarter of a century between the two writers, and as their point of view is in general respects almost identical and, indeed, suggests that the French critic has profited by the English, it is interesting to note the one matter over which they diverge, namely, the authorship of the Zohar.

It has been objected against Dr. Ginsburgh that he draws chiefly from Continental writers, reflects their views and shows little independent research. His quotations from the Zohar are, it is said, derived from Franck, and are open therefore to the harsh criticisms passed on them many years ago in Germany. These matters are of no importance to the reader who is in search only of elementary information, whose purpose is served well enough by the translations of Franck and for whom a digest of authoritative criticism is about the best text-book possible. The fact itself makes Dr. Ginsburgh's little treatise the English representative of a particular school of research, that of the hostile criticisms which refer the Zohar to the authorship, more or less exclusive, of Moses de Leon. In England Dr. Schiller-Szinessy's article on the *Midrashim* in the ninth edition of the " Encyclopædia Britannica," referring the nucleus of the book to Mishnic times and regarding Simeon ben Jochai as the author in the same sense that R. Johanan was the author of the Palestine Talmud, has helped to create another and more natural manner of regarding the Zohar. The critical objections of Dr. Ginsburgh derived from the work itself have been equally disposed of in the majority of cases, and the few which still remain can establish nothing conclusively. They have been noticed briefly in Book II., sec. 3. If we take in connection with this the fact that M. Isodore Loéb, who so closely reproduces Dr. Ginsburgh, abandons the theory of unqualified imposture, we shall see that some progress has been made with the subject during recent years, and as it is one of the purposes of the present study to place the evidence of this fact before the English reader, I feel warranted in giving space to the following synopsis of M. Isidore's Loeb's essay, as it may not be accessible to some who are acquainted with that of Dr. Ginsburgh. There is a literary excellence in the one which is fairly precluded by the circumstance that called the other into being, and it is really a matter of regret that the sole contribution of

M. Loëb towards the elucidation of Kabalistic literature occurs in *La Grande Encyclopédie*. M. Loeb was, however, for some time president of the publication committee of the French Society of Jewish Studies. His other literary work comprises a monograph on the Jewish chroniclers, a table of Jewish calendars, and some observations on the situation of the Israelites in Turkey, Servia and Roumania. In the essay with which we are here concerned he records the opinion that the term Kabalah may not be anterior to the tenth century and that the claim to antiquity which it signifies is supported by no written monument. It seems difficult in the nature of the case that it should be so substantiated. M. Loeb, however, makes a very proper distinction between the metaphysical or mystical Kabalah and the gross thaumaturgy connected with the practical branch. To the original elements of the first he ascribes, like all critics, a high antiquity, but not, as it need scarcely be said, of a kind which would permit it to be regarded as the perpetuation of an indigenous, much less an uncorrupted, tradition. As we have had occasion to see, this claim is no longer made by any competent student of the subject. For M. Loeb the Kabalah is a part of the universal mysticism which seeks to explain the disparity between an infinite God and a finite world by means of intermediate creations through which the Divine Power descends, diminishing in its spiritual qualities as it removes further from its source, and becoming more imperfect and material. The difficulty is removed by this process much in the same manner as the difficulty of a *terra firma* for the elephant which supports the universe is disposed of in Indian cosmology by assuming the tortoise. In other words, it is not removed at all. At the same time the explanation of emanationist mysticism, which is not all mysticism, as M. Loéb seems to assume, is not in the last analysis open to greater objection than any other philosophic attempt to bridge the gulf between finite and infinite. Passing from this consideration the French critic discovers the foundation of the Kabalistic theory of metaphysics in the Scriptural personification of Wisdom, and the chief elements of its symbolism in the prophetical books, about which points there is no question whatever, and they are matters of common knowledge. So also he refers correctly the name or catchword of the Zohar to Daniel xii. 3. He cites the number of the beast in the Apocalypse, as every one has cited it before him, as an example of *gèmatria*, but he raises a less hackneyed point by suggesting, on the authority of Munk, that *Temurah* was employed by Jeremiah. He does better service by reminding us that the Essenians attached great importance to symbolical angelology, and that each individual of that mystical fraternity was required to remember accurately the names of the angels. It is, however, among the Jews of Alexandria that, following several previous authorities, he discovers the germs of Kabalistic mysticism, but in this connection he cites only the Platonic doctrine of the Logos, its influence on the Greek Septuagint and on the Chaldee version of the Old Testament.

On the whole, I do not think that M. Loëb's critical faculty, or indeed his erudition, is at all comparable to his graceful synthetic talent. To cite a crucial instance, he dismisses one testimony to Kabalistic tradition by saying : " Despite the contrary assertions of the Talmud, we refuse to believe that Johanan ben Zoccai (*sic*) or his contemporaries devoted themselves to mystic doctrines or secret things." It is to the second century that he refers the " ravages " of Gnosticism among the Jews of Palestine, and cites various subtleties of the doctors which arose at that period. He sketches the decline of the Palestine schools and the rise of those of Babylon, "the traditional country of magic." He cites from Rab, the Babylonian, of the third century, that passage which I have mentioned elsewhere, and confesses that it is another germ of the mediæval Kabalah, that is, the doctrine of the *Sephiroth*. With a rapid pen he runs over the great impetus given to Jewish literature under Arabian influence from the middle of the seventh century. He refers to the ninth century that all-important treatise entitled " The Measures of the Stature of God," which is, in fact, as we have seen, the first form of the Zoharistic Macroprosopus, and is mentioned by Agobad. He places the alphabet of Akiba, dealing with the symbolism of the Hebrew letters, about the same period, together with a crowd of apocalyptic treatises, including *Pirke* of R. Eliezer, which has an elaborate doctrine of Pneumatology. Among all these he distinguishes the Sepher Yetzirah as occupying a place and deserving a rank apart. He admits its comparative antiquity, seeming to regard it as immediately posterior to the Talmud, which he affirms to have been finished A.D. 499. He describes it as a philosophy and a gnosis, and supposes it to have been written in Palestine under the direct influence of Christian and Pagan gnosticism. The opinion is interesting, but of course entirely conjectural, and as the doctrine of emanation is not very clear in the Sepher Yetzirah, we should not accept hastily the theory of an influence which assumes it. When he observes further that its fountain-heads must be sought in Azariel's Commentary on the *Sephiroth* and in the *Bahir*, I fail to understand the grounds on which he attributes a superior antiquity to those works. He assigns to the Zohar itself a Spanish origin, but does not press the authorship of Moses de Leon. Among the fine points of his criticism is a picture of the pure Talmudists of the period of Maimonides, especially those of the Peninsula and the south of France, living under the influence of Arabian philosophy, without philosophical doctrine, without perspective, having only the literature of the Law, and the anthropomorphic mysticism of the Jewish schools of Northern France, between which the Kabalah rose up as a mediator, "completing Talmudism by philosophy, correcting philosophy by theosophy, and anthropomorphic mysticism by philosophic mysticism."

XVIII. THE MODERN SCHOOL OF FRENCH KABALISM

Éliphas Lévi died in 1875, having founded, as it must be admitted, a new school of occult philosophy. For the ten years which preceded his death he had

made no outward sign.   There are rumours of the
initiations which were offered him and of the rites
which he remodelled, but all that is known certainly
is that he collected around him a small group of
private students who looked up to him as their
master, regarded his suggestive speculations almost
in the light of revelation, and, following his leading,
accepted the Kabalah as the great synthesis of
religious belief.   It was not till another ten years,
after his death, had elapsed that any visible result of
his influence became manifest.   During that period a
marked change had come over philosophic thought
in Paris ; the younger generation broke away from
the traditions of positivism and materialism, and,
without returning to the Church, passed off in the
direction of mysticism, and mysticism moderated by
science became the characteristic of the succeeding
epoch.   When about the year 1884 the Theosophical
Society opened a lodge in Paris and began the
publication of a monthly magazine, a proportion of
the French mystics gathered round it, and one of the
most noticeable in the group was Dr. Gérard
Encausse, the young *chef de laboratoire* of an eminent
doctor celebrated in connection with one of the
schools of hypnotism.   His first contributions
appeared in the pages of *Le Lotus* and his first work,
on the elements of occult science, under the auspices
of the Society.   A rupture, however, took place and
the seceding members, abandoning for the moment
their interest in *la métaphysique orientale*, established,
so to speak, a school of Western occultism, of which
Dr. Encausse became the moving and leading spirit
and Éliphas Lévi the most immediate inspiration of

the past. The ostensible characteristics of this school are Neo-Martinism and Neo-Rosicrucianism, but the transcendental conceptions associated with these names have undergone developments which have to some extent effaced their original outlines. So also the admired masterpieces of Eliphas Levi have been a point of departure quite as much as a guide. It is, broadly speaking, nevertheless, the work of Levi which has been continued, and along with other occult interests the study of the Kabalah has been revived under the reflected impulsion of his enthusiasm. It has not been so far an exhaustive study, nor has it, I think, been altogether a critical study, for it began by taking too much for granted and it has not shown a comprehensive acquaintance with the documents. There is, however, no writer of this group who has not had something to tell us concerning Jewish theosophy, while its activity has engendered consequences of much the same kind outside its immediate circle.

The two names which most call for notice in this connection are Dr. Gérard Encausse and Stanislas de Guaita. The literary and occult antecedents of the first writer are Saint Yves d'Alvedre, Fabre d'Olivet, Eliphas Levi and Adolphe Franck. From the first he has derived a systematic view of Jewish history, from the second his notion of esoteric mysteries concealed in the Hebrew language, from Lévi unfortunately a burden of historical suppositions, and from Franck an academic precedent for the antiquity of Kabalistic literature. On the other hand, Stanislas de Guaita belongs to what may be termed the literary school of occultism and as such he connects with Sar Péladan.   I propose to consider the position of both these writers in short sub-sections and to connect them with a third who is governed by very different motives and principles.

A.—PAPUS

The word Papus signifies physician, and according to a commentary of Eliphas Levi on the "Nuctemeron" of Apollonius, it is the title of a genius belonging to the first hour of that mystic period.   It is also the pseudonym adopted by Gerard Encausse, the head of the French Martinists and the leader of occult activity in Paris, presumably because he is a doctor of medicine.   Papus is a voluminous writer, methodical and laborious, and he has done work which along its own lines is admirable. From the beginning of his literary life he has been occupied with Kabalistic questions, and so far back as the year 1887 he made the first French trans lation of the Sepher Yetzirah, which appeared in the theosophical review *Lotus*.   It is not entirely a satisfactory translation and has been superseded by that of Meyer Lambert, which Papus himself recommends with the generosity of a true student.   The chief blemish of his own version is that by some misconception or error, founded apparently on the use of a dubious word in the Latin rendering of Postel, he has made this ancient work responsible for the doctrine of *Ain Soph* and it is a point of great critical importance that there is no such doctrine in the " Book of Formation."

DD

In 1892 Papus published a methodical summary of the Kabalah, together with a bibliography, which are both useful, but are again open to criticism. The bibliography has been constructed upon the most debatable of all principles, viz., the increase of the numerical importance by adventitious elements which are not Kabalistic at all, and again by the inclusion of works which are evidently unknown to the writer, with results which are occasionally ludicrous. Thus, in the one case, among books in the French language, we find Figuier's " Alchemy and the Alchemists," which contains no reference to the Kabalah ; Saint-Martin's " Crocodile," a clumsy satire open to the same objection ; Eckartshausen's " Cloud on the Sanctuary," also non-Kabalistic ; and a number of esoteric romances which have as much claim to insertion as Baudelaire's translation of Poe.* In the other case, Dr. Papus, who is only superficially acquainted with English, classifies Mr. Massey's translation of Du Prel's " Philosophy of Mysticism," my own " Lives of Alchemystical Philosophers," Dr. Hartmann's " White and Black Magic," a catalogue of second-hand books issued by Mr. Redway, and, unfortunate above all other instances, the once celebrated "Supernatural Religion." The bibliography of works in the Latin language is much better done, though it contains some useless numbers.

---

* Another instance is Julien Lejay : *La Science Occulte Appliquée à l' économie politique*, in a volume of composite authorship, entitled *La Science Secrète*. I may observe, however, that this volume contains a paper on the Kabalah by Papus, subsequently embodied in his larger work. Outside this, the only reference to the subject is in an essay by F. C. Barlet, which refers the origin of the Kabalah to the fourth century.

As regards the treatise itself it has the merit of extreme modesty ; it is, in fact, mainly a series of tabulated quotations from Franck, Loeb, de Guaita, Kircher and so forth, with a number of serviceable diagrams derived from similar sources. It is altogether excellent as a general introduction to the subject by an occultist and for the use of occultists. But it makes the mistake of attributing a real importance to the debased Hebrew influences found in the literature of Ceremonial Magic. Thus Dr. Papus says that " the practical part of the Kabalah is barely indicated in a few manuscripts dispersed through our great collections. At Paris the Bibliotheque Nationale possesses one of the finest examples, of which the origin is attributed to Solomon." Having appreciated in another section the claim of the clavicles to recognition in Kabalistic literature, it is here only necessary to say that in the work under notice there is no attempt to justify their inclusion, which is explained by the sympathies of the author, who in this connection owes something to the French version of Molitor.

Dr. Papus has also unfortunately a bias common to the majority of French and English occultists, and by this bias he is led irresistibly to prefer the imperfect equipment of past authority to the result of modern scholarship. In Egyptology he knows no higher name than that of Court de Gebelin ; in problems of Hebrew philology his great master is Fabre d'Olivet ; and hence, on the one hand, we shall not be surprised to find that he regards P. Christian as a source of serious information concerning the Egyptian mysteries of initiation, or, on the other,

that he considers the Hebrew of the Mosaic books
to be identical with the idiom of ancient Egypt.*
The position of writers who base their views on
language-studies undertaken at the beginning of this
century is not really more reasonable than would
be that of a person who should now attempt to
defend the antiquity of the Rowley poems. But
it might be scarcely worth while to speak of it were
it not for the consequences that it involves, at least
in the case of Papus, as, for example, the descent
of the esoteric tradition from Moses and its identity
-with the mysteries of Egypt, points which, debatable
or not, must not be determined after this unscholarly
fashion.

I have said sufficient to indicate that the
historical argument, so far as it exists in Papus, is
altogether unsatisfactory, and there is indeed no need

---

* He is not alone among recent French writers in taking this view.
M. Edouard Schure, in *Les Grands Inities, Esquisse de l'Histoire
Secrète des Réligions*, Paris, 1889, maintains that, "owing to the
education of Moses, there can be no doubt that he wrote Genesis in
Egyptian hieroglyphics, having three senses, and confided their keys
and oral explanations to his successors. In the time of Solomon it was
rendered into Phœnician characters, and after the captivity of Babylon
into Aramaic Chaldean characters by Esdras. The esoteric sense was
lost more and more, and the Greek translators had a very slight
acquaintance therewith." In this case it may have been the remnant
of this knowledge which made the Jews so hostile to the Septuagint.
M. Schure continues : "Jerome, despite his serious intention and his
great mind, penetrated only to the primitive sense when he made his
Latin translation. The secret sense does, however, remain buried in the
Hebrew text, which plunges by its roots into the sacred tongue of the
temples," and the writer affirms that it flashes forth at times for the
intuitive, that for seers it "shines forth once more in the phonetic
structure of the words adopted or created by Moses," and that by the
study of this phoneticism, by the keys which the Kabalah furnishes,
and by comparative esotericism, "it is permitted us at this day to
reconstruct the veritable Genesis." Pp. 180, 181.

to reckon with it. But his little work is useful as a summary of the content of the Kabalah, though even in this respect it might have been simplified with advantage. As regards the special motive of our own inquiry, the standpoint of Papus is that the Kabalah is the keystone of all the Western tradition of transcendentalism ; that the alchemists were Kabalists, and so also all mystic fraternities, whether Templars, Rosicrucians, Martinists, or Freemasons ; that the source of the Kabalah was Moses and that Moses drew from Egypt, whence the Kabalah is the most complete summary in existence of the Egyptian mysteries. Why those mysteries should have an absorbing claim on our respect does not appear from Papus, but the sub-surface understanding is undoubtedly that a tradition of absolute religion has been perpetuated from antiquity, and with all his dissemblings and palterings, with all the hindrance of his scepticism, that also is Lévi's standpoint.

B.—STANISLAS DE GUAITA

Associated with the literary work and much of the active propaganda of Dr. Gérard Encausse, the name of the Marquis Marie-Victor-Stanislas de Guaita, though scarcely known in England, was much valued in the occult circles of Paris, and his comparatively recent death at the early age of thirty-six years occasioned profound sorrow. I may perhaps observe that outside the immediate circle of his friends and admirers it is possible to say that he is a real loss to the esoteric literature of France.

It will perhaps scarcely be necessary to state that he was a disciple of Eliphas Lévi, whose works he regarded as constituting "the most cohesive, absolute and unimpeachable synthesis that can be dreamed by an occultist." If we add to this that De Guaita is described by Papus as occupying beyond contradiction the first rank among the pupils of Levi, we shall have a fair knowledge of his position. He began his literary life as a poet, and in that character connects with the school of Baudelaire. His mystic preoccupations appear, however, in his verses, and he soon devoted himself exclusively to the occult sciences. His works entitled "The Threshold of Mystery," "The Serpent of Genesis" and "The Key of Black Magic" are much admired for their "magisterial form," which recalls that of his master. In occult science de Guaita was chiefly attached to the Kabalistic tradition, and he considered that in "Neo-Mosaic Christianity, explained by the Holy Kabalah and Alexandrian Hermeticism (under certain reserves), the absolute truth must be sought in all knowledge.*

At an early period of his occult enthusiasm Stanislas de Guaita founded a Kabalistic Order of the Rose-Cross, comprehending three grades, to which entrance could be obtained only after successful examination, and the possession of the three grades of the Martinist Order was an indispensable preliminary condition. When the numerical strength of the association had attained the limits prescribed by

---

* From a *Lettre inédite* quoted in *L'Initiation*, tom. xxxviii., No. 4, Jan., 1898, pp. 12, 13.

its constitution, it was rigorously closed by decision
of the Grand Master. De Guaita is termed an
erudite orientalist by his friends, who also mention
the Hebrew folios which enriched his library.*
Finally, it is recorded that he believed himself more
thoroughly possessed of the Kabalah than all others.
But if we may accept the authority of Dr. Marc
Haven he seems to have distinguished two species of
Kabalah, the first a science which no one could teach
and no one could learn, except with the most arduous
toil and by years of sacrifice, for it is " more rugged
than Wronsky, more diffuse than Spanish Mysticism,
more complex than Gnostic analysis." And after all
it appears to be only a pseudo-Kabalah. The other
is apparently the Kabalah as presented by William
Postel, Nicholas Flamel, Khunrath, Saint-Martin and
so forth. I must confess that this distinction is a
puzzle. I know well enough that Saint-Martin was
not a Kabalist, except in the most phantasmal sense
and by a most remote derivation. I know that
Flamel the alchemist, if he ever wrote anything, was
concerned with the transmutation of metals and not
with the mysteries of *Ain Soph*. It is, however, the
Kabalah of such Kabalists that is said to illuminate
the pages of de Guaita and to have inspired his
active works.

Despite therefore of his accredited erudition,
the author of the "Serpent of Genesis" has no
message to the serious student of Kabalism ; the
Zohar has its difficulties, and by these he was clearly
intimidated. But the kind of distinction which

---

* *Ibid.*, p. 32 *et seq.*

de Guaita sought to establish offers at least one point of interest. Postel, Flamel, Khunrath, Saint-Martin, are names which stand in his mind for Kabalistic Christianity, for that marriage of the Zohar and the Gospel to which he refers expressly.* He differs therefore from his fellow propagandist Papus, who exhibits few Christian sympathies and is attached more consistently to the doctrine of Eliphas Levi. But in de Guaita, as in Levi, it is not the orthodox Christianity, as understood, on the one hand, by Mirandola and Postel, or, on the other, by Rosenroth, with which the Kabalah is connected, but Christianity permeated by Gnostic elements, and this is the special characteristic of all occult students who take any interest in the light cast on the religion of Jesus by the post-Christian developments of Jewish theosophy. Thus, the missionary enthusiasm of the early Christian schools of Kabalism, and the Messianic dream constructed by Jewry out of the wild elements of the Zohar, have been exchanged for an attempt to go back upon the path of doctrinal development and to discover in the analogies between the Kabalah and the Gnostics a practicable thoroughfare into the debated regions of esoteric religion. As disappointment waited on the mistaken ardour of the first zealots, so it is possibly in store for the revived zeal in Kabalism.

---

* "The Zohar has wedded the Gospel; the spirit has fructified the soul; and immortal works have been the fruits of this union. The Kabalah became Catholic in the school of St. John, the master of masters, incarnate in an admirable metaphysical form . . . the absolute spirit of the science of justice and love which vivifies internally the dead letter of all the orthodoxies."—*Le Serpent de la Genèse,* p. 183.

C.—LÉON MEURIN, S.J.

Having to establish some points of connection between the Kabalah and Freemasonry, it seems just to include among Kabalistic students the most laborious investigator of this subject, the late Archbishop of Port Louis. It is true that his large treatise, " Freemasonry the Synagogue of Satan," is a product of the troubled dream of the Papacy concerning the *Liberi Muratori* and is saved only by the sincerity of its intention from a place in bogus literature ; it is true also that it connects with a squalid imposture long since unmasked, but it shows a considerable acquaintance of the superficial order both with Kabalistic doctrine and Masonic symbolism, and it is worth noticing how the transcendental tradition of the Jews was appreciated quite recently by a Catholic critic who was also an ecclesiastic of some eminence and a member of the Society of Jesus.

It is unnecessary to say that it is an entirely hostile criticism. " In place of the orthodox synagogue and the true doctrine of Moses which God Himself inspired, modern Kabalists represent the paganism with which certain Jewish sectarians became imbued during the captivity of Babylon. We have only to study their doctrine and to compare it with those of civilised nations in antiquity—Indians, Persians, Babylonians, Assyrians, Egyptians, Greeks and so forth, to become assured that the same pantheistic system of emanation is inculcated by all. We find everywhere an eternal principle emanating a primeval triad and thereafter the entire universe, not by creation, but by substantial emanation. Hence we are compelled to recognise a close connection between Kabalistic philosophy and ancient paganism which is difficult to explain except by the inspiration of the same author, in other words, the Lying Spirit who is the enemy of mankind."

The entire treatise may be regarded as the development of this paragraph, which, it must be confessed, is the view that would be taken inevitably by the Latin Church. We have seen that under the auspices of Christian Kabalists, with Picus de Mirandola as their mouthpiece, there was for one moment a sign of *rapprochement* between the Church and the Jewish tradition, but it was impossible in the nature of both, and the Church was saved then, as it has been occasionally saved since, as if by some happy intuition which preceded any real knowledge of the interests at stake.

The general position being thus defined with perfect accuracy by Mgr. Meurin, he proceeds at a later stage to develop his impeachment by exhibiting the fundamental error of all pantheism, that, namely, which concerns the transition of the Infinite to the Finite, which wears, he tells us, for any serious thinker, the aspect of a fraudulent device. Basing his argument on the well-known verse in Wisdom: "Thou hast ordered all things in measure, and number, and weight," he advances that we musk seek in these the distinction between the Infinite and the Finite, for these categories do not exist in God, or rather they are "elevated above themselves and lost in a superior unity." Creation out of nothing is the only rational solution of the grand problem concerning the origin of a world which is governed by number, weight and measure, a doctrine which assumes no passage from Infinite to Finite, since it does not derive the universe from the divine substance by an emanation of any kind. "It is true that *ex nihilo nihil fit*. But in the creation there is not only the *nihilum*; there is also the *Omnipotens*, and it is untrue to say that with nothingness and the all-powerful, nothing can be made. *Ex nihilo nihil fit a Deo* would be a false axiom."

In a study like the present it would be entirely out of place to discuss the points at issue between emanationists and creationists. The Kabalah is a system of emanation, and it is so far opposed to the official doctrine of orthodox religion on a question of fundamental philosophy. I think personally that the better reason is on the side of the hypothesis of emanation on the simple ground that the conception of *nihilum* cannot co-exist with that of an infinite God. I shall be told, of course, that I am confusing the notion of endless space with that of the Divine Nature, but as God is everywhere by the hypothesis, there is no place which is not filled by His power and His presence, and then where is the *nihilum?* But the whole controversy concerns a *res ardua et diffic lis,* as Isaac de Loria would have termed it, which fortunately cannot produce a single consequence of importance to the human mind, though it is precisely to such arid speculations that official orthodoxy has always sought to attach an eternal consequence for the soul.

Mgr. Meurin remains, however, the consistent and correct exponent of the Church which he represents, and so far as this Church is concerned he has registered, as we must admit fully, the heretical nature of Kabalistic doctrine. We may go further and allow that in other places he scores occasionally a logical point against it. I think that no intelligent person can well deny the intellectual clumsiness with which the system of Sephirotic emanation is presented in works like the Greater Sacred Synod. We have, for example, such notions as the commencement of thought in *Ain Soph* which proceeds the emanation of understanding, thus reversing the psychological order, as the prelate well observes, besides formulating an absurdity concerning the one Being in whom there is no beginning. It may well be that in the last analysis these things are to be understood more profoundly than is suggested by their surface meaning, but they are crude and misleading enough in their outward sense.

XIX.—THE KABALAH AND ESOTERIC CHRISTIANITY

A discussion of the points of contact between Christianity and the mystical tradition of the Jews must not close without some reference to a scheme of mystical Christianity which obtained for a period a certain vogue in English occult circles and met with especial commendation from certain Kabalistic, students. I refer to the New Gospel of Interpretation, founded on illuminations received, or believed to have been received, by Anna Bonus Kingsford, and developed since her decease, not perhaps always acceptably, by her collaborator and co-recipient, Edward Maitland, now also passed away. The text books of this movement were, firstly, a small collection containing the illuminations, and, secondly a formal treatise which, under the title of " The Perfect Way," constituted a philosophical development and historical verification of the doctrines received by the seeress. Mr. S. L. McGregor Mathers dedicated his English translation of some of the Zoharistic books to the authors of this treatise on the ground that it was " one of the most deeply occult works that has (*sic*) been written for centuries." The dedication also described it as an " excellent and wonderful book," touching much on the doctrines of the Kabalah and laying great value upon its teachings. It was welcomed in terms of still higher appreciation by Baron Spedalieri, of Marseilles, the disciple of Eliphas Levi, who regarded it as " in complete accord with all mystical traditions, and especially with the great mother of these, the Kabalah." In connection with this appreciation the respectable French occultist observed : (*a*) That the Kabalistic tradition as we now possess it is far from genuine, and was much purer when it first emerged from the sanctuaries. (*b*) That when William Postel and his brother Hermetists predicted that the literature containing the secret tradition of the Jews would become known and understood at " the end of the era," they meant that it would be made the basis of " a new illumination," reinstating that tradition in its purity. (*c*) That this illumination and this restoration have been accomplished in " The Perfect Way." He adds : " In this book we find all that there is of truth in the

Kabalah, supplemented by new intuitions, such as present a body of doctrine at once complete, homogeneous, logical and inexpugnable. Since the whole tradition thus finds itself recovered or restored to its original purity, the prophecies of Postel and his fellow Hermetists are accomplished ; and I consider that from henceforth the study of the Kabalah will be but an object of curiosity and erudition, like that of Hebrew antiquities."

If this be the case, the inquiry with which we have been occupied at such considerable length is only prolegomenary to the New Gospel of Interpretation, and our concluding words should be simply to direct the student who is in search of the true meaning of esoteric tradition to the doctrines contained in this last word of revelation. Indeed, such a course would seem at first sight the only one which could be followed. I must add, however, that the opinion expressed by Baron Spedalieri has produced no consequence, that the Kabalistic School of occultists in England has not followed the lead thus indicated, and would not endorse the opinion, though committed to a certain extent in the same direction, while the New Gospel of Interpretation has taken no permanent hold on the occult thought of the time. It is still occasionally quoted with respect by writers who represent Kabalism, and notably by Dr. Wynn Westcott, the translator of the " Book of Formation," but this is the extent of its influence. I infer also that Baron Spedalieri's statement as to the adulteration of the genuine tradition in the Hebrew Kabalah would not be traversed seriously, but for its recovery occultists seem inclined to look backward towards Egypt rather than to any form of supplementary revelation.

I do not propose to recite here even the leading aspects of the system of esoteric Christianity developed in "The Perfect Way," for the work is well kn.own and its substance has been made accessible in many forms, thanks to the untiring devotion of Mr. Edward Maitland. It does offer some conspicuous points of contact with the tradition of the Kabalah, especially as to the dual nature of God, or the Divine-Feminine, and "the multiplicity of principles in the human system"; but it would be easy to exaggerate their extent, as also, in some less conspicuous cases, their importance. The traceable references are few and superficial. We may find, for example, the Kabalistic doctrine of *Ain Soph* and His emanations in the statement that "God unmanifest and abstract is the Primordial Mind, and the Kosmic universe is the ideation of that Mind," but it is not a far-reaching correspondence. So also the conception of Macroprosopus reflected in Microprosopus is thinly sketched by the following passage. "In 'the Lord' the Formless assumes a form, the Nameless a name, the Infinite the Definite, and these human. But, although 'the Lord is God manifested as a man' in and to the souls of those to whom the vision is vouchsafed, it is not as man in the exclusive sense of the term and masculine only, but as man both masculine and feminine" (Microprosopus it will be remembered is androgyne), "at once man and woman, as is Humanity itself." I should add that the "new Gospel" maintained the divinity of the Kabalah on the ground of the purity of its doctrine of correspondences, which shows that "this famous compendium belongs to a period prior to that destruction by the priesthoods of the equilibrium of the sexes which constituted in one sense the "Fall." With this statement of its Divine origin may be brought into contrast the interpretation of the claim made by the Kabalah as to the manner of its delivery. "When it is said that these Scriptures were delivered by God first of all to Adam in Paradise, and then to Moses on Sinai, it is meant that the doctrine contained in them is that which man always discerns when he succeeds in attaining to that inner and celestial region of his nature where he is taught directly of his own Divine Spirit, and knows even as he is known." As "The Perfect Way" and its connections assume to be the outcome of a similar quality of discernment, it follows, of course, that it is a recovery of "the doctrine commonly called the *Gnosis*, and variously entitled Hermetic and Kabbalistic."

I should add that many thoughtful persons have found in "The Perfect Way" a "fountain of light, interpretative and reconciliatory," that much of its interpretation indicates a rare quality of genius ; yet it was not free at the beginning from the fantastic element, and it depends to some extent on philological arguments which are more than fantastic. Also at the close of Mr. Maitland's life he wrote much which must have been regretted by his friends, bringing his earlier work into discredit by exaggerated claims concerning it. Taking it as a whole "The Perfect Way" cannot, I think, be regarded as a master-key to the Kabalah, or as anything indeed but a series of suggestions and glimpses concerning the hidden sense of many sacred scriptures, the full unfolding of which will not perhaps be accomplished even in the twentieth century.

XX.—THE KABALAH AND MODERN THEOSOPHY

The attempt which was made in the year 1875, by the foundation of the Theosophical Society, to extend and perhaps to centralise the study of Oriental Occult Philosophy, has, in spite of its chequered history, succeeded to a very large extent in that object. If we remove from consideration certain claims advanced by the founders, about which it would be unbecoming to speak positively, as it would be impossible and misplaced here to attempt their full discussion, and if we regard the Society rather as it assumes to regard itself, namely, as an organisation designed to promote a neglected branch of knowledge, we have only to survey its literature during the past twenty years to see how large a field it has succeeded in covering. No occult student will be inclined to overlook this fact, and as the Theosophical Society possesses at least this aspect of importance, it will be useful to ascertain how far the expositions of eastern philosophy which we owe to it connect with the subject of our inquiry.

It may be said in a general manner that the correspondences which I have already established are, of course, recognised. The cosmology and pueumatology of Jewish esoteric tradition are regarded, roughly speaking, as reflections or derivatives from an older knowledge and a higher teaching

EE

which has existed from time immemorial in the farthest East.* I suppose it would not be denied that the peculiar methods of the Kabalah are, so to speak, indigenous, but with these there is little sympathy and indeed little acquaintance.† Nor do I throughout trace a sufficient warrant in knowledge for the expression of particular opinions. The author of "Isis Unveiled" and "The Secret Doctrine" had, it must be confessed, an enormous budget of materials, but not very carefully selected. On the one hand, she gives us information which we are not able to check because we do not know her authorities ; on the other she makes statements occasionally with which it is difficult to agree. Thus, she distinguishes between the ordinary, or Judaistic, and the universal, or Oriental Kabalah. If little be known of the one, there is nothing, at least nothing that is definite, known of the other. " Its adepts are few ; but these heirs elect of the sages who first discovered ' the starry truths which shone on the great Shemaia of the Chaldæan lore' have solved the 'absolute' and are now resting from their grand labour." ‡ That is a statement which, of course, we cannot check, and for any critical study of the Jewish Kabalah it can,

---

* Compare the ignorant absurdity and assurance of the late W. Q. Judge, who did not scruple to affirm that Abraham, Moses and Solomon were members of the ancient lodge of adepts from whom this high teaching has been handed down. "The Ocean of Theosophy," New York, 1893, c. 1. "Echoes" of this kind "from the burnished and mysterious East," to quote Judge terminology ("Echoes from the Orient," p. 5, New York, 1890), do not find response among theosophical writers in England.

† It is, however, said that "there was at all times a Kabalistic Literature among the Jews." *Secret Doctrine*, iii., 166. This is simply without warrant, and is contradicted by the literature itself.

‡ "Isis Unveiled," i., 17.

therefore, carry no weight. It may be taken to indicate a growing feeling among occultists of all schools that the Hebrew tradition has been perverted.[*] It may be accepted also as evidence that because the term Kabalah signifies an oral reception it has come to be used in connection with any unwritten knowledge. Such a course is very inexact and misleading, but the same abuse of words is found in Paracelsus and many later writers. It serves, however, a purpose not intended by those who use it ; it distinguishes between scholar and sciolist. The statement which we cannot check is, however, usually accompanied by the statement that we can, In the present case we are told that the "Book of Occultation" is "the most ancient Hebrew document on occult learning,"[†] and I much doubt whether this would be countenanced by any student who was acquainted with the strong claims of the "Book of Formation," to say nothing of the literature which belongs to Talmudic times. It is added that the *Sepher Dzenioutha* was compiled from another and older work which is not named, but it is stated that there is only one "original copy" in existence, and that this is "so very old that our modern antiquarians might ponder over its pages an indefinite time, and still not quite agree as to the nature of the fabric upon which it is written."[‡] Till antiquaries

---

[*] One theosophical writer, however, maintains that "the collection of writings known as the Bible constitutes but one of a number of record, which are all derived from and based upon one unifying system, known at times as the Ancient Wisdom Religion, or Secret Doctrine." W. Kingsland. "The Esoteric Basis of Christianity," part l., p. 15, London, 1891.

[†] "Isis Unveiled," i., 1.   [‡] *Ibid.*

are furnished with the opportunity they will be
tempted to dismiss this claim. With both these
classes of statement we may connect the affirmation
that is not evident in itself and is supported by
doubtful reasoning, Thus we are told of Oriental
Kabalists who assert that the traditions of their
science are more than seventy thousand years old,
concerning which claim it is observed that modern
science cannot prove it to be false, but the question
is whether Kabalists, oriental or otherwise, have any
colourable pretence of evidence to produce in support
of its truth. We may pass over as circumspectly as
possible the writer's personal pretension to a first-
hand acquaintance with Kabalistic books once indis-
putably in existence, but now lost. Of such is the
Chaldæan Book of Numbers,* which, according to
another authority, is a companion to the *Æsh
Metzareph*,† but is declared in "Isis Unveiled" to
be a part of the great Oriental Kabalah, namely,
the patrimony of the persons previously described
as having "solved the absolute."‡ To the lesson
which is taught by observations of this kind we
may add the borrowed view which rests on bad
criticism, as, for example, that the Talmud is "the
darkest of enigmas even for most Jews,"§ thus
attributing a mystical sense to the commentaries

---

* This work is said to be much superior to the Zohar. "Secret
Doctrine," i., 214. It is, in fact, the only real Kabalah, *ib.*, iii., 170.
It appears to be now in possession of certain Persian sufis (*ib.*), an
interesting statement which I have not, however, felt authorised to
make use of in Book iii., § 6, of this study.

† This is Dr. Westcott's opinion. Madame Blavatsky adds that
the Sepher Yetzirah is also a portion of the Book of Numbers.

‡ *Ibid.*, i., 579.　　　§ *Ibid.*, i., 17.

on the exoteric laws of Israel, the value of which attribution has already been exhibited. I must admit, however, that many considerable names and one of great weight with occultists can be quoted in support of this opinion.*

It would serve no purpose to extend further the correction of such manifest errors or to enumerate all the singular assertions which rest more or less exclusively on the good authority of Madame Blavatsky. It will be sufficient to refer to her views upon the authenticity of the Zohar.† On the one hand the author is said to be R. Simeon ben Jochai ; ‡ again, it was "edited for the first time" between A.D. 70 and 110 ;§ and yet again, it was written, as it now stands, by R. Moses de Leon, the original being lost, though at the same time its contents were "scattered through a number of minor MSS." R. Moses had Syriac, Chaldaic, and Christian Gnostics to help him. Such opinions are without any warrant for serious criticism.‖

---

* The best test of Madame Blavatsky's first-hand knowledge of the subject is the fact that she calls the *Liber Drushim* of Isaac de Loria a part of the Talmud, and thence proceeds to exhibit the Sephirotic doctrine of that collection. "Secret Doctrine," i., 438. The symbolism of the Lesser Countenance is also referred to the Talmud. *Ibid.*, i., 350.

† It is characteristic that she should regard the Zohar as not sufficiently esoteric. *Ibid.*

‡ *Ibid.*, iii., 92. She also says that it was on account of his possession of the "secret knowledge" that R. Simeon was forced to take refuge in the cave. After this version of a matter of fact we shall not be surprised to learn that St. Peter was a Kabalist (*ib.*, iii., 125), that the Count de St. Germain had access to unknown Vatican MSS. on the Kabalah, which MSS. contain information regarding the Central Sun (*ib.*, ii., 237), or that the Zohar is "called also the Midrash," as if the last term were particular, and not generic (*ib.*, iii., 167).

§ *Ibid.*, iii., 167.   ‖ *Ibid.*, i., 114, 230; iii., 167.

BOOK VIII

THE KABALAH AND OTHER CHANNELS OF ESOTERIC TRADITION

ARGUMENT

Modern occultism regards all the secret sciences as vehicles of the great occult tradition, but this is outside the purpose of the present inquiry, which is confined to estimating the extent of the influence exercised by Kabalism on other branches of esoteric knowledge in the West. It is found that this influence has been much exaggerated in the West. It has been unquestionably large in the case of ceremonial magic, but very small in that of alchemy, of astrology, &c. Freemasonry has also been regarded by occultists as a channel of the secret tradition, but its connection with Kabalism is slight. The claims of the Tarot as a key of Kabalistic symbolism are set aside, without prejudice to their merits, because of an insuperable difficulty. As a conclusion to the whole research the doctrine of pure mysticism is contrasted with that of Kabalism and the points reached in the investigation are brought into a single focus.

I. THE KABALAH AND MAGIC

IT was established at the outset of our inquiry that occult speculations do not consider any single system as the exclusive depository of occult knowledge ; a variety of channels are recognised, and by the network of communications subsisting between these channels the occult sciences are methodised and their

identities and analogies exhibited.   There is an
enormous divergence of opinion as to what may and
may not constitute a path of the secret tradition,
individual predilection exercising, as will be supposed,
no inconsiderable influence.   We may conclude in a
general manner that the tradition being ubiquitous
by the hypothesis is thought to have assumed its
forms everywhere and at all times.   There was, for
example, no exoteric religion which did not possess
an esoteric interpretation* and there was no esoteric
interpretation which did not connect that religion
with all that is more especially understood here by
the secret teaching.   For this hypothesis the integral
connection of Kabalism with other systems belonging
to the far past would be evidence enough that it had
its root in the secret tradition, but, without denying
altogether that there may be a certain warrant for a
not dissimilar view, we have found that many of the
resemblances may be accounted for in a more natural
and spontaneous manner.   As, however, it was in the
western world that Kabalism was chiefly propagated,
and may be said roughly to have developed,† it is
necessary to observe its connections with other
channels by which the arcane knowledge is believed
to have been communicated to the West.   These are
Magic, Alchemy, Astrology, the occult associations
which culminated in Freemasonry, and, finally, an
obscure sheaf of hieroglyphs known as Tarot cards.

* John Yarker: "Notes on the Scientific and Religious M... ...
of Antiquity," p. 5.

† If the derivation of the Zohar from R. Simeon ben Jochai be
admitted, Palestine was, of course, the birthplace of that work.   Dr.
Schiller-Szinessy, who defends this derivation, accepts also what
follows therefrom.

There is also a side question as to whether devotional mysticism, apart from any formal initiation, shows any trace of Kabalism over and above that of unconscious analogy. Like the studies which have preceded it, the object of this concluding book is rather to correct misconceptions than to establish novel views. Far too much stress has been laid upon the common basis of all the occult sciences, while those who look for their enlightenment more especially to the Kabalistic apparatus have been unduly predisposed to discern Kabalism at the root of all. We shall see that in most instances the connection was accidental, a matter of adornment, late in its introduction, or chiefly of the historical order. The paramount exception to this statement is the first system with which we have here to deal. There is no doubt that Magic in the West * owes its processes and its complexion to Kabalism, though it would be folly to pretend that without Kabalism there would have been no Western Magic.†

I propose in the present section to restrict the use of the term Magic within the narrow limits of its common acceptation. To take it in its higher

---

* "The Kabalah is the source of all the vain imaginations which form the basis of Magic, and many Jews devoted to the Kabalah are also addicted thereto, abusing the names of God and the angels for the performance of things supernatural." Moreri : *Grand Dictionnaire Historique*, Tom. ii., s.v. *Cabale*. Amsterdam, 1740.

† The strength of the connection is exhibited by the modern literature of *colportage* in France. *La Grande et Véritable Science Cabalistique* is still *la Sorcellerie dévoilée*, and it is under such titles that the mutilated reprints of the "Great Albert," the "Little Albert" and the "Red Dragon" appear in the obscure by-ways of Paris, usually without place or date. Similar productions of the last century also exhibit it ; see the anonymous *Télescope de Zoroastre ou Clef de la Grande Cabale divinatoire des Mages, s.l.*, 1796.

sense,* as equivalent to Divine Wisdom, would make it superfluous to inquire whether it connects with a tradition which lays claim to the same definition. The question as it is understood here is rather historical than metaphysical, and is concerned only with the Western world. The White and Black Magic of the Middle Ages constitutes a kind of spurious practical Kabalah which represents Jewish esoteric science debased to the purposes of the sorcerer, and it is necessary that we should estimate it at its true worth, because it has been the subject of much misconception not only among uninstructed persons but even professed students.

A study of the Zoharistic writings, their developments and commentaries, even with the slender materials which are offered in this work, will show that the ends proposed by the speculative Kabalah are very different from the evocation of spirits, the raising of ghosts, the discovery of concealed treasures, the bewitchments and other mummeries of Ceremonial Magic. The Kabalah, does, however, countenance, as we have seen, the doctrine of the power resident in Divine Names,† and it is in fact one of the burdens of its inheritance. Of the antiquity and diffusion of that doctrine there can be no doubt ; in one or other of its forms it has obtained almost universally, and, like all universal beliefs, behind the insensate character which it exhibits externally

---

* It would be unwise to deny that there is a higher sense, but such attempts to present it as Dr. Franz Hartmann's " Magic White and Black " are much too highly coloured to possess any historical value.

† See the important chapter on the Name of God in J. Leusden's *Philologus Hebræus*, 1672.

there may be an inward reason which accounts for it. Without attempting an inquiry in which we should be probably baffled, it is sufficient here to indicate that at the sources to which Kabalistic tradition is generally referred, namely, Akkadia, Chaldæa and Babylonia, this doctrine prevailed; it was no doubt brought out of Babylon by the Jews, and they carried it with them into the dispersion of the third exile. It inspired a whole cycle of bizarre legends concerning Solomon and his marvels. More than this, it may be said to be directly connected with the Kabalistic symbolism concerning the divine powers and qualities attaching to the Hebrew alphabet. The worlds were made, so to speak, by the instrument of a single letter, and four letters are the living forces which actuate them. There can be therefore no question that every Kabalist accepted, symbolically at least, the doctrine of the power of words. It must have passed very early into un-fortunate applications;* sacred names were written on amulets and talismans which were used to heal diseases, to avert evil chances and so forth.† But it was a part also of the Chaldæan doctrine that the

---

* The *Sepher Raziel*, referred to Eleazer of Worms, and posing as an angelic revelation to Noah, has been already mentioned. With its talismans and philtres, its double seal of Solomon, its mystic or occult alphabetical symbols, its figures for the government of evil spirits, and its conjurations by means of the Divine Names, this work constitutes one of the storehouses of mediæval magic, besides being chiefly responsible for the whole of the practical Kabalah.

† So far as regards the early Christian centuries, the question is settled by a reference in the thirty-third Sermon of Origen by way of commentary on St. Matthew, wherein allusion is made to a book of exorcisms or adjurations of Demons passing under the name of Solomon, which was no doubt the prototype of the later *Keys* and *Grimoires*.

possessor of the Divine Name could, in some obscure way, influence the God to whom it was attributed. Above all, the demons and evil spirits became subservient to the power of such words. Here is the germ of which the last development, or rather the final corruption, is to be found in the French grimoires of Black Magic.

It was, broadly speaking, somewhere about the fourteenth century that a Latin literature rose up in Europe, passing subsequently into the vernaculars of various countries, containing processes for compelling spirits by means of Divine Names which are corruptions of Hebrew terms.* The processes pretend to be translated from the Hebrew, but, if so, the originals are not extant. The chief of them is known as the " Key of Solomon," of which there are two recensions, more correctly regarded as distinct works under an identical title.† Among the points which should be observed concerning them is the fact that while they are concerned with all classes of spirits, good and evil, for every variety of purpose, but mostly illicit, they contain no formulæ for dealing with the dead, and this, I think, indicates their Jewish origin, for the Jews had very strong feelings as to the sacred nature of the repose of the human

---

* Jean Wier, a demonologist of the sixteenth century, in his *Histoires, Disputes et Discours des Illusions et Impostures des Diables*, gives a list of magical works current at his period under great names of the past, and points out that the art which they deal with has depraved the most secret interpretation of the Divine Law, known as Kabalah among the Jews.—See the reprint of this work, Paris, 1885, i., 175.

† A work passing under this name was condemned in a Decree of Pope Gelasius....See Antonius van Dale : *De Origine et Progressu Idolatriæ*, Amsterdam, 1696, p. 558.

soul. Out of these two works there was developed subsequently a larger variety of processes, more distinctly spurious, which did enter into necromantic mysteries. They begot also many variations adapted for the use of Christian operators, and containing sacred words the efficacy of which would not have been so promptly acknowledged by a Hebrew.

It is one thing to note the existence of this literature and to confess its derivation; it is another, and as I think an unfortunate policy, to exalt works like the "Key of Solomon" into embodiments of genuine Kabalistic tradition. It is an insult to the rabbins of the Holy Synod to suggest their connection with the puerilities and imbecility of Ceremonial Magic. It has been done in England and is being done at this day in France.* The professed Kabalistic occultists of the latter country would actually seem to ascribe a superior importance and an additional aspect of mystery to the worthless Clavicles of Solomon, by representing that they are the only written memorials of a most secret oral branch of practical Kabalism instead of the final debasement of a perfectly traceable if not rationally accountable doctrine concerning Divine Names. Dr. Papus observes: "The practical part of the Kabalah is barely indicated in a few manuscripts scattered through our great libraries. At Paris, the *Bibliothèque Nationale* possesses one of the finest exemplars, of which the

---

* There is some ground for supposing that the first express attempts to identify Magic with Kabalism must be referred to Germany. There are numerous earlier examples, but Welling's *Opus Mago-Cabbalisticum*, Hamburg, 1765, is a good instance, and it is also a work of some interest.

origin is attributed to Solomon. These manuscripts,
generally known under the name of *Clavicles*, are the
basis of all the old grimoires which circulate in country
places (the Great and Little Albert, Red Dragon and
Enchiridion) and of those which drive priests into
mental alienation by sorcery (Grimoire of Honorius)."
The statement does not exhibit full acquaintance
with the works which it mentions ; the *Enchiridion*
in its earliest forms owes little to the "Keys of
Solomon," and the Grimoire of Honorius is not more
concerned with sorcery than are rituals like the Red
Dragon. Finally, the intellectual and moral difference
between the Clavicles and their derivatives is so slight
that it is scarcely worth labouring. As regards their
scope and intention, the Clavicles are themselves
grimoires. I have indicated the possibility that
behind the ancient doctrine of the virtue resident in
certain theurgic words and formulæ there may be
concealed a secret of the sanctuaries ; so also the
apparatus of Ceremonial Magic may be a travesty
and disfigurement of an occult practice known also
to the occult sanctuaries, but no one is on the track
of these mysteries who begins by mistaking *signum*
for *signatum* on the one hand or the mutilated
reflection for the original on the other.

The general fact remains that it is by the
perversion of the Kabalah that we have obtained the
grimoires, and that the sympathetic student of the
Jewish tradition must tolerate this unwelcome fact as
he best can.*

---

* A work belonging to this class, but more elaborate and
interesting than most of them, goes to show that a Jew in possession
of the " Holy Traditions of the Kabalah " and also of the secrets of

I should prefer to ignore altogether this so-called practical part of the Kabalah, but so much importance having been attributed to it by modern occultists, it seems necessary for the sake of completeness to say something briefly of its materials and its method. It was concerned above all with the names of God, firstly, as they are found in Holy Scripture, and, secondly, as their mysteries were developed by means of Kabalistic processes. It attributed certain names to the *Sephiroth*, and these were regarded as analogous to the divine forces and attributes associated with the *Sephiroth*.

The Divine Name connected with *Kether* was that signifying the essence of the Deity, *Eheieh* (AHIH). That of *Chokmah* is *Jod*, *Jah*, or *Tetragrammaton*, commonly rendered Jehovah (JHVH), and susceptible of twelve permutations, similar to the sealing names of IHV in the Sepher Yetzirah. These permutations are called Banners by the Kabalists. The name *Jehovah Elohim* (JHVH ALHIM) is attributed to *Binah* and signifies God of Gods. *El* (AL) is referred to *Chesed*, and its meaning, according to Rosenroth, is God of Grace and Ruler of Mercy. *Geburah* is in correspondence with *Elohim Gibor*, the strong God who avenges the

---

practical Magic, bequeathed the first to his elder and the second to his younger son. What happened when there were more than two sons does not appear.—See the "Book of the Sacred Magic," translated by S. L. MacGregor Mathers, London, 1898. The original is an MS. in the Arsenal Library, Paris, and belongs to the 18th century, but it claims to have been written in Hebrew in the year 1458, which claim, by the internal evidence, is manifestly imposture. Even its Jewish authorship is unlikely. Mr. Mathers, who has a certain erudition but is devoid of critical judgment, accepts every claim advanced by this work, as he accepts that of the "Key of Solomon."

crimes of the wicked. *Eloah va Daath* is the Divine Name of *Tiphereth* (ALVH V DATh); *Jehovah* or *Adonai Tzabaoth* (ADNI TsBAVTh), the God or Lord of Hosts, is connected with *Netzach; Elohim Tzabaoth*, of similar meaning, belongs to *Hod; Shaddai El Chai* (ShDI AL ChI), the omnipotent living God, is referable to *Jesod; Adonai Melekh* (ADNI MLK) to *Malchuth*.

But the ten *Sephiroth* are naturally connected with the ten numbers, and hence there was an occult power resident in numerals analogous to that which was inherent in the Hebrew letters; the divine names belonging to the *Sephiroth* were those also of the scale of the denary, but over and above these there were other names referred to the numbers based on the number of the letters which gave .expression to these names. Thus, the number one was represented by the single letter *Jod*, understood as a Divine Name, and not in its alphabetical order in which it is equivalent to ten. The number two was represented by JH and AL; the number three by ShDI = Shaddai; the number four by JHVH and AHIH; five by ALHIM, to which I presume that Christian Kabalism has added JHShVH = *Jehoshuah* or Jesus; six by ALVThIM and AL GBVR; seven by ARARITA and AShRAHIH; eight by ALVH V DATh and JHVH V DATh; nine by JHVH TsBAVTh, ALHIM GBVR, and JHVH TsDQNV; ten by ALHIM TsBAVTh and by the extended *Tetragrammaton* JVD HA VAV HA. It may be added in this connection that according to Cornelius Agrippa simple numbers were used to express divine things, numbers of ten were for celestial, numbers of one hundred for earthly, and numbers of a thousand for things to come. The Divine Names and their qualifications were also tabulated in reference to the twenty-two letters.

Of these names the greatest power and virtue were attributed to the *Tetragrammaton*, which was the root and foundation of all and the ruling force of the world ; its true pronunciation, as already seen, was one of the secrets of the sanctuary and for Kabalistic magic was the master key of all successful operation. With this was connected the name of 72 letters obtained by the Kabalistic computation of the numbers of the letters of *Tetragrammaton* after a conventional manner, as follows :—

$$\left.\begin{array}{l} \text{Jod} = 10 \\ \text{Jod He} = 15 \\ \text{Jod He Vau} = 21 \\ \text{Jod He Vau He} = 26 \end{array}\right\} = 72$$

After the Divine Names come those of the orders of the angels and the chiefs of the hierarchy, concerning which something has been said already in the section on Kabalistic Pneumatology. It would serve no purpose to enumerate all the complicated apparatus developed in this connection. The ten archangels and the ten angelic orders corresponded to the ten divine names connected with the *Sephiroth* and the name of 72 letters had 72 other angels attributed thereto, whose names were extracted by a conventional device from Exodus xiv. 19, 20, 21. There were angels of the cardinal points, rulers of the four elements, angels of the planets, angels of the Divine presence, and in opposition to all these there were also evil spirits, princes of Devils, held to be

"offensive in the elements," and so forth. This
apparatus passed bodily over to the ceremonial
magic of the middle ages, which the debased
Kabalah may be said to have constituted and ruled
throughout, and it is for this reason that Western
conventional magic has so little connection with
folk-lore.

II.—THE KABALAH AND ALCHEMY

Some reference has been made to the subject of
Hermetic tradition when considering the Kabalistic
treatise entitled " Purifying Fire." We have there
seen that the Hermetic and Kabalistic philosophies
are generally ascribed to a common source, and this
is the case with sympathetic as well as hostile critics.
The question, however, is exceedingly complicated,
and though I should have much hesitation in
differing from such a consensus of authorities,* I
am not less sure that as regards the branch of
Hermetic philosophy which is known under the
name of alchemy, we should be exceedingly
careful about making and accepting statements.
We must begin first of all by distinguishing the
earlier books ascribed to Hermes Trismegistus, and
not concerned with the transmutation of metals,†

---

* In a pamphlet entitled " The Science of Alchymy," by " Sapere
Aude," Fra. R.R. et A.C., the "sages of mediæval Europe are
said " to have derived their knowledge of this subject, (1) from the
Arabs, (2) from the heirs of the traditional lore now identified by the
name " Kabalah," (3) from ancient Egypt. Of these alleged sources,
the first only is historically certain.

† Compare, however, the anonymous preface to the first English
translation of the Divine Poimander, that of Dr. John Everard, 1650;

FF

from such late compositions, to make use of no stronger term, as the Emerald Table and the Golden Treatise. When Isaac Myer affirms that many of the doctrines of the Kabalah, more or less veiled, may be found in the books attributed to Hermes Trismegistus,* the reference obtains only, and can be intended only, to the *Divine Poimander*, the *Asclepios* and other tracts, the existence of which can be traced about or prior to the fourth century, A.D. We may search the Greek alchemists in vain for any definite doctrinal connection with these works, though Hermes is naturally included among the great names of antiquity who are associated with the making of gold, and there are also other references to this mystical personage. While we must discount altogether such extreme opinions as that of Isaac Casaubon, who represents the earlier Hermetic treatises as the work of a Kabalistic adept who was probably a Jew of Alexandria,† we have numerous general reasons for admitting that there were points of contact between Neo-Platonism

---

here the possession of "the great Elixir of the Philosophers" is ascribed to Hermes Termaximus. See also Dr. Westcott's observations prefixed to his verbatim reprint, Collectanea Hermetica, vol. 2, London, 1894.

    * "The Philosophy of Ibn Gebirol," pp. 166, 167.

    † M. Berthelot, however, observes that "the *role* attributed to the Jews in the propagation of alchemical ideas recalls that which they enjoyed at Alexandria during the contact of Greek culture with the culture of Egypt and Chaldea. It is known that the Jews exercised an influence of the first importance in this fusion of the religious and scientific doctrines of the East and of Greece, which presided at the birth of Christianity. The Alexandrian Jews were for one moment at the head of science and philosophy." — *Les Origines de l'Alchimie*, Paris, 1885.

and the Kabalah,* as seen in an earlier section.
The connection of alchemy with Hermes is not
through the Hermetic books of the Neo-Platonic
period, and its Kabalistic correspondences must also
be sought elsewhere. Among the writings of Zosimus
the Panopolite, which belong to the third century,†
there is a quotation from the "True Book of Sophe
the Egyptian" concerning the Divine Lord of the
Hebrews and the powers of Sabaoth, which affirms
that there are two sciences and two wisdoms, that
of the Egyptians and that of the Hebrews, the
second being rendered "more solid by Divine
Justice."‡ Both come from remote ages; they do
not investigate material and corruptible bodies; their
generation operates independently of any foreign
action, sustained by prayer and divine grace. Then
comes the following significant passage, which
accounts for the philosophical work of alchemy
being likened to that of God in the creation. "The
symbol of chemistry is drawn from creation (in the

* M. le Chevalier I. A. de Goulianov in his *Essai sur les
Hiéroglyphes d'Horapollon*, &c., Paris, 1827, connects Hermetic and
Kabalistic tradition on the fantastic ground that Enoch, who plays such
an important part in the revelation of the Kabalah, is identical with the
Edris of the Orientals and with Hermes (p. 48).

† As Louis Figuier's popular work, entitled *L'Alchimie et les
Alchimistes*, is much quoted by occultists, and is therefore presumably
in the hands of some of them, it will be well to point out that he classes
all Byzantine literature of alchemy as apocryphal, and the work of
monks belonging to the 8th, 9th, and 10th centuries. There was never
much excuse for this opinion, and it is only necessary to add that since
the researches of Berthelot it has become impossible. I may add that,
throughout, Figuier's work, though exceedingly interesting, is most
inaccurate as regards its facts, and of no consequence as to its opinions
and inferences. Consult, on the point involved, the third edition, p. 6,
Paris, 1860.

‡ *Collection des anciens alchimistes Grecs, livraison* ii., p. 206.

eyes of its adepts) who save and purify the divine
soul enchained in the elements, and, above all, who
separate the divine spirit confounded with the flesh.
As there is a sun, the flower of the fire, a celestial
sun, the right eye of the world, so copper, if it
become flower (that is, if it assume the colour of
gold) by purification, becomes then a terrestrial sun,
which is king on earth, as the sun is king in the
sky."* There is no doubt that this is a very
important citation. It shows why the early Hermetic
books came to be regarded as alchemical in later
times, and it institutes a striking parallel between
Egyptian and Jewish science. But that the latter
is the science of the Kabalah there is no evidence
to cite. So also the reference to the Labyrinth
of Solomon which occurs among the remains of
still earlier Greek alchemists is a mediæval inter-
polation.† In short, the celebrated Byzantine
collection, which is so far the source of all
alchemy, shows no traces of acquaintance with
the Jewish secret tradition. The same observation
applies to the early Arabian and Syriac alchemists
who drew from Greek sources, though some extracts
from Zosimus, with analyses, in a Syriac MS.
possessed by the University of Cambridge, mention
the talismans of Solomon, referred to the seven
planets, and the power which they exercise over
demons. When we add to this that in spite of such
evidence for the connection between alchemy and the
Kabalah as is offered by the late *Æsh Metzareph*
there is very little, as already seen, to support it in
the Zohar, it must be inferred that these two esoteric

---

* *Ibid.*   † *Ibid.*

traditions grew up for a long peried in independence of one another.* Furthermore, there is no trace of any science of transmutation in ancient Egypt, and it is worth noting that the claim of alchemy rose into prominence precisely at that period when certain Chinese ports were first thrown open to Western commerce. If it be true, as it has been affirmed, that alchemy flourished in China from a remote period, that it possessed a literature, and that the terminology of this literature offers analogies with that which afterwards prevailed in the West, it may well be that we must look to the furthest East for the cradle of what is usually understood by Hermetic Science, namely, that of transmutation.† The subject is far too large to enter on in this place, but we shall do well to remember that the doctrine of the Macrocosm and the Microcosm, the analogy between spiritual and material, the Zoharistic symbolism of the balance, have all been traced to the oldest sacred books of the Chinese.‡ The analogies may not be so striking

---

* It is fair, however, to state that the Leyden papyrus which contains the earliest known process of alchemical sophistication forms part of a Gnostic and theurgic collection. On this point, see Berthelot's *Collection des Anciens Alchimistes Grees, livraison, Ie.*, p. 6 *et seq.* Albert Poisson, whose *Théories et Symboles des Alchimistes* is a contribution of real importance to the elucidation of Hermetic science, observes that "Alchemy among the Greeks was, by reason of its very origin, mixed up with magic and theurgy. Later on, thanks to the philosophic Arabs, this science became purified, and it was not till the fifteenth or sixteenth century that it allied itself afresh with the occult sciences properly so called. Thenceforth a considerable number of alchemists demanded the Key of the Great Work from the Kabalah, Magic and Alchemy."—*Op. cit.*, p. 27. Paris, 1891.

† See "The Chinese," by Dr. W. A. P. Martin, New York, 1881.

‡ The most accessible work of reference is Isaac Myer's "Philosophy of Ibn Gebriol," appendix B. I mention this hypothesis so that it may be taken for what it is worth. See Book iii., § 5.

as the scholars who have discovered them have thought; as to this, we have no real means of deciding; but they indicate at least the possibility of a common source for both esoteric traditions at a centre not as yet acknowledged and at a very far epoch of the past.

Of course, as time went on, and as alchemical literature developed in Europe, a connection undoubtedly arose with the Kabalah.* The *Æsh Metzareph* is one of its evidences; many Kabalists became alchemists; a few alchemists studied the Kabalah. But it is still a slight and occasional connection which we must be careful not to exaggerate: there is also very little trace of it prior to the seventeenth century,† when writers like Fludd concerned themselves with both subjects, and Khunrath ‡ introduced Kabalistic symbolism into the pictorial emblems of transmutation. §

The best proof of these statements is the literary history of the *Æsh Metzareph* itself. Mr.

---

* "Alchemy, a science of observation, could not profit in any way by its alliance with the Kabalah, which was purely a speculative science."—Poisson, *Théories et Symboles des Alchimistes*, p. 28.

† Poisson refers this confusion of one occult science with another mainly to Paracelsus, but I have already given full proof of the very slender connection between this adept and the esoteric tradition of the Jews.

‡ *Amphitheatrum Sapientiæ Æternæ*, with which compare the second tract of the *Trinum Chemicum Secundum*. Strasbourg, 1700.

§ There is a treatise entitled "The Azoth of the Philosophers" which passes under the name of Basil Valentine, and suggests a certain connection with Kabalism, because the term Azoth is composed of the first and final letters of the Greek, Latin and Hebrew alphabets. It has been called into requisition accordingly, but the foundation is exceedingly slight. Moreover, the term is at least as old as pseudo-Geber, while the treatise attributed to Basil Valentine is of doubtful authenticity, and was excluded from the collection of Mangetus.

Mathers observes that it is "known to few, and when known is understood by still fewer."* If this were its position in the year 1887, it may be truly said that when alchemy most flourished in the West, the treatise had never been heard of, being first mentioned by Rosenroth at the end of the seventeenth century. Prior to that date there is no case within my knowledge of its quotation by any alchemist, and although the *Kabbala Denudata* was described on its title-page as *Scriptum omnibus philologis, philosophis, theologis omnium religionum, atque* PHILOCHYMICIS *quam utilissimum*, I believe that only one alchemical writer concerned himself with it after the appearance of its fragments among the *Apparatus in Librum Sohar.* This was the "Lover of Philalethes," who collected and translated the fragments in 1714 and also published in the same year "A Short Enquiry Concerning the Hermetic Art,"† which introduces certain citations from the *Æsh Metzareph* and connects them with the symbolism of the Doves of Diana first introduced into alchemy by Eirenæus Philalethes.

It follows, however, from what has been stated previously that the literary connection between the Kabalah and alchemy does not begin so late as

---

* "The Kabbalah Unveiled," Introduction, p. 15.

† Reprinted in Dr. Wynn Westcott's *Collectanea Hermetica*, vol. 3, London, 1894; the preface, which is not by the editor, states that the "Short Enquiry" was "written with special reference" to the *Æsh Metzareph*, but there seems no foundation for this view. The little tract is largely a collection of opinions and quotations, not always derived from the best sources, for its author appears to regard Edward Kelley and Elias Ashmole as of equal authority with the acknowledged adepts of alchemy.

the first quarter of the eighteenth century* and though the *Æsh Metzareph* seems to have been cited methodically by only one writer, the influence of the *Kabbala Denudata* may be traced in Germany soon after its publication by means of an anonymous tract which pretends to treat of the chemical Kabalah† (*cabala chymica*) and has these words on its headline. This little work is incidentally of importance in more than one respect. On p. 16 there is a curious *Figura Cabalæ* where the light from the *Ens Entium* falls on a bearded figure holding the compass in the right and the square in the left hand, thus giving the characteristic symbols of emblematic Masonry in connection with the secret sciences at a date when such a connection would scarcely be expected on the Continent by modern scholarship. There are also some observations worth noting on the subject of regeneration which are useful for the mystical aspects of alchemy.‡ Unfortunately the correspondences between the Kabalah and transmutation seem to be confined to the title which I have quoted.

---

* I except such slender analogies as the correspondence traced by *Sapere Aude* between the three worlds of Jean D'Espagnet and the four worlds of the Kabalists. See " Hermetic Arcanum," Collectanea Chemica, vol. 1 (Westcott's Edition), London, 1893.

† *Cabalæ verior Descriptio : das ist, Brundliche Beschriebungund Enveisung aller naturalischcn und uber naturalischen Dingen boiedurch das Verbum Fiat das alles erschasun* . . . Hamburg, 1680. There was a later edition, Frankfort, 1761.

‡ A work of similar pretensions is F. Kiern's *Cabala Chymica : concordantia chymica, Azoth Philosophicum Solificatum*, Mülhausen, 1606. Here the term Cabala is simply a catchword derived from Paracelsus, and is used in this sense by a compiler belonging to the group of Paracelsian exponents, of whom Benedictus Figulus and Alexander von Suchten are the names now most remembered or least forgotten.

The most important information on the subject might be expected in Hoefer's "History of Chemistry,"* which claims to include an exposition of Kabalistic doctrines concerning the philosophical stone, but the term proves on examination to be used in the loose sense of the period, and out of two very large volumes there are only two pages devoted to the subject of the Kabalah.† The authorship of the Sepher Yetzirah is attributed to R. Akiba, and that of the Zohar to R. Simeon. It is also affirmed that Jewish and Arabian alchemists possessed an old knowledge of Kabalistic books, and that they were held by adepts in as much honour as those of Hermes Trismigestus. The evidence is unfortunately wanting, and as M. Hoefer also maintains that the science of transmutation was pursued in ancient Egypt, it would be unsafe to accept his opinion unsupported by other authority.‡

Before dismissing the Kabalistic connections of alchemy, a word must be said concerning two works which have been supposed to be examples of that connection, and to which some importance has been

---

* Ferdinand Hoefer: *Histoire de la Chimie depuis les temps les plus reculés jusqu'a notre époque ; comprenant une analyse detaillée des MSS. alchimiques de la Bibliotheque Royale de Paris ; un exposé des doctrines cabalistiques sur la Pierre Philosophale*, etc., 2 vols., Paris, 1842, 1843. Mr. H. C. Bolton observes that this great work is superseded so far as the MSS. are concerned by the researches of Berthelot. See "A Select Bibliography of Chemistry, Smithsonian Miscellaneous Collections, Washington, 1893, p. 119.

† T. i., pp. 242-244.

‡ There is indeed one authority cited, namely, the *Apparatus* of Rosenroth, *Kab. Den.*, i., 441-443, and this is a quotation from the *Æsh Metzareph*, c. 7.

attached.*   Both have the advantage, which they
share in common with Khunrath and his *Amphitheatrum*, of precedence over the publication of
Rosenroth's *Kabbala Denudata*, and one is prior to
any printed edition of the Zohar.   It will be needless
to say that neither shows an acquaintance with the
Æsh Metzareph, nor do I observe in their contents
anything to connect them with the Sephirotic
attribution of the metals which is characteristic of
that work.   One is a treatise by Joannes Augustinus
Pantheus, a Venetian priest, entitled *Ars et Theoria
Transmutationis Metallicæ, cum Voarchadumia Pro-
portionibus, muneris et iconibus rei accomodis illus-
trata.*   It was published at Venice in April 1530.†
Following the author himself, the Hermetic Lexicons
interpret Voarchadumia, (*a*) as "a liberal art gifted
with the virtues of occult science," a definition which
leaves something to be desired ; (*b*) as the Kabalistic
science of metals.   It is further a species of alchemical
metallurgy, concerning "auriferous metallic veins ;"
it explains "the intrinsic fixed form and the natural
yellow colour of gold ; it distinguishes the heterogeneous, combustible, volatile parts, and exhibits

* There are others naturally in the large literature of alchemy,
but they are not of Hermetic value, and, as in all cases, the Kabalistic
connection is thin and elusive.   Such is the *Philosophia Salomonis*, o
Secret Cabinet of Nature, a German anonymous treatise published at
Augsburg in 1753.   Here the royal stone of alchemy is connected
with the art of King Solomon, but there is no Kabalistic knowledge,
and the work is quite worthless.   See also : Cabala : *Spiegel der Kunst
und Natur in Alchymia*, Augsburg, 1690, remarkable for its curious
folding plates.

† Rare in the original edition, but rendered accessible by the
reprint in Lazarus Zetner's *Theatrum Chemicum*, Argentorati, 1613,
etc., second edition, 1659.   See vol. ii., p. 459 *et seq.*   A Paris edition
is also mentioned, date 1550.

how the same may be conducted to the grade of perfection. It defines, lastly, the Matter of the work, "a heavy, corporeal, fixed, fusible, ductile, tinged, rarefied and arcane substance of Quicksilver or Mercury, and of an incombustible Metallic Sulphur, educed and transmuted into true gold by means of cementation."* It will be seen from this specimen of style that the work is very nearly unreadable, even for an alchemical treatise, and it will be enough for the present purpose to note the fact of its existence and to observe that it seeks to throw light on the mysteries of transmutation by calculations of *Gematria*. It exercised no influence, and no importance can be reasonably ascribed to it.

The other work is much better known to fame and it offers several interesting, and so far unsolved, problems to the student. This is the *Monas Hieroglyphica* of Dr. John Dee, first published in 1564, and containing an analysis of the planetary symbols attributed to the metals.† Thus, the symbol of Mercury ☿ is composed of the crescent ☽, which is the sign of silver, the circle ☉, which is that of gold, and the cross representing the four elements. Special alchemical importance is attributed to their union in the sign which represents the fundamental matter of the philosophers as well as metallic quicksilver. It

---

* See the anonymous English translation of Martinus Rulandus : *Lexicon Alchemiæ, sive Dictionarium Alchemisticum*, the edition of 1612. This translation, without date or place, was restricted to six copies, and includes a large "Supplement to the Alchemical Lexicon of Martinus Rulandus." The explanation of *Voarchadumia* occurs on p. 438.

† For the astrological aspect of this analysis, see some curious speculations in Alan Leo's " Practical Astrology," second edition, *n. d.*

will be seen that this is not in any sense information which helps to connect alchemy with Kabalism, though it is highly important for the obscure question of the origin and history of the astronomical signs.*

I may observe in conclusion that there is one possible connection between alchemy and Kabalism which would appear to be overlooked by all those who have instituted a comparison between them. It is supplied by the obscure but subsisting analogies between the ancient document of Latin alchemy known as the *Turba Philosophorum*† and the two Synods of the Zohar, I am not, of course, referring to the accidental similarity of form, though, having regard to the history of the *Turba*, this accident is certainly a feature of interest. There are statements and allusions in this obscure colloquy, more especially regarding the four elements of ancient chemistry, which offer curious points of contact with Kabalism. When we add to this that some scholars have referred the *Turba* in the guise that we at present possess it to a Hebrew original, now lost, and that its date, so far as it can be assigned, is somewhere between the promulgation of the Book of Formation and the Zohar, enough has been said in indication of a possibility upon which there is no need, as indeed there are few materials, to insist further.‡

---

* For information and references see § xliv. of the *Eclaircissement Astronomique* appended to M. Bailly's *Histoire de l'Astronomie Ancienne*, 2nd edition, Paris, 1781.

† See the " *Turba Philosophorum*, or Assembly of the Sages, called also the book of Truth in the Art, and the third Pythagorical Synod . . . Translated from the Latin . . . By A. E. Waite, London, 1896. I must confess that I have no theory as to the two previous Synods.

‡ It is due to my readers, and to the subject, to confess that I have not made an exhaustive examination of alchemical literature in

III. THE KABALAH AND ASTROLOGY

The modern school of Kabalism is inclined, as already remarked, to claim that all the occult sciences arise out of their own, but it seems more correct to infer that the Kabalah has been engrafted on some of them, and in this manner we have Kabalistic astrology, as we have also Kabalistic alchemy. To determine the superior accuracy of either view we must have recourse exclusively to history and literature. It is only in the instance of Ceremonial Magic that the voice of both is unanimously in favour

---

reference to its connections with Kabalism. I have made myself acquainted with all sources which have been cited by those who affirm them, but as their observations have not been based upon a wide study of the alchemists, it is possible that my future researches may discover something which has, so far, been overlooked on both sides. I should note also that, according to M. Berthelot, "the Kabalah was bound up during the middle ages with alchemy, and the connection goes far back," that is, to the Leyden Papyrus as well as to the Greek alchemists. But I infer that this great authority has, so far as the mediæval period is concerned, received only a derived impression, or that at least his notion of the Kabalah has been obtained as such notions most commonly are. All his instances as to the earlier connections must be rejected decisively. Some of them, such as the "Labyrinth of Solomon," have been already dealt with; others are mere names—Abraham, Isaac, Jacob and the word Sabaoth "in papyri of the same family as No. 75 of Reuvens." It is further obvious that a reference by Zosimus to Solomon and his wisdom establishes no Kabalistic analogy. Finally, when the Greek alchemist traces the revelation of the sacred art from the Egyptians to the Jews, "who published it to the rest of the world," we must remember that this view belongs to a period which referred all science and philosophy to the chosen people on the principle of Aristobulus and Philo, so that this also proves nothing. *Les Origines de l'Alchimie* . . . Observe that W *Bibliotheca Britannica*, ii., 179 n, gives a reference to a work by H. C. van Byler, entitled, Tractatus Cabbalistico—Chymico—Philosophico—Magicus, Cologne, 1729, but I am not acquainted with its contents.

of a Kabalistic origin as regards the Western world.
From *a priori* considerations we shall be disposed to
believe that the case of astrology will prove something like that of alchemy, namely, that its history
and literature contain little to connect it essentially
with Jewry. It has the air of an exact science and
seems to suggest few possible analogies with the
speculations of a theosophical system. There are two
facts, however, which it must be admitted are above
challenge, firstly, that the Jews were much addicted
to astrology,* and, secondly, that the prophetic
science of the stars, as it is known in the West, has
derived something from the later Hebrews. Against
these must be placed two other facts, not of less
significance, namely, that ancient Israel contributed
very little to the science of astronomy, that Jewish
astronomical writings belonging to the Christian
centuries draw chiefly from Arabia, and that as
regards astrology in Jewry, during the Kabalistic
period, it was imbedded in fastastic notions and
puerile processes. We are not called to deal here
with the history of the science; we know that
Josephus traces it to Seth and assures us that he
himself had visited the two famous pillars
reported to have survived the deluge, and on
which all the rules of astrology are said to
have been engraved. Josephus may have been

---

* The question whether the art was condemned by the Law of
Israel has been a subject of some debate. Perhaps the best opinion
considered that it was. See on this point the *Conciliator* of Menasseh
ben Israel, *Sive de conventia locorum S. Scripturæ quæ pugnare inter
se Videntur*, Frankfort, 1633, p. 142. It was also debated by Gaffarel,
writing from the Christian standpoint. He contrived to defend the
art by distinguishing it into two branches.

deceived easily, or he may have been tempted to claim for his nation on the warrant of a fable the precedence in a study to which the notion of learning was attached.   Seth and the pillars set apart, we know also that antique Chaldea was a great centre of astrology, that it flourished among the Babylonians, that it was practised in Egypt, and it is natural to suppose that the Jews must have had their share in the knowledge of each of these peoples.   There may have been even a Kabalah of astrological procedure communicated to Christian times.*   All this is, however, beside the real question ; we are not justified in looking for the Zohar or its influence in Jewish writings on mathematics or natural philosophy, for the simple reason that the Zohar does not connect seriously with these subjects.   It has also little concern with astrology.   We are at liberty, however, to ask ourselves one question. Astrology works upon data which are very obscure in their history,† and there are doctrines connected with it which even to the occult student may seem insufficiently grounded.   It would be interesting to ascertain whether they have any Kabalistic correspondences.   As to the data, I suppose no one has attempted to institute a parallel, but it has been thought that some astrological theorems may have

---

I Christian affirms that there was, but he offers no evidence in support of his assertion that the *Speculum Astrologiæ* of Junctin was a kind of synthesis of the astrological labours of the "Arabian and Hebrew Kabalists."—*Histoire de la Magie*, l. vii., *Clefs générales de L'Astrologie*, p. 579.

† Which history, moreover, has never been elucidated by any writer on the subject.   Mr. W. Gorn Old's "New Manual," perhaps the latest work on Astrology (London, 1898), does not attempt to account for the grounds on which the old judgments are based.

a connection with Kabalistic apparatus. Let us see, therefore, what is said upon this subject by its students.

The attribution of metals to the *Sephiroth* in the *Æsh Metzareph* suggests planetary attribution, and a tabulation has been constructed by Papus,[*] following the authority of Kircher :—

1. *Kether* corresponds to the Empyrean.
2. *Chokmah* 　 ,, 　 　 ,, 　 Primum Mobile.
3. *Binah* 　 　 ,, 　 　 ,, 　 Firmament.
4. *Chesed* 　 　 ,, 　 　 ,, 　 Saturn.
5. *Geburah* 　 　 ,, 　 　 ,, 　 Jupiter.
6. *Tiphereth* 　 ,, 　 　 ,, 　 Mars.
7. *Netzach* 　 　 ,, 　 　 ,, 　 Sun.
8. *Hod* 　 　 　 ,, 　 　 ,, 　 Venus.
9. *Jesod* 　 　 　 ,, 　 　 ,, 　 Mercury.
10. *Malkuth* 　 　 ,, 　 　 ,, 　 Moon.

It is possible, as the *Æsh Metzareph* shows, that "all systems tend to the one truth," but this scheme is not in accordance with either of its own attributions. These are followed by Rosenroth, but the R. P. Esprit Sabathier, in that strange little treatise on Kabalism which still exercises so much fascination on French students of the subject, refers Mars to *Geburah* and Mercury to *Hod*.[†] When there is

---

* For Papus consult *La Kabbale*, already cited frequently ; for Kircher *Œdipus Œgyptiacus*. The synopsis of the Kabalah in this rare work has been recently translated into French.

† See *L'Ombre Ideale de la Sagesse Universelle*, 1679. A reprint of this work has been promised in Paris. The original is rare, and there is no copy in the British Museum, but the reader may consult the Table given by Papus at pp. 80, 81 of his treatise on the Kabalah, where the attribution in question will be found.

no unanimity we must infer that there is no point of importance involved and that attributions and tabulations of this kind are less or more conventional and can have little application to astrology itself. In modern times, however, all the divinatory sciences, which in every case possess or suggest astrological connections,* have received some kind of Kabalistic attribution. Thus, the planetary correspondences of the figures used in geomancy have been adjusted to the *Sephiroth*; Kabalistic principles have been applied to chiromancy; physiognomy alone, possibly because it has never had much attention at the hands of professed occultists, seems an exception to this rule, although, as we have previously seen, there is direct warrant for it in the Zohar.†

The most accessible information on astrology among the Jews is in the "Curiosities" of James Gaffarel, who based his observations on a direct knowledge of its chief rabbinical exponents during the Christian centuries.‡ To reduce what he says to a sentence, the Jewish astrologers read the heavens like a book, they regarded it as a book, and, for the

---

* Thus, the "Principles of Astrological Geomancy" have been the subject of a special treatise by Franz Hartmann, M.D. (London, 1899), while Miss Rosa Baughan has compiled a curious medley of chiromancy and astrology under the title of "The Influence of the Stars."

† Physiognomy has been, of course, connected with astrology, and an old work published about the beginning of the seventeenth century under the title of "Book of Palmistry, Physiognomy, and Natural Astrology" illustrates this connection. See also "A Treatise on Zodiacal Physiognomy," by John Varley, London, 1828.

‡ A summary of Gaffarel's information, with some pertinent criticisms, will be found in Eliphas Levi's *Rituel de la Haute Magie*. See also "Transcendental Magic," part ii., and "Mysteries of Magic," pp. 248, 252, 253, 254. Second Edition, 1897.

GG

purposes of methodising its contents with a view to its interpretation, they collected the stars into hieroglyphic characters, which were, in fact, the Hebrew alphabet. Their process was therefore not an astrological process, but more correctly one of divination, and as to its value, we have only to glance at the Hebrew planisphere furnished by Gaffarel to see how arbitrary was the nature of the arrangement. At the same time it must be admitted that it suggests a correspondence with the fundamental notion of the Sepher Yetzirah, though the fact has not been observed by any previous writer. There could be nothing more natural for those who believed that the heavens and the earth were made by the inscription of letters in the air than to discover these letters in the configuration, apparently fortuitous, of the starry heavens. In place, therefore, of the unmeaning mythological figures of pagan antiquity they imagined the twenty-two elements of the divine word manifested to the chosen people, and the imagination once justified by the apparent delineation of the characters it became part of the scheme of the universe ;* to read the sense of the heavens so that they could give the meaning thereof was an operation no less sacred in its intention, mysterious in its methods, and strange in its results† than the application of

---

* This is the Zoharic notion, and it was claimed that by means of the signs and figures in the heavens most profound secrets and mysteries could be discovered. So regarded, the stars and constellations are a subject of contemplation, and a source of mysterious delight for the sage.—Zohar, ii., 76a, Mantua.

† Compare those other strange results in symbolical astrology of which Ruysbrœck the Mystic speaks in the "Book of the Twelve Beguines," Latinised by Surius under the title *De Vera Contemplatione.*

Zoharistic processes to the disentangling of the mystic meaning beneath the letter of the Scriptures. This is the true Kabalistic astrology,* based on a Kabalistic doctrine which is its justification and of which it is in turn the logical development. Outside the Sepher Yetzirah, it has the countenance of the Zohar itself. But it has little in common with the science of the stars, as it has been pursued in the western world ; it can offer nothing in evidence of its considerations, even as astrology in the West has nothing to tell us concerning the Kabalistic mystery of *Ain Soph*. It is better therefore not to confuse further the complicated issues of the secret sciences by the suggestion of fantastic influences and un-realisable communications.†

It will, of course, be anticipated that a literature so large as that of the Jews and embracing, as we said at the inception of our inquiry, so wide a range of subjects could not have grown up without con-tributing anything to the knowledge of the heavens. In the third century the Jews of Babylon were famous as doctors and astronomers and, partly for this reason, were in high credit at the Persian Court during the reign of the usurper Artaxerxes. Samuel

Needless to say this astrology is not judicial. The late Mr. Hargrave Jennings has also some pleasing fantasies on the "astronomy of the mind" in "The Indian Religions," p. 207 *et seq.*, London, 1890.

* Which astrology, as Levi rightly observes, must be distinguished from what is commonly understood by judicial astrology. See "Mysteries of Magic," p. 247.

† As an instance of the extraordinary lengths to which speculations of this kind have been carried outside astronomical connections, see Dr. J. Lamb's "Hebrew characters derived from Hieroglyphs," London, 1835. The hieroghyphics in question are re-constituted, and various doctrines, passages and words of the sacred writings are inter preted by recourse to them.

Lunaticus, famous for the astronomical tables attributed to him, and head of the academy of Naharden, is an instance in point, and R. Ada, also of Naharden, is another. Abba Aricha, better known as the Babylonion Rav, founder of the academy of Sora, was again a deep student of astronomy, and names might be multiplied easily. Side by side with medicine and the interpretarion of dreams, astrology was much pursued by the Eastern Jews of the tenth and eleventh centuries. In 1150, or thereabouts, R. Avi Joseph wrote a treatise on the intelligences which move the heavens and concerning the judgment of the stars. Aben Ezra, about the same period, is a great name among the astronomers of Jewry as well as in doctrine and philosophy. Abraham Chiia and Abraham Nasi are also contemporary students of the same science. In the second half of the thirteenth century, during the reign of Alphonso the 10th, King of Castile, himself called the astrologer, the rabbins were in high estimation for their knowledge of the heavens, and the Tables attributed to Alphonso were the work of a Jew whom he employed. In the fifteenth century the family of Alcadet produced two famous astronomers, and Abraham Zacut, author of the *Sepher Yuhasin*, was another student of the subject in the days of Ferdinand and Isabella.

Meagre as are these indications, having regard to the fact that astronomy was usually pursued in connection with the judgment of the stars, *i.e.*, with judicial astrology, they are sufficient to establish that this occult science is to be found in Jewry during most of the Christian centuries.

The reader who desires to become acquainted with the first principles and procedure of Jewish astrology may consult the "Curiosities" of Gaffarel, whose information is drawn from R. Moses, R. Aben Ezra, R. Jacob Kapol ben Samuel, &c. This learned but pedantic writer wholly rejected what is called Kabalistic astrology, with its Sephirotic attributions,[*] but the system which he develops is not less fantastic, and is that indeed which we have described briefly in the earlier part of the present section. It would be out of place to extend our references, for, as on the one hand Sephirotic astrology is rejected even by so determined a Kabalist as Gaffarel, so, on the other, the secrets of the Hebrew planisphere and the mysteries of stellar writing do not connect with the practice of the art in the West.

It may be added that a recent writer, Mr. W. Gorn Old, has published a Kabalistic astrology,[†] but it is merely a process of divination, like that attributed to Cagliostro, which was developed at great length and applied to the science of the stars by P. Christian.[‡] It is obvious that the use of the term Kabalistic in such a connection is merely a *façon de parler*, unfortunately in very common use. This

---

[*] So far as I am aware, no astrological work developing these connections has ever been printed in any European language, but books like John Bishop's "Marrow of Astrology," London, 1688, with its list of the governing angels of the signs and the planets, suggest Kabalistic connections through the vehicle of Ceremonial Magic.

[†] "Kabalistic Astrology, or Your Fortune in your Name," by Sepharial, London, n.d. (? 1892).

[‡] In his *Histoire de la Magie*, books ii., iii., and vi. Also in *L'Homme Rouge des Tuileries*. Some account of Cagliostro's Method will also be found in Grand Orient's "Manual of Cartomancy," &c., of which several editions have appeared.

is made further evident by the parallel use of the term Hermetic, not only as an analogue, but an actual equivalent. Mr. Old's process is affirmed to have been "in use among the ancient Kabalists," but this is merely speculative and an inference from certain Tarotic connections.

IV. THE KABALAH AND FREEMASONRY

It is generally agreed among occultists that the Masonic Fraternity is an institution of mystic origin, but that it has lost its real secrets and is interesting only as a survival. As such, it continues to preserve certain legends and symbols of occult philosophy, but it applies to them a conventional meaning of an obvious and meagre character. As to its historical origin, there is also a general opinion prevailing in the same circles, namely, that Freemasonry, after some manner that is not wholly apparent, is a survival of the ancient mysteries, but this term is used in a catholic sense, not as signifying the initiations of Egypt, of Greece, or of Rome, but rather the secret power and intelligence which is thought to have been present behind the philosophical associations of all ages and most civilised countries. During the Christian period the knowledge which would otherwise have perished was preserved among successive occult fraternities, some known to history, such as Templars and Rosicrucians, the rest working in complete silence. Corporately or otherwise, they were all affiliated with each other and symbolic Freemasonry forms the last link in the Western chain of transmission.

No presentation of this hypothesis has so far been able to survive analysis, and the inductive student must be content to recognise, (*a*) the mystic nature of most Masonic symbolism to which the fraternity now attaches only elementary meanings belonging to the ethical primer ; (*b*) a certain analogy of ostensible purpose as regards the ends of human existence, but it is not worth while to insist strongly on this point ; (*c*) the affinity for Mysticism which has always been shown by Masonry during its historical period. It may be added that there are certain indications which point to a possible connection between Masonry and Rosicrucianism, and this, if admitted, would constitute the first link in its connection with the past. The evidence is, however, inconclusive, or at least unextricated. Freemasonry *per se*, in spite of the affinity with Mysticism which I have just mentioned, has never exhibited any mystic character, nor has it a clear notion how it came by its symbols; though occultists at all times have gravitated towards it, and though it has tolerated and even received them, it has shown no sense of understanding on occult subjects. This being the state of the case, and the claim which is made for Freemasonry having never been urged by the institution on its own behalf, there is nothing *prima facie* to accredit the idea that it has ever been a channel of the secret tradition or to warrant us in supposing *à priori* that it should have any distinct analogies with Kabalism. And as a fact its position in this respect is much like that of alchemy, seemingly fortuitous, a question of subsequent introduction, as much imputation as reality, a varnish rather than a permeating tincture, and yet, like all such positions, interesting. To establish my point, I must refer for a third time to the fact that since Masonry appeared on the historical plane, occultists and mystics have always tended towards it, that it has received them all amiably, and that all have elaborated the system in accordance with their particular notions. During the prevalence of the passion for rites we know that alchemists, Swedenborgians,* Martinists, theurgists, astrologers, all invented new grades and new orders, and as at this period there were also Kabalists, so in one or two instances we hear of Kabalistic rites, and especially of rites and grades which exhibit Kabalistic influences. As Free-masonry is not Swedenborgianism, as it is not alchemy, as in spite of the Elect Cohens, the evocations and rituals of Pasqually, and all the magical marvels of Schrœpfer, it is not theurgy, as it is still less the mysticism of any of the true Mystics, so it is not Kabalism, but it has been developed somewhat in Kabalistic as in other interests.

It must be added that the few Kabalistic degrees which have left any record behind them beyond their name, and the uncommon swiftness with which they passed into extinction, give no evidence of acquaintance with the Jewish esoteric tradition. They represent the Kabalism of the period. There is no need to speculate as to its quality; it has bequeathed its literary remains in grimoires and

---

* The history of the Swedenborgian Rite being exceedingly obscure, and yet possessing considerable occult interest, it may be observed that some account of it was published at New York in 1870 by Samuel Berwick.

grand clavicles, in the spurious thaumaturgic processes of Abramelin, and in amusing Kabalistic
correspondence with the Seigneur Astaroth,* the
lees and lavations of the rabbinical conduits. As
it will be well to enforce these statements by means
of documentary evidence, I will add an account of
one Kabalistic grade which may be taken to
represent the whole.

A degree of Knight of the Kabalah once
existed among those innumerable decorative developments of the Fraternity which were termed high
by their disciples and spurious by some who
resented innovations, and especially those which
led to nothing. It has long since fallen into disuse.
The object of the candidate, according to the
catechism of the degree, was "to know, by means
of numbers, the admirable harmony which subsists
between nature and religion." It defines the Kabalist
as a man who has acquired the Sacerdotal Art and
the Royal Art by the communication of the tradition.
The device was *Omnia in numeris sita sunt.* The
Master of the Lodge in which the degree was
imparted seems to have been called the President
of the Sanhedrim and the Rabbi. The mystical
significance of numbers† was developed by the

---

* See D'Argens: *Lettres Cabalistiques, ou Correspondance Philosophique . . . entre deux Cabalistes,* &c., 7 vols., La Haye, 1754.

† The numerical mysticism of the Kabalah is based, of course,
on the *Sephiroth* ; most of its developments are very late, and possess
a magical complexion, for which reasons they do not enter into the
scheme of this study. Some of these developments are quite unknown
to occultists, as, for example, the attempt to simplify chronology by
Kabalistic figures in Michael Aitsinger's *Pentaplus Regnorum Mundi,*
Antwerp, 1579. On the general subject, see Petrus Bargus : *Mysticæ
numerorum significationis liber,* Bergomi, 1585.

catechism in a somewhat curious manner, which it may be worth while to summarise.

I = In the moral order, a word incarnate in the bosom of a virgin, otherwise, Religion; in the physical order, a spirit embodied in the virgin earth, or Nature. It is the generative number in the order of Divinity, apparently a false symbolism, because the monad neither generates nor is generated, whence Eliphas Levi more correctly says that the monad supposes the duad, and thence, through the triad, all numbers are evolved.

II = In the moral order, man and woman; in the physical, active and passive. It is the generative number in created things.

III = In the moral order, the three theological virtues; in the physical, the three principles of bodies. The reference here is to salt, sulphur and mercury, thus indicating the Hermetic connections of this grade. Three also denotes the triple divine essence.

IV = the four cardinal virtues, the four elementary qualities—another Hermetic reference—and it is, moreover, the most mysterious of numbers, because it contains all the mysteries of nature.

V = the quintessence of religion, and the quintessence of matter—which again is alchemical. It is also the most occult number, " because it is enclosed in the centre of the series." The precise meaning of this last statement does not appear, but it may possibly refer to the pentagram as one of the emblems of the grade.

VI = the theological cube and the physical cube. It is the most salutary number, " because it contains

the source of our spiritual and corporeal happiness."
Is this a reference to the mystical adultery of the
first man whereby the coming of the Liberator was
necessitated ?

VII = the seven sacraments and the seven
planets. It is the most fortunate number, " because
it leads us to the decade, the perfect number."

VIII=the small number of the elect or the
wise. It is the most desirable number, " because
he who possesses it is of the number of the *Elves*
and Sages."

IX=the exaltation of religion and the exaltation
of matter. It is the most sublime number, because
religion and nature are both exalted thereby.

X=the ten commandments and the ten precepts
of nature. It is the most perfect number, " because
it includes unity, which created everything, and zero,
symbol of matter and chaos, whence everything
emerged. In its figures it comprehends the created
and uncreated, the beginning and end, power and
force, life and annihilation. By the study of this
number we find the relations of all things, the power
of the Creator, the faculties of the creature, the Alpha
and Omega of divine knowledge.

XI = the multiplication of religion and the
multiplication of nature. It is the most multiplying
number, " because with the possession of two units,
we arrive at the multiplication of things."

XII=the twelve articles of faith ; the twelve
apostles, foundation of the Holy City, who preached
throughout the whole world for our happiness and
spiritual joy; the twelve operations of nature ; the
twelve signs of the Zodiac, foundation of the

Primum Mobile, extending it throughout the universe for our temporal felicity. It is thus the most solid number, being the basis of our spiritual and corporeal happiness.

The numbers after twelve were left to the discernment of the candidate. The catechism also shows that this order concerned itself with the universal spirit of alchemy and even with the quadrature of the circle. The history of the Knights of the Kabalah is unfortunately involved in obscurity, but it will be seen that it was Christian and Catholic, which furnishes a resemblance to other and later institutions professing similar purposes and having similar religious sympathies.*

Had the "Book of Occultation" been made in the eighteenth century the theme of a Masonic grade, had the lodge represented *Atziluth*, the Master *Ain Soph*, his throne in the East *Kether*, and the officers the remaining *Sephiroth ;* had the ritual been constructed from the Zohar and the catechism from the Apparatus of Rosenroth, all this would have proved nothing as to the Kabalistic connections of Masonry. Within recent years a powerful Masonic order has undergone a species of development in this direction through the labours of Albert Pike, and there can be little doubt that it was his intention to transform the Ancient and Accepted Scottish Rite into a seminary of occult study. There may be many of its own brethren at the present time in whom this statement will excite only incredulity,

---

* Among the degrees collected by the French Mason Peuvret, there was that of *Maçon Cabbalistique.* The Metropolitan Chapter of France dignified its 80th Grade by the title of *Chevalier de Cabale.*

but it is not the less certain that Albert Pike was
more than an ardent admirer and far more than an
unqualified follower of the occult philosophies, or that
he pursued it into regions of which Masonry has now
no conception. He was also seconded by numerous
like-minded persons who occupied high dignities in
the United States' Southern Jurisdiction, and some
of whom still survive.

The evidence of all these things is to be found
in the vast body of instruction which he compiled,
chiefly from sources in occult literature, for all the
grades of the order. No person who is acquainted
with the " Morals and Dogma " can fail to trace the
hand of the occultist therein, and it is to be especially
observed that, passing from grade to grade in the
direction of the highest, this instruction becomes
more and more Kabalistic. It matters little that
the sources from which Pike drew were not of the
best, or that, though a man of wide reading, he
was not a skilled critic; for we are concerned only
with a tendency and its development. He accepted,
for example, without due caution, the construction
placed on Kabalism by the most unsafe of all its
expounders, Eliphas Lévi, from whom he translated
verbatim at great length, and, following his professed
habit, with no specific acknowledgment, while for
the rest his only source of further information was
the *Kabbala Denudata*, of which, however, he shows
no analytical knowledge, seeming to regard the
Liber Drushim as entitled to rank in authority
with the *Sepher Dzenioutha*. In spite of these
limitations he made available an amount of information on occult subjects with which no previous

scheme had ever provided Masonry. Yet with all his strenuous efforts it must be doubted whether the seal of occultism has been impressed effectually on the Ancient and Accepted Scottish Rite, in which case, if we except such interesting minor instances as the *Societas Rosicruciana in Anglia*, with which I have dealt elsewhere, it must be confessed that the Ancient and Primitive Rite of Memphis* and Misraim† is the only section of high-grade Masonry which claims a distinct purpose of an occult kind ; it is not necessary to say that in England, at least, it has failed wholly in obtaining recognition as a genuine development of Masonry, and it remains practically in abeyance. ‡

We see therefore that Kabalistic influence is confined to the so-called high grades. It would be absurd to discuss the possibility of its conscious presence in the blue lodges, or seek to interpret the legend of the master grade in connection with Jewish tradition. The symbols, however, which are familiar to the initiates of these lodges do connect . with Kabalism, among other forms of occult philosophy, but the presence of the seal of Solomon among the heirlooms of the brotherhood being, so far, unaccountable, it is useless to insist on the connection,

---

* See Marconis et Moultet : *L' Hiérophante, développement complet des Mystères Maçonniques*, Paris, 1839. *Le Rameau d' or d' Eleusis*, another work by Marconis is also interesting as the views of an amiable student upon the Mysteries in connection with Masonry.

† A history of this institution, with all the romantic elements which might be expected, was written by Marc Bedarride and published in two volumes at Paris, 1845, under the title, *De L' Ordre Maçonnique de Misraïm, depuis sa creation jusuq'a nos jours*, &c.

‡ The fourth Series of the Rite of Misraïm is designated Kabalistic.

because nothing logically follows from it. So far as history is concerned, Kabalism and Masonry have joined hands in the sphere of the higher grades, and as a historical fact this is interesting, but that it is otherwise significant must be left to those who affirm it.

V. THE KABALAH AND THE TAROT

It is very well known to all occult students at the present day that the Tarot is a method of divination* by means of seventy-eight symbolical picture-cards, to which great antiquity and high importance are attributed by several authorities. Their literary history is also equally well known. They were first mentioned by the French archæologist Court de Gebelin at the close of the eighteenth century, and were attributed by him to an Egyptian origin. Much about the same time the subject was taken up by a professed cartomancer, named Alliette, who wrote a great deal about them in several illiterate tracts, and endeavoured to trace their connection with Egypt through the Jewish Kabalah. The inquiry then fell into neglect, except in so far as Continental fortune-tellers were concerned, until the year 1854, when Eliphas Lévi made his first contributions to occult science.

---

* As there may, however, be some readers who are not acquainted with this matter, I may observe that Mr. S. L. MacGregor Mathers is the author of a small explanatory treatise, entitled, "The Tarot; its Occult Signification," &c., published with a set of the cards, London, 1888.

In 1857, J. A. Vaillant* endeavoured to prove their Chinese origin† and transmission by means of the gipsies ; their connection with these nomads was subsequently adopted by Lévi, who gave great prominence to the Tarot in all his writings up to the year 1865. The subject was also taken in hand by P. Christian, who published a large history of Magic in 1870. He developed still further the Egyptian theory, but no statement which he makes can be accepted with any confidence. In the year 1887 I was the first who introduced the claims of the Tarot to English readers in a digest of the chief works of Eliphas Levi. An important contribution to the inquiry was made shortly after by the French occultist Papus, whose elaborate work entitled the "Tarot of the Bohemians," though scarcely of critical value on the historical side, remains the most comprehensive and attractive summary of all the arguments.

The point which concerns us here is, of course, the Kabalistic connections. Eliphas Lévi says that

---

* *Histoire Vraie des Vrais Bohémiens.* As a notice of the gipsies this work is exceedingly good for its period ; its Tarot speculations are worthless, and its philological arguments absurd. M. Vaillant described the Tarot as "the synthesis of ancient faith, a deduction from the sidereal book of Enoch" (412). Its origin he affirms to be lost in the night of time (413). He only mentions the Kabalah to establish its connection with Cabul ! (p. 54).

† Occult writers mostly favour Egypt as the birthplace of the Tarot, and this is consistent with their views on the origin of the Kabalah. So Mons. Z. Lismon has recently published a version of the cards under the title of *Livre de Thot, Jeu des 78 Tarots Egyptiens*, with explanatory booklet. Compare R. Falconnier : *Les xxii. Lames Hermétiques du Tarot divinatoire*, which pretend to be re-constituted exactly according to "the sacred texts and translation" of the Magic of old Egypt !

the Tarot cards are the key to the esoteric tradition
of the Jews, and "the primitive source of divine and
human tradition"; he institutes an analogy between
the symbols of its four suits and the four letters of
the Divine Name *Tetragrammaton*, and between the
ten *Sephiroth* and the ten small cards belonging to
each suit. He gives also the correspondences
between the twenty-two trump cards and the letters
of the Hebrew alphabet, for which he quotes the
authority of "divers Kabalistic Jews," which must
not, however, be interpreted too strictly, as although
the symbolism of the Hebrew alphabet has been
much dwelt on by such authorities there is no trace
of any reference to the Tarot by Kabalistic writers of
the past. It must be admitted, on the other hand,
that the analogies are exceedingly striking, and that
although the historic evidences can scarcely be said
to exist, and have been supplied from the treasures of
imagination, there can be no doubt that the Tarot is
actually, as it is claimed to be, of considerable
importance symbolically. I may perhaps be permitted also to register my personal belief that it has
distinct Kabalistic connections, some of which were
broadly outlined by Eliphas Lévi. Unfortunately,
the interpretations of its symbolism which have
been attempted by various writers are nearly worthless, in the first place because they have all proved
themselves incapable of conducting a dispassionate
historical inquiry; they have allowed affirmation to
take the place of evidence; they have regarded a
hint as a sufficient ground of conviction; they have
made conjecture certitude. Setting aside Court de
Gebelin, who was merely an inquirer hampered by

IIII

the limitations of his period ; setting aside Lévi, who seldom made an accurate statement about any matter of fact ; observe how Dr. Papus pursues his inquiry into the origin of the Tarot. It is by an appeal to the writers who preceded him, as if their authority were final; to Court de Gebelin, who was a groper in the dark during the childhood of archæological reasoning ; to Vaillant, with his fascinating theory of gipsy transmission which is about as conclusive as Godfrey Higgins on the " Celtic Druids"; to Lévi, whose "marvellous learning" is so much and so unsafely insisted on by the whole French school. Papus contributes nothing himself to the problem on its historical side except an affirmation that "the game called the Tarot, which the Gypsies possess, is the Bible of Bibles." Obviously, the historical question calls for treatment by some independent scholar who will begin by releasing its present fantastic connections.

In the second place, the symbolism of the Tarot, which, to do justice to Dr. Papus, is most patiently and skilfully elaborated in his work, is at once disorganised if there be any doubt as to the attribution of its trump cards to the Hebrew alphabet. Now there is one card which bears no number and is therefore allocated according to the discretion of the interpreter. It has been allocated in all cases wrongly, by the uninstructed because they had nothing but their private judgment to guide them, and by those who knew better because they desired to mislead. I may go further and say that the true nature of Tarot symbolism is perhaps a secret in the hands of a very few persons, and outside that circle

operators and writers may combine the cards as
they like and attribute them as they like, but they
will never find the right way. The symbolism is,
however, so rich that it will give meanings of a kind
in whatever way it may be disposed, and some of
these may be strikingly suggestive, but they are
illusory none the less. The purpose of this short
paper is therefore to show that the published Tarots
and the methods of using them may be very serviceable for divination, fortune-telling and other trifles,
but they are not the key of the Kabalah, and that
the Royal Game of Goose may be recommended with
almost as much reason for the same purpose. Dr.
Papus is therefore unconsciously misdirecting his
many followers when he advertises his laborious
readings as the "Absolute Key to Occult Science."

VI. THE KABALAH AND MYSTICISM

It is a task of no inconsiderable difficulty to
attempt a judgment upon the Kabalah from the
purely mystic standpoint. On the one hand the
history of Kabalism is so imbedded in that of
mysticism, that it is scarcely known or admitted in
any distinct connection. On the other hand, to the
pure mystic, there is so much in the Kabalistic
system which seems extrinsic to the subject of
mysticism, that there is a temptation to underrate its
real influence. The correspondence and the difference
may perhaps be brought into harmony if it be
permissible to regard mysticism in two ways—as a
philosopical system, that is to say, an ordered

metaphysics, held intellectually,* but also as a mode
of conduct practised with a defined purpose, in a word,
as transcendental doctrine and transcendental life.
The practical mystic is the saint on the path of his
ascent into the mystery of the eternal union, concerning whom it is consonant with the purpose of our
present inquiry to speak only with great reservation,
because the mysteries of the Divine Life do not fall
within the limits of historical research. I conceive
that the sum of Kabalistic instruction is of no real
service to the disciple of this secret path, after every
allowance has been made for the Zoharic doctrine
that a science of that Holy Unity into which all
things return as all come forth therefrom can be
attained by man.† *Invenit sanctum.* Like all other
studies, and perhaps not more so than any other
methodised theosophy, it has a certain office in the
sanctum facit. For that far larger class to whom the
possibility of sanctity is denied, who are in search
rather of a guide for thought upon questions of
fundamental philosophy, I conceive that the Kabalah
—but again, like other metaphysics—has some useful
and reassuring lights. It is a source of intellectual
consolation that one of the most barren of all the ways
pursued by the human mind has its own strange
flowers and fruit. There is no book, and there is no
system, to which this moderate office can be denied.
It is also, as I have sought to show, something more

---

* And this would be the correspondence of the Zohar with
mysticism. For example, the doctrine of ecstasy is assuredly found
therein, but not in the same way that we find it in Ruysbroeck or St.
John of the Cross. It is more especially a rationalised system of mystic
thought.

† Zohar, i., 51a, Mantua.

than an inheritance from the past, even an inheritance that has been transmitted from a period far back in human history. The Zohar at least has the power of stirring those depths in the human heart which are beyond the "plummet of the sense"; it seems occasionally to "strike beyond all time, and backward sweep through all intelligence," and to say this, is to confess that it is the eternal soul speaking, here under the common influence of right reason, there in ecstacy and vision, and again, as it would seem in somnambulism or even in frenzy. Now, the speech of the human soul, in what state soever, must be a message to the mystic. There is no need to add that on the philosophical side the Kabalah connects assuredly with mysticism.*

With occultism, of course, it connects wholly, throughout all its history. The difference between occultism and mysticism is much more than that of a Latin equivalent for a Greek term, as might appear at first sight. We are all acquainted with the distinction which is made between the magnetic and hypnotic sleep. They have much in common, but they are pathologically separate, having diverse characteristics and a divergent mode of induction. Sleep, however, is obtained in both, and this is their

---

* M. Anatole Leroy Beaulieu says that the Jew is not inclined to mysticism, and seems never to have been so. "Judaism has always been a law, a religion of the mind, an intellectual creed not favourable to mystic transports or divine languors." He denies also that Kabalism was indigenous in Jewry. "The mysteries of the Kabalah, and those of the Hassidim, the neo-Kabalists, seem to have been a foreign importation; according to the best judges, the Cabala itself is not rooted in Judaism."—*Israel among the Nations*, translated by Francis Hillman, London, 1895, p. 292. This view shows little first-hand acquaintance with the subject.

superficial and obvious point of union—so superficial and so obvious that the ordinary observer would scarcely fail to identify them, while they have also been identified on grounds which are not precisely those of ordinary observation. Between occult science and mystic science there is the common point of union which is created, let us say, by their secrecy. Beneath this fantastic resemblance there is the more important fact that they both profess to deal with the inner and otherwise uninvestigated forces of the human soul. In the case of occult science it is, however, for the kind of end which we connect with the notions of magic. For example, Talismanic Magic, so called, is ostensibly the art of infusing a certain recondite spiritual power into some object composed artificially. This is an operation of occult science because it deals with a power which is, by the hypothesis, of an occult or generally unknown nature and applies it in accordance with the formulæ of a concealed instruction. A knowledge of the powers which are latent in human nature is not unlikely to lead to mysticism, which is the development of the latent powers in the direction of divine union. There is usually, however, no person less really mystic than the occultist conventionally understood.

The points of contact between occult science and the Kabalah are very numerous, but between Mysticism and the Kabalah they are, comparatively speaking, few. It is difficult to name a branch of occult science which is not indebted for some development, though not as we have seen in most cases for a governing direction, to the tradition of the Jews, so far at least as the West is concerned. This is true in a degree even of astrology, though it must be said frankly that its rabbinical aspects are often highly fantastic, confined by their ignorance to the most general conclusions and based upon absurd principles, as appears most explicitly, though not with intention, in the defence of Gaffarel. Ceremonial Magic in the West had, as we have seen, its root in Kabalism; so had all methodised Divination, while the connections of alchemy with the *Æsh Metzareph* have been the subject of a special study. It seems unnecessary to prolong the thesis of the present section. The end of Mysticism is the recovery or attainment of consciousness in God. The secret doctrine of the creation, as that of the emanation of souls, written symbolically, cannot in the absence of the Key which will open its mysteries, be of any use to the mystic, nor can the Key itself, which is the successful methodising of the confused Kabalistic medley, provide more than intellectual knowledge, even by the most extreme hypothesis. Should he enter within the circle of initiation where that Key is said to be obtained the student will in due time be in a position to know whether the secret knowledge which underlies such symbolism can contribute to the success of his enterprise. But it is not impossible that a knowledge so obtained will take him far from any traditions of Israel. I have never met with any mystic, except those of the natural order, owing, as such, nothing to literature or traditions, who ignored the possibilities concealed behind Kabalistic symbolism, or on the other hand owed anything of importance to the Kabalah. I have never met with any mystic, as distinguished from occult students concerned with the offices of Magic, who had so much as a tolerable acquaintance with the subject. Finally, the greatest students of occult science within my acquaintance have been invariably taken further afield. It must be confessed, however, that the question is complicated by a number of issues to which it is impossible to do justice in a brief space. But it may be clearly set down that as mysticism, properly disengaged from its adventitious associations and regarded essentially, is a sacramental experience of the soul, not a system of cosmology, not a doctrine of spiritual essences constructed hypothetically, so it has at best but an extrinsic connection with *Bereshith* and *Mercavah*, as, in like manner, with all that we understand conventionally by the occult sciences.

We have now reached the term of our inquiry, and a small space only can be spared to a summary of its results. As regards the documents of Kabalism we take our stand with that later and better scholarship the position of which is indicated by Dr. Schiller-Szinessy's admirable article on the *Midrashim*. We reject entirely the German school of Dr. Graetz, whose popular English exponent is Dr. Ginsburgh. We regard the Zoharic writings as the growth of some centuries. We believe that they represent a tradition which connects with Talmudic times. We respect the legend by which that tradition is identified with the name of R. Simeon ben Jochai, but we are not pledged thereto. We admit that the final shape assumed by the Zohar may not have been much

anterior to the date of its publication. We do not
deny that it may have received additions which
deserve to be described as spurious, or that some
of its increment may be attributable to Moses de
Leon, but we receive every statement with regard
to this personage tentatively and under all reservation,
ascribing little evidential value to the account in the
Sepher Yuhasin, and confessing that outside it there
is perhaps no ground for supposing that such a rabbi
flourished in the thirteenth century. We consider
that the period of R. Akiba is not an unwarrantable
date to ascribe to the Sepher Yetzirah, or to some
earlier form of that document, but the extent to
which it antedated the ninth century must remain
conjectural. We observe in the Sepher Yetzirah
and the Zohar certain doctrines which in some form
or other belong to all occultism ; they are part of
its burden, but they go far back into antiquity. We
believe these doctrines to have been derived by the
Jew in his early settlements and captivities. We
regard the other doctrines of the Zohar, in so far
as they follow from Scripture, to be of various and
chiefly unassignable dates and periods, but in so far
as they are philosophical subtleties or theosophical
fantasies we regard them as largely post-Talmudic.
We look upon the Kabalistic writings as documents
of humanity, and among such as memorials of the
genius of Israel, possessing their connections with
other systems and other modes of thought, but by
correspondence, by affiliation, by filtration, by causal
identity, rather than by historic descent. We look
upon the Zohar in particular as one of the most
attractive curiosities of the human mind, full of great-

ness and littleness, of sublimity and folly. The interest which it aroused on its appearance has in some measure survived all criticism, and the work itself has lived down even the admiration of its believers. We hold that it can be accounted for naturally and historically as a genuine growth of its age and not either as an imposture or as the key of all esoteric knowledge. It contains few or no traces of that doctrine of secret religion which occultists look for therein. It is the theosophical doctrine of Jewry. It supposes and involves the whole claim of Jewry, and as such its acceptation in any serious teaching sense is intolerable to the modern mind and would not be worth arguing were it not for the strong trend of occult thought in its direction. The existence of a concealed doctrine of religion perpetuated from antiquity cannot be proved by recourse to Kabalistic literature, and in so far as this notion has been rested thereon, it is to that extent discounted, yet the question itself does not stand or fall by the Kabalah. Speaking from the transcendental standpoint for the first time, as I feel warranted to do in concluding, I venture to say that it is in Christian channels that this doctrine must be sought by those who assume it, by which I mean that the transcendental succession has passed into the Church of Christ. The question, however, is not approachable from the historical side, and in no real sense of the term can it be said to possess such a side. It is therefore outside the common channels of inquiry, and assuming for the moment that any person now living in the flesh is entitled to affirm its existence, then he best of all, though not he only, is aware that the secret doctrine is not of this world. The historical association of the Kabalah with occult science in the West could not, of course, have taken place without a common ground between them, and the occult students who are concerned practically with the alleged efficacy of theurgic formulæ, with the physical possibilities said to be indicated under alchemical symbolism, with certain side issues of astrology, as with the historical aspect of all these subjects, must not ignore the Kabalah, for which reasons the rigid demarcation of its sphere of influence and operation has been much needed, and has been here attempted, as it is ·believed, for the first time.

INDEX

Ishmael, R., ⁱ author of the "Delineation of the Heavenly Temples," 157.

Issachar ben Napthali, his synopsis of the Zohar, 84, 195, 307, 308.

JAMI of Herat, his "Seven Thrones," 140.

Jechidah, fifth principle of the soul, 85; its unique character, 177; quintessence of the soul, 232; the mystic daughter, 233; as a name of Neshamah, 242; according to Isaac de Loria, 300.

Jellinek, on the term *Sephira*, 42; on the names of the Zohar, 111; his citations from Moses de Leon, 114; from the *Beth Hammadresh*, 267.

Jesod, *see Sephiroth.*

Jehovah, *see Tetragrammaton.*

Joel, on emanationism and the Kabalah, 40, 41.

T. ⁻ . R., hi- Arabic translation of the Talmud, 138.

Joshua ben Chananga, the n. . . . Akiba, 91.

Judge, W. O., on a secret lodge of adepts, 434.

Judgment, Last, 263, 264.

KABALAH, suggested derivations, 3; true derivation of the term, 3, 4; a secret traditional knowledge, 4; the hidden thought of Israel, 5; the conceal· of the Pentateuch, 6; difficulty of its literary methods, 7; two ways of regarding its importance, 10; its interest not exegetical or historical for the occult student, 12; failure of occult expositions, *ib.*; whether a channel of the secret tradition, 13; popular identification with magic, 23; four groups of Hebrew tradition, 26-28; mystery infused by the Kabalah into the Bible, 31; . of a liberal and Catholic doctrine, 54; the understanding of man methodised, 71; limitation of, 88; authority of, 90; the Kabalah and the Zohar, 98; ·i " ʷʸ .nism, 103; sources of its doctrine, 122 Kabalah and mystic tradition, 153, 440, 463 *et seq.*; Kabalah and Magic, 323, 324, 351, 438

.h and Agrippa, 347, 348; Kabalah and c ,65 *et seq.*; Modern ᵇ Kabalism, 414 ι. : ᵇ ·ιιι Christianity, 428 *et seq.*; Kabalah and Modern . 433 *et seq.*; Kabalah and Alchemy, 449 *et seq.*; Kabalah and Astrology, 461 *et seq.*; Kabalah and Freemasonry, 470 *et seq.*, the inquiry summ d, 488-491.

Kabbala Denudata of Rosenroth, motives which led to it, 380; of the preface, 383, ,84: sacrifices involved by the work. : ritical standpoint, 385, 386; its ambitious design, 188; excerpts and references, ᶜ, 31, 33, 39, 45, 47, 48, 51, 54, 65, 75, 76, 88, 192, 194, 213, 214, 225, 227, 228, 291, 293, 294, 304, 306, 307, 383, 457.

Kairites, 143.

Kapila, 4.

Karppe, Dr. S., preface, xviii-xx.

Kenealy, E. V., on the rr Kabalah, 3; on the wisdom of Adam, 6.

Kerner, Justinus, the revelations of his seeress, 84.

Kether, *see Sephiroth.*

Key of Solomon, a transparent forgery, 100; nonsensical pro-ᶜ , 150; its two recensions, 443; as an embodiment of Kabalistic tradition, 444.

Khunrath, reference by Eliphas Lévi, 382, by Stanislas de Guaita, 424; his connection with Kabalism, 454.

Kiern, F., his Kabalah of alchemy, 456.

ᵢin . C. W., on the ancient traditions of the Zo r 128; on the anal ι ·n Gnosticism and the Kabalah, 120.

Kingsford, Anna. 2ᵇ

Kingsland, W., on the A.. nt Wisdom Religion, 435.

Kircher, Athanasius, on the G. t. ᶠ ιιι , ᴢ ι Kabalistic corre . 132.

ᵇ .. a defendant of the Kabalah, 97.

ᵥ ᵃⁱ ι ι. the Sephir ᵥ irah, 159.

394 ; not a student of the Kabalah, 395 ; Kabalistic complexion of his lesser doctrines, *ib.* ; error of French occultists, 396 ; *see also* 424.

Salomon and Absal, 140.

Samael, averse correspondence of *Hod*, 81 ; according to the Zohar, 244, 245.

Sapere Aude on the *Æsh Metzareph* and Alchemy, 309, 312 ; on the Kabala and Chaldean philosophy, 125 ; on the derivation of alchemical knowledge to the West, 449.

Scaliger and the Knights of the Temple, 146.

Schiller-Szinessy, on the authorship of the Sepher Yetzirah, 92 ; on modern criticism of the *Targumim* and *Midrashim*, 103 ; on the late date and origin of the Zohar, 112, 439 ; on the original writings of Moses de Leon, 114 ; on the latest date which can be ascribed to the Zohar, 112, 119 ; on the Mishnic period of its nucleus, 410 ; *see also* 488.

Schiur Komah, 154.

Schœttgenius, Christianus, on the Christianity of R. Simeon ben Jochai, 115.

Sealing Names, permutations of the Tetragram in the Sepher Yetzirah, 171, 172.

Schure, Edouard, on a triple sense in Genesis, 420.

Secret Commentary, fragments extant in the Zohar, 260 ; on the connection between soul and body, 261 ; on the soul at death, 262 ; on the two Edens, 2... retributive justice, 263 ; on future happiness, 264-267 ; on the resurrection, 267-269 ; on angel... 27... to the Secret Commentary, 285.

Secret Doctrine, alleged transmission from antiquity, xv., xvi., 11, 13 ; the Kabalah not demonstrably a part of such tradition, 86 ; the affirmative view was not held in the past, 323, 324, and Bk. vii. *passim* ; *see also* 192.

Secret Learning, an alleged early name of the Zohar, 114.

Secret of S... quoted in Zohar, 276 ; concerns Kabal

istic physiogonomy, 276, 277 ; *see also* 192.

Secret Societies in the Middle Ages —Ghoolat Sect, 138.

Seder Ha Kabalah, an important orthodox apology, 160, 161 ; *see also* 179.

Sepher Dzenioutha, *i.e.*, Book of Concealment, on *Ain Soph*, 33 ; on a holy intelligence and an animal soul in man, 75 ; probably the oldest part of the Zohar, 119, 136 ; its antithesis, 154 ; place in the Zohar, 212 ; summary of its contents, 213-216 ; *see also* 192, 435.

Sepher Raziel, not the earliest form of occultism in Israel, 211 ; debased apparatus of, 369 ; a storehouse of mediæval magic, 444 ; *see also* 6.

Sepher Yetzirah, as a vehicle of the philosophic tradition of Kabalism, 28 ; part of a large mystical literature, 29 ; contains the germ of the Sephirotic scheme, 44 ; its description of the *Sephiroth*, 45-49 ; does not mention the Four Worlds of later Kabalism, 53 ; nor yet the doctrine of the Countenances, 59 ; on the letters of the Hebrew alphabet, 60, 131 ; on the instruments of creation, 60-62 ; the Paths of Wisdom as a dependency of the Sepher Yetzirah, 65 ; contains no reference to Kabalistic pneumatology, 74 ; traditional authorship, 91, 116, ascribed to Akiba, 92, 146 ; the reference to a Sepher Yetzirah in the Talmuds, 93, 94 ; its different influence on Christian minds as compared with the Zohar, 97 ; commentary of R. Abraham, 111, 174, 180-182 ; latest possible date, 93, 122 ; commentary of Saadya Gaon, 157, 175-178, 180 ; commentary of Azariel, 167, 174, 182-184 ; general analysis, 168-174 ; its connections and dependencies, 174-186 ; commentary of Nachmanides, 184 ; other commentaries, 185 ; the Sephir Yetzirah said to end where the Zohar begins, 211 ; not a magical work, 324 ; *see also* xii., xiii., 63, 90, 96, 136, 153, 162, 187, 345, 346,

More Metaphysical Books from Cornerstone

Esoteric Christianity
by Annie Besant
6x9 Softcover 170 pages
ISBN 1-934935-47-6

Raja Yoga
by Yogi Ramacharaka
6x9 Softcover 190 pages
ISBN: 161342065X

The Divine Origin of the Craft of the Herbalist
by E. A. Wallis Budge
6x9 Softcover 116 pages
ISBN 1613421222

The Masters and The Path
by C.W. Leadbeater
Foreword by Annie Besant
6x9 Softcover 252 pages
ISBN: 1-887560-80-7

The Rosetta Stone
by E. A. Wallis Budge
6x9 Softcover 210 pages
ISBN 1613421540

The Diaries of Leonardo Da Vinci
Jean Paul Richter, Translator
Michael R. Poll, Editor
Large Format, 7 x 10 Softcover 610 pages
ISBN: 1-887560-84-X

Cornerstone Book Publishers
www.cornerstonepublishers.com

More Metaphysical Books from Cornerstone

The Gates of Knowledge
by Rudolf Steiner
6x9 Softcover 192 pages
ISBN: 1613420935

History of the Secret Societies of the Army
by Charles Nodier
6x9 Softcover 260 pages
ISBN: 1-934935-24-7

The Magical Writings of Thomas Vaughan
by Arthur Edward Waite
Softcover 196 pages
ISBN 1613420773

The Interpretation of Dreams
by Sigmund Freud
6x9 Softcover 524 pages
ISBN 1613420811

Control of Mind and Body
by Frances Gulick Jewett
6x9 Softcover 280 pages
ISBN 161342079X

The Hand-Book of Astrology
by Zadkiel Tao-Sze
6x9 Softcover 126 pages
ISBN 1613420897

Letters on Occult Meditation
by Alice A. Bailey
6x9 Softcover 372 pages
ISBN 1613420978

Cornerstone Book Publishers
www.cornerstonepublishers.com

CPSIA information can be obtained
at www.ICGtesting.com
Printed in the USA
LVHW090146010322
712302LV00004B/29

9 781613 422397